CRITICAL SURVEY
OF
POETRY

CRITICAL SURVEY
OF
POETRY

English Language Series

Essays
Index

8

Edited by
FRANK N. MAGILL

Academic Director
WALTON BEACHAM

SALEM PRESS
Englewood Cliffs, N. J.

Library of Congress Catalog Card Number: 82-62168

Complete Set: ISBN 0-89356-340-4
Volume 8:   ISBN 0-89356-348-X

PRINTED IN THE UNITED STATES OF AMERICA

LIST OF ESSAYS

CRITICAL SURVEY
OF
POETRY

POETRY: PATTERN AS DEFINITION

The boundaries and definitions of poetry have changed so often throughout literary history that it is obvious that much of the vitality of poetry is derived from its flexibility. In modern times, as formal constrictions have disappeared and as contemporary poets have experimented with video, lazers, and three dimensional forms, readers have been confronted with innovative, often radical departures from more conventional concepts of poetry. Modern critics, therefore, have been careful not to prescribe what a poem should be, but instead, have chosen to describe only how it functions; and one of the most useful means for explaining function is to show how the poem establishes pattern. By examining pattern, which to some extent reflects the poet's attitude toward logic, the critic can extrapolate the artist's vision of order.

Pattern in poetry can be created in several ways, and those ways change as society changes. Traditionally, pattern has been most easily described through meter and rhyme, compounded by more subtle patterns of image, symbol, and recurring themes, but visual and phonic patterns are important as well. *Carmen figuratum*, or picture poetry, though not traditionally important, has interested contemporary poets for its three-dimensional qualities, resulting in "concrete poetry" that has moved the art form from the purely conceptual to the partially tactile. Contemporary sculptors create word objects that would not have qualified as poems under traditional expectations of pattern. Visual pattern in traditional poems has been more commonly established by the poem's length, stanzation, and balance. Readers coming to a long poem may expect a narrative, whereas readers of a sonnet will expect balance. Some modern readers cannot tolerate end rhyme, whereas others take delight in seeing end rhyme but not in being forced to focus on it through couplets or strong caesura.

Related to visual patterns are phonic ones, which are established not only through formal rhymes but also more subtly through internal sound associations. In "Speech After Long Silence," William Butler Yeats binds each word in the first line to the others, and continues to do so in most of the other lines. In "Speech after long silence, it is right," the "s" and "t" consonants alliterate, and the "n's" in "long" and "silence" resonate. Poets use sound not only to bind ideas together but also to arouse emotions, as in *Paradise Lost* (1667) where each character speaks in a distinctive phonic pattern. Children's verse is an obvious example of how sound functions on a primary level to excite response; the words may be nonsense but the child discerns a pleasurable pattern. The oral tradition in literature also illustrates how sound can be used to create repetition and pattern to build the poem to its climax.

The bases for establishing pattern in poetry, rhythmical, visual, and phonic, suggest that poetry is highly sensory, and there is little doubt that readers first respond to poetry emotionally, then intellectually, and finally returning to a higher emotional or aesthetic appreciation. The Metaphysical poets and many modern poets, however, have attempted to isolate the intellectual qualities from the emotional to establish pattern through ideas, such as in T. S. Eliot's *The Waste Land* (1922), which creates symphonic intellectual movements and depends upon obscure allusions. In "Anyone Live in a Pretty How Town," E. E. Cummings alters syntax for the purpose of focusing on the meaning of individual words, so that the placement pattern is crucial to understanding the theme. Contemporary poets have made poems conceptual by creating "cubist" and "minimalist" works in order to reestablish the way in which modern man perceives his reality.

Still other poets have created pattern through incantation, especially with ritual verse: the tribal priest was often the tribal poet. The words of the gods have frequently been recorded and interpreted in poetic language, not only to evoke immediate responses but also to create permanent impressions, often of awe, respect, fear, or mystery.

The rhythm of poetry accounts for much of the listener's initial response, and, remembering that for most of literary history poetry was recited rather than printed, it is clear that the power of incantation and memory served more important functions than any close analysis of metaphor and symbol. Rhythm in both poetry and music can affect listeners without words, but when the human voice is used as the instrument, language seems to combine the ethereal nature of music with the strictly human quality of words. Even if the words themselves are not particularly significant, the process of utterance causes people to be aware of their humanness. In that sense, music may cause listeners to think more about other worlds than about their function and obligation to this one. Knowing this, priests have learned to use poetry to instill certain behavorial responses as well as to lead people to a deeper understanding of themselves. Because poetry can be so mnemonic, the poet/priest can establish certain associations between verse and related religious activities, making the ritual a part of one's daily activity even when the priest is not present to conduct a ceremony.

Combined with rhythm, abbreviated language is used to create the effect of poetry. That is, words are presented more as symbols than as a complete logical sequence, a characteristic that distinguishes poetry from the other arts. When combined with ritual, abbreviated language alleviates the expectations of cause and effect and of the explanation and resolution typical of ordinary communication. When people do not demand that logic prevail, they are free to believe rather than question, and to accept circumstances that are beyond their rational comprehension. That is not to say that poems are not logical, but that their logic is more implied than stated as a consequence of the brevity of language. This quality of implication assists in releasing the imagination.

Abbreviated language must accept as its premise for communication the fact that it can be only suggestive, not exhaustive. The way it suggests is through a triggering mechanism which activates then associates emotions. Other than sound and meter, which work subconsciously, imagery furnishes the most direct access to readers; consequently, poets use imagistic patterns to release emotional responses. In the lines "Listen! you hear the grating roar/ Of pebbles which the waves draw back, and fling," Matthew Arnold is working on three levels of imagery. First, he instructs the reader to listen as the pebbles are raised from their natural resting place on the sea's floor—an absolutely silent world—and slung against one another so violently that they clack with the solid thud of rocks, which Arnold combines with the repetitious sound of waves thumping the shore. As a result of these sea sounds, many readers will bring to the poem their own associations of the sea and their particular feelings about it. The poet has suggested an image which the reader completes with his own experience.

The second sensory experience in the poem is tactile. If the reader can hear the pebbles and sea, he will probably feel them as well and bring to the image the force of rocks and waves beating the shore, and perhaps beating him. He may also feel (and smell) the spray. The reader's third imagistic response is visual; he may be able to see the retreating tide as it meets the incoming waves, the rising water and stones, and the inevitable fling. Visually, the pebbles have no means of escaping the continual, seemingly eternal cycle.

Whatever emotional patterns these lines evoke are in part activated by the images. The pebbles are clearly under the power of the tide and have been thrust from their silent sea world into turmoil. They are being acted upon brutally, and although the reader does not care about the stones themselves, he may transfer their condition to his own. Historically, Arnold and the post-Darwinian Victorians felt that the world was falling apart and that man was a victim of an indifferent universe. Phonically, the stones grate upon one another and on the listener's nerves; tactily, they are crushed against one another and the shore; and, visually, they are flung brutally and indifferently. The words create the images, but the reader's emotional response may reach far deeper than the abbreviated language denotes.

In addition to the power to suggest, abbreviated language also has the capability of comparing, and thereby it becomes philosophical. Images are used primarily to transfer the experience of the poem, while metaphor is often created to provoke ideas about the nature of life. In the lines cited from "Dover Beach," images alone are suggested, and yet, if the reader empathizes with the conditions of entrapment and violence that characterize the stones' environment, then he has created a metaphor that says: "I am like stones in a tremulous sea," a statement not much different in form from the famous metaphor (simile) "My love is like a red, red rose." At the close of "Dover Beach," Arnold writes: "And we are here as on a darkling plain . . . where ignorant armies clash by night," with which he extends the image of the randomly victimized pebbles to soldiers engaged in senseless battle (the Crimean War); the soldiers are symbols for all of mankind. The poem thus opens with imagery, progresses to metaphor, and closes with symbol, each stage leading the reader from the sensual to the intellectual.

Abbreviated language enhances rather than hinders this developing process. To be sure, "Dover Beach" is composed in complete sentences and is not written in the telegraphic language that typifies many poems, but there is still an absence of transition which complete prose requires. Whatever connections the reader makes comes largely as a result of imagistic patterns, which the reader infers as a result of his own experience and philosophy.

A more recent example of abbreviated language is William Carlos Williams' "The Red Wheelbarrow," in which the juxtaposition of colors, textures, and objects creates a metaphor which lies outside the poem. A still more contemporary example is Mary Ellen Solt's "Forsythia," which on the surface appears to be nothing more than a loose pictorial re-creation of the plant, using only the letters contained in its name. Whether or not readers are willing to accept this as a literary rather than a visual art form depends on their ability to establish metaphor which falls outside the poem. First, it is essential that the reader be familiar with forsythia and connect some associations with it. In temperate North American climates, forsythia is the first sign of spring. Its branches are spindly, its flowers delicate though hardy, and its name is languid. The base of the poem, like the base of the plant, is solid and sturdy, while the branches seem whimsical. The poet breaks apart the name in the same manner that E. E. Cummings breaks apart "grasshopper" to re-create the insect's movement and thus establish something about the essence of the creature. It is language, though, that helps to interpret this essence, and by breaking words into their basic components (letters), the poet reminds the reader of the importance of nuance. It is not only the essence of forsythia or grasshoppers that is important but also the reader's verbal association with the natural world. Man has named these organisms and in that role must not forget that he, too, has been named and is a composite of parts.

Another Cummings poem, "a leaf falls," illustrates the principle of pattern and metaphor. Ignoring its placement of letters on the page, the entire poem reads "a leaf falls/ loneliness." Considering only the meaning (rather than the placement), there is only poetic inspiration here; the poem has not yet emerged. As with "Forsythia," most readers associate falling leaves with a season, and those seasons possess strong emotional qualities. One leaf falling might suggest either autumn's first leaf, or its last; in either case, the leaf suggests points of embarkation. To other readers, "a" leaf might not be the first or last but an isolated leaf that has been cut away from its natural affinity with other leaves: where there is one leaf, either on the tree or ground, there should be others. A falling leaf might also suggest death because of its inevitable decay and because falling leaves are associated with the coming of winter, which also suggests death. Decay, death, and isolation might all add up to loneliness for many readers.

Cummings, however, presents another theme and by altering the syntactical pattern creates an entirely different poem. Visually, the poem's strong vertical character, which flattens on the bottom, suggests a leaf's flight and arrival on the ground, and because of the placement of letters, the poem cannot be read aloud, thereby defying sound and reinforcing the leaf's silent path. More important, by denying the reader any possibility of reciting the poem, Cummings forces a silent response and makes the reader as mute as the leaf.

Because the poem is entirely visual, Cummings can play out the real conflict, which is to emphasize the "l's" and "i's." Paired to read down the page, the "l" characters look like ones ("1's"), and in the second stanza there is a preponderance of ones ("1's"). Even the strict pairing of characters in the first stanza has been broken so that the lines in stanza 2 are composed of one, three, or five characters, and each of the lines emphasizes that when the word "loneliness" is broken apart, "oneness" is the basic component. Cummings seems to suggest that people feel lonely because they are one rather than two (that is, attached to someone else). The poem, however, twists itself with the last line: it is not being alone that causes loneliness but egocentricity—the "iness" of existence. People look at falling leaves and think that the leaves suggest some violation of their own importance. That is, if leaves fall unheralded to their grave, people must too. It is only in the viewer's mind that falling leaves are pathetic. In fact, falling leaves are part of a natural process. The tree is not dead. It does not need its leaves for winter survival, and it will grow healthy in the spring. It is only man's "iness" that creates this pathetic fallacy; "iness," then, becomes the poem's message, and without typography to establish the pattern, the poem does not exist.

One of the major differences between traditional and avant-garde critics is the extent to which each group believes that language must be used as an integral part of the poem. In "a leaf falls" there is no question about the vitality of language; "Forsythia" is not as clearly dependent on language for its theme. A question that the traditional critic would ask of "Forsythia" is whether the poem would have been any different had it been written using the word "azalea." No other language could have been substituted in "a leaf falls"; the difference between "forsythia" and "azalea" is more difficult to distinguish. Both are spring plants, both are hardy but delicate and have spindly branches. If language can be substituted without any loss of meaning, then most critics would agree that the language is not essential.

If language is not essential for meaning, is it acceptable for poems to use the shape of letters as a basis for creating visual pattern? Nonsense verse, which uses vowels and consonants to establish pattern, is accepted as a genre of poetry, but visual patterns are not yet as acceptable. At the present time, the critical attitude leans toward the infallibility of denotation and connotation as essential elements of poetry. Even nonsense verse, such as Dr. Seuss's children's books, use word meanings in very distorted ways, and in doing so deny or reverse the usual meaning. In this respect, Dr. Seuss's poetry depends on definition, as well as sound, for its effect.

Even so, any open-minded study of poetry must recognize the vast differences between the poetry produced in different historical periods and by different cultures. William Wordsworth defined poetry as "the spontaneous overflow of powerful feelings recollected in tranquility"; Miller Williams describes it as "an encounter between poet and reader." However poetry is defined, it functions to help man order his perceptions of his life, and in doing so challenges his assumptions about universal order. Most poems can be approached from the perspective of pattern as long as the reader is constantly aware that pattern is philosophical as well as functional, and that it can take many shapes to achieve its higher ordering.

Walton Beacham

THE ORAL TRADITION

Literature, as the word is now most often used, means *written* works—poetry, drama, prose. Derived from the Latin word for "letter of the alphabet," the word enshrines a particular notion of what literature involves; namely, texts. The concept of a nonwritten, "oral" literature, therefore, might seem a contradiction in terms. Literature implies writing and often "good" writing as opposed to the writing found in popular novels or the like. "Oral literature," if it is considered at all in the teaching of literature, tends to be considered in terms of the act of reciting a written work, or of literature meant for performance, such as drama. Even so, no literature, however tied to written means of transmission or composition, can be completely divorced from the spoken word, since verbal art is itself a specialized use of language, and language exists independently of any mode of transcription. Doubtless, spoken language and written language have developed different conventions, expressions, even grammars; the modern Greek distinction between "demotic" and "pure" (*katharevousa*) is not an uncommon phenomenon when one considers languages throughout the world. Nevertheless, before modern literate culture valued one form of language (written) above the other, before there was even any one word such as "literature" to cover the disparate forms of verbal art often tied to social functions, there existed poems and songs, dramas and narratives. In contemporary nonliterate societies, there are many examples of flourishing "literary" forms. Even in modern Western society, the most popular verbal artistic modes are "oral" in that they are transmitted without the use of writing. How many persons, for example, read the text of a popular hit song, a Broadway play, or a television show, compared with the mass of viewers or auditors? The status of the text, in such cases, becomes merely a legal, copyright question, and a disputed right at that. The fundamental orality of all literature, then, can be seen to reassert itself, even in the most literate of all cultures. Indeed, the audio-visual revolution has helped to broaden the notion of literature; no longer does one consider literature to be only that which can be printed and cataloged in libraries. Consequently, it is easier in this century than in the last several to conceive of an oral traditional literature that lies at the roots of modern written Western literature.

The term "oral literature" can refer to a vast range of verbal products. It can include modern blues lyrics, African drum songs, ancient Greek epic poetry, the latest jokes or limericks, ballads, folksongs, folktales, children's rhymes or street-corner games, such as the "Dozens" (a series of rhyming insult verses that can be extended to any length by improvisation). On one hand, it is very useful for an investigator to know about all these genres of oral literature, to take the term at its most inclusive, so that one can learn by comparison precisely what defines each given composition as "oral" and therefore different from its written counterpart. On the other hand, some restriction of the term is needed in order to examine in any detail the workings of such literature. This article, then, will focus on a narrow area of disproportionately influential oral literature. Although referring to African and Asian literature at times, most of the article will deal with Western literature. Unfortunately, this means excluding such great compositions as the Babylonian *Gilgamesh* story, the Iranian *Shāhnāma*, and the Sanskrit *Rāmāyana* (c. 350 B.C.) and *Mahābhārata* (c. fifth century B.C.), as well as the hymns of the *Rig Veda*, all of which have importance for the student of epic poetry in the Western tradition. Second, only poetry will be discussed; in most Western literature, poetic compositions are attested as being much older than compositions in prose. Nevertheless, some old European traditions, like that of Ireland, contain heroic sagas written in a combination of prose and verse. They are thought to have been orally composed; yet they can be dealt with here only secondarily. The third focus of the article is on that poetry thought to be composed, and not merely transmitted, without the aid of writing. This restriction necessarily raises some questions: What of ballads or songs which change as they are transmitted? Is not this a form of composition without writing, even if the original composition were "written"? Such questions might be answered when discussion turns to longer compositions, such as narrative songs, which seem at times to exhibit the same behavior. It will be seen that the interplay of oral and written literature forms a separate problem within the field of oral poetics, and ballad study requires critical notions different from those applied to other oral genres. Finally, this article makes a further distinction between *freely improvised* poetry, which exists within a literate culture alongside written work—for example, the work songs or insult contest verses that can be heard today—and preliterate compositions, which necessarily transmit large amounts of traditional language, motifs, and themes, and so cannot be termed "improvisation" in the same way. These poems, usually lengthy and narrative in nature, demand trained composers using generations-old techniques; at every turn of the poem, one comes across fusions of the individual's creative improvisation with *traditional* material.

The traditional poem to be discussed here is the Old English epic *Beowulf* (c. sixth century). There will be some selective analysis of the function of poetry in the society, of the formulaic nature of the poem, and of the influences of other compositions outside the indigenous language.

Beowulf

"One might say that each song in oral tradition has its original within it and even reflects the origin of the very genre to which it belongs." This observation by A. B. Lord, though meant to be general, might apply specifically to *Beowulf*, the earliest full-length Germanic language epic that has survived. Although this poem was probably composed in the eighth century, its historical context is that of the early sixth century on the Continent and in Scandinavia; the story was likely brought to England by the migrating Angles and Saxons. This is *prima facie* evidence for the conservative nature of the poem, a trait often noticed in other oral compositions: the Serbo-Croatian songs that Lord and Milman Parry found were often about battles fought five hundred years previously, such as that at Kosovo Polje in the fourteenth century. *The Nibelungenlied* (c. 1200, *The Lay of the Nibelungs*), *Poem of the Cid* (from the twelfth century) and *Chanson de Roland* (c. 1100, *The Song of Roland*) all share this characteristic.

In the case of *Beowulf*, as clearly as in the Greek epics, the oral origin of the poem is made explicit by the poet's own references to oral poems in the narrative, so that *Beowulf* is conservative in its view of poetry as well as in its historical outlook. As in the *Iliad* and the *Odyssey* (both c. 800 B.C.), when bards are presented composing poetry, one should not expect exact depiction of the process by which the narrative itself was composed: there is always the possibility that the poet is archaizing, recalling the more glorious poetic as well as heroic past, when oral composers held a higher place in society. Yet the very fact of this "backward look" is important. It is the seal of a poem's traditional content.

The origin of a poem such as *Beowulf* can be viewed within the Old English epic in the important scene starting at line 867. As the Danes return on horseback from the site of Grendel's plunge, a retainer of their king recites the exploit,

> A man proved of old, evoker of stories,
> Who held in his memory multitude on multitude
> Of the sagas of the dead, found now a new song
> In words well-linked: the man began again
> To weave in his subtlety the exploit of Beowulf.

This sort of instant praise-poetry is not, however, simply a direct restatement of the hero's deed. The "evoker of stories" instead praises Beowulf by beginning with the story of Sigemund, who had a similar exploit (killing a dragon), and he ends with a mention of the blameworthy Heremod, an early Danish king, the complete opposite of Beowulf. There is no mention of the way in which he actually praised the maiming of Grendel by the contemporary hero; it could well be that what the old retainer composed in fact made little or no reference to Beowulf. Surprising as this might seem, it would fit with what can be seen in the *Iliad*, in the episode just mentioned above: the present is continually set into its past heroic context in this oral traditional material.

That something like the horseback poem of the retainer could have occurred in early times is suggested by the Roman historian Tacitus' account of Germanic tribesmen, who, he reported, sang the histories of their ancestors before battles and at night in their camps. This urge to turn the past into incentive for the present lies at the root of heroic poetry as well as praise-poetry, the kernel form of the epic. In the song of the retainer, which resembles Greek praise-poetry in its use of a "negative foil" figure (the blamed character), one can see the kernel blossoming into a full-fledged narrative.

As in the analysis of the Greek epics, the notion of type-scene and theme proves useful in establishing connections between *Beowulf* and oral composition. The analysis of the low-level formula—the repeated phrase or word—is less conclusive; *Beowulf* appears to be oral because it appears to have a high percentage of formulas or formula-types (repeated syntactical groupings such as epithet and noun), but the statistical method should not be relied on completely. It has recently been shown that poems known to have been written and signed by Cynewulf, probably in the ninth century, would have to be classified as "oral" if the same counting methods were applied. It could be that both Cynewulf's poems and the epic *Beowulf* are transitional products of the meeting of an oral tradition with a learned, Christianized, literate society. This would explain the seemingly incongruous elements of Christian faith in the heroic poem. Whatever the results of the diction-oriented analysis, the occurrence of traditional type-scenes and themes in *Beowulf* is important in itself and may be taken to show the poem's oral heritage.

Beowulf has its start in an arrangement of type-scenes remarkably like that of the *Odyssey*: a hero sets out by boat, is met on landing, is greeted and entertained, finds important information, and acts on it to the advancement of his own heroic career. In the *Odyssey*, the sequence is repeated, once for Telemachus (like *Beowulf*, a young hero accompanied by a small group) and once for Odysseus (Books Five through Thirteen). Beowulf, however, acts immediately; the poem is consequently much shorter. Odysseus and Telemachus, on the other hand, act only on return to Ithaca, where their reunion and slaying of the suitors forms the grand finale. In this development, conditions of performance must dictate which themes will be doubled and which contracted, how many type-scenes will be inserted, and how large they will be allowed to grow.

The *Beowulf*-poet handles themes with as much dexterity as Homer, although his stock of type-scenes seems smaller. An example is the "taunt of Unferth" scene. The taunt is itself a genre in oral society, as the Homeric epics and modern African examples make clear. Here, the taunt is expanded to contain a thematic narrative remarkably like the theme of the surrounding poem: the underwater exploits of Beowulf. Unferth, a retainer of the Danish king Hrothgar, asks Beowulf on arrival whether he is the man who lost a swimming-match against Breca. Beowulf's reply is an elaborate, suspenseful narrative of a fight with sea-demons—the "correct" version of the story, unlike Unferth's, and a foreshadowing of his defeat of Grendel's mother beneath the lake. Beowulf (like Odysseus in the *Odyssey*) acts the part of the oral poet. Is it not significant, then, that he wins over the final monster, not with Unferth's donated sword Hrunting, but with the "blade of old-time" found in the den of Grendel, which only Beowulf among heroes can lift? His personal weapon, like his personal story, is the one to surpass the competing stories of heroic action; fame, in an oral culture, tunes out the noise of rumor.

As well as containing hints of its own origin, *Beowulf* has one scene that might point to the kind of poetry that ultimately replaced it: the introduction of Grendel into the narrative describes his approach to the hall of the Danes where he had daily heard singing—and the song consists of nothing less than the creation of the world by God. As such, this singing strongly resembles the compositions attributed to Caedmon in a well-known section of Bede's history of the English Church. Caedmon was in the habit of leaving the nightly entertainments at Whitby Abbey because he had never learned songs, Bede reports. One night, guarding the stables, Caedmon dreamt that he was asked to sing the creation of the world; he did so, and the next morning recited the poem to his superiors, who from that time on used him to put stories from religious works into verse. Caedmon clearly was an oral composer; from Bede's viewpoint, his gift was "divine," since he knew no literature. Yet it was through such recruits to Christian tradition that the oral art of the older native singers eventually was lost—the beginning of the end can be seen in the *Beowulf*-poet's knowledge of this theological genre.

Bibliography

Duggan, J. J., ed. *Oral Literature: 7 Essays*, 1977.

Finnegan, R. *Oral Poetry: Its Nature, Significance, and Social Context*, 1977.

Lord, A. B. "Beowulf and Odysseus," in *Franciplegius: Studies in Honor of F. P. Magoun*, 1965. Edited by J. Bessinger and R. Creedy.

Oinas, F., ed. *Heroic Epic and Saga*, 1978.

Opland, J. *Anglo-Saxon Oral Poetry*, 1980.

Stevens, M., and J. Mandel, eds. *Old English Literature: 22 Analytical Essays*, 1968.

Stolz, B., and R. Shannon. *Oral Literature and the Formula*, 1976.

Richard P. Martin

THE FOURTEENTH CENTURY

Whan that Aprill with his shoures soote
The droghte of March hath perced to the roote . . .
Thanne longen folk to goon on pilgrimages,
And palmeres for to seken straunge strondes,
To ferne halwes, kowthe in sondry londes;
And specially from every shires ende
Of Engelond to Caunterbury they wende,
The hooly blisful martir for to seke,
That hem hath holpen whan that they were seeke.

With these words Geoffrey Chaucer begins *The Canterbury Tales* (1387-1400), arguably the poetic masterpiece of fourteenth century England and certainly a stout cornerstone in the monumental edifice of the English literary tradition. Critics have long praised Chaucer's choice of the pilgrimage as the overarching frame for a highly varied collection of individual tales, and readers are often advised of its particular virtues of providing a theme of religious renewal and community enterprise against which are set, for example, the delightful boorishness of the Miller, the outrageous iconoclasm of the Wife of Bath, the earnest pondering of how man and woman are to live together in what G. L. Kittredge called the "Marriage Group," and the insouciant extortion of the wily Pardoner. Yet perhaps readers are not often enough reminded of the milieu in which *The Canterbury Tales* were created, the context which they in part reflect. It is crucial to a faithful reading of any literary work that readers take a moment to review its cultural and historical background, and never is such a review more needed than for this tumultuous period that proved to be the poetic flowering of the late Middle Ages.

Historical and Cultural Context

The fourteenth century was an era of great literary achievement in the face of governmental, economic, and religious near-apocalypse. No sooner had Boniface VIII declared his own gaudy papal jubilee in the year 1300 than his chief secular opponents, Philip IV of France and Edward I of England, began to contest his power. Working from the solid church and state amalgam that was the bequest of the thirteenth century, Boniface had aroused the kings' resistance in 1296 with the *Clericis laicos* papal bull, which asserted the Church's right to levy taxes. Two years after the jubilee he issued the more famous *Unam sanctam*, intended to establish the primacy of the Church in unambiguous terms by subordinating all human creation to the authority of the Pope in Rome. This anachronistic attempt at absolutism, destined to fail in an era in which social and political evolution was ever accelerating, precipitated the withdrawal of the Papacy from Rome to Avignon, initiating in 1309 the "Babylonian Captivity" of Popes that was to last until 1376 and presaging the ultimate schism in the Church, which was healed only two decades into the fifteenth century at the Council of Constance. With the loss of a generally accepted central government for Christianity, as well as numerous other disasters, many of the philosophical and religious syntheses of the previous century also foundered.

As prominent as any dogma inherited from the thirteenth century was Thomas Aquinas' apparent reconciliation of faith and reason in his *Summa Theologica* (c. 1265-1274). Blending the newly rediscovered Aristotelian logic and his own brand of Christian humanism, Thomas erected a cathedral-like intellectual monument to celebrate the fusion of human reason and divine grace. John Duns Scotus (c. 1265-1308), a Franciscan, had begun to pry faith and reason apart, however, and William of Ockham (c. 1280-1350) finished the dismantling through the application of his well-known "razor." Ockham insisted that human knowledge should be restricted to the immediately evident, thus making it necessary to discard the grand latticework of categories assembled by Aquinas and others. The Nominalist movement, so called because of its dismissal of the Thomistic *nominae* (or categories), also provided the impetus for a series of scientific developments at the universities of Oxford and Paris. To replace the Aristotelian notions of streams of air as the medium for physical motion, for example, John Buridan (c. 1300-1358) offered a theory of original forces that was to be transferred fruitfully to studies of heavenly bodies. Remarkably, Nicholas of Oresme (c. 1330-1382) described the universe as a mechanical clock, an idea all the more brilliant since such timepieces had been perfected only in his century. Along with these discoveries, and others such as the cannon, eyeglasses, and the mariner's compass, came the evolution of modern scientific method in the nominalist emphasis on observed phenomena.

To be sure, however, Ockham's was not the only heresy to come to prominence in the vacuum of formal religious authority created by the withdrawal of the Papacy. As rationalism lost its footing in the Christian world view, mysticism increased markedly and became a pan-European movement, finding its focus in Germany, for example, with the writings of Meister Eckhart (c. 1260-1327). Interest in astrology and alchemy was likewise on the rise; and Chaucer especially revealed a fascination with the courses of the stars and planets and their supposed influence on the world of men. One of the more engaging and curiously modern heresies involved the professions of the Free Spirit reformers, who advocated unrestrained sexual freedom and other apparent vices in the pursuit of individually achieved deification. Nearly as influential as Ockham's nominalist beliefs were the attacks of John Wycliffe (c. 1320-1384) on the presumptions of the Avignon Popes. Refusing to credit any clergy with the power they claimed unless they were in a state of divine grace, he championed the Englishmen who resisted the financial demands of the Papacy and later questioned the existence of Church government and even the Eucharist itself. In many ways Wycliffe, a strident religious dissenter and yet the originator of the first English Bible, well represents the maelstrom that was Christianity in the age of Chaucer and his contemporaries.

As religion passed through a series of challenges, reforms, and counter-reforms, losing in the process the comparatively well-regulated syntheses of the preceding century, secular developments followed suit. England and France entered the fourteenth century with their governments reasonably intact, but in both cases a succession of less than qualified leaders and a sequence of catastrophic events brought the countries to their political knees and, not inconsequently, to the Hundred Years War. On the French side, Philip the Fair (IV), opponent of Boniface, had placed the monarchy in a position of strength at the cost of considerable financial strain on his constituency. When he died in 1314, his successor Louis X was quickly forced to agree to charters limiting his power and transferring a great deal of authority to a confused baronial system. After two more Capetian kings of unremarkable achievement, the rule passed to the inept Philip VI, who set about establishing an adversary relationship with his English counterpart Edward III, an ongoing conflict that led eventually to open warfare. In mid-century, John the Good assumed the throne, only to be taken prisoner at the Battle of Poitiers. Even as these monarchs followed one another to death or infamy, Edward III was in the process of declaring himself king of France; the French, in a weakened condition, had to curb his presumptuousness in 1360 by consenting to the conditions of the Treaty of Brétigny, awarding Gascony, Calais, and Ponthieu to the English in return for Edward's renunciation of his claim to their monarchy. While John's son Charles V (ruled 1364-1380) was able to reorganize his country and help the English to exhaust themselves and relinquish newly won territories, the century ended with France in the hands of the incompetent Charles VI and the advantage once more passed to her opponent.

England likewise started the fourteenth century struggling with Boniface. Edward I (ruled 1272-1307) fostered a typical thirteenth century cooperation between the monarchy and the legislative powers, reformed the judicial system, gave order to ecclesiastical activity, and controlled feudal tendencies. His son Edward II, however, was at best a shadow of his father. He suffered a humiliating defeat by the Scots at Bannockburn in 1314 and gave no evidence whatever that he was qualified for leadership. In 1327, he was forcibly deposed by the parliament, and his fourteen-year-old son, Edward III, was appointed the nominal regent. At first the young man was only a figurehead manipulated by his mother Queen Isabella and her lover Roger Mortimer, but three years after his accession he toppled them both, sentencing Mortimer to death and stripping the Queen of all power and holdings. With the monarchy in hand, this English Orestes then set about providing a focus for growing English nationalism by erasing the "Shameful Peace" with Scotland from popular memory through a series of successful battles to the north. Thus, Edward III showed his ambitions and talents early in his fifty-year reign and also revealed, not incidentally, a penchant for nationalistic assertion that was to lead to severe, even crippling, problems for the nation he so stoutly defended.

The most serious and debilitating result of this martial activity was the Hundred Years War with France, which opened in 1337 when Edward ordered the Gascon fleet to attack shipping in the ports of Normandy. As mentioned above, a context for these actions already existed in the quarrel over the French crown and the efforts of Flanders to gain its independence, and this single event was merely one of many subsequent skirmishes along the English Channel. Important events included the naval encounter of 1340, the Treaty of Brétigny in 1360, and the gradual reversal in favor of the French in the late fourteenth century. At the same time, the spirit of British nationalism that fueled Edward's war machine also manifested itself in other ways: the Statute of Praemuniere (1353) forbade Englishmen to bring their appeals to a foreign (that is, papal) court, and the first of the Navigation Acts (1382) stipulated that English goods must be carried by domestic ships only. When the official change from French to English as the language of the law courts (1361) is added to this list, it becomes apparent that the rising tide of nationalism was nearing its peak. Unfortunately, the advent of Richard II in 1377 created another incompetent monarch to rival Edward II. The century closed in an undistinguished manner, with Richard desperately resorting to execution of his enemies in 1397 and suffering his own death two years later.

In Germany the political situation was even worse. The inheritor of an unwieldy coalition of states headed by scheming princes and under attack by the Papacy, Albert of Hapsburg tried to bring order to the Empire but was murdered in 1308 by his nephew. The puppet emperor Henry of Luxemburg (VII) made a foolish expedition to Rome in an attempt to bring Italy back into the fold but was poisoned in 1313. His successor, Charles of Bohemia, dismissed papal claims with his Golden Bull of 1356, but his concentration on Bohemia at the expense of the Empire as a whole left his nation vulnerable to attack, and the French and Swiss made steady gains throughout the fourteenth century. Notwithstanding this unrest, the German cities made some strides forward in urban management in the form of administrative innovations, paved streets, fire protection, and public health. At about the same time, the Serbian people made their first heroic effort to throw off the Ottoman yoke at the celebrated Battle of Kosovo (1389), where the Serbs and their leader Knez Lazar went down to a defeat that was to serve as the seedbed of a fierce nationalism and an extensive cycle of heroic poems.

In Italy, the internal strife characteristic of the period stemmed primarily from the withdrawal of the Popes to Avignon. With Philip IV and Edward I in open defiance of Boniface's edicts, and with the time of absolute clerical authority on the wane, there was little choice but to abandon the politics of

Rome and to seek refuge under the French imperial banner. Meanwhile, the customary infighting in Italy grew worse, with the merest and most superficial unity existing between the southern Kingdom of Naples and the northern despots. A touch of neoclassicism emerged for a moment in the reforms of Cola di Rienzi, who rose to power in 1347, but the age made his visions of reinstating antiquity anachronistic, and he was driven into exile and murdered in 1354. The Popes began to try to return to Rome and reinstall themselves in 1367; nine years later, when Urban VI resisted all attempts to depose him, and his "successor" Clement VII retreated to Avignon to establish a rival Papacy, the Great Schism was begun. All in all, Italy was not a pleasant place to live in the fourteenth century, as the writings of Dante confirm.

Almost precisely in the middle of the century the Black Death struck Europe, reducing the total population of most countries by half to two-thirds. As the frequency of themes of morbidity, pessimism, and death in all of the arts indicates, this pestilence had a profound effect on the medieval mind, in addition to its decimation of the populace. Traveling along trade routes from China through Italy, Spain, and southern France, by July, 1348, it had reached Normandy and the English coast. Medieval medicine was apparently powerless against the more virulent of the disease's two forms and it passed unchecked into Ireland and Wales over the next two years, only to return periodically throughout the rest of the century. In addition, people had earlier had to contend with the disastrous crop failure and famine of 1315, caused by floods which were also to recur regularly for many years to come. For these and other reasons, economic disaster became the rule of the day, and overtaxed market systems, alternating surpluses and shortfalls of agricultural and manufactured goods, the backsliding of emancipated serfs into the feudal equivalent of slavery, and general social upheaval led to the Peasants' Revolt of 1381.

As the authority of the Church and of secular government languished, the Thomistic unity of faith and reason unraveled, the Black Death claimed half of Europe, antifeminist and anti-Semitic movements gained momentum, and the economic and social institutions of the thirteenth century trembled and then fell, people were forced to experiment and adapt in order to survive. Reform and renovation proceeded in all areas, with various degrees of success and almost no visible effect until the fifteenth century. Yet, in the middle of the worst confusion and turmoil the Middle Ages was to know, the arts underwent truly radical change and produced a remarkable number of discoveries and true masters. Emblematic of this transformation was the Italian painter Giotto (c. 1266-1337), a genius who cast aside his shepherd's crook to become the first great postclassical painter. What Giotto accomplished was phenomenal: he replaced the formal, stylized, two-dimensional Byzantine representations with a more realistic artistic idiom that imitated nature in all her beauty and with all her flaws. His "Madonna Enthroned" (c. 1310) and

"Death of St. Francis" (c. 1318-1320), for example, illustrate his technique of creating depth, movement, and fidelity to nature. While the Italo-Byzantine style continued in a modest way on a separate line (an example is Simone Martini's "Annunciation" of 1333), Giotto's techniques spread north rather quickly, first in the form of manuscript illumination (as in the work of Jean Pucelle, beginning c. 1325) and later to architecture and portraiture. Giotto's painting played a large part in bringing Europe to the brink of the Renaissance.

As the conventional use of Latin declined and the vernaculars became more prominent all over Europe, great authors began to mold the new tongues for literary purposes. Like Giotto, the Italian poet Dante (1265-1321) reached beyond traditional models and the tenor of the times to create his masterpiece, *The Divine Comedy* (c. 1320). Dante wrote his epic poem while he was a political exile wandering through northern Italian cities in search of a patron; however, even though topical allusions to the political and social problems of his beloved Florence abound, his work rises above contemporary strife to glimpse the path to God: in the hands of his guides Vergil, representing human reason, and then Beatrice, who as the symbol of divine love leads the pilgrim Dante to the heaven where reason cannot take him, he accomplishes the journey of Everyman and allegorically points the way to the Christian's true reward. Dante's countryman Francisco Petrarch (1304-1374), who, in addition to establishing so many of the Italian sonnet conventions, contributed to most of the literary and philosophical genres of his day, stressed the importance of human mortality in the face of theological dogma and displayed an atavistic tendency to return to the ancient philosophers in his search for truth. Giovanni Boccaccio (1313-1375), author of *The Decameron* (1353), a collection of ten "days" of ten stories each, tried to develop a more worldly poetic language. His famous tales are told by seven young women and three young men who flee Florence to escape the ravages of the Black Death and for ten days amuse themselves with stories of cuckolding, murder, and other fantastic pursuits. Especially since it now appears that Chaucer had not read *The Decameron* and thus conceived the analogous structure of his *The Canterbury Tales* independently, the genre of tales unified by a framing story should be considered a typically fourteenth century form in its originality and response to the demands of individuality upon traditional genres.

The Nature of Medieval Texts

Before beginning a description of fourteenth century poetry per se, it is well to take a moment to note some special characteristics of medieval texts that were particularly prominent in this age of experimentation and reaction to change. Authors in this period suffered very little from the more modern "anxiety of influence," and there were compelling reasons for their resistance to this literary disease. In the fourteenth century—and virtually throughout the Middle Ages—there was no special value placed on "originality": stories, characters, events, and situations were almost always either borrowed, from another source or from the wordhoard of convention, or simply translated from Latin or one of the vernacular tongues, in whole or selectively. Poets did not so much strive after fresh and mysteriously engaging material as they molded known material to their own designs; they were in the main retellers rather than creators, and this procedure characterized not only their subject matter but also the ways in which they shaped it. As has been shown time and again, the rhetoric of medieval poetry was codified by such writers as Geoffrey of Vinsauf, Bernard Silvestris, and Alanus de Insulis. Fourteenth century poets had available to them handbooks concerning such topics as the proper method of picturing a woman's beauty—proceeding vertically through a catalog of her features from "tip to toe." These conventional methods of description were advocated by poets and expected by their audiences, as were what Ernst R. Curtius has called *topoi*, or narrative commonplaces, such as the ubiquitous garden of earthly delights, the *locus amoenus*. Form as well as content was traditional, and each aspect of the poetry was all the more expressive because of its typicality in other works and consequent connotative power. Twice-told tales and time-tested rhetoric were the order of the day, and so modern notions of aesthetics must be adjusted to take faithful account of these medieval values.

Such stories and established methods of telling them imply a particular kind of text no longer extant in a modern literary milieu consisting of finely crafted objects virtually complete in themselves. The Romantic legacy of originality marks the end of texts with an active history behind them, but the poem that reaches out into its traditional context to complete its form and content is, *par excellence*, a medieval phenomenon. The process had begun with earlier medieval oral traditions—Anglo-Saxon, Old French, and Hispanic; in the case of the oldest texts, such as *Beowulf* (c. 1000) and the *Chanson de Roland* (c. 1100, *The Song of Roland*), the tradition is paramount and the poet is a member of a succession of bards who transmit more than they compose. With later medieval texts, the individual author is of course firmly the master of his own literary fate, and yet his debt to tradition is still great. The medieval text, in short has diachrony: it reaches back to earlier narratives or lyric moments and it speaks through a grammar of commonplaces and rhetorical figures assembled and approved by tradition. The more innovative writers of the fourteenth century grasped tradition with consummate ease, reformulating its lexicon of tales and grammar of rhetoric, and passed beyond it to create formerly unheard harmonies on the basic melodies of the canon. These original melodies remain, however, and give the newer compositions a fundamental strength. Indeed, it is well to remember that even the great iconoclast and innovator, Chaucer, was the inheritor of a rich traditional legacy, which he invested brilliantly with his often startlingly fresh ideas for literary works, and that both the intensely dramatic and psychological *Troilus and Criseyde* (1382) and the great send-up of medieval romance "Sir Thopas" bear testimony to his creative use of poetic tradition.

Arthurian Legend

One of the strongest of medieval traditions, and one that was to reach forward to the Medieval Revival of the Victorian nineteenth century, to the classic American tale-telling of Mark Twain, and beyond into the modern era, was the cycle of legends surrounding King Arthur and his knights. This central character of countless tales was probably a sixth century historical figure celebrated in Britain for his heroic defense against Saxon invaders; like the Serbian Knez Lazar after his fall at Kosovo in the late fourteenth century, Arthur was especially revered after the Celts were defeated and subjugated by the Germanic attackers. Of his earliest history little is known—some Welsh sources from about 600 (such as the elegy *Gododdin*) refer to his martial accomplishments, and the priest Nennius chronicles the victories over the Saxons as well as local legends, but by 1100 in Wales he had become a full-blown legendary hero of romantic adventure and the leader of a band of men themselves also larger than life. From this Welsh origin, the legend of Arthur spread to the Cornish, who claimed him for their own, and then to the Bretons, who through their French-Celtic bilingualism were able to spread the insular tradition to the Continent: Largely by means of oral transmission, a medium that was to remain a channel for diffusion of romance materials throughout the Middle Ages, the tales soon passed from Wales to France, Provence, Italy, Sicily, Germany, and parts of Asia Minor. Even the great Arthurian masterworks of Chrétien de Troyes in France and Wolfram von Eschenbach and Gottfried von Strassburg in Germany trace their origins to this Breton connection.

Arthurian legend entered the learned tradition through Geoffrey of Monmouth's *Historia regum Britanniae* (1136, *History of the Kings of England*), a delightful, wholesale fabrication that passed as the standard historical account until the sixteenth century and was even adapted into French by the Norman poet Wace in 1155 (*Le Roman de Brut* or *Geste des Bretons*), in which form it also enjoyed wide currency as a source for English romances, directly and through Layamon's *Brut* (c. 1205). Meanwhile, the French romancers were developing the attached legends of Lancelot, Tristram, Gawain, and the Grail. In the twelfth century, Arthur's knights and court occupied the center of their attentions, while in the thirteenth they combined individual tales, greatly expanded the contemporary cycles of tales, and further Christianized the originally animistic and magical Grail stories. It is from this French efflorescence that the English tales of Arthur begin to develop in the second half of the thirteenth century, the legends having come full circle back to their origins in Britain, albeit in much modified form.

Of the considerable number of fourteenth century poems concerning Arthur or his knights, a handful stand out as deserving of special attention. Perhaps foremost among them are *Sir Gawain and the Green Knight* (c. 1375-1400) to be treated below in its own section, and the two poetic tales of Arthur's death, the alliterative *Morte Arthure* (c. 1360) and the stanzaic *Le Morte Arthur* (c. 1400). The former, composed in alliterative long lines in the same Northwest Midlands dialect that characterizes *Sir Gawain and the Green Knight* and the stanzaic version, derives mainly from Wace's translation of Geoffrey and legends of Alexander, and presents its portrait in both epic and tragic terms. Because of its relatively high density of conventional diction and typical scenes, it has been described as either a memorized or a traditionally composed poem; it is not far removed from the oral tradition that spawned its phraseology and narrative design. The alliterative poem represents what Larry Benson calls the "chronical tradition," an ostensibly historical account of battles and warriors rather than of romance and carefully drawn, individualized characters. The stanzaic version, on the other hand, is a true romance composed in eight-line stanzas of four-stress lines and represents a deftly managed condensation of the French prose *La Mort Artu* (c. 1225-1230). It includes Lancelot's encounter with the maid Astolat, his defense of the queen, the usurpation of the kingdom by Mordred, and the events leading up to Arthur's death. Unlike the alliterative version, this poem depends more on a fast-paced, streamlined narrative with emphasis on action than on conventional romance tropes, an economical texture that no doubt played a part in attracting the close attention of Malory as he composed his classic Arthurian works in the next century.

While no fourteenth century poems specifically about the wizard Merlin survive, owing perhaps to the lesser influence of Geoffrey's *Vita Merlini* as compared to his seminal *History of the Kings of England*, and while the only verse tale involving Lancelot in any significant role is the stanzaic *Le Morte Arthur*, a great many poems about Arthur's knight Gawain survive from the late medieval period. Primarily because Gawain was prominent in both Geoffrey and Wace, as well as in the French romances of Chrétien de Troyes, the English romancers celebrated his chivalric prowess and, it may be safely said, by their literary attention assigned him the highest rank of all who honored Arthur at the famous Roundtable. Apart from *Sir Gawain and the Green Knight*, the best known of these tales is *Ywain and Gawain* (c. 1300-1350), a translation and condensation of Chrétien de Troyes' *Yvain, ou le chevalier au lion* (c. 1170, *Yvain: Or, The Knight with the Lion*) and the only extant Middle English version of any of the great French romancer's works. As is the general rule with Anglo-Norman or French originals and their English descendants, the continental poem bristles with sophisticated literary conventions which reflect its intended courtly audience, while the English adaptation often uses proverbial or colloquial expressions more in keeping with its popular constitutency. *Syre Gawene and the Carle of Carelyle* (c. 1400) is also aimed at a popular audience and shares with its better-known counterpart the elements of temptation and beheading. In addition, the second episode of *The Awntyrs off Arthure at the Terne Wathelyne* (after 1375) consists of the common challege to Gawain and incorporates the hunting scenes that are juxtaposed to scenes of courtly wooing in *Sir Gawain and the Green Knight.* Finally, the *Libeaus Desconus* (c. second quarter of the fourteenth century), not much read today but extremely popular in its time, included the story of Gawain's bastard son Guinglain, whose emergence from personal obscurity combines the biographies of his father and Perceval. Possibly the work of Thomas Chestre, the author of *Sir Launfal* (c. 1430), this romance is ordinary enough in its execution but boasts a fair number of analogues, among them the Middle High German *Wigalois* (c. 1209) by Wirnt Von Grafenberg and the Italian *Carduino* (c. 1375) in addition to the inevitable French parallel *Le bel inconnu* (c. 1190).

The Perceval legend is rare in the medieval English poetic tradition, but alongside Malory's later prose is found the fourteenth century romance *Sir Perceval of Galles* (c. 1300-1340) and the more ambitious and justly famous German *Parzival* (1200-1212) of Wolfram and the French *Le Conte du graal* (c. 1182), the last romance composed by Chrétien. The Grail poems, Christianized in twelfth century French versions by association of the magic platter, and later cup, with already existing legends surrounding the Eucharist, are likewise few in English during this period, the only avatar being the fragmentary *Joseph of Arimathie* (c. 1350). Tales of Sir Tristram prove scarcer still, the sole examples being found in the thirteenth century *Sir Tristram*, in Thomas Malory's *Le Morte d'Arthur* (1485), and in a phantom twelfth century text by one Thomas of Britain that provided the basis for Gottfried von Strassburg's monumental but incomplete *Tristan* (c. 1210). If the relative paucity of Arthurian poems in certain areas is frustrating, caused in part by the eternal problem of damaged, destroyed, and lost manuscripts, it should be remembered how freely and widely these tales circulated even without the aid of writing throughout the Middle Ages, and therefore how rich the Arthurian tradition must have been.

The Alliterative Revival

Part of the richness of poems such as the Alexander fragments, the alliterative version of the death of Arthur, *Sir Gawain and the Green Knight, The Vision of William, Concerning Piers the Plowman* (1362-1393), and other works by the *Gawain*-poet stems from a literary phenomenon or movement that proceeded hand in hand with the development of Arthurian legend in the latter half of the fourteenth century—the burgeoning of unrhymed alliterative verse commonly called the Alliterative Revival. Like many terms canonized by usage in literary histories, this rubric is in some ways a misnomer.

In the absence of hard and unambiguous information, it is customarily assumed that the rejuvenation of the alliterative verse form reflects a kind of continuity not only with the thirteenth century *Brut* of Layamon but also, *ceteris paribus*, with the poems in the Anglo-Saxon type of alliterative meter five centuries earlier. Although the former connection is generally acknowledged, the latter is much more tenuous and cannot at present be demonstrated. It would be better to consider the Revival essentially a Middle English phenomenon, a poetic renaissance that took place when the cultural, linguistic, and historical time was right.

To appreciate the explosion which took place about the year 1350, one should note Derek Pearsall's striking observation that, while only twenty-eight lines of unrhymed alliterative verse survive, from the period of 1275 to 1350, the figure rises to more than forty thousand lines during the period from 1350 to 1425. Clearly something significant happened to precipitate this poetic deluge, and scholars have long been laboring to uncover and describe the forces that were or might have been at work. One suggestion is primarily historical, although with innumerable ramifications in other areas: it explains the rapid rise of English alliterative poetry as a response to the vacuum created by the demise of the Anglo-Norman tradition, a reflex of the progressive reaffirmation of things English, and especially English language and literature. Other critics locate the impetus of the Revival in the activity of monastic orders, which in the later Middle Ages were much involved in the social and economic as well as religious spheres. Still others have attributed this resurgence to the patronage of the ruling classes of the west of England, and some have found the verse to be propagandistic of this or that group or opinion. Whatever the complex of origins at the root of the movement, however, most critics agree that the Revival was a phenomenon that began in the north and soon spread to the Northwest and Southwest Midlands areas, that it was a typically fourteenth century flowering of literary excellence far outstripping anything immediately before or after it, that the movement was transitional between oral and written composition and transmission in its often consciously artistic permutations of traditional conventions and patterns, and that it represents the increasingly English character of literary tradition.

Genre in Fourteenth Century Poetry

Literary traditions seldom follow well-worn or predictable pathways; rather, they seem to meander this way and that, ever evolving and changing their own defining characteristics. As so many editors of anthologies and teachers of medieval survey courses have too painfully come to recognize, this truism is particularly apt for the fourteenth century. Although the period was never at a loss for models in the various European literatures, and although not a few contemporary writers were content to follow quite unrebelliously the rules of composition bequeathed to them implicitly in the assortment of genres at hand and explicitly in sources such as the handbooks mentioned above, many poets struck out bravely beyond the frontiers of generic and rhetorical propriety to discover new modes of artistic expression. The result of this iconoclasm is at once a rich legacy of experimentation and a correspondingly heterogeneous mix of poetic types. In confronting this achievement one must be careful not to diminish its richness and complexity by insisting on too rigid a taxonomy to contain it. Some of the commonly used labels, such as the venerable *romance*, do have *bona fide* literary identities and deserve the title of genre on the basis of classical critical criteria. Others, such as *didactic poetry*, are obviously the offspring of descriptive necessity and can lay no claim to constituting an integral group within the poetic tradition; clearly, it would be difficult to locate many medieval poems that are not in some manner didactic. With this caveat in mind, then, some general remarks about the maze of fourteenth century genres can be made.

The Romance

Although it may boast of being the most widespread and significant poetic form of the fourteenth century, the romance is not a genre that lends itself easily to brief definition. A general profile of the English romance can be assembled, however, and certain cycles or groups among its extant representatives can be distinguished. The English romance, a creature of the mid-thirteenth through the fifteenth century, was composed in a bewildering variety of verse forms as well as in prose, the major types of versification being the four-stress couplet, the tail-rhyme stanza (with a large number of different ryhme schemes), and the four-beat alliterative meter, sometimes in stanzaic format. The romancer followed the typical medieval method of borrowing *par excellence*, the source most often being a French original that was adapted into English, with original touches added by the poet, or simply translated in whole or in part. Stories concerned the adventures, both martial and amorous, of knights and their opponents and ladies, and were told with the greatest "willful suspension of disbelief" imaginable, a fantastic quality that fairly characterizes the genre as a whole. The narrative voice of most romances leads one to the conclusion that the primary aim of their composers was entertainment, and in fact there is evidence that many of the poems were meant to be read before audiences, both popular and courtly. This tendency did not, however, absolutely preclude a didactic intent; in some of the more finely crafted romances, such as *Sir Gawain and the Green Knight*, the chivalric and religious undercurrents are plain in the overall design of the work.

Hand in hand with the fantasy element in medieval romance goes idealization, readily transmuted to instructive purpose, and convention. Because the genre made use of oral traditional forms by cultivating stock characters, attitudes, and action patterns, it tended to present the immediate and particular against the larger canvas of the generic. Commonplaces, story patterns, verbal tags and formulas, and stock scenes were all among the elements at the romancer's disposal, and the fantastic, the ideal, and the typical merge in a text enlivened by its traditional context. The responses of heroes, the undertaking of quests, the wooing of ladies, and the games of courtly love are expected subjects; the audience read (or better, listened) to the story of Sir Launfal or Morgan Le Fay with a deep sense of its "reality" in the romance tradition and without nagging worry that its content was in modern terms quite unrealistic. To enter the world of medieval romance, to join the poet's quest, was willfully to renounce the corporeal and mundane in favor of the mysterious, the adventurous, and the magical.

More often than not the quest proved successful, the journey culminating in the medieval equivalent of a Hollywood ending. Innocence and even naïveté prevail, as the Perceval tradition well illustrates, and virtue is almost always rewarded. With little regard for historical accuracy, the romancer felt free to embroider a dull sequence of events either with his own personal literary design or, more frequently, with a pattern that was part of his poetic inheritance. He favored feasts and public ceremonies of all sorts for his courtly audience, more worldly embellishments for a popular group. In either case, however, his English poems were, as remarked above, generally less sophisticated than their French originals, in part because their intended audience was also less sophisticated.

As the useful taxonomy in *Manual of the Writings in Middle English* (1967) by John Wells and J. Burke Severs indicates, the great variety of English romances can profitably be viewed in ten groups: poems that derive from legends concerning (1) early Britain, (2) King Arthur, (3) Charlemagne, (4) Godfrey of Bouillon, (5) Alexander the Great, (6) Troy, (7) Thebes, and (8) the long-suffering Eustace, Constance, Florence, or Griselda, as well as (9) those stories that belong to the genre of the Breton lay and (10) a miscellaneous category that includes works of Eastern origin, historical poems, and didactic pieces. An alternate method for classifying and interrelating romances is the approach of Laura H. Loomis and Maldwyn Mills, a tripartite division of chivalric, heroic, and edifying. The first group contains those verse tales most like earlier French romances in their primary concern with love and chivalry, inorganic combination and recombination of stock elements, and typical location in a magical or exotic domain. The second type characteristically treats the hero as a member of a collective force and highlights societal expectation in addition to heroic achievement. In the third group the most important values are suffering and endurance in the face of just or unjust punishment, with the possibility of eventual transcendence as the protagonist's reward.

The most famous entry in the first Wells/Severs category, that of native English romances, must certainly be *King Horn* (c. 1225), a tale told and retold in many forms throughout the medieval period. Within the fourteenth century are *The Tale of Gamelyn* (c. 1350-1370) and *Aethelston* (c. 1355-1380), two poems that are probably English in origin and for which, unlike most other works in this group, no surviving sources in French have been discovered. *The Tale of Gamelyn* presents a lively composite of a number of familiar folktale elements, most prominently the benevolent outlaw behavior associated in the popular imagination with Robin Hood, and contemporary social commentary, as imaged in the hero's overturning of a corrupt judge and court. Moreover, there are criticisms of monastic and mendicant orders of clergy, humor, psychological realism, and the cherished happy ending, the last perhaps as much the gift of folktale as the emblem of the romance genre as a whole. The quite Anglo-Saxon *Aethelston*, a patently unhistorical tale of the victorious leader at the Battle of Brunanburh, is even more qualified for inclusion in the Loomis-Mills group of "heroic" romances, for not only is it unrelieved by episodes of love and chivalry but it also figures forth community values and obligations at the expense of individuals. Aethelston stands falsely accused until a trial by fire proves his innocence; the same trial determines the treason of his blood brother Wymound and matters are soon set right through execution. A third verse romance, *William of Palerne* (c. 1350-1361), amounts to a popularized translation of the French *Guillaume de Palerne* (1194-1197) and follows the return pattern so common in this and other categories.

The Lyric
   The miscellany of surviving Middle English lyrics extends throughout the period 1200-1500 and resists the application of general ordering principles and specific dating. Many of these works, however, take on a variety of identifiable aspects, even though the poets are themselves generally anonymous, and with good reason since many of the poems and virtually all of the constituent motifs and phraseology were in the public domain. As Raymond Oliver puts it, the poems have three intentions: to celebrate, to persuade, and to define. In the first case, the setting is a ritual occasion, such as the spring season, a wedding, Easter, or, preeminently, Christmas; the large collection of traditional carols belongs to this category. Lyrics intended to persuade customarily adopt a stance on particular actions and explain them in a coherent fashion, the *contemptus mundi* theme being a common subject for treatment. The third case, definition, bears on a position or doctrine and is almost always religious in nature. Other characteristics of the lyrics include their impersonal, generalized attitude and lack of interest in personality and psychology, features reflecting the poems' presentation in oral performance.
   Many of the topics and themes common to other fourteenth century literature can be found in much abbreviated form in the lyrics. An example is the courtly lover's plaint, such as the justly famous "Blow, Northern Wynd" (c. 1320), or, perhaps most classically, in "Now Springs the Spray" (c. 1300):

"Nou sprinkes the sprai./ Al for love Icche am so seek/ That slepen I ne mai."
The employing of a seasonal marker to impart an archetypal momentum to
a brief narrative, another familiar medieval device, also typifies many of the
lyrics, such as

> Somer is i-comen in,
> Loude syng cuckow!
> Groweth seed and bloweth meed
> And spryngeth the wode now . . . (c. 1320).

This famous poem preserves, as do others of the period, an elaborate set of
instructions for performing its music. More than other contemporary genres,
however, these poems manifest the influence of French and Latin traditions
in their multilingual phraseology: Where they are not straighforwardly
macaronic, they are often brimful of borrowings. Their rhetoric is also very
different from that of other forms; again in keeping with their customary
composition for oral performance, the rhetorical figures ordering the poems
lean toward the paratactic in structures such as anaphora, parallelism, and
repetition of words and phrases. Larger patterns follow suit, with emphasis
on stanzaic organization, narrative patterns based on ritual, liturgical, or
seasonal events, and repetition of segments. Alliteration and assonance occur
frequently, and the meter is accentual; as a rule, Rossell Hope Robbins'
suggestion that the levels of prosody and versification are commensurate with
the complexity of the subject well summarizes the matter and takes account
of the whole spectrum of lyrics, from the plainest and most popular song to
the most sophisticated tract on human mutability.

As Oliver notes, surviving Middle English lyrics differ considerably from
contemporary continental traditions in their anonymity and lack of concern
with individual psychology. German, Latin, and French lyrics of the period
often treated ostensibly biographical or other personal issues, most notably
the poems of François Villon (c. 1431-?) written in the form of a last will and
testament, but also the works of Walther von der Vogelweide (c. 1170-1230),
Hugh Primas of Orléans (wrote c. 1150), and the German "Archpoet" (died
c. 1165). Comparisons with Old English material, particularly with elegiac
lyrics and gnomic poetry, show a large number of alliterative and rhetorical
features in common, and the further development of the Middle English lyric
can be seen in the poetry of John Skelton and William Dunbar in the late
fifteenth and early sixteenth century. Those lyrics that can be placed in the
fourteenth century (at least on the evidence of surviving manuscripts) show
a representative spread of topics and concerns, from the sometimes vulgar
recountings of nature in all its earthiness, to Christmas carols that have managed to survive to this day, to celebrations of spring and religious renewal,
to earnest contemplations of the transience of human life and meditations on
liturgical moments and their meaning. The lyrics constitute a rich miscellany,

a backdrop of tradition that helps to contextualize the entire medieval period.

Didactic Poetry

Under this heading are grouped, for the sake of convenience, poems whose intent is chiefly religious and instructional and that do not easily stand alongside more better-defined counterparts in other genres. Although it is quite true that much of fourteenth century verse could be called didactic, this category should include only works not generically appropriate for inclusion elsewhere. One such work is Robert Mannyng's *Handlyng Synne* (1303-c. 1317), a thorough recasting of the Anglo-Norman *Le Manuel des péchés* (by William of Wadington in the thirteenth century). The subject of Mannyng's poem is vast: a good deal of Christian church doctrine, including the Ten Commandments, the Seven Deadly Sins, the Sins of Sacrilege, the Seven Sacraments, the Twelve Points of Shrift, and the Eight Joys of Grace, comes under his scrutiny. He occasionally leavens his theological lessons, perhaps intended for a specific audience of novices of Sempringham, with realistic detail and reaction, and, like Chaucer after him, he knows the edifying potential of a good story:

> For lewde men Y undyrtoke
> On Engylssh tunge to make thys boke;
> For many ben of swyche manere
> That talys and rymys wyl blethly here.

Mannyng also composed *The Story of England* (c. 1338), a chronicle of historical events from the Flood to the reign of Edward I, and he may be responsible for an adaptation of St. Bonaventure's *Meditations on the Life of Christ* (mid-thirteenth century).

Another primarily didactic poem of this century is the anonymous *Parlement of the Three Ages* (c. 1350), which employs two of the most characteristic medieval narrative devices, the dream vision and the debate. An example from the Alliterative Revival described earlier, this tale concerns the Nine Worthies and thus connects itself with the Alexander legends and their form as romances, but the most fundamental structure of the poem is as a moral lesson on the transience and mutability of all things earthly. The poet reviews the Worthies, wise men, and lovers, all from the perspective of the "vanity of human wishes," combining tried and true stories, topoi, and narrative patterns with a vigorous alliterative language that recalls at points the hearty realism of Anglo-Saxon heroic poetry as well as the later *Sir Gawain and the Green Knight*.

Less realistic but perhaps more rewarding stylistically and aesthetically, the elegiac *The Pearl* (c. 1380), attributed to the anonymous *Gawain*-poet, concerns the author's infant daughter who dies in her second year and inspires in her father a debate over divine wisdom and mortal expectation. After ascending to heaven, she tells him of her spiritual happiness and explains temporal misconceptions in God's ordering of the universe. Just as he tries to cross over to her, the poet awakes from his dream vision with his head on her grave, forever reconciled to her loss. A highly allegorical work, *The Pearl* recalls numerous biblical figurations from Revelations and elsewhere and presents its simple dream-vision narrative and complex allegorical latticework in a style both nominally typical of the Alliterative Revival and yet uniquely its own in the concomitant development of stanzaic patterns. Many critics have sought, and arguably found, numerological sequences that relate in some way to biblical and patristic sources, a not uncommon phenomenon in medieval texts. Other poets likewise turned to the dream and debate as methods for active mediation of the earthly and spiritual worlds, but few achieved the delicate interweaving of alliterative idiom and theological instruction that the *Pearl*-poet displays.

The same author is also credited with two other poems in the *Gawain* manuscript, *Cleanness* and *Patience*. The former presents the tales of the Flood, a popular subject since Anglo-Saxon times and usually thought to prefigure the Apocalypse, the destruction of Sodom and Gomorrah, and the fall of the sacriligious Belshazzar, concerning itself chiefly with the impurity of the situations that incurred God's punishment. The poet counterposes the sinful figures in these three biblical stories—and again the numerology seems more than accidental—to the three positive figures of Noah, Abraham, and Nebuchadnezzar, whose respect toward God is rewarded with mercy. Although not so intensely allegorical as *The Pearl*, *Cleanness* still motivates the reader to compare the three main stories with other biblical sources and, perhaps most of all, to consider the tropological implications for his own life. Similarly, *Patience*, the fourth of the poems in the *Gawain* manuscript, retells the narrative of the Book of Jonah, although the general medieval fascination with steadfast faith throughout the worst imaginable adversity, as evidenced so widely in the edifying romances of Griselda and company, must also serve as a background for this alliterative expatiation. This shorter poem is also the most personal of the four, portraying each of its characters with considerable realism and finesse, and offering a glimpse into the psychology of Jonah, particularly his human frailty. As a whole, the works of the *Pearl*-poet must be numbered among both the best and most memorable of the didactic poems of the fourteenth century and the most complicated representatives of the Alliterative Revival.

Political-Historical Poetry

During the fourteenth century there arose a fair number of poems that chronicled various historical epochs and events with a political purpose in mind. The earliest of these are eleven poems by Laurence Minot, written between 1333 and 1352, on the successful campaigns by Edward III against the Scots and the French. Responding to earlier English defeats, in particular the "Shameful Peace" with Scotland following Edward II's defeat at Bannockburn in 1314, Minot sought to eulogize the king's achievement and foster the cause of nationalism. The first and best known of his works, *Halidon Hill* (c. 1333), commemorates the young monarch's retributive victory that regained control of the northern border and soothed the political as well as territorial wounds inflicted on the English psyche, but warns against thoughtless celebration lest the nation be deceived by Scottish "gile."

John Barbour's *The Bruce* (c. 1375), on the other hand, celebrates Scottish nationalism in an account of the heroic actions of King Robert the Bruce and his faithful comrade-in-arms Sir James Douglas that stretches to more than thirteen thousand lines. Beginning with historical facts and bringing to his work classical and medieval models as well as a lively sense of mythic narrative, Barbour recounts the heroic accomplishments of Robert, including the Battle of Bannockburn, and Douglas' unsuccessful attempt to bear the fallen king's heart to the Holy Land. As Charles Dunn and Edward Byrnes observe in *Middle English Literature* (1973), the poem finds its thematic center in Robert as the quintessential defender of Scottish liberty and in Douglas as the equally paradigmatic loyal follower. In this and other ways, *The Bruce* eludes categorization, whether as chronicle, political poem, epic, or myth; in the final analysis it remains a work *sui generis*, one most typical of the mélange of later fourteenth century verse forms.

The anonymous author of *Thomas of Erceldoun* (c. 1388-1401) also combined a number of stock medieval generic characteristics to forge a unique kind of narrative. Although parts of the story share with *Halidon Hill* and *The Bruce* certain real battles as subjects, and although the hero of the work, one Thomas Rymor of Earlston, is historical, the poem also interweaves common folktale elements and other features typical of medieval romance. The main narrative frame concerns Thomas' love affair with an underworld queen and his consequent ability to foretell the future. As well as the queen's predictions about clashes between Scotland and England, the poet presents certain other auguries of indistinct relation to the first group. Dunn and Byrnes note that *Thomas of Erceldoun* typifies a pan-European medieval technique in its assignment of known historical facts to the visions of a seer or prophet and attachment of especially attractive prophecies not yet fulfilled to the historical record; once assembled, the entire package was apparently submitted as a political tour de force.

Great Individual Authors and Works

Apart from the many engaging and accomplished poems treated above under various generic categories stand some individual authors and works that, by virtue of both their own artistic excellence and their influence and modern appeal, deserve special attention. Among this latter group are William

Langland's *The Vision of William, Concerning Piers the Plowman*, the anonymous *Sir Gawain and the Green Knight*, and John Gower's *Confessio Amantis* (1390, *The Lover's Confession*). Each in its own way helps to set the standard of poetic achievement that is the legacy of the late fourteenth century or "Ricardian" period, as J. A. Burrow has named it, and together these three poems constitute a crucial context for the genius of Chaucer.

The Vision of William, Concerning Piers the Plowman is extant in three recensions, labeled the A, B, and C texts. The three combined are divided into two parts, "The Vision of William, Concerning Piers the Plowman" and "The Life of Do-Well, Do-Better, and Do-Best," which articulate, respectively, general and individual problems of evil and corruption, both offering solutions for the good Christian during his stay on earth. The vision portrays the ruin of contemporary society in allegorical terms and, perhaps responding in part to the social upheaval that wracked the everyday lives of fourteenth century humanity, suggests the humble and simple virtue and obedience of the plowman as an antidote to temporal discord. In the second section, the poet conducts an allegorical search for the ideal Christian existence, starting within himself and then undertaking a quest through various liturgical and philosophical domains under the guidance of a series of mentors. With his journey complete, the dreamer's vision turns from its focus on higher abstract truths to their practical implementation in contemporary society.

Langland's poem is, as much as any medieval work, uniquely his own, but one can trace a few analogues and parallels to fill out its literary context. Tracts such as Mannyng's *Handlyng Synne*, described above in the section on didactic poetry, are typical of many such instructional poems and prose works of the period; some of the most familiar include Dan Michel of Northgate's *Ayenbite of Inwyt* (1340, a translation of *La somme des vices et des vertues* by Laurentius Gallus) and Chaucer's "Parson's Tale." These poems and similar works were commonly consulted by writers for liturgical details and traditional literary accounts associated with church dogma. Also of influence was the well-developed sermon tradition of the later Middle Ages, which became a learned craft memorialized in handbooks (*Ars praedicandi*), much like the *Ars rhetoricae* or *Ars poeticae* employed by poets in search of commonplaces of description or narrative action. In fact, several whole works are at least formally similar to *The Vision of William, Concerning Piers the Plowman*, such as Guillaume de Deguileville's *The Pilgrimage of Human Life, of the Soul, and of Jesus Christ* (c. 1330-1358), as well as more general classical and other foreign models of allegorical quests and seeking after divine truth. Although superficially *The Vision of William, Concerning Piers the Plowman* and *Sir Gawain and the Green Knight* are strange bedfellows, the fact remains that Langland's poem is also a manifestation, and a brilliantly executed one, of the Alliterative Revival. Even so, as with all of the best works of the late fourteenth century, *The Vision of William, Concerning Piers the Plowman* is best assessed on its own merits as an earnest and able contemplation of its time, in this instance against the backdrop of the Christian drama.

To appreciate the earnestness of this finely crafted allegorical latticework, it is necessary to view the poem in its literary historical milieu. Recalling the desperate state of affairs in late fourteenth century England—the Church in corrupt disarray since the preceding century, the Avignon Papacy just coming to an end, the Black Death having run rampant only twenty-five years before, the longstanding social discontent crystallizing in the Peasants' Rebellion of 1381, the condemnation of Wycliffe's teaching in 1382, and the blatantly incompetent rule of Richard II, one can well imagine how a poem such as *The Vision of William, Concerning Piers the Plowman* came to be composed and why, if the extremely large number of extant manuscripts is any testimony, it found a large and sympathetic audience long before being taken up by scholars and critics as one of the masterpieces of its time. In a century wracked by uncertainty, the spiritual journey of Everyman in search of truth must have served a social as well as aesthetic purpose; given the prevailing problems, it may not be too daring to characterize one function of this "poem of apocalypse," as Morton Bloomfield calls it, as cathartic or therapeutic. In the medium of poetic art, Langland and, vicariously, his countrymen could respond to a sometimes corrupt and vacuous clergy with satire and wit; they could counter a monumentally intransigent and self-centered government with lessons on taming Lady Meed; and, most crucial, they could combat the socially exacerbated sickness of mortality by imagining, in great allegorical detail, a religious restorative. Langland proposed a journey not unlike that of Dante, a dream of transcendence of the earthly sphere, and a vision of God uncomplicated and unsullied by the catastrophic events of his time. Even if *The Vision of William, Concerning Piers the Plowman* ends with the Antichrist in power, the Church under attack, and the world as yet unredeemed, the dreamer has a new understanding of what lies beyond his immediate environment as a defense against apocalypse. The search will continue.

Sir Gawain and the Green Knight

Another of the jewels in the crown of the Alliterative Revival, *Sir Gawain and the Green Knight* represents a very different sort of literary masterpiece from *The Vision of William, Concerning Piers the Plowman*. Melding together games and story patterns from Celtic folklore, attitudes and values from a highly developed and thoughtful Christianity, and the ritualistic procedures of courtly love, it achieves a fusion of medieval ideas unique in the fourteenth century. An Arthurian hero, Gawain, in place of his monarch, takes up the challenge to behead the Green Knight and, should the marvelous fellow survive, to allow him the same privilege a year hence. Gawain accepts what critics have viewed as both a Christmas prank and the initial act in a story of vegetative renewal and cleanly lops off the Green Knight's head; not the least discouraged, his adversary gathers up his lost part and, reminding Gawain of his pledge, rides off to unknown regions. Too soon the annual cycle is complete and the day arrives for the honorable knight's departure to fulfill the bargain; Gawain leaves Arthur's court and eventually finds himself at the castle of one Bercilak and his lady, an honored guest enjoying their hospitality. Here the plot begins to thicken ominously. While the lord and master is off on his daily hunting expedition, not incidentally for three successive days, his wife acts as courtly temptress of their guest. Gawain finds himself suspended between two medieval romantic codes: either he must follow the precepts of chivalric behavior and, refusing the lady's advances, honor his host's hospitality as a true knight of the Round Table, or he must gallantly bow to the pressures of courtly love and, accepting the lady, fulfill another set of expectations. Of course he cannot do both, especially since he agreed with Bercilak to exchange any booty won on their respective hunts, and so he is caught in a logically insoluble quandary. After weakening the third day and accepting a kiss, Gawain leaves the castle and soon encounters the Green Knight, who turns out to be Bercilak in disguise. Submitting to the promised return blow, the hero flinches once, receives a second feint, and on the third swing of the ax is slightly injured, just enough to compensate for his minor indiscretion on the third day of the earlier test. The Green Knight then gives him the lady's "girdle" or sash, a symbol of femininity since classical times, to wear around his belt in remembrance of the whole affair, and Gawain heads back to Arthur's court with his life and his knighthood intact.

The sources behind this lively tale include a mixture of originally Celtic elements and common romance motifs, but whatever the actual source materials with which he worked, the artistic achievement of the *Gawain*-poet remains uniquely his own. The archetypal frame provided by the self-renewing Green Knight promotes ideas of recurrence and inevitability and is made to surround a series of ironic and playful games engaged in by the much-tried hero, the lady temptress, and the lord Bercilak. There is clearly no escape for Gawain, nor is there meant to be: the fall of Gawain as Everyman is in fact remarkably innocuous given the pressing circumstances, as the Green Knight's mercy (but justice) with his sharp edge illustrates. Gawain loses a battle as, from one point of view, the entrapment made inevitable by his mortality eventually draws blood; the Green Knight must be repaid, just as surely as the next Christmas season will announce the rebirth of God. Yet the hero's fallibility also becomes his religious and moral sinecure. Chastised by a natural, postlapsarian error, he shows himself—and in the process humanity—to be the better for the test. What he loses with a kiss and a flinch from the blade he repays, Christ-like, with his wound, and ever afterward the girdle remains as a symbol of his transcendence of mere mortal frailty. Gawain, like Oedipus, solves a riddle and wins a contest; by surviving the complex contest of conventions and circumstances, he comes to epitomize the triumph not only presaged by Christ but also, optimally, mirrored in Every-man's experience of earthly life. For all this, the vehicle for this highly serious investigation of mysteries remains a virtual *cadeau*, a Christmas jest: when all is over, when the tale is done and the poet adds "Honi soyt qui mal pence" ("Evil be to him who thinks evil"), Chaucer's immoral morality and playful hermeneutics seem very near indeed.

John Gower's *Confessio Amantis*

John Gower's much praised *Confessio Amantis* forms one third of a trilogy of poems by Gower on the evils that assail the individual and state and on methods for overcoming them and achieving virtue. He first completed the Anglo-Norman *Mirour de l'Omne* (1374-1378), and the Latin *Vox Clamantis* followed in 1381; the first version of *Confessio Amantis*, universally pro-claimed his masterpiece, was finished in 1390. A straightforwardly and severely moral work, it functions chiefly through a barer and more economical allegory than does *The Vision of William, Concerning Piers the Plowman*, but one that is in its way equally powerful. Again, there is the familiar dream-vision structure in Book I, with the poet Gower imagining a meeting with the God of Love, the Queen of Love, and the Queen's priest Genius. The priest then treats the dangers of earthly love and the Seven Deadly Sins, one after the other, for most of the remainder of the work, teaching the poet-lover in good medieval style through a series of illustrative stories. Finding himself absolved of his afflictions, the poet is able to bid Venus farewell, turn to reason for guidance, and pursue the lasting spiritual rewards of moral virtue.

Several features of the *Confessio Amantis* deserve special comment. First, in addition to the dream vision, allegorical commonplaces, and discussion of the Seven Deadly Sins, the poem is thoroughly medieval in its juxtaposition of human versus divine love, a topic as old as the Anglo-Saxon elegies *The Wife's Lament* or *The Seafarer* (both c. tenth century). Of course, no poem could well function more differently from *Sir Gawain and the Green Knight*, but the two works do share the story of medieval man learning his human shortcomings and profiting from the lesson. The *Confessio Amantis* delivers its instruction in a less immediate, more austere manner, agreeing in tone and structure with *The Vision of William, Concerning Piers the Plowman*, but it seems worthwhile to note that John Gower's moral allegory and the *Gawain*-poet's romance do affirm the same values and, once the particulars deriving from generic differences are deemphasized, can be seen to offer similar pre-scriptions for getting on in the world. At the same time, one should remember that the *Confessio Amantis* is not, like *The Vision of William, Concerning Piers the Plowman* and *Sir Gawain and the Green Knight*, a product of the Alliterative Revival, and that both its subject and the rhymed couplets of its verse hark back to foreign as well as native models, as indicated by the vision's considerable debt for its story-line to the *Roman de la Rose* (the first portion written in the first half of the thirteenth century by Guillaume de Lorris, the second portion written between 1275 and 1280 by Jean de Meurq). As an obviously well-educated and widely read man, Gower had no shortage of models for his poetry, and he turned his conception of proper human attainments into a clear and readable narrative intended both to instruct and to entertain. That such a work, rigorously formal in attitude and design yet a paragon of literary attractiveness, could exist beside *Sir Gawain and the Green Knight* and even complement its purpose is a measure of the poetic cornucopia of the fourteenth century.

Geoffrey Chaucer's *The Canterbury Tales*

Towering over all of fourteenth century poetry are the poems of Geoffrey Chaucer. In nearly every imaginable manner Chaucer epitomizes his age and its literature: in the midst of social anguish and turmoil he focused his genius on matters of supreme and permanent importance; as a thoroughly medieval author he borrowed freely and imaginatively from English, French, Italian, and Latin sources; refusing even more than his contemporaries to be hidebound by generic or rhetorical constraints, he frequently pushed the rules of genre and poetic composition to the breaking point, creating in the process some works that defy classification in their brilliant originality; and, especially typical of late fourteenth century or Ricardian masters, he managed to achieve affecting and enduring *aperçus* into the pilgrimage of humanity and the ceaseless ritual games between men and women.

Chaucer's most ambitious work is also the most typical literary document of its age. At a time when uncertainty and doubt threatened to send most social and political institutions careening into disaster or disrepute, when Langland was composing his monumental allegory of salvation as a bulwark against religious and cultural apocalypse, Chaucer managed to assemble a company of remarkably disparate individuals and to lead them on a pilgrimage of hope, a journey that would discover their common humanity in a startlingly novel fashion. If creative response to the breakdown of hard-won but outmoded syntheses was an important theme in this period, then *The Canterbury Tales* epitomize that solution: in presenting his panorama, Chaucer uses most of the major contemporary genres but subordinates them to a new design; he introduces God's plenty of personalities but finds a way to integrate them into a believable community; he has his pilgrims discuss many of the burning social, religious, and philosophical issues of the day but never lets debate or pedantry obtrude on the collective function of the group; and he achieves a realism and naturalism of characterization far beyond that of any contemporary work without ever abandoning either his finely crafted, brilliantly conceived narrative voice or the structure, large and small, of the stories themselves and the work as a whole. When one adds the tremendous range of his learning, so apparent in the variety of sources and the skill with which he re-creates them, and the outright appeal of the poem for generations of audiences, it becomes no exaggeration to call *The Canterbury Tales* both Chaucer's masterpiece and the masterwork of the entire fourteenth century.

As might be expected, such a poem seems to have been largely the product of the poet's later years, of his mature style. Still influenced by the French tradition of romances and *dits amoreux* which served so importantly as models in his earlier writings, and having digested the contributions of the Italian poets and transmuted this literary gold into an indigenous English coin, Chaucer struck out on the kind of creative, original venture that only a lifetime of exposure to experience with traditional materials could foster. Scholars customarily associate the year 1386 with his conception of the plan for *The Canterbury Tales*, but he may well have been working on the project beforehand. Perhaps the next year he composed the immortal "General Prologue," from a textual viewpoint the key to all that follows. Opinions on other aspects of chronology vary as well, but the tales themselves probably occupied Chaucer for most of the rest of his life. The unfinished state of the work and its tangle of manuscripts indicate that he probably composed significant parts of the poem up until his death, but one should also remember that *The Canterbury Tales* were, like most medieval poetry, intended for oral performance and not primarily as a written text.

One of the influences on Chaucer's poem was the Italian *novelle* tradition, a loose aggregation of tales brought together by an outwardly unifying fiction. Although Giovanni Sercambi did write such a collection in the general form of a pilgrimage about 1374, it is important to note that neither this nor any other group of *novelle* could have provided more than a suggestion for the complex and dynamic frame of *The Canterbury Tales*. Likewise, the richness of the "General Prologue" derives not from the considerable number of sketches written at the time, but most vitally from Chaucer's genius for weaving conventional topoi, rhetorical rules, character types, and at least some real personalities into a fabric distinctly his own. Of the sources and analogues for the tales themselves, it may be said that the mélange of genres and possible parallels is as diverse as the company of pilgrims, including, besides the *novelle*, the French *fabliau* tradition, the romance, the saint's life, the folktale, the medieval sermon, the miracle story, the epic, and the mock-heroic poem. No form passed through Chaucer's hands without considerable elaboration or some sort of modification; often his contribution consisted of turning the genre to his favorite purpose of social satire, and at times his reworking was so complete that, as in the case of the superbly farcical "Sir Thopas," he created a virtually new genre.

To surround his tales of life and love, Chaucer constructed what is frequently called a frame but which might better be labeled a purpose or context. Unlike the Italian analogues that postulate a nominal unifying fiction and leave the matter quite undeveloped, the pilgrimage is ever evolving, with the poet shifting the focus this way and that to sustain the fiction and to allow his characters their remarkable range of expression and interaction. Intimately allied to the pilgrimage conceit is the naïve, impressionable narrator who keeps it alive—the poet-pilgrim Chaucer who mourns his lack of literary aptitude ("My wit is short, ye may wel understonde"). Behind this wide-eyed, good-natured fellow, of course, stands the poet Chaucer, manipulating the unbounded enthusiasm of his narrator with consummate skill and a keen sense of irony, allowing his audience a double perspective on characters and events. Indeed, it is impossible to separate the pilgrimage context from its somewhat clumsy but ever-willing rhapsode. If Chaucer's characters come alive and interact in ways unique to *The Canterbury Tales*, a large part of the credit is due to a combination of his narrator's unfailing and irrepressible humanity with the poet's own perspectives on the fascinating heterogeneity of mankind.

From this union of authorial design and naturalistic narration springs the vivacity of the "General Prologue." After setting the scene and creating the rationalizing fiction, the narrator begins an exacting introduction of his society in microcosm, epitomizing each character type and endowing each pilgrim with a memorable individuality. His small community allegorizes fourteenth century society—and it does not: taking advantage of traditional associations, Chaucer not infrequently adorns a character with the "tell-tale detail," such as the Prioress' brooch, the Miller's wart, the Wife's deafness or scarlet hose, or the Pardoner's waxy yellow hair. Details and the actions and habits that they either imply or actually represent come nimbly into play, as the narrator balances expectations based on character types against the exceptions to those *règles du jeu*. Such is Chaucer's mastery of the poetic medium, however, that he expresses even these singularities in the form of medieval rhetorical commonplaces. Drawing on conventional techniques of poetic description, and especially on the *notatio-effictio* method of portraying inner qualities or liabilities in a character's specific physical features, he encodes some of his most subtle and iconoclastic observations on a character in the metalanguage prescribed by poetic handbooks. Sometimes an overabundance of one of the four humors—blood, phlegm, yellow bile, and black bile, postulated since the Greek physician Galen and common in medieval medical lore—leads to a judgment on a person; in another case a term with lascivious associations, such as the Wife's quality of being "gat-toothed," mitigates or seconds other aspects of a description. Employing to the hilt the narrator's unremittingly naïve euphemisms (only he could call as notorious a swindler and reprobate as the Pardoner a "noble ecclesiaste"), Chaucer delicately balances traditional expectation and individual design, managing to make time for implicit commentary that ranges from ironic to bawdy to sincerely religious.

Chaucer's portraits are elaborately crafted, to be sure, and just as certainly very carefully hung. Critics have pointed out various possible schemes for the arrangement, many of them founded on the ideas of the various estates or social classes of medieval provenance. Donald Howard suggests that the order of presentation is a mnemonic structure or *aide-mémoire* analogous to medieval formulations reported by Frances Yates; that is, three groups of seven, each group headed by an ideal figure: the Knight, followed by the Squire, Yeoman, Prioress, Monk, Friar, and Merchant; the Clerk, followed by the Man of Law, Franklin, Guildsman, Shipman, Physician, and Wife; and the Parson and Plowman (brothers), followed by the Miller, Manciple, Reeve, Summoner, Pardoner, and Host. Howard argues that these mnemonic constructs were so much a part of medieval literary consciousness that it would be only natural for Chaucer to employ them in his art. This scheme for the introduction of the characters seems credible enough. It does, however, leave out a character who is in many ways the most important of all: Chaucer the pilgrim. Throughout the "General Prologue," but particularly in the thirty-two lines that intervene between the introductions of the Pardoner and the Host, the narrator is introduced as another in the company, an appealing fellow who begs his readers not to hold him directly responsible for what he reports because he can only repeat what was said by others. It is very much in the innocent nature of Chaucer the pilgrim to issue such a disclaimer before he begins the recital of romance, *fabliau*, and the other genres that make up *The Canterbury Tales*, and the reader may also sense the guiding hand of the poet finishing off the characterization of yet another pilgrim, the narrative liaison between poet and poem and the lifeblood of the pilgrimage frame.

Harry Bailly, the Host, soon takes nominal charge of the enterprise, sets the rules for tale-telling (two while riding to Canterbury and two on the way back from each pilgrim), and has the participants draw lots to determine who will start. The cut falls to the Knight, and the tales begin as they should in the social sphere of fourteenth century England with the pilgrim of highest rank opening the proceedings. "The Knight's Tale" turns out to be a story and a type of poem appropriate both to its teller and to its position in the work as a whole. As an adventurer in the service of the Christian God, and as "a verray, parfit gentil knyght" quite the opposite of that over-courtly *bon vivant* his Squire, he lends dignity and a sense of purpose to the community by relating an intricate Boethian romance that reaffirms the social order that he leads. Drawn primarily from Boccaccio's *La Teseide* (1340-1345), or epic of Theseus, with a great deal of the favorite medieval device of compression, this chivalric tale was probably first composed as a separate piece unconnected with *The Canterbury Tales* and only later fitted into its present place. Whatever the nature of the lost version mentioned in the Prologue to *The Legend of Good Women* (1380-1386), the extant tale chronicles the tragic and eventually ennobling love of the young knights Palamon and Arcite for a lady Emelye. The misfortunes of earthly life are seen as "perturbations of the spheres" and the story moves like Chaucer's *Troilus and Criseyde* from mortal myopia to a larger perspective under the aegis of Theseus. The variety of contributions to follow are to an extent rationalized by this tale, which remains a philosophical anchor and moral standard for the entire work.

No sooner has the stately knight finished justifying the ways of God to his fellow pilgrims than the drunken Miller counters the propriety and high style of the initial tale with his coarse, irreverent *fabliau* of carpenter John's cuckolding. The Miller is so impatient and rude, in every way the antithesis of the first teller, that he interrupts the Host's request that the Monk be next and, ever so characteristically, barges straight ahead to "quite the Knyghtes Tale." His own words introduce an important structural principle, that of "quiting" or repaying, which will account for the presence of the tale to follow as well. This low-life character offers the furthest remove imaginable from the philosophical complexity of "The Knight's Tale" by telling an uproarious story of how Nicholas the clerk planned and carried off the seduction of the carpenter's wife virtually before her husband's eyes. Not only is the Miller "quiting" the Knight; in addition, the lower class is challenging the views and values of the upper, animal instincts and scheming are being played off against higher passions and earnest moral deliberations, and, perhaps most significantly, the dynamics of the community of pilgrims—both as individuals and as representatives of their vocations or types—are starting to take shape. "The Miller's Tale" deals not with Boethius but with bawdiness: the clever Nicholas, the doltish John, the unspeakably fey parish clerk Absolon, and the concupiscible young wife Alison engage in a fast-paced charade that rides roughshod over courtly love, religious duty, matrimonial fidelity, and all available aspects of contemporary morality. At the same time, the Miller stumbles through a real, if homely, alternative to the deep pondering and austerity of "The Knight's Tale" and helps to set the tone and outer limits of Chaucer's investigation of humanity.

The lonely Reeve, who brings up the rear of the assemblage, then reacts violently against what he judges to be the Miller's personal insult of a trade he has practiced and, "quiting" his foe, responds with a *fabliau* about the cuckolding of a dishonest miller. Some tales later Chaucer introduces a justly famous character, Dame Alys or the Wife of Bath, as vigorous, self-serving, and lecherous as the Reeve is biting, sarcastic, and "colerik." Her Prologue consists of a boisterous, happy biography complete with accounts of her five husbands and how she achieved mastery over all of them. Often linked to the antifeminist sentiment of the period, ironically evident in her fifth husband's book of misogynist exempla, the Wife commands the stage of *The Canterbury Tales* by misquoting and misapplying biblical and patristic authorities, by celebrating the lustful nature that led her to ogle Jankyn (her fifth husband) during her fourth mate's funeral, by discoursing on male and female genitalia with a crudity that would do the blockhead Miller proud, and generally by providing the community of pilgrims with an inextinguishable source of gleeful iconoclasm, good will, and high spirits. Very rarely in any literary period is there so vivacious and singular a character as the Dame; like a medieval Falstaff, she stands astride the work of which she is a part, to be remembered and cherished as a patroness of its art.

As the Wife boasts of her conquests in the Prologue, the reader begins to understand that she is offering one possible solution to the problem of the contest for mastery between men and women. "The Wife of Bath's Prologue and Tale" is one in a series of seven tales that Kittredge identified as the "Marriage Group," a sequence that, he argued, was intended to present various possibilities for the seat of authority in marriage. The four most important members of this group are the Wife, the Clerk, the Merchant, and the Franklin. The Clerk tells a story of male dominance over a painfully patient Griselda which "quites" the Wife, and the Merchant spins the ubiquitous medieval tale of the elderly January and his young wife May, warning of the consequences that such a doomed alliance must bring. For her part, the Wife fashions a Prologue that finds distant analogues in the very antifeminist writings that it parodies, but which remains after all a brilliant original; her tale, on the other hand, is the common story of the Loathly Lady and her miraculous transformation, analogues of which are found in Gower's *Confessio Amantis* and numerous contemporary romances. With the Knight under the thumb of the hag, whom he has promised to marry after she saves his life, Dame Alys makes her exit, no doubt supremely confident of the influence of her words on the audience she has been both entertaining and instructing. Even so, the reader may ask how well she has succeeded in making the patently outrageous palatable.

If the Wife, Clerk, and Merchant offer what are finally unsatisfactory alternatives for the problem of sovereignty in marriage, the Franklin, "Epicurus owene sone" and knight of the shire, provides a final solution in a tale that Chaucer adapted from Boccaccio's *Il Filostrato* (1335-1340), with elements from Geoffrey of Monmouth, the Breton lay tradition, and the common folktale motif of the rash promise. As Paul Ruggiers puts it in *Art of The Canterbury Tales* (1965), "The view of marriage which has in a sense been dismembered is reconstituted in terms of a balance between service and dominance, between human weakness and strength of character, between respect for self and respect for others." Even the announced genre of the tale, a Breton lay, promotes the resolution by creating a fairy-tale world wherein forbidding complexities can be magically simplified and the nagging temporal concerns of an imperfect world dissolved in a romantic suspension of disbelief. Taking as his topic and argument the already demonstrated reality that "Love wold not been constreyned by maistrye," the Franklin tells the story of Arveragus and his faithful wife Dorigen, whom Aurelius, the courtly lover *par excellence*, is, characteristically enough, pursuing. In resisting his suit, a rare abstinence in the world of *The Canterbury Tales*, she sets him a task seemingly impossible of fulfillment, saying that she will accede only if he manages to remove each and every stone from the coast of Britain. By consulting a clerk versed in Chaucer's favorite science of astronomy, the resourceful Aurelius accomplishes the task and calls the lady's hand.

The dilemma that now presents itself to Arveragus and Dorigen is clear-cut but morally insoluble: if she refuses Aurelius' love, she violates her solemn promise; if she accepts him, he violates her contract of fidelity with her husband. As much as the outcome seems "agayns the proces of nature," the quandary is real, at least for people as honorable and devoted to each other as this couple. Arveragus selflessly counsels his wife to uphold her part of the bargain and she reluctantly agrees, but such is the self-correcting nature of the world of "The Franklin's Tale" that the once crafty and unabashed suitor takes pity on Dorigen's obvious suffering and releases her from the promise, even proclaiming her fidelity as a virtue implicitly superior to the code of courtly love. True to its genre, the poem then completes the resolution by releasing Aurelius from his financial obligations through the kindness and mercy of the clerk he had surreptitiously hired to perform the impossible feat. *Gentilesse*, the Chaucerian idiom for nobility and delicacy of character, replaces *governance* as the ruling principle of conjugal relations, and the Marriage Group finds the answer it has been seeking throughout the community of pilgrims. "The Franklin's Tale" thus represents a kind of testament to order in the world of man as well as a coda to a set of literary preludes. In the midst of real and expectable social chaos there is a bit of magic, a moment of harmony in a generaly discordant world.

That discord is never more baldly evident than in the shameless words of the Pardoner, a marvelously vile and altogether reprehensible character who will offer, so he claims, a "moral tale." It is difficult to see how such a man could bring it off: a seller of bogus absolutions and false relics, he takes as his theme the oft-quoted aphorism "Radix malorum est Cupiditas" ("The root of all evils is Greed") and goes on to make a case for himself as the contemporary personification of Cupiditas. He straightforwardly and pride-fully boasts of swindling well-meaning people searching for religious comfort in the form of supposedly genuine pardons, happy to deprive even the poorest widow of the money that would keep her children from starvation. Ironically true to his claim to be able to instruct although he is himself fast-fettered by sin, the Pardoner launches into a moral exemplum presented as a sermon. His tale, designed to illustrate the eventual retribution to be visited on gluttons and revelers and, by extension, on all those guilty of the deadly sins, is crudely told and leads into hollow apostrophes against what are of course his own flaws, followed by his customary shameless plea for money. His direct address of the Host as the pilgrim most in need of his services inflames Bailly and evokes his memorable threat to denature the Pardoner, a sentiment that the audience—especially the contemporary audience, who had to deal more and more with false sellers of writs as the authority of the Church continued to decline—must have applauded. It remains for the Knight, the embodiment of honor and social protocol and a tale-teller whose words have already served as balm for the ephemeral wounds of Everyman, to brave the verbal fray between these two and restore order to the pilgrim's community.

As an entire work, *The Canterbury Tales* seems to stand incomplete. Only twenty-three of the thirty pilgrims mentioned actually tell a tale, even though the Host's original arrangement called for no fewer than four apiece. The framing device, however, is a fiction that provides unity to a heterogenous collection; it is not a legal document. Especially since *The Canterbury Tales* were composed primarily for reading aloud before an audience, individual stories or groups of stories may well have enjoyed an existence of their own apart from the text as a whole. Chaucer may never have intended to "complete" his most lasting poem at all; having invented the fiction that would cause any number of tales to cohere, he may simply have turned his hand to those characters, issues, genres, and narratives that most attracted him. It seems more than a little pedantic, then, to insist that *The Canterbury Tales* remain incomplete, in the sense of "partial," for Chaucer's vision reached far beyond anything created by even his most talented contemporaries, and the tales he did compose bear eloquent testimony to the fertility of his design.

At the close of "The Parson's Tale" there is one final twist of the narrative thread in *The Canterbury Tales*. Here Chaucer places his "retraction," ostensibly a profession of faith accompanied by a confession of self-proclaimed wrongdoings in some of his poetic works. Critics have pointed out how the retraction has numerous literary precedents and analogues, perhaps the most striking of which is Boccaccio's own rejection of his often bawdy tales in Italian in favor of learned Latin treatises. A reader may also take Chaucer's protestation as another in a series of clever manipulations of his audience, accepting his prayer at face value as both a pious expostulation and a traditional tour de force but recognizing the retraction itself as a form of disclaimer—only this time on the part of Chaucer the poet rather than Chaucer the pilgrim. As has been seen, the narrator is more than adequate to the task of presenting *The Canterbury Tales* in a naturalistic and blameless way, and now the poet further relativizes not only this work but also all others that treat in any way lecherous, scatological, or otherwise irreligious subjects. If Chaucer's retraction honestly professes faith in Christ and hope for eternal salvation, it also allows the poet and audience yet another perspective on the wonderful variety of pilgrims who have trod the stage of *The Canterbury Tales*: they are real, they are complete in themselves, and they collectively figure forth a uniquely engaging pastiche of characteristics, attitudes, values, and beliefs typical of the fourteenth century in particular and of humanity in general. Chaucer cannot retract that achievement.

John Miles Foley

THE FIFTEENTH CENTURY

Dwarfed by the mighty accomplishments of Geoffrey Chaucer at one end and the great Elizabethans at the other, fifteenth century poetry has often seemed to stretch like a lesser plain between mountain ranges. There is some truth to this view: by no standard was this a distinguished age in the history of English verse. The English Chaucerian tradition, running from John Lydgate and Thomas Occleve to Stephen Hawes, can boast no major poet and only a paucity of significant minor ones, and rarely did fifteenth century works in the well-established popular genres of metrical romance, saint's life, and lyric match the high achievements of the century before. Indeed, the best-known literary productions of the 1400's, the prose Arthurian romances of Thomas Malory and the dramatic cycles of the Corpus Christi season, belong to genres other than poetry. On the other hand, poetry in this period may have suffered a general undervaluation owing to comparisons which it cannot sustain; if one approaches fifteenth century poetry with chastened expectations and sensitivities attuned to the artistic aims of this period as distinct from others, one can find work of real interest and value. For example, although the age found little original stimulus in matters of poetic form, the carol attained its fullest development during this time, and the ballad was beginning to take shape. Finally, at the turn of the century, three Scots "makars," Robert Henryson, William Dunbar, and Gavin Douglas, produced verse of a sufficiently high order to warrant labeling the reign of James IV a brief "golden age" of literary Scotland.

Forces and Influences

Although it is always hazardous to speculate on the connections between history and artistic felicity, it remains true that the political and social climate in the fifteenth century did not favor literary achievement. The international stage was still dominated by the Hundred Years' War with France; Henry V's successful invasion, crowned by the victory of Agincourt in 1415, committed his successors to a costly, protracted, and ultimately futile defense of this new French territory against the onslaughts of Joan of Arc and the French king. Meanwhile, in England itself the weakness of Henry VI encouraged factionalism and intrigue which finally erupted in the Wars of the Roses between the Lancastrians and the Yorkists. It was a nation tired of war and depopulated of much of its nobility that welcomed the restoration of civil order in 1485 with the crowning of Henry VII and the establishment of the Tudor dynasty.

This political turbulence severely disrupted the patronage system upon which art throughout the Middle Ages and into the Renaissance had always relied. Early in the century Henry V had encouraged literary production, as had his brother, Humphrey of Gloucester. Yet the decimation and financial impoverishment that subsequently exhausted the aristocracy could hardly serve to foster an atmosphere of courtly refinement such as had supported Chaucer and John Gower. Indeed, it is notable that the fifteenth century witnessed a contraction in most aspects of intellectual and cultural life. Architecture, the visual arts, philosophy, and theology all declined; only in music did the English excel, principally through the harmonic innovations of John Dunstable (1370?-1453). At the same time, the role of the poet seems to have been evolving from that of an entertainer in the tradition of medieval minstrelsy to one of an adviser to princes. Thus the prestige of erudition rose while the indigenous oral traditions fell further into disrepute.

The rise of the middle class was another factor in the determination of literary tastes. Though depressed economically by the disorders in the middle of the century, this constituency ultimately gained in power as the aristocracy depleted its own ranks and resources. Simultaneously, education and literacy were spreading down the social pyramid. The gradual infiltration of humanism from the Continent, particularly during the 1480's and 1490's, had as yet made no impression on the literary sensibility: what this new, conservative readership demanded was the familiar and time-honored—such as the lives of saints, or works of the revered Chaucer. This appetite fueled extensive copying of manuscripts, an activity culminating, as chance would have it, in a technological revolution when William Caxton established England's first printing press in 1476. The discovery of printing radically and permanently altered the availability of literary works and finally established the written text as the principal medium of poetic exchange.

In their cumulative effect, these factors produced a literary conservatism that persisted throughout the century. Poets of this era turned to their own native tradition, particularly to Chaucer and Gower, for their models and stimulus, a practice contrasting radically with that of Chaucer himself, who wove into his verse many Continental influences. Thus Chaucer's meters, the iambic pentameter and tetrameter, and his rhyme patterns, notably the ballade (ababbcbc) and rhyme royal (ababbcc) stanzas and the couplet, were widely imitated, even by poets with a most imperfect grasp of what they were imitating. These same poets likewise admired the poetic diction and the rhetorical elevation that Chaucer and Gower had standardized. This influence produced the inflated sententiousness, the rhetorical pomp, and the "aureation" (use of polysyllabic Latinisms) that modern readers often deplore in the verse of Lydgate and his followers.

Yet fifteenth century poets adopted larger poetic forms as well. The many allegories and dream visions of the period clearly model themselves on Chaucer's work and that of his contemporaries. Other genres, such as the romance and lyric, continued to draw upon the same reserve of verse forms, topoi, story patterns, and subjects. Nowhere is the conservative character of the period better revealed than in the inclination toward verse translation. Of course, this was nothing new: the Middle Ages always had great respect for authority, and most writers—even the best—worked from sources. Yet the sheer bulk of fifteenth century translation obtrudes nevertheless, particularly in the number of major works that fall into this class. Lydgate's 36,365-line *Falls of Princes* (1430-1438, printed 1494), for example, was his longest poetic effort. Further, with the exception of Gavin Douglas' version of the *Aeneid* (1553) seldom do the translations, depite their frequent expansion and supplementation of the originals, stand as significant poetic works in their own right; John Walton's competent yet poetically uninspired rendering of Boethius' *The Consolation of Philosophy* (523) represents the best that the age produced. However sympathetically perceived, this widespread tendency to rely on the matter and inspiration of the past must ultimately be admitted as a weakness in much fifteenth century poetry, translated or otherwise. Rarely do the versifiers exhibit the ability of great traditional poets to return to and re-create the myths embedded in the traditional material.

The English Chaucerian Tradition

In the late fourteenth century Geoffrey Chaucer, drawing on the French tradition of courtly love and allegory that he found in *Roman de la Rose* (c. 1370, *The Romance of the Rose*) brought courtly poetry in England to its fullest perfection. His precedent inspired many imitations; allegories, love-debates, and dream visions throughout the fifteenth century attempted to recapture the Chaucerian magic. Although several of these labors show talent, one finds in this tradition little innovation or development beyond the point that Chaucer had reached.

Chaucer's first and historically most significant heir was John Lydgate (1370?-1450?), the prolific monk of Bury St. Edmunds whose influence and prestige over the next two hundred years rivaled those of his master. Written in almost every form and mode available to him, Lydgate's poetic corpus is staggering in its volume and variety: taken collectively, his many allegories, romances, histories, courtly love poems, fables, epics, lyrics, hymns, prayers, didactic and homiletic works, and occasional pieces total some 145,000 lines. Lydgate's debt to Chaucer and the courtly love tradition appears most plainly in his early work of the first decade of the 1400's. *Complaint of the Black Knight* (c. 1400) and *The Floure of Courtesy* (c. 1400-1402) both feature lovers' complaints in dream-vision garden settings; in the 1,403-line *Temple of Glas* (c. 1410, printed 1477) the poet in a dream visits a temple, styled after Chaucer's House of Fame, in which Venus joins a love-distressed knight and a lady. An allegorical cast and landscape in the manner of *The Romance of the Rose* give texture to the narrative in *Reson and Sensuallyte* (c. 1408), a pleasant and unfinished 7,042-line translation of the beginning of a long French poem, *Les Echecs Amoureux*. To this early period also belong versions of seven of Aesop's Fables, representative of several didactic works in this vein composed by Lydgate at various times. Tales of Mariolatry loosely strung amid much digressive material constitute the 5,932-line *The Life of Our Lady* (c. 1409) another early work, and the harbinger of many later efforts in the genre of the legend or saint's life.

Yet Lydgate's major works were the prodigious translations completed in his later years. Undertaken at the behest of Henry V, the *Troy Book* (1513) rendered Guido delle Colonne's Latin prose history of Troy into 30,117 lines in decasyllabic couplets. The tale of Oedipus and the rivalry of his two sons furnished the matter of the 4,176-line *The Story of Thebes* (c. 1500), a tale embedded in a narrative frame attaching it to *The Canterbury Tales* (1387-1400). Begun in France in 1426 and probably completed two years later, the 24,832-line *The Pilgrimage of Man* translates and slightly expands Guillaume de Deguileville's fourteenth century *Pélerinage de la vie humaine* (c. 1340). The lengthy and popular *Falls of Princes*, composed for Humphrey of Gloucester between 1430 and 1438, generously renders into English Laurent de Premierfait's version of Giovanni Boccaccio's *De Casibus Illustrium Virorum* (1358), a compendium of medieval "tragedies" of men of greatness whom fickle fortune humbled. In addition to these major works, one finds myriad shorter pieces of every description poured forth profusely throughout the poet's long career.

Time has not smiled upon Lydgate's literary reputation over the last two hundred years. Chief among his alleged sins is his prolixity, but critics also remark a prosodic weakness (especially in the prevalence of "broken-backed" lines), a tendency toward syntactic incoherence, and an infatuation with rhetoric and aureation. Other readers, however, finding these condemnations unduly harsh, note a human empathy, passages of lyric smoothness, and occasionally felicitous imagery, and a few have competently defended the poet's often-slandered craftsmanship. Although it is probable that Lydgate's poetic star will never rise to its former ascendency, it is also likely that future generations will find in his work merits which its amplitude has sometimes tended to obscure.

Less important historically yet in some regards more interesting is Thomas Occleve (1368?-1430?), a clerk of the Privy Seal whose attempts to secure patronage and pecuniary recompense would seem to have been less successful than desired. His *magnum opus*, the *Regement of Princes* (1412), occupies 777 stanzas of rhyme royal after the three-stanza envoy dedicating the work to Henry, Prince of Wales. The body of the *Regement of Princes*, conflating material from three Latin sources, urges the young prince by means of exemplary tales to aspire toward virtue and to eschew vice. Yet the most characteristic portion is the 288-stanza prologue, which amounts to an elaborate begging plea with many melancholy digressions and allusions to contemporary conditions. This autobiographical strain, allied with the many topical references and the poet's endearing love for Chaucer, whom he seems to have known personally, endow Occleve's verse with a human and historical interest that constitutes his main claim on posterity. On the other hand, his work, lacks serious artistic intention, a sense of structural design, and stylistic distinction. Along with several shorter pieces, his other main poems are *La Male Règle* (1406), the *Letter of Cupid* (1402), and an autobiographically linked series including the *Complaint* (1422); the *Dialogue with a Friend* (1422); the *Tale of Jereslaus' Wife* (1422); *Knowing How to Die*; and the *Tale of Jonathas*.

Three further early "Chaucerians" require mention. Foremost among them is James I of Scotland (1394-1437), who spent most of his childhood as a prisoner of the English. Composed during his captivity, *The Kingis Quair* (1423-1424, *The King's Choir*) pays tribute in 197 stanzas of rhyme royal to Lady Joan Beaufort, whom James married the next year (1424). In the poem the young monarch, complaining about his bad fortune, sees a beautiful woman through his cell window and is smitten with love. That night in a dream he visits Venus, Minerva, and Fortune, the last of whom promises the betterment of his affairs; on this hopeful note he awakes. Betraying a clear debt to Boethius' *The Consolation of Philosophy*, Chaucer's "The Knight's Tale," and Lydgate's *Temple of Glas*, *The King's Choir* was written in the Scots dialect with Midlands admixtures and so occupies an important role in the emerging Scottish tradition. Another captive nobleman, Charles of Orleans (1394-1465) sprang directly from the French courtly tradition in which language and traditional idiom he wrote. The main English translation, which Charles may have authored, is a three-part sequence of ballads and rondels dealing conventionally with the progress of several love affairs. One further work from this early period was Sir John Thomas Clanvowe's *The Boke of Cupide* (1391). This May-time dream vision is dominated by a debate between a cuckoo, who slanders lovers, and a nightingale, who lauds them; the nightingale prevails, and the dream concludes with an assembly of birds. Composed in an unusual five-line stanza (aabba), this poem recalls such earlier works in the bird-debate tradition as the thirteenth century *Owl and the Nightingale* (c. 1250) and Chaucer's *The Parliament of Fowls* (1380).

The allegorical tendency found in the *Temple of Glas* emerges again in a group of poems from the later fifteenth century, most of which were at one time or another apocryphally attributed to Chaucer. One of the finest of these, *The Flower and the Leaf*, depicts through the eyes of a female narrator an amusing incident involving the followers of the Leaf (the laurel) and the followers of the Flower (the daisy). Skillfully composed in 595 lines of rhyme royal, *The Flower and the Leaf* invests its lightly allegorized narrative with much charm of image and detail. Somewhat heavier in its allegorical machinery, the 756-line *Assembly of Ladies* features such characters as Perseverence, Diligence, Countenance, Largesse, Remembrance, and Loyalty. Less courtly and more didactic, the *Court of Sapience*, sometimes attributed to Stephen Hawes, confronts a traveler with a more scholastic variety of allegorical personifications—such as Peace, Mercy, Righteousness, Truth, and the seven arts. Hawes's *Pastime of Pleasure*, composed shortly before its publication in 1506, recounts the allegorical adventures of Graunde Amour on his road toward knightly perfection and the love of La Belle Pucel. Another early sixteenth century work, *The Court of Love*, far more skillfully narrates Philogenet's visit with Alcestis and Admetus at the Court of Love and recounts his successful wooing of Rosiall; the action closes with a celebration and birdsongs of praise. Thoroughly Chaucerian in form and intention, these poems mark the end of the courtly tradition in medieval English literature.

The Lyric

The term "lyric" suggests to most modern readers a highly individualized expression of some personal feeling in concrete language treating a subject of the poet's choice, yet this notion proves misleading in the case of the medieval English lyric. Although this body of poems indeed concerns itself with feelings, the individuality of the poet has been largely effaced; thus most of the surviving pieces are anonymous, not merely because the names of the authors are unknown (with a few exceptions, such as John Audelay and James Ryman), but in the nature of the expression. Moreover, the subjects, on which basis these poems are usually classified, belong to a common cultural wordhoard that also provides much of the standard imagery and diction. The consequence is a poetic genre expressive of what might be called "public experience"—moods, thoughts, and emotions defined and recognized in the public mind.

The essential continuity of the English medieval lyric from its beginnings in the mid-thirteenth century to the closing of the Middle Ages reveals itself in the persistence of certain lyric types, such as the Passion poem, the hymn to Mary, and the praise and complaint of lovers. Yet the fifteenth century brought its share of changes. One new development was a growing literary self-awareness with a corresponding loss of freshness and spontaneity, characteristics that had distinguished early English lyrics from their more artificial French counterparts. New motifs came into prominence, such as the Marian lament; other poems elaborated old themes to greater lengths with an increasingly aureate diction.

The fifteenth century's most distinctive contribution lay in the flowering of a relatively new lyric form, the carol. Medieval English lyrics in general, employing a variety of metrical and stanzaic patterns, share no defining formal characteristics. The carol differs in this regard: R. L. Greene, the editor of the standard anthology, defines this lyric type as "a song on any subject, composed of uniform stanzas and provided with a burden." Sung at the beginning and repeated after every stanza, the burden is a group of lines, most often a couplet, that usually signals a major theme or subject in the poem. Some claim that the carol originated as a dance song. In any event, it is clear that during the fifteenth century the carol was developing a connection with the Christmas season; many explicitly celebrated the Nativity in a manner familiar to modern readers from Christmas carols of the present era. The genre was not restricted to this subject, however; one of the most beautiful and haunting of all carols is a Passion elegy whose burden runs,, "Lulley, lulley, lulley, lulley;/ The fawcon hath born my mak away."

Medieval lyrics are usually classified on the basis of subject into two groups, the religious and the secular, with the religious poems being far more numerous. The most popular subject was the Virgin, whose cult still flourished in the late Middle Ages. Some of these Marian poems, adopting the conventions of secular love verse, proclaimed her inexpressible beauty, or praised her bodily parts, or begged for her mercy, or presented her with a Valentine's Day offering. More often, however, these lyrics derived from the Latin liturgical tradition. Many such pieces celebrated various of the Virgin's five joys— the Annunciation, the Nativity, the Resurrection, the Ascension, and the Assumption; "The Maiden Makeles" is a particularly famous Nativity song. God and Christ were often the objects of address; "Close in my Breast thy Perfect Love" harks in its intimate tenderness back to the fourteenth century mystical tradition of Richard Rolle. Christ's Passion provided another major subject in poems that tended toward a more extended narrative treatment and greater didactism than in previous periods. In one common and distinctive type of Passion poem, Christ Himself addresses humanity directly from the Cross. A new fifteenth century trend introduced the theme of Mary's compassion and her participation in Christ's suffering. Lyrics in the *planctus* mode give expression to her grief; other poems present this theme through dialogues between the Virgin and Son.

Turning to the secular lyrics, one finds in the fifteenth century, as in most ages, a preponderance of love songs. All the expected types appear: praise to a lady and enumeration of her beauties, complaints about her cruelty and fickleness, laments on a lover's absence, and epistles, such as the one that opens "Go, litull bill, and command me hertely/ Unto her. . . ." Some lyrics take the form of antifeminist diatribes; others are plainly pornographic. One interesting anonymous series, *The Lover's Mass*, tastefully mimics the liturgy in fine love poems bearing such titles as the *Introibo*, *Kyrie*, and *Gloria*. A dramatic framework informs the highly praised "Nut Brown Maid," a debate between a woman and an earl's son disguised as a knightly outlaw which culminates in a self-revelation and a marriage offer. Other types of secular lyrics include drinking songs, charms and gnomes, and poems on historical events. In the meditations on fortune and worldly happiness, one can once more discern a growing religious tone in the contemplation of human affairs, a tone that emerges explicitly in the songs on death, the penitential confessions, and the homilies on virtue and vice. Cutting across this entire dichotomy of the secular and the religious are lyric types distinguishable by their objects of address. Poems addressed to the reader tend toward didacticism; lyrics addressing a third party (such as the Virgin or a human beloved) define themselves between the polarities of celebration and of complaint or petition. An appreciation for both strains, the didactic and the celebratory, is an essential prerequisite to any competent reading of medieval lyrics.

Popular Narrative: The Romance and the Ballad

During the fifteenth century two forms of popular narrative overlapped as the metrical romance declined and the ballad rose to supplant it. Though the relationship between these genres remain unsettled, both were probably circulated orally, and the traveling minstrel performers may have provided a line of continuity between them. This context of oral performance helps to explain in both cases the frequent verbal and narrative formulas that overly sophisticated readers are likely to condemn as "trite" and "stereotyped." At the same time, difference in subject matter and narrative technique clearly distinguish the two forms.

The first English romances appeared in the middle of the thirteenth century, at the very time when this aristocratic form had begun its decline in France. Descended from the *chanson de geste*, the French romance was a tale of knightly adventure that celebrated the ideals of bravery in battle, chivalric honor, courtesy, and service to a lady. Showing little concern for verisimilitude or psychological realism, these stories pitted their shallowly portrayed heroes against frequently supernatural and fabulous adversaries in a string of encounters joined less by a sense of "organic unity" than by a technique of narrative interlace. The English romances were regularly "translations" of such French works and exhibit many of these same characteristics. They also borrow most of their stories from the French cycles, specifically the "matters" of Britain (including the Arthurian cycle and unrelated "English" tales such as *Haveloc* written in the early thirteenth century), France (the Charlemagne cycle), and antiquity (including the cycles of Alexander, Troy, and Thebes). Other tales deal with the Orient, and a few bear no relation to any major cycle.

Fifteenth century romances have been relatively neglected in favor of Sir Thomas Malory's *Le Morte d'Arthur* (c. 1469, printed 1485), the greatest of the many prose narratives published by Caxton, yet the metrical romance persisted as a popular form: according to the *Wells Manual*, some thirty can be dated roughly from the fifteenth century, with a growing number from Scotland in the later decades. Lengths ranged from 516 lines in the case of *The Grene Knight*, an unhappy condensation of *Sir Gawain and the Green Knight* (c. 1370), to the 27,852 lines of Henry Lovelich's *Merlin*, a translation of the prose French *Vulgate*. The most common verse patterns were rhyming octosyllabic couplets and tail-rhyme stanzas, although occasionally other forms, such as the rhyme royal or ballade stanza, made their appearance. Although the alliterative revival had passed its prime, alliterative tendencies still persisted in Northumbria and Scotland, yielding late in the century such

Middle Scots works as *Golagrus and Gawain* (c. 1500) and *The Taill of Rauf Coilyear*.

In their choice of subjects, fifteenth century romancers followed the established channels described earlier. One of the best-known Arthurian romances is the stanzaic *Morte Arthur* (c. 1360), a 3,969-line account of Lancelot's role in Arthur's downfall. Most of the romances from the Arthurian cycle depict the deeds of Gawain, who in the English tradition (unlike the French) remained for the most part a model knight. Two of the best Gawain romances are *The Avowynge of King Arthur, Sir Gawan, Sir Kaye, and Sir Bawdewyn of Bretan* (c. 1425), which follows each knight's separate path of adventure, and *Golagrus and Gawain*, whose plot hinges on a noble act of self-effacement by Gawain. After the Arthurian cycle, the next most popular source of lore for romance was the life of Alexander. *The Alliterative Alexander Fragment C* (c. 1450) verges toward the epic manner; far more leisurely and episodic in its narrative style, the 11,138-line *Scottish Alexander Buik* (1438) is surpassed in length by another bulky Middle Scots poem, Gilbert Hay's 20,000-line *Buik of Alexander*. In other areas, the wars of Troy and Thebes inspired a handful of romances, two by Lydgate; a small group, including only *The Taill of Rauf Coilyear* and a Middle English *Song of Roland* (c. 1100), belong to the Charlemagne cycle; five or six others, such as *Eger and Grime* (c. 1450) and John Metham's *Amoryus and Cleopes* (c. 1448), treat miscellaneous subjects. By 1500, the 250-year-old English metrical romance tradition had, with a few minor exceptions, reached an end.

David Fowler has argued that in the late Middle Ages, as the medieval minstrels were increasingly denied access to the courts of the higher nobility, the romance converged with the folksong to produce a shorter, simplified, less episodic narrative form that we now call the ballad. While origins of balladry remain a controversial subject, it is certainly the case that the ballad is one of the few medieval forms that did not perish with the Renaissance and its aftermath; and as such it has a special claim to modern interest. The most thoroughly oral of the genres so far considered, the ballad could be defined as a short narrative poem, usually composed in two- or four-line stanzas, and distinguished by its concentration on a single event or episode. Unlike romances, which characteristically "tell" their stories, ballads tend to "show" their action directly through dramatic dialogue stripped of descriptive scene-setting. The ballad style is formulaic: tags, phrases, motifs, and episodes are repeated throughout the ballad tradition, and the poems themselves have survived in multiple versions. The general impersonality of the formulaic style is reinforced by the absence of a distinctive narrative persona. Although current opinion favors individual and not group composition, in its cumulative effect balladry strikes one as reflecting the outlook of a community and tradition, not that of some particular person.

Although most extant ballads survive in collections from the seventeenth century and later, many of these poems may have originated in the fifteenth century or even before, for oral traditions have a well-demonstrated ability to transmit story patterns over remarkably long periods of time. The reconstruction of a specific ballad's evolution remains a speculative and subjective process, however, and there are a mere handful of documentably fifteenth century ballads, most of which narrate the adventures of Robin Hood. The choice of this legendary outlaw as a hero presents a departure from the usual practice of romancers with their knightly, aristocratic adventurers; indeed, later ballads do tend to draw subjects from middle-class life more often than romances had done. This point, however, should not be overemphasized: ballads and romances retain many similarities of motif, story pattern, and even metrical form; in several cases, such as *Hind Horn* and *King Horn* (c. 1250), a ballad and romance relate the same story. Yet during the fifteenth century the ballad had begun a life of its own that would lead in its peregrinations down to the modern day to a point far from its medieval origins.

Other Fifteenth Century Poetry

The prestige of the courtly tradition did not obscure the power that religious narrative continued to exercise over the popular imagination. Indeed, collections of saints' lives of the type represented in the *South English Legendary* and the *Golden Legend* enjoyed immense popularity throughout the century although original composition in this vein was on the decline. One of the most prolific of the religious versifiers, Osbern Bokenham, composed between 1443 and 1447 a group of thirteen saints' lives under the title *The Lives of Saints: Or, Legends of Holy Women*. The versatile Lydgate several times turned his hand to this genre; even John Capgrave, a learned friar who customarily wrote in prose, composed lives of St. Norbert and St. Katharine in rhyme royal. One must further note the numerous translations and verse paraphrases of books of the Bible, both Old and New Testaments, even if their literary achievement is slight.

A number of shorter poems address themselves to the events or conditions of the day. Major military conflicts such as Agincourt and the Wars of the Roses inspired commemorative ballads and lyrics. A spirited series in prose and crude poetry, *Jack Upland*, *Friar Daw's Reply*, and *Jack Upland's Rejoinder*, exchange blows on the subjects of friars and Lollardy. Long attributed to Lydgate, *London Lickpenny* (1515) vividly depicts life in the late medieval metropolis. Other poems in this satirical vein lament the state of the clergy and the general evils of the age.

A considerable bulk of the surviving poetry seems to be little more than versified prose. *The Libel of English Policy*, for example, makes recommendations on foreign trade policy in couplets and rhyme royal stanzas totaling 1,141 lines. Similarly, pragmatic intentions appear in John Russell's *Book of Carving and Nature*, an *Ordinal of Alchemy*, and *The Babees Book*, the latter an instruction on points of etiquette. By far the longest of these poems is Peter Idley's 7,000-line *Instructions to His Son*, which gives advice on a variety of subjects.

The Scottish Makars

In the fifteenth century in Scotland, an era concluding in military cataclysm as England crushed James IV and his Scottish forces at the Battle of Flodden Field in 1513, one finds a burgeoning literature with several poets or "makars" of real greatness. John Barbour, in many respects the founder of the English-language poetic tradition in Scotland, had already sounded a patriotic note in *The Bruce* (c. 1375), an epic romance celebrating the deeds of Robert the Bruce, national liberator and victor at the Battle of Bannockburn (1314). In 1423-1424 James I introduced a courtlier, more Chaucerian strain in *The King's Choir*. Two further poems sometimes ascribed to James, *Christis Kirk on the Green* and *Peblis to the Play*, initiate a Scottish comic tradition that continues in such works as *Sym and His Brudir*, *The Wyf of Auchtiramuchty*, *Cockelbie's Sow*, and even the romance *The Taill of Rauf Coilyear*. Exhibiting the superb mastery of an intricate, interlocking stanzaic pattern, *Christis Kirk on the Green* and *Peblis to the Play* are both distinguished for their vividly sketched rustic settings and their rough-and-tumble humor.

Meanwhile, the nationalistic and historical tradition of Barbour was carried on by Andrew of Wyntoun (1350?-1424) in his *Orygynale Chronikil of Scotland*, a lifeless history of the nation from Creation to the time of writing. Composed in octosyllabic couplets, Wyntoun's chronicle is best known now as the source of the Macbeth story that William Shakespeare found in Raphael Holinshed's *Chronicles of England, Scotland, and Ireland* (1577). By far the most popular and influential Scottish poem of the century was *The Wallace*, ascribed to a certain Blind Harry and completed before 1488. A companion piece to *The Bruce*, Harry's eleven-book heroic romance is based on the life of William Wallace (1272-1305), an unsuccessful Scottish insurgent a generation before Robert the Bruce. The first sustained Scottish work in decasyllabic couplets, *The Wallace* often irks modern readers with its chauvinistic romanticization, its repetitiveness, and its lack of psychological depth. At the same time, the poem does not lack enthusiasm, and many passages show real poetic power.

The work of Robert Henryson (1430?-1506?) and William Dunbar (1460?-1520?) is unrivaled in fifteenth century poetry, Scottish or English. The label "Scottish Chaucerians" attached to these and other Middle Scots poets should be rejected, for it clouds their essential originality. Nevertheless, the poem for which Henryson is best known, the *Testament of Cresseid*, (1593), is a 615-line continuation of the fifth book of Chaucer's *Troilus and Criseyde* (1382) in rhyme royal stanzas. Cresseid, rejected by Diomede, blasphemes against the gods, who accordingly punish her with leprosy. Troilus rides past one day and, pitying the wretched woman whom he fails to recognize, tosses her a purse; learning the name of her benefactor, Cresseid repents, sends him a ring token, and dies. A poetic tour de force, the *Testament of Cresseid* presents a stern and uncompromising moral vision in which Cresseid falls as the result of her own wrongdoing; nevertheless, she ultimately finds redemption. Another major effort, the 633-line *Tale of Orpheus* (1508) interprets the Orpheus myth in a standard allegorical fashion. Of Henryson's some dozen minor poems, perhaps the best is "Robene and Makyne," a debate of wooing and rebuttal with an amusing dramatic reversal.

Henryson's *magnum opus* was his 2,975-line collection, *Fables* (1621). The didactic character of these thirteen fables of Aesop is reflected in the twenty- to seventy-line *moralitas* following each one; composed in rhyme royal, the fables show in their ordering an awareness of total design. Henryson's poetry in general lacks the dazzling stylistic virtuosity of Dunbar's, although his meticulous craftsmanship cannot be faulted. His greatness lies more in his moral profundity; his detached, ironic humor; and his ability to depict the small and commonplace. In the sources of his learning and the tendency to allegorize, Henryson looks more to the Middle Ages than to the Renaissance; despite the usual Chaucerian influence and a competence in handling aristocratic themes, he belongs more to the parish pulpit than to the court.

Henryson's temperamental opposite, William Dunbar, flourished in the court of James IV during the first decade of the sixteenth century until the demise of his royal patron at Flodden Field. Although he never attempted a work of much more than five hundred lines, his range of form and manner was otherwise matched only by the apparent fluctuations of his mood. "The Thistle and the Rose" (1503), a dream vision in the Chaucerian allegorical fashion, celebrates the marriage of Margaret Tudor (the "Rose") and James IV (the "Thistle"). Another allegory of love, "The Goldyn Targe," (c. 1508, "The Golden Shield"), launches its poet-narrator into another dream vision before the court of Venus, where he is wounded by the arrows of Dame Beauty. Similar in spirit is *The Merle and the Nightingale*, in which the two birds debate on the subject of love. "The Two Married Women and the Widow" treats love more satirically, as these depraved discussants contemplate sex and their husbands. Satire turns to invective in "The Flyting of Dunbar and Kennedy," a distinctively Scottish form in which the poetic contestants hurl at one another volleys of extravagant verbal abuse.

Dunbar also had his darker moments, as in "The Dance of the Seven Deadly Sins" (c. 1503-1508), in which the dreaming poet watches Mohammed preside over the grotesque festivities of his fiendish crew. *The Lament for the Makaris*, with its refrain "Timor Mortis conturbat me" ("the fear of death disturbs me"), evokes the elegiac strain and the theme of the world's ephemerality that recur again in *This World Unstabille* and *In Winter*; a sonorous musical power adds weight to poems on the Nativity and the Resurrection. Among

Dunbar's numerous remaining shorter poems, many were addressed to the king and the royal family. Some readers find Dunbar deficient in human sympathy and in his vision, but none can deny his imaginative inventiveness, tonal and emotional range, satricial humor tending toward the grotesque, and prosodic and stylistic genius that finds few equals in any period.

Although Gavin Douglas (1475?-1522) turned to the classical world for his greatest literary attempt, the generality of his work, like that of his immediate peers and predecessors, belongs more to the Middle Ages than to the humanistic movements then stirring on the Continent and in England. His debt to the Chaucerian tradition appears in his early poems, *The Palice of Honour* and *King Hart*, both love allegories in the tired French and Chaucerian manner. His rendering of the *Aeneid* into heroic couplets, completed just before Flodden Field in 1513, was the first; it remains one of the finest of all verse translations of this Vergilian masterpiece. Matching poetic style to social degree, Douglas employed heavy alliteration in passages relating to rustic characters and reserved a "noble" style for aristocratic matters. He also contributed an original prologue to each book. The total result, less a translation than a re-creation of the Roman epic into the Middle Scots language and idiom, exerted a regrettably minor influence on later poetry because of Scotland's political collapse and the rapid linguistic changes that followed. Flodden Field sounded the death knell to a literary era, but even as it did, English-language poetry was about to experience fresh influences and the revitalization of the Renaissance.

Ward Parks

THE SIXTEENTH CENTURY

The poetry of the sixteenth century defies facile generalizations. Although the same can obviously be said for the poetry of other periods as well, this elusiveness of categorization is particularly characteristic of the sixteenth century. It is difficult to pinpoint a century encompassing both the growling meter of John Skelton and the polished prosody of Sir Philip Sidney, and, consequently, past efforts to provide overviews of the period have proven unhelpful. Most notably, C. S. Lewis in his *English Literature in the Sixteenth Century Excluding Drama* (1954) contrived an unfortunate division between what he called "drab" poetry and "Golden" poetry. What he means by this distinction is never entirely clear, and Lewis himself further confuses the dichotomy by occasionally suggesting that his own term "drab" need not have a perjorative connotation, although when he applies it to specific poets, it is clear that he intends it to be damaging. Furthermore, his distinction leads him into absurd oversimplifications. As Lewis would have it, George Gascoigne is mostly drab (a condition that he sees as befitting a poet of the "drab" mid-century) though blessed with occasional "Golden" tendencies, while Robert Southwell, squarely placed in the "Golden" period, is really a mediocre throwback to earlier "drab" poetry. Such distinctions are hazy and not helpful to the reader, who suspects that Lewis defines "drab" and "Golden" simply as what he himself dislikes or prefers in poetry.

The muddle created by Lewis' terminology has led to inadequate treatments of the sixteenth century in the classroom. Perhaps reinforced by the simplicity of his dichotomy, teachers have traditionally depicted the fruits of the century as not blossoming until the 1580's, with the sonneteers finally possessing the talent and good sense to perfect the experiments with the Petrarchan sonnet form first begun by Sir Thomas Wyatt early in the century. Students have been inevitably taught that between Wyatt and Sidney stretched a wasteland of mediocre poetry, disappointing primarily because so many poets failed to apply their talents to continuing the Petrarchan experiments begun by Wyatt. Thus, indoctrinated in the "axiom" that, as concerns the sixteenth century, "good" poetry is Petrarchan and "bad" poetry is that which fails to work with Petrarchan conceits, teachers deal in the classroom mostly with the poets of the 1580's and later, ignoring the other poetic currents of the early and mid-century. It has been difficult indeed to overcome Lewis' dichotomy of "drab" and "Golden."

Fortunately, there have been studies of sixteenth century poetry that are sensitive to non-Petrarchan efforts, and these studies deserve recognition as providing a better perspective for viewing the sixteenth century. In 1939, Yvor Winters' essay "The 16th Century Lyric in England: A Critical and Historical Reinterpretation" focused on some of the less notable poets of the period, such as Barnabe Googe, George Turberville, and George Gascoigne, who, until Winters' essay, had been dismissed simply because they were not Petrarchan in sentiment, and the essay also helped to dispel the notion that the aphoristic, proverbial content of their poetry was symptomatic of their simplemindedness and lack of talent. By pointing out how their sparse style contributes to, rather than detracts from, the moral content of their poetry, Winters' essay is instrumental in helping the reader develop a sense of appreciation for these often-overlooked poets. In addition to Winters' essay, Douglas L. Peterson's book *The English Lyric from Wyatt to Donne: A History of the Plain and Eloquent Styles* (1967), taking up where Winters left off, identifies two major poetic currents in the sixteenth century: the plain style and the eloquent style. Peterson provides a more realistic and less judgmental assessment of the non-Petrarchans as practitioners of the "plain" rhetorical style, a term that is a welcome relief from Lewis' "drab." Thus, Winters' and Peterson's efforts have been helpful in destroying the damaging stereotypes about the "bad" poets of the mid-century.

Despite the difficulties inherent in summarizing a century as diverse as the sixteenth, it is possible to discern a unifying thread running through the poetry of the period. The unity stems from the fact that, perhaps more than any other time, the sixteenth century was consistently "poetic"; that is, the poets were constantly aware of themselves as poetic craftsmen. From Skelton to Edmund Spenser, poets were self-conscious of their pursuits, regardless of theme. This poetic self-consciousness was manifested primarily in the dazzling display of metrical, stanzaic, and prosodic experimentation that characterized the efforts of all the poets, from the most talented to the most mediocre. In particular, the century experienced the development of, or refinement upon, for example, the poulter's measure (alternate twelve- and fourteen-syllable lines), blank verse, heroic couplets, rime royal, ottava rima, terza rima, Spenserian stanza, douzains, fourteeners—all appearing in a variety of genres. Characteristic of the century was the poet watching himself be a poet, and every poet of the century would have found himself in agreement with Sidney's assessment of the poet in his *Defense of Poesie* (1595) as prophet or seer, whose craft is suffused with divine inspiration.

This process of conscious invention and self-monitoring is one key to understanding the poetry of the sixteenth century. It is a curious fact that whereas in other periods, historical and social factors play a large role in shaping poetic themes, in the sixteenth century, such extraliterary influences did little to dictate the nature of the poetry. Surprisingly, even though Copernicus' theory of a heliocentric universe was known by mid-century, the poetry barely nodded to the New Science or to the new geographical discoveries. Certainly, the century experienced almost constant political and religious turbulence, providing abundant fare for topical themes; a less apolitical period one can hardly imagine. It was the prose, however, more than the poetry, that sought to record the buffetings created by the fact that the official religion in England changed four times between 1530 and 1560. It seems that the instability created by this uneasiness had the effect of turning the poets inward, rather than outward to political, social, and religious commentary (with the exceptions of the Broadside Ballads, pseudojournalistic poems intended for the uncultivated, and the verse chronicle history so popular at the close of the century), bearing out the hypothesis that good satire can flourish only in periods of relative stability. For example, despite the number of obvious targets, the genre of political satire did not flourish in the sixteenth century, and its sporadic representatives, in particular anticlerical satire, a warhorse left over from the Middle Ages, are barely noteworthy. A major figure in Spenser's *The Faerie Queene* (1590-1596) is Gloriana, a figure depicting Queen Elizabeth, but she is an idealized rendering, only one of many such celebrations in poetry of Queen Elizabeth, not intended to provide a realistic insight into her character.

Thus, to the poet of the sixteenth century, the primary consideration of the poetic pursuit was not who or what to write about, but rather how to write. The reason for this emphasis on style over content is simple enough to isolate. By the middle of the sixteenth century, the English language was experiencing severe growing pains. In fact, throughout Europe the vernacular was struggling to overthrow the tyranny of Latin and to discover its essential identity. Nationalism was a phenomenon taking root everywhere, and, inevitably, the cultivation of native languages was seen as the logical instrument of expediting the development of national identity. Italy and France were undergoing revolts against Latin, and Joachim Du Bellay's *Défense et illustration de la langue française* (1549) proclaimed explicitly that great works can be written in the vernacular. In England, the invention of new words was encouraged, and war was waged on "inkhornisms," terms of affectation usually held over from the old Latin or French, used liberally by Skelton. Thus, George Puttenham, an influential critical theorist of the period, discusses the question of whether or not a poet would be better advised to use "pierce" rather than "penetrate," and Richard Mulcaster, Spenser's old headmaster, was moved to announce, "I honor the Latin, but I worship English."

It was no easy task, however, to legislate prescribed changes in something as malleable as language, and the grandeur of the effort nevertheless often produced comic results. Sixteenth century English vernacular, trying to weed out both Latin and French influences, produced such inelegant and uneasy bastardizations as "mannerlier," "newelties," "hable" (a hangover from Latin "habilis"), and "semblably," leading William Webbe in his *Discourse of English Poetry* (1586) to rail in a sneering pun about "this brutish poetry," with "brutish" looming as a veiled reference to "British." Although the sixteenth century was constantly discovering that the subtleties of perfecting a new language could not be mastered overnight, the effort was nevertheless sustained and paved the way for a future confidence in what the vernacular could achieve. Words that often strike the modern reader as outdated, stodgy pedantry are, in fact, the uncertain by-products of innovative experimentation.

Thus, to understand sixteenth century poetry is to ignore the stability of language, which is taken for granted in later centuries, and to understand the challenge that the poets experienced in shaping the new language to fit their poetry. Working with new words meant changes in the old classical syntax, and, in turn, changes in the syntax meant changes in the old classical versifications. These changes often resulted in frustration for the poet (and for the reader), but, depending on the skills of the poet, the result of all this experimentation could mean new rhyme schemes, new meters, and new stanzaic structures. In the wake of all the excitement generated by this constant experimentation, the poets cannot be blamed for often judging innovations in content as secondary to the new prosody. The volatility and flux of the language siphoned all energies into perfecting new styles not into content.

The zeal for metrical experimentation which characterized the sixteenth century is manifested not only in the original poetry of the period but also in the numerous translations that were being turned out. The primary purpose of the translations was to record the works of the venerable authorities in the new vernacular, and it is significant that Webbe refers to these works not as being "translated" but as being "Englished." The *Aeneid* (c. 29-19 B.C.) was a favorite target for the translators, with the Earl of Surrey publishing a translation in 1554, Thomas Phaer in 1558, and Richard Stanyhurst in 1582. Stanyhurst translated only the first four books, and he achieved a metrical monstrosity by attempting to translate Vergil in English hexameters, reflecting the tensions of cramming old subject matter into new forms. Ovid was another favorite of the translators. Arthur Golding translated the *Metamorphoses* in 1567, and also in that year, George Turberville translated the *Heroides*, featuring elaborate experiments with the poulter's measure, fourteeners, and blank verse. Most of the translations of the period may be dismissed as the works of versifiers, not poets (with the exception of George Chapman's Homer, which has the power of an original poem), but they are valuable reflections of the constant metrical experimentations taking place and, subsequently, of the ongoing process of shaping the new vernacular.

An overview of the poetry of the 1500's would be incomplete without an introduction to the critical theory of the period and the ways in which it recorded the successes and failures of the new vernacular experimentations. Not surprisingly, critical theory of the age was abundant. An obvious representative is Sidney's *Defense of Poesie*. The elegance and polish of this argument for the superiority of poetry over any other aesthetic pursuit has made it the most outstanding example of Renaissance critical theory. The easy grace of the work, however, tends to obscure the fact that the new experiments in prosody had created a lively, often nasty debate in critical theory between the guardians of the old and the spokesmen for the new. There were many other works of critical theory closer than the *Defense of Poesie* to the pulse rate of the arguments.

The turbulent nature of the critical theory of the period (and, by implications, the turbulence of the poetry itself) is reflected by George Gascoigne, who in his *Certain Notes of Instruction Concerning the Making of Verse or Rime in English* (1575) serves as a hearty spokesman for the new vernacular, advocating a more widespread use of monosyllables in poetry and a rejection of words derived from foreign vocabularies so that "the truer Englishman you shall seem and the less you shall smell of the inkhorn," and decrying poets who cling to the old Latin syntax by placing their adjectives after the noun. In his *Art of English Poesy* (1589), George Puttenham scolds those poets who "wrench" their words to fit the rhyme, "for it is a sign that such a maker is not copious in his own language." Not every critic, however, was so enchanted with the new experimentation. In his *Art of Rhetorique* (1553), Thomas Wilson called for continued practice of the old classical forms, and he sought to remind poets that words of Latin and Greek derivation are useful in composition. Contempt for new techniques in versification pervades Roger Ascham's *The Schoolmaster* (1570). He condemns innovations in rhyming, which he dismisses as derived from the "Gothes and Hunnes," and calls for renewed imitation of classical forms. In his *Discourse of English Poetry*, William Webbe is even less charitable. He scorns the new experiments in prosody as "this tinkerly verse," and he campaigns for keeping alive the old, classical quantitative verse, in which the meter is governed by the time required to pronounce a syllable, not by accentuation. Clearly the severity of the critical debate needs to be kept in the forefront as one begins consideration of the poetry of the period; to fail to do so is to overlook what the poets were trying to accomplish.

The opening of the sixteenth century, however, was anything but a harbinger of new developments to come. Like most centuries, the sixteenth began on a conservative, even reactionary note, looking backward to medieval literature, rather than forward to the new century. Allegories and dream visions written in seven-line stanzas, favorite vehicles of the medieval poets, dominated the opening years of the sixteenth century. Under Henry VII the best poets were Scottish—William Dunbar, Gavin Douglas, and Sir David Lindsay—and they were devoted imitators of Geoffrey Chaucer. The first English poet to assert himself in the new century was Stephen Hawes, who wrote *The Pastime of Pleasure* in 1509, representing uninspired medievalism at its worst. The work is constructed as a dream-vision allegory. An almost direct imitation of John Lydgate, *The Pastime of Pleasure* narrates the hero Grand Amour's instruction in the Tower of Doctrine, employing a profusion of stock, allegorical characters reminiscent of the morality plays. The old medieval forms, especially those combining allegory and church satire, were hard to die. In

1536, Robert Shyngleton wrote *The Pilgrim's Tale*, a vulgar, anticlerical satire directly evocative of Chaucer, and as late as 1556, John Heywood wrote *The Spider and the Fly*, a lengthy allegory depicting the Roman Catholics as flies, the Protestants as spiders, and Queen Mary as wielding a cleaning broom.

Another heavy practitioner of the dream allegory was John Skelton, one of the most puzzling figures of the century. Skelton has long been an object of negative fascination for literary historians—and with good reason. He deserves a close look, however, because, despite his reactionary themes, he was the first metrical experimenter of the century. His paradoxical undertaking of being both metrical innovator and medieval reactionary has produced some of the oddest, even comic, poetry in the English language. His infamous "Skeltonic meter," a bewildering mixture of short, irregular lines and an array of varying rhyme schemes, relies on stress, alliteration, and rhyme, rather than on syllabic count, and as a result, the reader is left either outraged or amused. His subject matter was inevitably a throwback to earlier medieval themes. He wrote two dream-vision allegories, *The Bouge of Court* (1499), a court satire, and *The Garland of Laurel* (1523). Skelton is still read today, however, because of his fractured meter. The theme of his *Colin Clout* (1522), a savage satire on the corruption of the English clergy (whose title, incidentally, was the inspiration for Spenser's *Colin Clout's Come Home Again*, 1591), is of interest to the modern reader not so much for its content as for its versification. In the work, Skelton describes his own rhyme a being "Tatterèd and jaggèd/ Rudely rain-beaten/ Rusty and moth-eaten." Skelton's rhyme arrives fast and furious, and it is possible to conclude that he may have been the object of Puttenham's attack on poets who "wrench" their words to fit the rhyme.

Despite his original metrical experimentation, Skelton was still entrenched in inkhornisms and looked backward for his themes. Paradoxically, as is often the case, it can be the poet with the least talent who nevertheless injects into his poetry vague hints of things to come. Alexander Barclay wrote no poetry of the slightest worth, but embedded in the mediocrity lay the beginnings of a new respect for the vernacular. To the literary historian, Barclay is of interest for two reasons. First, he was the sixteenth century's first borrower from the Continent. Specifically, in his *Certayn Egloges* (1570), he was the first to imitate the eclogues of Mantuan, which were first printed in 1498 and which revolutionized the genre of the pastoral eclogue by making it a vehicle for anticlerical satire, although such satire was of course nothing new in England at that time. Barclay's second importance, however (and perhaps the more significant), lies in the fact that he was the first to use the vernacular for the pastoral.

It was not until mid-century that English borrowings from the Continent were put on full display. In 1557, a collection of lyrics known as *Tottel's Miscellany* was published, and the importance of this work cannot be overemphasized. It was innovative not only in its function as a collection of poems by various authors, some of them anonymous, but also in the profusion of prosodic experimentation that it offered. *Tottel's Miscellany* represented nothing less than England's many-faceted response to the Continental Renaissance. In this collection, every conceivable metrical style (including some strange and not wholly successful experiments with structural alliteration) was attempted in an array of genres, including sonnets, epigrams, elegies, eulogies, and poems of praise and Christian consolation, often resulting in changes in the older Continental forms. Truly there is no better representation of poets self-consciously watching themselves be poets.

Nevertheless, unfair stereotypes about the collection abound. Perhaps because of Lewis' distinction between "drab" age and "Golden" age poetry, students are often taught that the sole merit of *Tottel's Miscellany* is its inclusion of the lyrics of Sir Thomas Wyatt and Henry Howard, Earl of Surrey (which had been composed years earlier), in particular, their imitations of the amatory verse of Petrarch. The standard classroom presentation lauds Wyatt and Surrey for introducing Petrarch and his sonnet form into England. Students are further taught that the long-range effects of *Tottel's Miscellany* proved to be disappointing since no poet was motivated to continue Wyatt's and Surrey's experiments with Petrarch for decades thereafter. Thus, *Tottel's Miscellany* is blamed for being essentially a "flash in the pan" work lacking in any significant, literary influence. Such disappointment is absurdly unjustified, however, in view of what the publisher Richard Tottel and Wyatt and Surrey were trying to accomplish. Tottel published his collection "to the honor of the English tong," and in that sense the work was a success, as the conscious goal of all its contributors was to improve the vernacular. Furthermore, its most talented contributors, Wyatt and Surrey, accomplished what they set out to do: to investigate fully the possibilities of the short lyric, something that had never before been attempted in England, and, in Surrey's case, to experiment further with blank verse and the poulter's measure.

By no stretch of the imagination did Wyatt view himself as the precursor of a Petrarchan movement in England, and he made no attempt to cultivate followers. In fact, despite the superficial similarity of subject matter, Wyatt's poetry has little in common with the Petrarchan sonneteers of the close of the century, and he most assuredly would have resented any implication that his poetry was merely an unpolished harbinger of grander efforts to come. As Douglas L. Peterson has pointed out, Wyatt used Petrarch to suit his own purposes, mainly to perfect his "plain" style; and Yvor Winters maintains that Wyatt is closer to Gascoigne than Sidney. Whereas the sonneteers of the close of the century composed decidedly in the "eloquent" style, Wyatt expressed contempt for trussed-up images and pursued the virtues of a simple, unadorned style.

Thus, far from attempting to initiate a new "movement" of Petrarchan eloquence, many of the poems in *Tottel's Miscellany* sought to refine the possibilities of the plain style. As Peterson defines it, the plain style is characterized by plain, proverbial, aphoristic sentiments. It is a style often unappreciated by modern readers because its obvious simplicity is often mistaken for simplemindedness. The practitioners of the plain style, however, were very skilled in tailoring their verse to fit the needs of the poem's message, the pursuit of simplicity becoming a challenge, not a symptom of flagging inspiration. Skelton unwittingly summarizes the philosophy of the plain style when, commenting on his rhyme in *Colin Clout*, he instructs the reader: "If ye take well therewith/ It hath in it some pith." Thus, a plain-style poet expressing disillusionment with the excesses of love or extolling the virtues of frugality, rather than adorning his poem with an abundance of extravagant images, he instead pared his sentiments down to the minimum, with the intense restraint itself illuminating the poet's true feelings about love or money. The desiderata of the plain style were tightness and disciplined restraint. In the hands of an untalented poet, like John Heywood, who published his *Dialogue of Proverbs* in 1546 and a collection of epigrams in 1556, the aphoristic messages could easily become stultifying; but as practiced by a poet with the skill of Wyatt, the economy of rendering a truth simply could produce a pleasurable effect. Interestingly, near the close of the century, when the eloquent style was all the rage, Sir Walter Raleigh, Thomas Nashe, and Fulke Greville often employed the techniques of the plain style.

The three decades following the publication of *Tottel's Miscellany* have been stereotyped as a wasteland when poetry languished desultorily until the advent of the sonneteers in the 1580's. Nothing could be more unfair to the poetry of the period than to view it as struggling in an inspirational darkness. Amazingly, such a stereotype manages to overlook the profusion of poetry collections that *Tottel's Miscellany* spawned. Though admittedly the poetry of some of these collections is forgettable, nevertheless, the continual appearance of these collections for the next fifty years is an impressive indication of the extent to which Tottel's philosophy of prosodic experimentation continued to exert an influence.

The first imitation of Tottel to be published was *The Paradise of Dainty Devices* (1576), the most popular of the imitations. As its title would indicate, a number of amatory poems were included, but the predominant poems had didactic, often pious themes, which offered ample opportunity for further experimentation in the plain style. A number of reasonably accomplished poets contributed to the collection, including Sir Richard Grenville, Jaspar Heywood, Thomas Churchyard, and Barnabe Rich. Another successful collection was *Breton's Bower of Delights* (1591), interesting for its wide range of metrical experimentation, especially involving poulter's measure and the six-line iambic pentameter stanza. Imitations of Tottel's works did not always prove successful. In 1577, *A Gorgeous Gallery of Gallant Inventions* appeared, a monotonous collection of poems whose oppressive theme was the vanity of love and pleasure, and it was as plagued with affectations and jargon as *Breton's Bower of Delights* was blessed with fresh experimentation. Not everyone was pleased, however, with the new direction the lyric was taking after Tottel. In 1565, John Hall published his *Court of Virtue*, an anti-Tottel endeavor designed to preach that literature must be moral. In his work the poet is instructed by Lady Arete to cease pandering to the vulgar tastes of the public and instead to write moral, instructive lyrics, an appeal which results in the poet's moralizing of Wyatt's lyrics.

The experimental spirit of Tottel carried over into the works of individual poets, as well. From such an unlikely source as Thomas Tusser's *A Hundreth Good Points of Husbandry* (1557), an unassuming almanac of farming tips, explodes a variety of metrical experimentation, including Skeltonics, acrostics, and other complicated stanzaic forms. Despite his willingness to experiment, however, Tusser was not an accomplished talent, and thus there are three poets, Barnabe Googe, George Turberville, and George Gascoigne, to whom one must turn to refute the stereotype of the mid-century "wasteland." Too often viewed as bungling imitators of Tottel, these poets deserve a closer look as vital talents who were keeping poetry alive during the so-called wasteland years.

In his *Eclogues, Epitaphs, and Sonnets* (1563), Barnabe Googe's explicit poetic mission was to imitate Tottel. Working mostly in the didactic tradition, he wrote some epitaphs and poems in praise of friends, but his eclogues are of primary interest to the literary historian. He revived the Mantuan eclogue, which had been lying dormant in England after Barclay, and his eclogues were good enough to offer anticipations of Spenser's *The Shepheardes Calender* (1579). Another noteworthy work is his *Cupido Conquered* (1563), a dream-vision allegory, which Lewis dismissed as "purely medieval." The dismissal is unfair, however, because, despite the throwback to medieval devices, the plot, in which the languishing, lovesick poet is chided by his Muses for his shameful unproductivity, reveals Googe's self-consciousness of himself as craftsman, a characteristic pose for a poet of the sixteenth century. George Turberville's dexterity with metrics in his translation of Ovid has already been mentioned. Like Googe, Turberville, in his *Epitaphs, Epigrams, Songs, and Sonnets* (1567), carried on with Tottelian experimentation, primarily in didactic poems employing poulter's measure and fourteeners written in the plain style.

George Gascoigne has only recently received the attention that he deserves, his poetry serving as the most impressive evidence disproving the existence of a post-Tottel wasteland. Predictably, Lewis describes him as a precursor of golden age poetry, ignoring Gascoigne's contributions to the plain style. In his *A Hundreth Sundry Flowers Bound Up in One Small Posy* (1573), Gascoigne was the first to experiment with Petrarch and the sonnet form since

Wyatt and Surrey, but he was no slavish imitator. Gascoigne's poetry is often coarser and more lewd than that of Petrarch, but he never sacrifices a robust wit. In addition, he is an interesting figure for his variations in the sonnet form, featuring the octave-sestet division of the Petrarchan form, but in an English, or abab rhyme scheme. Puttenham refers to his "good meter" and "plentiful vein."

Thus, the poetry of the latter part of the century, the great age of the eloquent style, must not be viewed as a semimiraculous Phoenix, rising from the ashes between Wyatt's experiments with Petrarch and the advent of Sidney. Nevertheless, it must be noted that the Elizabethan era ranks as one of the outstanding poetic periods of any century, its development of the eloquent style ranking as an outstanding achievement. A valuable representative of what the eloquent style was trying to accomplish is Sir John Davies' *Orchestra: Or, A Poem of Dauncing* (1596). In his *Elizabethan World Picture* (1943), E. M. W. Tillyard analyzes the poem at length as a fitting symbol of the Elizabethans' obsession with cosmic order. Though accurate enough, Tillyard's discussion places too much emphasis on the poem's content and does not pay enough attention to the style in which the message is delivered. In the poem, the suitor Antinous launches an elaborate discourse designed to persuade Penelope, waiting for her Odysseus to return, to dance. Through Antinous' lengthy and involved encomium to cosmic order and rhythm, Davies was not attempting a literal plea to Penelope to get up and dance. Rather, he was using Antinous as a vehicle for an ingenious argument, ostentatious in its erudition and profusion of images; in effect, Antinous' argument is the repository of Davies' experiments in the eloquent style. It is the dazzling display of the process of argumentation itself, not the literal effort to persuade Penelope, that is the essence of the poem. The way in which the poem is written is more important than its content, and in that sense (but in that sense only) the goal of the eloquent style is no different from that of the plain style.

When one thinks of sixteenth century poetry and the eloquent style, however, one almost immediately thinks of the Petrarchan sonnet sequence, and one explanation for the almost fanatic renewal of interest in Petrarch was the inevitable shift of interests in poetic style. The plain style, so dominant for almost half a century, was beginning to play itself out, a primary indication being the decline in use of the epigram, whose pithy wit held little appeal for Elizabethan poets. The more skillful among them were anxious to perfect a new style, specifically the "eloquent" style, almost the total antithesis of the plain style. Not particularly concerned with expressing universal truths, the eloquent style, as practiced by Davies, sought embellishment, rather than pithy restraint; profusion of images, rather than minimal, tight expression. The eloquent style effected some interesting changes in the handling of the old Petrarchan themes, as well. It should be noted that in his experiments with Petrarch, Wyatt chafed at the indignities suffered by the courtly lover.

By contrast, the sonneteers emphasized with relish the travails of the lover, who almost luxuriates in his state of rejection. In fact, there is no small trace of fin de siècle decadence in the cult of the spurned lover that characterized so many of the sonnets of the period, most notably Sidney's *Astrophel and Stella* (1591), and it decidedly signaled the end of the plain style.

The sonnet sequence, a collection of sonnets recording the lover's successes and failures in courting his frequently unsympathetic mistress, was practiced by the brilliant and mediocre alike. Of course, the two most outstanding poets of the century pioneered the form—Sidney in his *Astrophel and Stella*, who in the true spirit of the poetic self-consciousness of the century wrote sonnets about the writing of sonnets and wrote some sonnets entirely in Alexandrines, and Edmund Spenser in his *Amoretti* (1595), who, in addition to introducing refinements in the sonnet structure, also intellectualized the cult of the rejected lover by analyzing the causes of rejection. In the next twenty years the contributions to the genre were dizzying: Fulke Greville's *Caelica* (written in 1577); Thomas Watson's *Passionate Century of Love* (1582); Samuel Daniel's *Delia* (1592); Henry Constable's *Diana* (1592); Thomas Lodge's *Phillis* (1593); Giles Fletcher's *Licia* (1593); Barnabe Barnes's *Parthenophil and Parthenophe* (1593); Bartholomew Griffin's *Fidessa* (1593); Michael Drayton's *Idea's Mirror* (1594), noteworthy for its experiments with rhyme; *The Phoenix Nest* (1593), a collection of Petrarchan sonnets in a wide variety of meters by George Peele, Nicholas Breton, Thomas Lodge, and others— the list of accomplished poets and tinkering poetasters was almost endless.

By the close of the century, so many mediocre poets had turned out sonnet sequences, and the plight of the rejected lover had reached such lugubrious proportions that the form inevitably decayed. Not only was the cult of the masochistic lover becoming tediously commonplace, but also one of the major triumphs of the eloquent style, the Petrarchan paradox (for example, Wyatt's "I burn, and freeze like ice") lost its appeal of surprise and tension as it became overworked, predictable, and trite. The genre had lost all traces of originality, and it is interesting to consider the fact that the modern definition of a sonneteer is an inferior poet. As early as 1577, Fulke Greville in his *Caelica* had perceived how easily in the sonnet sequence numbing repetition could replace fresh invention, and to maintain some vitality in his sequence his subject matter evolves from the complaints of the rejected lover to a renunciation of worldly vanity and expressions of disappointment in the disparity between "ideal" love and the imperfect love that exists in reality. (For this reason, of all the sonneteers Greville is the only precursor of the themes so prevalent in seventeenth century devotional poetry.)

The success and subsequent decline of the sonnet sequence left it wide open to parody. Many of the sonnets of William Shakespeare, who himself revolutionized the sonnet structure in England, are veiled satiric statements on the trite excesses of Petrarchan images ("My mistress' eyes are nothing like the sun"), indicating his impatience with the old, worn-out sentiments. Sir John Davies' collection of *Gulling Sonnets* (1873) was an explicit parody of Petrarchan absurdities and weary lack of invention, and, following their publication, the genre spun into an irreversible decline.

As the sonnet declined, however, another form of amatory verse was being developed: the mythological-erotic narrative. This form chose erotic themes from mythology, embellishing the narrative with sensuous conceits and quasi-pornographic descriptions. It was a difficult form to master because it required titillation without descending into vulgarity and light touches of sophisticated humor without descending into burlesque. Successful examples of the mythological-erotic narrative are Christopher Marlowe's *Hero and Leander* (1598), Shakespeare's *Venus and Adonis* (1593), Chapman's *Ovid's Banquet of Sense* (1595), Drayton's *Endimion and Phoebe* (1595), and Lodge's *Scillaes Metamorphosis* (1589). Like the sonnet the mythological narrative fell into decline, as evidenced by John Marston's *The Metamorphosis of Pygmalion's Image and Certain Satires* (1598), in which the decadence of the sculptor drooling lustfully over his statue was too absurdly indelicate for the fragile limits of the genre.

As the mythological narrative and the sonnet declined, both social satire and religious verse experienced a corresponding upswing. The steady growth of a middle-class reading audience precipitated an increased interest in satire, a genre which had not been represented with any distinction since Gascoigne's *The Steel Glass* (1576). Understandably, though inaccurately, Joseph Hall labeled himself the first Englsh satirist. Juvenalian satire flourished in his *Virgidemiarum* (1597), similar to Davies' *Gulling Sonnets*, followed by Everard Guilpin's *Skialetheia: Or, Shadow of Truth in Certain Epigrams and Satyres* (1598), which attacks the "wimpring sonnets" and "puling Elegies" of the love poets, and Marston's *The Scourge of Villainy* (1598).

Perhaps feeling reinforced by the indignation of the satirists, religious verse proliferated at the end of the century. Bedazzled by the great age of the sonnet, the modern reader tends to generalize that the latter decades of the century were a purely secular period for poetry. Such a view, however, overlooks the staggering amount of religious verse that was being turned out, and it should be remembered by the modern reader that to the reader of the sixteenth century, verse was typified not by a Sidney sonnet, but by a versified psalm. Throughout the century, experiments with Petrarch ebbed and flowed, but the reading public was never without religious writings, including enormous numbers of sermons, devotional manuals, collections of prayers and meditations, verse saints' lives, devotional verse, and, of course, an overflow of rhyming psalters. Versifying the psalter had begun as early as the fourteenth century, but its popularity and practice went unsurpassed in the sixteenth. Although many excellent poets tried their hand at the Psalms, including Wyatt, Spenser, and Sidney, who saw them as legitimate sources of poetry, these versifications were led by the Thomas Sternhold and John Hopkins edition of 1549, and it represents a mediocre collection of verse. Nevertheless, the uncultivated reading public hailed it as an inspired work, and people who refused to read any poetry at all devoured the Sternhold and Hopkins edition. Popular collections among the Elizabethans were William Hunnis' *Seven Sobs of a Sorrowfull Soule for Sinne* (1583) and William Byrd's *Psalmes, Sonnets, and Songs of Sadnes and Pietie* (1588).

By the close of the century, attempts at religious verse by more accomplished poets were surpassing the efforts of hack versifiers. While the satirists were ridiculing the atrophied sonnet sequence on aesthetic grounds, other writers were attacking it on moral grounds, and perceptions of what poetry should be and do were shifting as the sonnet lost its influence. Having put a distance of four years between his *Astrophel and Stella* and the publication of his *Defense of Poesie*, Sidney authoritatively proclaimed in the latter work that poetry should celebrate God and Divine Love. Thomas Nashe attacks verse in which "lust is the tractate of so many leaves." Physical love was no longer *au courant*. In his "A Coronet for his Mistress Philosophy," George Chapman reflects the new vogue of Neoplatonism by carefully identifying the differences between divine and physical love, also investigated meticulously by Spenser in his *Fowre Hymnes* (1596). Joshua Sylvester's translations between 1590 and 1605 of the works of the French Huguenot poet Guillaume du Bartas helped to reinforce Protestant piety and further counteracted the Petrarchans. The most saintly poet of the period was the Jesuit, Robert Southwell. In his Preface to his *St. Peter's Complaint* (1595), Southwell laments that the teachings of Christ go unheeded as poets would rather celebrate the glories of Venus. In *St. Peter's Complaint* itself, Peter excoriates himself for his denial of Christ, and the fact that the work is oddly adorned with sensuous conceits is an interesting indication that Petrarchan images managed to survive stubbornly, even in works inimical to their spirit. Finally, in 1599, Sir John Davies published his *Nosce Teipsum*, whose theme was self-knowledge, rather than carnal knowledge of one's mistress, as well as the proper relationship between the soul and the body.

The tug of war between the sonneteers and the religious poets was only one of several noteworthy poetic developments near the close of the century. Spenser, the most talented poet of the century, contributed to both sides of the battle (the *Amoretti* and *Fowre Hymnes*), but his versatility as a poet enabled him to transcend any one category. Spenser's early poetic career is not without its mysteries. No literary historian would have predicted that at a time when a new poetry was being refined by means of the sonnet form, someone would choose to revive the old medieval forms, but that is what Spenser did. *The Shepheardes Calender* is a throwback to the Mantuan eclogues, at this point almost a century old, and *Colin Clout's Come Home Again* is reminiscent of Skelton's anticlerical satires. His *Mother Hubberds*

Tale (1590) is an imitation of a medieval beast fable, and even *The Faerie Queene*, his most famous work, is essentially a compendium of medieval allegory and Italian epic forms derived from Ludovico Ariosto and Torquato Tasso. Furthermore, many of Spenser's works were written in a deliberately archaic style.

Thus a major contribution to Spenser's fame is not the originality of his themes, but the range of his metrical and stanzaic experimentations. In a century characterized by poets self-consciously aware of themselves exercising their craft, Spenser was the apotheosis of the poetic craftsman. Though his archaic diction violated the tenets of many critics who believed that the vernacular must grow, Spenser's experiments in versification furthered the cause of making English more vital. Despite its reactionary themes, *The Shepheardes Calender* explodes with experimentation in poetic forms. The "January" eclogue is written in the six-line ballad or "Venus and Adonis" stanza, "February" is written in Anglo-Saxon accentual verse, "March" is written in the romance stanza of Chaucer's "Sir Topaz," "July" is written in a rough, vulgar ballad meter, and "August" is a contrast of undisciplined folk rhythms and elegant sestinas. Though not Spenser's most famous work, *The Shepheardes Calender* is nevertheless a remarkable symbol and culmination of the poetic self-consciousness of the sixteenth century and a fusion of the experiments in poetic versification that had helped to shape English as a suitable vehicle for poetry.

As the century was drawing to a close, a popular genre flourishing outside the continuing battle between amatory and religious verse was the verse chronicle history. Of all the genres popular in the sixteenth century, the verse chronicle history is probably the most difficult for the modern reader to appreciate, probably because of its excruciating length; but more than any other genre, it serves as a repository for Elizabethan intellectual, historical, and social thought, especially as it reflects the Elizabethan desire for political order, so amply documented by Tillyard in his *Elizabethan World Picture*.

The first treatment of English history in poetry was the landmark publication of *A Mirror for Magistrates* in 1559. it was a collection of tragedies of famous leaders in the medieval tradition of people brought low by the turning wheel of Fortune and was written in rime royal, the favorite stanzaic vehicle of medieval narrative. The structure of its tragedies was imitated from Giovanni Boccaccio and from John Lydgate's *Falls of Princes* (1494), and the constant themes of the tragedies were both the subject's responsibility to his king and the king's responsibility to God; if either the ruler or the subject should fail in his proper allegiance, disorder and tragedy would inevitably ensue. *A Mirror for Magistrates* was extraordinarily popular with a reading public desiring both entertainment and instruction. It went through eight editions in thirty years, with Thomas Sackville's "Induction" being considered at the time the best poem between Chaucer and Spenser.

The major importance of *A Mirror for Magistrates* is the fact that it fulfilled Sidney's mandate in his *Defense of Poesie* that the poet take over the task of the historian, and *A Mirror for Magistrates* exerted a powerful influence on the late Elizabethan poets. Pride in the royal Tudor lineage led not only the prose chroniclers but also the poets of the Elizabethan period to develop a strong sense of Britain's history. Shakespeare's history plays are widely recognized as reflections of England's growing nationalistic fervor, and because of the magnitude of the plays, it is easy to overlook the contributions of the poets to English history, or, perhaps more accurately, pseudohistory. The troublesome murkiness of Britain's origins were efficiently, if somewhat questionably, cleared up by exhaustive embellishments of the legends of Brut and King Arthur, legends that spurred England on to a sharpened sense of patriotism and nationalism. An obvious example is Spenser's chronicle of early British history at the end of Book II of *The Faerie Queene*. In 1586 William Warner published his *Albion's England*, a long work ambitiously taking as its province all of historical time from Noah's Flood down to the execution of Mary, Queen of Scots.

The following years saw the publication of Samuel Daniel's *The First Fowre Bookes of the Civile Warres* (1595, 1599, 1601), whose books represented the apotheosis of all attempts at versified history. Like Shakespeare in his history plays, Daniel focused on a theme common in Elizabethan political theory, the evil that inevitably results from civil and moral disorder—specifically, the overthrow of Richard II. The modern reader has a natural antipathy toward the Elizabethan verse chronicles because of their length and because of the chroniclers' penchant for moral allegorizing, for their tedious accounts of past civil disorder as illustrative of present moral chaos, and for their far-reaching, interweaving parallels among mythological, biblical, and British history (for example, the Titan's defeat of Saturn being contrasted with the victory of Henry V at Agincourt in Thomas Heywood's *Troia Britannica*, 1609). Nevertheless, these versified histories and their championing of moral order and nationalism constituted much of the most popular poetry of the Elizabethan period, and their impact cannot be over-emphasized.

In retrospect, it is indeed astonishing to consider precisely how much the poetry of the sixteenth century grew after Stephen Hawes's allegories first limped onto the scene in 1509. The pressing need for most poets at the beginning of the century was to imitate medieval forms as faithfully as possible. There was no question as to the superiority of the classical authorities, and there was no "English" poetry as such. In 1531, Sir Thomas Elyot mentions Ovid and Martial but not English poets, and, as late as 1553, Thomas Wilson was defending the rhetoric of the authorities Cicero and Quintilian. Gradually, however, by struggling with the new language and continuing to experiment with verse forms both new and original, poets were starting to shape a new English poetry and were achieving recognition as craftsmen in their own right. By 1586, William Webbe respectfully addressed the Preface to his *Discourse of English Poetry* to "the Noble Poets of England" and made mention of Skelton, Gascoigne, and Googe, finally recognizing Spenser as "the rightest English poet that ever I read." Thus, by the end of the century the question of whether there could be an English poesy had been replaced by the question of what were the limits of the great English poets.

Because of the struggle to shape the new vernacular, the sixteenth century differs from other centuries in that many innovations were coming from the pens of not particularly gifted poets. Thus, working in a period of volatility and flux in the language, such men as Barclay and Skelton could exert an impact on the shaping of the poetry and earn their place in literary history. The first half of the sixteenth century did not witness the formation of new genres. The old reliables, dream-vision allegories, anticlerical satires, pastorals, ballads, versified psalms, and neomedieval tragedies, were the favorite vehicles of most poets. The extraordinary development of this period was the metrical experimentation, which never stopped, no matter how limited the poet. Perhaps more than any other period, therefore, the first half of the sixteenth century reveals as many noteworthy developments in its bad poets as in its talented ones.

After the publication of *Tottel's Miscellany*, poetry began to settle down somewhat from its pattern of groping experimentation as it gained confidence and stability working with the vernacular. Perhaps the surest indication that poetry had hit its stride in England was the parody of the Petrarchan sonnet. The parody of the first truly great lyric form in England was a significant landmark because only widely popular forms tend to serve as targets for parody. A further indication of the vitality of the poetry was the fact that its poets survived the parody and went on to create new forms. Furthermore, poetic tastes were flexible enough to produce a Spenser who, while forging ahead with prosodic experimentation, looked backward to the archaisms that English poetry had originally utilized.

As the sixteenth century waned and old genres, such as the sonnet, the pastoral, and the verse chronicle, faded, there were numerous hints of what the poets of the new century would be attempting. In particular, there were several suggestions of the Metaphysicals. The decline in popularity of the Petrarchan sonnet and its subsequent ridicule paved the way for John Donne's satires of the form in many of his secular lyrics. As was seen earlier, Greville's religious themes in his *Caelica* were a precursor of devotional poetry. The sensuous conceits of Southwell heralded the baroque extravagances of Richard Crashaw. The pastoral, a favorite Elizabethan genre, was fast fading, as indicated by Sir Walter Raleigh's cynical response to Christopher Marlowe's "The Passionate Shepherd to His Love," a plea for living a romantic life in pastoral bliss. In his "Nymph's Reply to the Shepherd," Raleigh makes it clear that such idyllic bliss does not exist. The pastoral was being replaced, however, by a less idealized, more rational mode, the theme of self-contained, rural retirement, as embodied at the close of the century in Sir Edward Dyer's "My Mind to Me a Kingdom Is," a theme that became increasingly popular in the new century. Finally, the proliferation of songs and airs, found in such collections as Nicholas Yonge's *Musica Transalpina* (1588), John Dowland's *The First Book of Songs or Airs* (1597), and Thomas Campion's *A Book of Airs* (1601), created a vogue that influenced the lyrics of Ben Jonson and his followers.

The true worth of the poetry of the sixteenth century, however, lies not in the legacies that were inherited from it by the next century but rather in the sheer exuberance for the poetic undertaking that characterized the century from beginning to end. Because of the continuing process of shaping the new vernacular, the tools of the poetic craft are evident in every work, and in no other century did the poets better embody the original etymology of the word "poet," which comes from the Greek word for "maker." to use Webbe's term, they "Englished" the old poetry and proved to be untiring "makers" of a new.

Elizabeth J. Bellamy

THE SEVENTEENTH CENTURY

The Century's Antipodes: Donne and Dryden

A question which can be asked of any century's poetry is whether it owes its character to "forces"—nonliterary developments to which the poets respond more or less sensitively—or whether, on the other hand, the practice of innovative and influential poets mainly determines the poetry of the period. Clearly, great poets do not always shape the literature of their century, as the cases of the twin towers of seventeenth century England, William Shakespeare and John Milton, indicate. What Ben Jonson wrote of Shakespeare is true of both: they are "not of an age, but for all time!" John Donne and John Dryden, however, are poets who seem to have stamped their personalities on much of the poetry of their own and succeeding generations.

In most libraries the two are neighbors. If not the shaper of poetry in the first half of the century, Donne stands at least as its representative poet, while Dryden, born just a few months after Donne died in 1631, probably has an even more secure claim to the same position in the final decades of the century. They may indeed have determined the poetic climate; certainly they serve as barometers on which modern readers can see that climate registered. The distinctive differences between the writings of the two men testify to the diversity of seventeenth century poetry and to the likelihood that powerful forces for change were at work in the interim.

The differences are apparent even when—perhaps particularly when—roughly similar types of poems (and parallels between the two are inevitably rough) are chosen. Donne wrote two sequences of religious sonnets. One begins:

> Thou hast made me, and shall thy work decay?
> Repair me now, for now mine end doth haste,
> I run to death, and death meets me as fast,
> And all my pleasures are like yesterday.

Dryden is known for two longer religious poems, one of which *Religio Laici: Or, A Layman's Faith* (1682), begins: "Dim as the borrowed beams of moons and stars/ To lonely, weary, wand'ring travelers,/ Is Reason to the soul. . . ." A long list of contrasts might be drawn up, most of which would hold true of entire poems and, for that matter, of the works of the two poets generally.

Donne addresses God directly, for example, and even ventures to command Him, while neither in his opening nor anywhere else in 456 lines does Dryden apostrophize his maker, although several times he refers circumspectly to "God," "Godhead," or "Omnipotence." Donne not only personifies but also personalizes the abstraction *death*, which "runs fast" and "meets" the speaker. Dryden's chief abstraction, *Reason*, is grand but "dim," and another which he introduces soon thereafter, *Religion*, though described as "bright," remains inanimate. Donne's sonnet has an immediate, even urgent, quality; Dryden sets out in a more deliberate and measured way, as if any necessary relationships will be established in due time. Donne achieves that immediacy through a plain, simple vocabulary, thirty-one of his first thirty-five words having only one syllable. While there are no striking irregularities after the first line, rhetorical stresses govern the rhythm. Dryden's diction is also simple, but there are more polysyllables, and their arrangement, as in "lonely, weary, wand'ring travelers," creates a smoother, more regular cadence.

In other ways the poems elicit different responses. Donne is paradoxical. The reader senses in his third line that rigorous demands are being made on him. What does "I run to death" mean exactly? How can that be? Why is death said to do the same? Such questions have answers, no doubt, but the reader anticipates that he will have to work for them, that he must stay alert and get involved. Dryden, on the other hand, begins by making a statement that can be accepted without any particular mental activity (which is not necessarily to say that it should be, or is intended to be, so accepted). Whereas the person setting out to read Donne suspects that obscurities may lie ahead, the beginner at Dryden finds nothing to raise such expectations. (The reader will hardly be surprised to find Dryden saying, near the end of the poem: "Thus have I made my own opinions clear.")

Samplers of other poems by the two poets reveal similar contrasts right from the beginning. Frequently in Donne's poems a speaker is addressing someone or something—God, a woman, a friend, a rival, the sun—in a tone which is often abrupt, questioning, or imperious. The poems are often dramatic in the sense of implying a situation and a relationship. They make demands, both on the addressee and the reader, who is present in somewhat the same way as an audience in a theater. Dryden was a dramatist, and a highly successful one, but he seems to have reserved drama for his plays. In his poems he is inclined to begin, as in *Religio Laici*, with statements, often in the form of generalizations: "All human things are subject to decay." "From harmony, from heavenly harmony,/ This universal frame began." "How blest is he who leads a country life." While not condescending to his readers, Dryden is much more likely to go on to *tell* them something—something clear, measured, plausible.

Donne turned twenty-nine in the year 1601. Dryden, busy to the last, died in 1700. Thus a century brimming with good poetry may be said to begin with Donne and end with Dryden.

The Elizabethan Heritage

The Renaissance had come to England late. Sixteenth century Italian poetry is dotted with famous names—Ludovico Ariosto, Pietro Bembo, Michelangelo Buonarroti, Torquato Tasso—and French poets distinguished themselves throughout the century, Pierre de Ronsard and the Pléiade group overshadowing others of whom today's readers would hear much more but for that brilliant constellation of poets. The Elizabethan poets' debt to these older literatures, particularly to that created by their French elders and contemporaries, has been well documented.

From the time of Edmund Spenser's *The Shepheardes Calender* (1579), English poetry came on with a rush, while the post-Renaissance baroque movement was already rising on the European continent. By 1600, Spenser and Sir Philip Sidney, both born in the 1550's, were dead, but many of their contemporaries from the 1550's and 1560's worked on, with many of their brightest achievements still ahead. As relief from the earlier but continuing Elizabethan tradition of ponderous, prosaic moralizing exemplified by the incessantly reprinted and expanded *A Mirror for Magistrates*, whose first extant edition dates from 1559, the poets of later Elizabethan decades favored pastoral, love sonnets, mythological narratives, and of course songs and the verse drama.

As part of the last wave of poets to come of age under Elizabeth, Donne and Ben Jonson might have been expected to rebel against their elders. Fifteen years or so of hobnobbing with Hobbinol and other literary shepherds and of agonizing with woebegone Petrarchan lovers over their unattainable or recalcitrant golden ladies goaded the new generation into staking out new territory. The sweetness and naïveté of much Elizabethan verse cloyed their literary taste buds. The serious side of Elizabethan endeavor ran wearyingly to themes of transience and mutability. There was room for more realism and sophistication, and new forms and conventions.

Donne responded by parodying the ideal Petrarchan mistress in his paean to indiscriminate love, "I can love both fair and brown," meanwhile reserving that standard vehicle for love laments, the sonnet, for religious purposes. Jonson refused to write sonnets at all, coolly praised a goddess named Celia, and claimed, with some exaggeration, that he did not write of love. As mythologizers, Elizabethans were accustomed to plunder from Ovid and the Ovidians, but Donne did not conduct his raids on the *Metamorphoses*, with its wistful accounts of lovers vanished into foliage and feathers; instead, he concentrated on Ovid's saucy prescriptions for both lovemaking and love-breaking in the *Amores* (*Loves*), *Ars amatoria* (*Art of Love*), and *Remedium amoris* (*Love's Remedy*). Later (or perhaps just alternatively) he drew on the pre-Petrarchan traditions, including Platonism and Scholasticism, to write of love as a refining and exalting experience. As for Jonson, where the Elizabethans were amply decorous, he tended to be blunt and epigrammatic. More rigorously than Donne, he rejected the medieval trappings that clung to Elizabethan poetry.

Yet neither man made anything like a clean break with Elizabethan values. In satirizing Petrarchan conventions, Donne was only continuing a tendency implicit in the Petrarchan mode almost from its beginning, Shakespeare already preceding him in English poetry in his sonnet "My mistress' eyes are nothing like the sun." The man most responsible for the English sonnet-writing mania, Sir Philip Sidney, had, in his *Astrophel and Stella* (1591) suggested all sorts of latent possibilities for the deployment of wit which the Elizabethans had barely begun to exploit. Elizabethan moral earnestness awaited poets who could bring fresh resources to its expression. The student of the drama can hardly escape the conclusion that Donne owed something of his penchant for dramatizing love and religious conflict to the fact that he grew up in London at a time of flourishing theatrical activity, when even writers deficient in dramatic talent strove to turn out plays. Jonson must have learned much about friendship from Sidney's *Arcadia* (1590), the Fourth Book of Spenser's *The Faerie Queene* (1590-1596), and other romances of the sort before turning this subject to account in poetic forms more congenial to him. Again, Jonson's distinctive contribution to songwriting depended on his good fortune in maturing at a time when music was everywhere in the air, as Willa McClung Evans has shown in *Ben Jonson and Elizabethan Music* (1929). In short, Elizabethan influences on these Jacobean poets were very far from exclusively negative ones.

Seventeenth century developments originating with Donne and Jonson have absorbed much of the attention of literary students, but the Spenserian tradition must not be underrated. Its master having been a many-faceted poet, it is a rich and diverse one. Michael Drayton carried his adaptations of Spenserian pastoral to the verge of the new century's fourth decade. The greatest English poet after Shakespeare found in *The Faerie Queene* the best model for his own epic. Some poets imitated Spenser's idealism, some his sensuous and even sensual music, some his achievement in romantic narrative, and some his demanding stanza. No one like Spenser wrote in the seventeenth century, but the rays of his genius shone over the century and long afterwards. The twentieth century emphasis on Donne and the Metaphysical poets has had the unfortunate effect of obscuring the illumination that Spenser furnished generations of respectful and admiring followers.

In few European countries was there such a concentration of talent and creative energy as in Renaissance London. England had no city to rival it in size or cultural pretensions, and to the city or to the court came all aspiring writers and all ambitious men. Literary associations blossomed easily in its square mile, as did rivalries and jealousies. Although London did not boast a university, many of its creative men came to know one another in school. Beginning in the last quarter of the sixteenth century, for example, and extending over the next seventy years, the roster of poets who attended just one school, Westminster, includes Jonson, Richard Corbett, Giles Fletcher, Henry King, George Herbert, William Strode, Thomas Randolph, William Cartwright, Abraham Cowley, and Dryden. Half of these men later gravitated to one Cambridge college, Trinity. A similar list of poets who claimed residence at London's Inns of Court might be made. It is likely that the richness of late Elizabethan and seventeenth century English poetry owes much to the cross-fertilization that is almost inevitable when virtually all of the poets of any given time know one another more or less intimately. Although poets have always come together for mutual support and stimulation, in the seventeenth century the poets who did so were not beleaguered minorities without status in the intellectual world or insulated coteries intent on defending the purity of their theory and practice against one another. Poets constituted something of a brotherhood—although brothers are known to fight—and not a school or club where narrowness can prevail along with good manners.

Realizing the essentially close relationships among poets whose work scholars tend to classify and mark off from one another, modern commentators on seventeenth century poetry have recently emphasized the common heritage and shared concerns of writers once assumed to be disparate and even antagonistic. It is well to recall this shared heritage and common cause when distinguishing—as criticism must distinguish—among individual achievements and ascertainable poetic movements.

The "Metaphysical School": Donne and His Followers

After Sir Herbert Grierson's edition of Donne's poems in 1912, critics spent some decades attempting to define and delineate "Metaphysical poetry." T. S. Eliot, in a 1921 essay, lent his prestige to the endeavor, and such studies as George Williamson's *The Donne Tradition* (1930), Joan Bennett's *Four Metaphysical Poets* (1934), J. B. Leishman's *Metaphysical Poets* (1934), Helen C. White's *The Metaphysical Poets* (1936), and Rosemond Tuve's *Elizabethan and Metaphysical Imagery* (1947) refined readers' understanding of the movement but created such a vogue that the term "metaphysical" came to acquire a bewildering variety of applications and connotations, with the understandable result that some critics, including Leishman, came to view it with suspicion. Nevertheless, it remains useful for the purpose of designating the kind of poetry written by Donne, Herbert, Richard Crashaw, Henry Vaughan, Thomas Traherne, Andrew Marvell (at least some of the time), and a considerable number of other seventeenth century poets, including the American, Edward Taylor. The earlier tendency to call these poets a "school" has also fallen into disrepute since the term suggests a much more formal and schematic set of relationships than existed among these poets. Douglas Bush, in his valuable contribution to the *Oxford History of English Literature* series, *English Literature in the Earlier Seventeenth Century, 1600-1660* (1962), refers to the Metaphysicals after Donne as his "successors," while Joseph H. Summers prefers another designation, as the title of his 1970 study, *The Heirs of Donne and Jonson*, indicates.

Because the bulk of English Metaphysical poetry after Donne tends to be religious, it has been studied profitably under extraliterary rubrics, especially by Louis L. Martz as *The Poetry of Meditation* (1954), in which the author demonstrates how many distinctive features of such poetry derive from the Christian art of meditation, especially from such manuals of Catholic devotion as St. Ignatius Loyola's *Spiritual Exercises* (1548) and St. Francis de Sales' *An Introduction to the Devout Life* (c. 1608). More recently, Barbara Kiefer Lewalski has argued for the importance of Protestant devotional literature in her *Protestant Poetics and the Seventeenth Century Religious Lyric* (1979). Donne and some of his followers have been profitably studied as poets of wit, a classification that connects them with Jonson and the Jonsonians, in later books by Leishman (*The Monarch of Wit*, 1951) and Williamson (*The Proper Wit of Poetry*, 1961), as well as in the aforementioned book by Summers.

Students of literature continue to be intrigued by the word "metaphysical," however, and by the challenge of pinpointing its essential denotation. One of the most distinctive traits of this poetry is the Metaphysical conceit, an image which, as its name suggests, is intended to convey an idea rather than a sensory quality. The conceit, as exemplified by Donne's comparison of the quality of two lovers' devotion to the draftsman's compass in "A Valediction: Forbidding Mourning," or the pulley image in Herbert's poem of that title used to express the speaker's sense of the relationship between God and man, is likely to be ingenious, unexpected, and apparently unpromising; the poet is inclined to develop it at considerale length (Donne uses three stanzas for his compass conceit, while Herbert builds his whole poem on the pulley image) and in a number of particulars; and the result, often arrived at through argumentation, justifies the seeming incongruity of the image. An interesting comparison between Donne's imagery and that of Shakespeare has been made by Cleanth Brooks (in *The Well Wrought Urn*, 1947) with the view of demonstrating the use of similar conceits by Shakespeare, who is never thought of as a Metaphysical.

Describers of Metaphysical poetry have most often cited a cluster of traits, no one of which differentiates this mode from others. Metaphysical poems are often dramatic, colloquial in diction and rhythm, and set forth in intricate and varied forms with respect to line lengths, rhyme schemes, and stanzaic configurations. Whether dealing with sexual or religious love, Metaphysical love poems develop the psychological aspects of loving which are always implicit, sometimes explicit in the Petrarchan tradition. Sexual, Platonic, and religious love are frequently explored in terms seemingly more appropriate to one of the other types. Thus Donne assures God that he will never be "chaste, except you ravish me," and a lady that "all shall approve/ Us canonized for love." Crashaw can refer to a mistress as a "divine idea" in a "shrine of crystal flesh," and, in another poem, to God as a rival lover of St. Teresa.

The chief trait of Metaphysical poetry in the eyes of Earl Miner (*The Metaphysical Mode from Donne to Cowley*, 1969) is its "private mode." He considers the most distinctive aspect of the love or religious experience in this poetry to be its individual and private character. Either because the poet senses a breakdown of social bonds or because these bonds threaten the integrity of private experience, the Metaphysical poet is in self-conscious retreat from the social realm. Thus Donne's love poems often evoke third parties only to banish them as early as the first line: "For God's sake, hold your tongue, and let me love." The earlier Metaphysicals, however, are familiar with the world that they reject, and its immanence contributes to the dramatic quality in their poetry. In later poets such as Vaughan and Traherne the interfering world has receded; as a result the dramatic tension largely disappears.

Metaphysical poetry's reputed taste for the obscure and the "far-fetched" has been overemphasized by critics from Dryden to the twentieth century. That it is intellectual and that its allusions are likely to necessitate numerous glosses for modern readers there can be little doubt. The ideal audience for Metaphysical poetry was small and select. To Pre-Restoration readers, however, the poems probably did not seem especially difficult. It is simply that Renaissance learning was replaced by a different learning. As the century waned a gap widened between the old and new learning; as a result Dryden had more difficulty reading Donne than do modern readers, who enjoy the benefit of modern scholars' recovery of much of that older learning. The continuing popularity of Metaphysical poetry demonstrates readers' continuing willingness to absorb glosses without which the richness of the poetry is lost.

European Metaphysical Poetry (1961), an anthology by Frank J. Warnke with a long critical introduction, presents French, German, Spanish, Dutch, and Italian texts of selected poems with facing verse translations. The volume includes a number of poems analogous to the works of Donne and his followers and distinguishes between the Metaphysical and baroque traditions, although clearly they overlap. A Mexican nun, Sor Juana Inés de la Cruz (1651-1695), rivals Edward Taylor, who came to America in 1668, as the first Metaphysical poet of the New World. Like Crashaw, Sor Juana writes emotional, sexually charged religious verse, but, also like him, she was a keen student of theology and something of an intellectual. In Taylor the Metaphysical manner and a Puritan religious outlook produced a body of poetry unique in the American colonies or elsewhere. The influence of Richard Baxter's famous book *The Saints' Everlasting Rest* (1692) is heavier on Taylor than on any other Metaphysical poet, and many of his poems are cast as meditations. The language is that of a man who lived and worked on the late seventeenth century American frontier, cut off from the society of the learned and the artistic. Even his conceits, such as the one on which he bases "Huswifery"—"Make me, O Lord, thy spinning wheel complete"—have a homely, rough-hewn air.

Finally, the seventeenth century produced a body of poetry not usually classified as Metaphysical but having some affinities with that tradition. Much of it is religious. Emblem poetry, best exemplified by Francis Quarles, was a mixed-media art including a print which depicted a scene of religious or moral significance, a biblical quotation, a related poem, another quotation, and, in most cases, a concluding epigram. The engravings in emblem books are frequently more interesting than the poems, but the form seems to have made its mark on Spenser, Shakespeare, and several of the Metaphysical poets, notably Herbert and Crashaw; Herbert's great book *The Temple* (1633) contains several poems which, arranged to form figures, become in effect emblems of their subject matter. Another poet, Henry More, in his fondness for allegory and the Spenserian stanza points to one large influence, but often reminds the reader of the Metaphysicals in his choice and handling of imagery, even though his work is more justly charged with obscurity than theirs. At the same time More is one of the few seventeenth century poets who is known to have studied René Descartes and to have been directly influenced by the Cartesian dualism of mind and matter. If, as Basil Willey has argued in *The Seventeenth Century Background* (1934), Cartesian thought undermined confidence in the "truth" of poetry, it is in More that one should be able to read the signs of the decline, but More seems as sure of the truth of his poetical utterances as of his *Divine Dialogues* (1668) in prose. Other Metaphysically tinged poetry will be considered as part of the "Mid-Century Transition" below.

Ben Jonson and Renaissance Classicism

From a twentieth century perspective Ben Jonson was overshadowed by Shakespeare as a playwright and by Donne as a lyric and reflective poet, but his importance in his time is difficult to overestimate. Before his time England had produced classical scholars who edited texts, produced grammars and other educational tools, and wrote significant prose. Not until Jonson, however, did an Englishman combine classical learning with great poetic ability. Jonson's interpretation of the classical heritage, which involved (besides the drama) imitations of such distinctly classical forms as the epigram, ode, and verse epistle; the translation into verse of Horace's *Ars Poetica* (13-8 B.C., *The Art of Poetry*); and the employment of poetry as an ethical, civilizing influence not only enriched poetry but also defined classicism itself for generations of Englishmen. Even today classicists are likely to conceive of its essential spirit as comprising such virtues as simplicity, clarity, symmetry, detachment, and restraint, although such qualities are hardly the hallmarks of Euripides, Pindar, Ovid, and any number of other Greek and Roman poets. Jonsonian classicism proved to be a timely antidote to Elizabethan verbosity and extravagance, however, and generated some of the best poetry of the seventeenth century.

All of Jonson's favorite classical forms had been practiced in the sixteenth century, though often in an eclectic and self-indulgent way. Jonson showed that the discipline of strict classicism could be liberating. Douglas Bush has pointed out that his imitations of Martial not only capture the temper of the greatest Roman epigrammatist better than did any of his predecessors, but also display more originality than earlier poems in this genre. Although not a great love poet, Jonson wrote a series of song lyrics that are models of their type, one of them, "Drink to me only with thine eyes" being familiar to millions of people who know nothing of classicism or of Jonson himself. His verse letter "To Penshurst," though initially unexciting to a reader accustomed to Donne's pyrotechnics, achieves an unobtrusive but unforgettable effect. When, at the end he contrasts the Sidney family mansion with other houses—"their lords have built, but thy lord dwells"—he has accomplished a tribute worth all the fulsome compliments that Elizabethans heaped upon their bene-factors. It was through his study of Horace, a quiet bastion of civility in the noisy Roman Empire, that Jonson was able to produce such an effect.

Like Donne, Jonson not only wrote fine poems but inspired others of a high order as well. Robert Herrick, to whom Jonson was "St. Ben," sometimes approached his master in the art of epigram and sometimes exceeded him in the writing of cool, elegant lyrics. Poets such as Edmund Waller who reached the heights only infrequently probably could not have done so at all without Jonson's example (and occasionally Donne's also). The delicacy of Waller's "Go, lovely rose" is an inheritance of the Tribe of Ben. If the same poet's Penshurst poems fall short of Jonson's, Andrew Marvell's *Upon Appleton House* is both marvelously original and indebted to Jonson. William Alex-ander McClung, in *The Country House in English Renaissance Poetry* (1977), has shown how the poets after Jonson were able to set forth both an ideal of environment and an ideal of virtue through their reflection in a house.

Neither Jonson nor his followers necessarily came by their Horatian restraint and moderation naturally. As a young man Jonson flashed the same hot temper that many another Elizabethan did not bother to control. In 1598 he plunged a rapier six inches into the side of a fellow actor named Gabriel Spencer, killing him instantly. He escaped with a branding on the thumb by pleading benefit of clergy—a dubious privilege possible for an educated man in or out of holy orders. Pen in hand, however, he modeled his work on that of Horace, who counseled, and perhaps practiced, moderation as a "golden mean." Horace did not prevent Jonson from lashing out verbally at his critics from time to time, but the Roman poet probably saved the impetuous Jonson from many a poetical gaucherie.

Many of Jonson's followers were political conservatives, advocates of royal supremacy and others who had most to fear from the intransigent Puritans, whose power grew steadily throughout the first half of the century until they forced Charles I from his throne and, in 1649, beheaded him for treason. Thus Jonsonian classicists overlapped, but did not subsume, the Cavalier lyric poets, who celebrated the not particularly Horatian virtues of war, chivalry, and loyalty to the monarchy. Just as paradoxically, the great classicist of the generation after Jonson turned out to be Latin Secretary of Oliver Cromwell's Commonwealth, the militant Puritan John Milton.

At their best the Jonsonians wrote graceful and civilized lyrics reflecting a philosophy that was, in the best sense of the term, Epicurean. Like the Elizabethans, they were attracted to the theme of man's mortality, but whereas the earlier poets had responded to the inevitability of decline and death with lugubrious melancholy, the Tribe of Ben had imbibed Horace's advice: *carpe diem*, "seize the day." They wrote the most beautiful lyrics on this theme ever written in English: Herrick's "To Daffodils," "To the Virgins, to Make Much of Time," and "Corinna's going A-Maying," Waller's "Go, lovely rose," and Andrew Marvell's "To His Coy Mistress."

Another subject dear to the heart of Jonsonians was one relatively rare in previous (and many later) eras: children. Jonson wrote, with deep feeling yet immense restraint, of the deaths of two children. "On My First Daughter" does not repeat the personal pronoun of the title, although the reader learns that her name was Mary. The parents, however, are referred to in the third person, only the final phrase, "cover lightly, gentle earth!" betraying the speaker's involvement in the child's demise. An even finer poem, "On My First Son," has only six couplets and yet achieves enormous poignancy through the most economical means. Jonson could have expressed his love no more forcefully than by saying: "Here doth lie/ Ben Jonson his best piece of poetry." The lesson he draws is more Horatian than Christian: "For whose sake, henceforth, all his vows be such/ As what he loves may never like too much." Although Jonson wrote a few religious lyrics, it seems to be the classical legacy that he cherished most deeply.

Among those who gathered with Jonson at the Mermaid Tavern, Richard Corbett also wrote of family members, including one poem "To His Son, Vincent" in which he characteristically sets forth moderate wishes for his offspring, "not too much wealth, nor wit," and on the positive side, the graces of his mother, friends, peace, and innocence at the last. Among the poets who wrote poems about other people's children was William Cartwright, who expressed wishes for a friend's new-born son, and Robert Herrick, who penned two short epitaphs and two graces for children to recite at meals. Obviously the range of childhood poems in the seventeenth century is very narrow, even if Traherne's mystical poems, "Shadows in the Water," "Innocence," and others are included. Even so, that children figure in poetry at all is an indication that Jonson's disciples do not consider commonplace subjects beneath their notice.

As might be expected of admirers of Horace and Martial, Jonsonians favored short lines and short stanzas, though without the intricacy and irregularity often seen in Metaphysical lyrics. They often wrote in couplets, though the form known as the heroic couplet does not appear much before mid-century and does not become important until the age of Dryden. The couplets mirror the unassuming quality of so much early English classicism but commonly betray careful craftsmanship. The diction is rather plain, the metaphors few and not often unusual. The words and images are carefully chosen, however, with an eye to precision and euphony. The tone is tender and affectionate toward friends and loved ones, sarcastic toward those who, like fools, deserve it. There are few high flights, but neither are Jonsonian lapses likely to be very gross. Speech, Jonson wrote, in *Timber: Or, Discoveries* (1641) is "the instrument of society." Furthermore, "words are the people's." The poet is someone who uses the people's resources for the people's good.

Baroque Poetry

Probably because it arose as a reaction against a Renaissance classicism that had no parallel in England before Ben Jonson, the movement called the "baroque," beginning around 1580 and continuing for the better part of a century, had few manifestations in English poetry. Originally applied to architecture and later to sculpture and painting, the term came to designate in particular the style of certain sixteenth century Venetian painters, particularly Jacopo Robusti Tintoretto, and of those, such as El Greco, who were influenced by the Venetian school. The baroque disdained formal beauty and placidity in favor of asymmetrical composition, rich color, energy, and even contortion.

Applied to prose style, *baroque* signifies the revolt against full and rounded Ciceronian elegance, a tendency to place the main sentence element first, the avoidance of symmetry by varying the form and length of constructions, and a greater autonomy for subordinate constructions, which tend to follow the main sentence element. English had developed a Ciceronian prose style, but a recognizably anti-Ciceronian prose arose in the seventeenth century, notably in such works as Robert Burton's *The Anatomy of Melancholy* (1621) and Sir Thomas Browne's *Religio Medici* (1642).

In poetry the baroque has some affinities with the Metaphysical, but the differences are suggested by the adjectives used to describe the baroque: "ornate," "sensuous," "pictorial," and "emotional." The baroque is more likely to reject logic and reason, which are useful to Metaphysical poets of an argumentative bent. In his *European Metaphysical Poetry* Frank J. Warnke distinguishes between a baroque inclination to use contrast and antithesis for the purpose of separating opposites and a Metaphysical preference for paradox and synthesis to produce a fusion of opposites. The baroque was cultivated chiefly—not exclusively—by Roman Catholics as an expression of the Counter Reformation spirit; it stands in contrast to the austerity of much northern European Protestant art.

The only English poets commonly associated with the baroque are Giles

Fletcher (1585-1623) and Richard Crashaw (1612-1649). Although Crashaw left more than four hundred poems, he is best known for his St. Teresa poems, especially his florid "Upon the book and picture of the seraphical Saint Teresa" called "The Flaming Heart." The poem blazes to a finish in a series of oaths that illustrate the baroque manner:

> By thy large draughts of intellectual day,
> And by thy thirsts of love more large than they;
> By all thy brim-filled bowls of fierce desire
> By thy last morning's draught of liquid fire. . . .

By these and other oaths he asked to be emptied of self and enabled to imitate her example. It is no surprise to learn that Crashaw lived for some years on the Continent, that he renounced his Anglican priesthood to become a Roman Catholic, and that he died in Italy. Fletcher, on the other hand, stands as a caution against too facile generalizations. He remained English and Anglican, and although his poetry reminds some readers of the baroque pioneer Guillaume du Bartas, he usually causes readers of Spenser to think of *The Faerie Queene*. The case of Giles Fletcher underlines the fact that English writers of the earlier seventeenth century felt no compulsion to wage war with the Renaissance, since its greatest nondramatic poet, far from being a doctrinaire classicist, synthesized elements classical, medieval, and Renaissance.

The baroque style in poetry, as in the visual arts, contained more than the usual number of the seeds of decadence. Baroque poets were liable to grotesqueness, obscurity, melodrama, and triviality. Its excesses no doubt helped pave the way for the later neoclassical resurgence. Again by analogy with architecture, some literary historians have seen the baroque also leading to the rococo, understood as a fussy, overdecorative, playful style which nevertheless might serve a serious purpose for a neoclassicist engaged in playful satire. The most obvious example in English literature, Alexander Pope's *The Rape of the Lock* (1712), comes early in the eighteenth century.

Mid-Century Transition

To argue for too neat a mid-century transition between the earlier classical, Metaphysical, and baroque styles, on the one hand, and the Neoclassical Age on the other, is perhaps to betray an obsession with the neoclassical virtue of symmetry, but in a number of ways the mid-century marks a turning point. England's only interregnum straddles the century's midpoint, while on the Continent the Thirty Years' War came to an end with the treaties of the Peace of Westphalia in 1648. Both of these political events involved poetry and poets, the English Civil War more strikingly. The continental wars, insofar as they involved Protestant-Catholic clashes, represented nothing new, but they exhibited several modern features. Because they involved most European states in one way or another and required a general congress of nations to achieve even temporary peace, these conflicts augured the modern situation, in which local conflicts can trigger unforeseen large-scale involvement. Armorers preparing soldiers for battle had to devise protection against traditional weapons such as the sword and also new ones such as the pistol; the latter were often used as a kind of last resort, as clubs, or thrown at enemies more often than they were fired. All over Europe men were getting a preview of the mass destruction they could expect in future wars. The necessity of compromise and toleration—never before recognized as virtues—was beginning to dawn. More and more it seemed essential that reason and judgment, not passion and force, reign.

England had embarked on its internal war in 1642. The Puritans, who had already succeeded in closing London's theaters, alarmed conservative Englishmen by closing down the monarchy itself. The execution of Charles I and the proclamation of the Commonwealth in 1649 culminated nearly a decade of violence that had driven Sir John Denham, Sir William Davenant, and Thomas Hobbes, among others, into exile, and the Cavalier poet Richard Lovelace into prison, where he penned several immortal poems. The political transition ended in 1660. Young John Dryden wrote *Astrea Redux* (1660), an elaborate poetic tribute to a great event: the return of Charles II, son of the executed king, in glory. The adjustments made by all the former belligerents signal a new era. The next revolution, in 1688, despite ingredients seemingly as volatile as those which had precipitated the mid-century war, was unbloody.

Earl Miner (*The Metaphysical Mode from Donne to Cowley*) has referred to the decade between 1645 and 1655 as a "microcosm" of the century as a whole. Certainly it was a productive time for poets. In only the first half of that decade appeared Waller's *Poems* (1645), Sir John Suckling's *Fragmenta Aurea* (1646), Crashaw's *Steps to the Temple* (1646), Herrick's *Hesperides* (1648), Lovelace's *Lucasta* (1649), and Vaughan's *Silex Scintillans* (1650, 1655), all studded with still familiar anthology favorites. Although Marvell's posthumous poems are difficult to date, at least some of his best are presumed to have been written in the early 1650's, as were a number of the finest of Milton's sonnets, while *Paradise Lost* (1667) was evolving in Milton's imagination. Miner's point, however, is that the poets at work at this time are difficult to classify as "Cavalier" or "Puritan" or "Metaphysical" or "neoclassical." The distinctive earlier voices—those of Donne and Jonson and Herbert—had been stilled, and the most distinctive later one had not yet developed. The teenage Dryden's notorious foray into Metaphysical imagery in his 1649 poem "Upon the Death of the Lord Hastings," where Hastings' smallpox blisters are compared to "rosebuds stuck in the lily-skin about," and where "Each little pimple had a tear in it/ To wail the fault its rising did commit," presages the great neoclassicist only in its use of rhymed pentameter couplets—and those are not yet particularly "heroic."

That particular form, the end-stopped couplet with its potential for balance, antithesis, and memorable precision, was being hammered out in the 1640's by such poets as Edmund Waller, Sir John Denham, and John Cleveland (otherwise remembered chiefly as a decadent Metaphysical) in a series of spirited anti-Puritan satires. The latter's 1642 poem, "Cooper's Hill," now faded, looks forward to the Augustan Age with its blend of Horatian and Vergilian sentiments, its lofty abstractions, and its skillful handling of rhythm. The pentameter couplet was as old as Geoffrey Chaucer, but as a distinct unit, sometimes virtually a stanza in itself, it was capable of generating quite different effects. Detachable, quotable, suited for uttering the common wisdom, the great truths apparent to all, it embodied the neoclassical concept of wit, which was variously defined from this period on, but most memorably (because so well-expressed in a couplet, of course) by Pope in 1711: "True wit is nature to advantage dressed,/ What oft was thought, but ne'er so well expressed."

At the very middle of the century appeared a work by a man whose profession was neither poet nor critic but whose terse genealogy of a poem marks off the distance between the ages of Donne and Dryden. Thomas Hobbes was responding to remarks on epic made by Sir William Davenant in the Preface to his fragmentary heroic poem *Gondibert* (1651) when he wrote: "Time and education beget experience; experience begets memory; memory begets judgment and fancy; judgment begets the strength and structure, and fancy begets the ornaments of a poem." It is impossible to imagine Donne countenancing the splitting asunder of "structure" and "ornaments," or for that matter acknowledging "ornaments" at all—for where were they in his poetry?

The following year, 1651, saw the publication of Hobbes's *magnum opus*, the *Leviathan*. There he made explicit what his answer to Davenant had implied: "In a good poem . . . both judgment and fancy are required: but the fancy must be more eminent." In other words, "ornament" is more important than "structure." To be sure, Hobbes was only stating succinctly a view that had already surfaced in Francis Bacon's philosophy: poetry is make-believe ("feigned history," as Bacon put it in *The Advancement of Learning* back in 1605) and has nothing to do with truth. This reproach becomes more damning when seen in the context of the linguistic theories set forth elsewhere by Hobbes and by the Royal Society of London in the following decade.

Another work of the mid-century marks a beginning rather than a transition. In 1650 there was published in London a book with the title of *The Tenth Muse Lately Sprung Up in America*. Supposedly the manuscript had been spirited across the Atlantic without its author's consent. It was the first book of poems by an American woman. Discounting the doggerel of such works of piety as *The Bay Psalm Book* (1640), it was in fact the first book of poems by any American. Over two hundred years would pass before another woman poet would do as well as the woman who had emigrated to Massachusetts as a teenage bride twenty years earlier, Anne Bradstreet.

Poetry and the Scientific Revolution

Of the nonliterary forces on seventeeth century poets, the New Science may well have been the most uniformly pervasive throughout the Western world. Whereas social, political, and even religious developments varied considerably in nature and scope, the scientists were busy discovering laws that applied everywhere and affected the prevailing world view impartially. Some artists and thinkers discovered the New Science and pondered its implications before others, but no poet could fall very many decades behind the vanguard and continue to be taken seriously. The modern reader of, say, C. S. Lewis' *The Discarded Image* (1964) and E. M. W. Tillyard's *The Elizabethan World Picture* (1943) observes that the Elizabethan "picture" had not changed substantially from the medieval "image" described by Lewis. Between 1600 and 1700, however, the world view of educated people changed more dramatically than in any previous century. Early in the century John Donne signaled his awareness of science's challenge to the old certitudes about the world. By Dryden's maturity the new learning had rendered the Elizabethan brand of erudition disreputable and its literary imagination largely incomprehensible.

In *The Breaking of the Circle* (1960) Marjorie Hope Nicolson uses a popular medieval symbol, the circle of perfection, to demonstrate the effect of the New Science on the poets' perception of their world. The universe was a circle; so was the earth and man's head. The circle was God's perfect form, unending like Himself, and all its manifestations shared in the perfection. It was easy—one might almost say "natural"—for Donne to begin one of his sonnets: "I am a little world made cunningly." Significantly, Donne did not say that he was *like* a little world. Not only did he use a metaphor instead of a simile, but also he used the metaphor confident that he was expressing a *truth*. In another sonnet Shakespeare refers to his soul as "the center of my sinful earth." Two thousand years earlier Aristotle had said that "to make metaphors well is to perceive likeness," and this judgment still stood firm. Already, however, a succession of thinkers from Copernicus in 1543 to Sir Isaac Newton in 1687 were at work breaking up the circle of perfection.

A special irony attaches to the contribution of Copernicus, a pious Roman Catholic who took the concept of the circle of perfection for granted when he set forth his heliocentric theory of the solar system. His insight was to see the sun, not the earth, as the center of God's operations in the visible world. To him it was perfectly obvious that God would impart perfect circular motion to the planets. Unfortunately his new model provided even less accurate predictability of planetary motions than the old geocentric theory that it was intended to replace. Thus he had to invent an ingenious system of subordinate circles—"eccentrics" and "epicycles"—to account for the discrepancies between the simple version of his model and his observations of what actually went on in the heavens. Thus, although his heliocentric theory incurred condemnation by Protestant and Catholic alike, his cumbersome model did not attract many adherents, and for decades intelligent men remained ignorant of his theory and its implications.

Two contemporaries of Donne changed all that. In 1609 Galileo built a telescope; by the next year he was systematically examining not just our solar system but other suns beyond it. Johann Kepler discovered, virtually at the same time, the elliptical orbit of Mars. He did this by breaking the old habit—his own as well as mankind's—of regarding physical events as symbols of divine mysteries, and thereby swept Copernicus' eccentrics and epicycles into a rubbish heap. When Donne wrote his "First Anniversary" poem, *An Anatomy of the World*, in 1611, he showed his familiarity with the new astronomy:

> And new philosophy calls all in doubt,
> The element of fire is quite put out;
> The sun is lost, and the earth, and no man's wit
> Can well direct him where to look for it.

Even before the confirmation of Copernicus' theory, the greatest literary geniuses of his century raised in their masterpieces versions of the great question provoked by the new science. Michel de Montaigne put it most simply in his *Essais* (1580, *Essays*): "What do I know?" The word *essays* signifies "attempts," and the work can be described as a series of attempts to answer his question. Miguel de Cervantes, setting out with the rather routine literary motive of satirizing a particularly silly type of chivalric romance, stumbled on his theme: the difficulty of distinguishing appearance from reality—even for those who, unlike Don Quixote, are not mad. The second part of Cervantes' novel, written like the first out of an understandable but pedestrian literary ambition (to reclaim his hero from the clutches of a plagiarist) raises the disturbing possibility that the madman interprets at least some aspects of reality more sensibly that the "sane" people among whom the idealistic Don Quixote was floundering. Shakespeare, having already endorsed the ancient concept of the poet as a divinely inspired madman in *A Midsummer Night's Dream* (1595-1596), created, at the very beginning of the new century, a "mad" hero who raises an even more profound question: Can knowledge of the truth, even if attainable (and Hamlet gains the knowledge of the truth that concerns him most—the circumstances of his father's death—through ghostly intervention), lead to madness and paralysis of the will?

Unlike J. Alfred Prufrock, who asks, "Do I dare disturb the universe?," medieval man did not disturb, and was not disturbed by, the universe. Even the presumed decay of the world from its original golden age did not alarm him, for it was all part of the plan of a wise and loving Creator. In *An Anatomy of the World*, the decay of the world has become profoundly disturbing, for the very cosmic order itself seems to be coming apart: "'Tis all in pieces, all coherence gone." Shortly before writing this poem—and perhaps afterwards—Donne was able to write poetry of the sort quoted earlier, in which he moves easily from macrocosm to microcosm; but he also recognized that the "new philosophy calls all in doubt."

Astronomical discoveries were not the only form of knowledge. In 1600 William Gilbert wrote a book on magnetism. He was, like Copernicus, a good sixteenth century man and could talk about lodestones as possessing souls; his important discovery, however, was that the earth *is* a lodestone. In 1628, when William Harvey published his findings on the circulation of the blood, he referred to the heart as the body's "sovereign" and "inmost home," but in the process he taught the world to regard it as a mechanism—a pump. The old world view was being destroyed quite unintentionally by men whose traditional assumptions often hampered their progress, but whose achievement made it impossible for their own grandchildren to make the same assumptions or to take the old learning seriously. As a result of Robert Boyle's work, chemistry was banishing alchemy, a subject taken seriously not only by poets but also by the scientists of an earlier day. At century's end, to talk of a person as a "little world" was mere quaintness, for Harvey had taught everyone to regard the body as one sort of mechanism, while the astronomers insisted that the solar system was another. It was merely idle to make connections between them.

As the scientists focused more clearly on their subjects, the poets' vision became more blurred. Astronomy is only one such subject area, but it is a particularly useful one for the purpose of demonstrating the change. Around 1582 Sir Philip Sidney's Astrophel could exclaim: "With how sad steps, O moon, thou climb'st the skies,/ How silently, and with how wan a face." Astrophel is a disappointed lover, of course, and need not be taken too seriously. What strikes the reader is the ease with which his creator sees parallels between the moon and the earthbound lover. In a more serious context George Herbert addresses a star: "Bright spark, shot from a brighter place/ Where beams surround my Savior's face." Herbert almost surely knew what Galileo had been doing, but his "brighter place" still lay, as it were, beyond the reach of the telescope. In 1650 Henry Vaughan could begin a poem: "I saw Eternity the other night/ Like a great Ring of pure and endless light,/ All calm, as it was bright." The reader's first inclination is perhaps to marvel at the facility of the utterance, but is the tone as matter-of-fact as it seems? Might not Donne and Herbert have seen eternity every night? On second thought one wonders whether the moments of insight are getting rarer. Five years later Vaughan published "They are all gone into the world of light," a poem reflecting an awareness of the transience of the heavenly vision:

And yet, as Angels in some brighter dreams

> Call the soul, when man doth sleep:
> So some strange thoughts transcend our wonted themes,
> And into glory peep.

At the end of the poem the speaker begs God to "disperse these mists." Any reader can verify that in later Metaphysical poetry the view of heaven gets cloudier. Thomas Traherne, almost surely writing in the Restoration, sees heaven not through the earthly eye but mystically with a sight often blurred by dream, shadows, and mists. In "My Spirit," for example, his soul "saw infinity/ 'Twas not a sphere, but 'twas a power/ Invisible." In *Religio Laici* Dryden can see none of this and counsels submission to the Church. By 1733 Pope has banished all thought of reading heavenly meanings in the heavens: "The proper study of Mankind is Man"—unless, of course, one happens to be an astronomer.

Neoclassicism from 1660 to 1700

By the Restoration the poets had turned their attention primarily to public and social themes. The comedy of this period has given readers the impression of a licentious age determined to bury the memory of Puritanistic domination and live as fast and loose an existence as possible. Such behavior could not have characterized more than a tiny percentage of the people of later Stuart England. It was an age struggling for order through compromise. Wit might entertain, but life required sober judgment.

The classical tradition survived the New Science better than did the Metaphysical. It did not aspire to compete with science in the realm beyond everyday human and social experience. The Jonsonian tradition of short lyric and reflective poems no longer flourished, but the neoclassicists of the Restoration rediscovered satire and the heroic poem—the latter primarily in the remarkable triad of Miltonic poems published between 1667 and 1671: *Paradise Lost*, *Paradise Regained*, and *Samson Agonistes*. Horace was not neglected, but the study and translation of the Homeric and Vergilian epics gained in popularity. The time might have been ripe for a great patriotic epic (Milton considered a true Arthurian epic that would rectify the deficiencies of Spenser's episodic one before he finally settled on the yet nobler idea of justifying God's way to men), but whether because Milton's accomplishment had preempted the field or because history as Restoration poets knew it could not be hammered into the Vergilian mold, it was not written. Instead, Dryden produced something new: a political satire in a heroic style based on a contemporary controversy over the attempt to exclude Charles II's Roman Catholic brother James from the royal succession. It was a serious matter, laden with danger for the principal in the struggle, for Dryden, and for the nation. He did not use blank verse, as Shakespeare and Milton had in their greatest works, but the heroic couplet, a form which Dryden had been honing for twenty years.

The result is a poem of peculiar urgency, yet by virtue of Dryden's skillful representation of Charles II as the biblical King David and of the Earl of Shaftesbury as "false Achitophel," who attempts to turn Absalom (Charles's illegitimate son, the Duke of Monmouth) against his father, the poem takes on universality. It is by far the most impressive poem of the period: *Absalom and Achitophel* (1681).

The drama aside, satire is the greatest literary achievement of the Restoration, and it is also the most diverse. From Samuel Butler's low burlesque of the Puritans in *Hudibras* (1663) to Dryden's sustained high style in *Absalom and Achitophel*, from a butt as small as one undistinguished playwright (Thomas Shadwell in Dryden's 1682 mock-epic *MacFlecknoe*) to one as large as mankind, vain aspirer to the status of rational being (the Earl of Rochester's "A Satire Against Mankind," printed in 1675), verse satire flourished, providing models for even greater achievements in the first part of the following century. The Renaissance notion of decorum as the delicate adjustment of literary means to ends, of the suitability of the parts to the whole, governed these diverse attempts at diminishing the wickedness and folly that Restoration poets considered it their duty to expose and correct. Even *Hudibras*, with its slam-bang tetrameter couplets and quirky rhymes, seems the perfect vehicle for flaying the routed Puritans, and its levels of irony are far more complex than superficial readers suspect. When satire began to invade prose, as it increasingly did in the eighteenth century, its narrative possibilities increased, but it lost subtle effects of rhythm, timing, and rhyme.

Compared with the first sixty years of the century, the Restoration seems a prosaic age. A considerable number of its most accomplished writers—John Bunyan, the diarists Samuel Pepys and John Evelyn, Sir William Temple, John Locke—wrote no poetry worth preserving, and Dryden himself wrote a large proportion of prose. Does the preponderance of prose and satire confirm T. S. Eliot's early charge that a "dissociation of sensibility" had set in by the time of the Restoration? Is it true that writers no longer could fuse thought and feeling, with the consequence that prose was used for conveying truth and poetry for the setting forth of delightful lies?

Hobbes, who had little use for poetry in general, praised the epic as conducive to moral truth, and he admitted that satire can be defended on moral grounds also. The Restoration poets in England were the successors of a classical tradition that emphasized the ethical value of poetry, so they might as plausibly be considered carrying out, on a somewhat larger scale, the dictates of Jonson as those of Hobbes. The Royal Society of London, of which Dryden was a member, was founded in 1662 for "the improving of natural knowledge," and among its ambitions it numbered the improving of the language by waging war against "tropes" and "figures" and "metaphors." One cannot imagine Donne having anything to do with such an organization, all the more because the Society on principle did not discuss "such subjects as God and the soul." It is difficult to see how Dryden's association with it substantiates the charge of dissociated sensibility, however, for there is certainly both thought and feeling together in *Absalom and Achitophel*, even if it is, like the Royal Society itself, earthbound and relatively unmetaphorical, and, while it is no doubt instructive, generations of readers have taken delight in it also.

One is tempted to offer a different explanation for Restoration writers' greater attachment to prose and to satire. The reading audience expanded greatly in the seventeenth century, and increasingly it became the business of the writer to satisfy its interests, which for a variety of reasons were political and social. The early Metaphysical writers possessed a very small audience (one another and a few more who shared the same interests); very much the same situation obtained for Jonson and his followers. When the readership increased, poets modified their work accordingly. When Dryden did write of religion, he wrote of it as he and his contemporaries understood it. That Dryden took little delight in Donne's poetry is clear from his remarks in "A Discourse Concerning the Original and Progress of Satire" (1693): "Donne affects the metaphysics, not only in his amorous verses, where nature only should reign; and perplexes the minds of the fair sex with nice speculations of philosophy, when he should engage their hearts and entertain them with the softnesses of love." Dryden did not understand Donne's intentions very well, but he understood his own political intentions very well indeed.

In his own and the century's final years Dryden worked primarily at translation, promising in his Preface to *Fables Ancient and Modern* (1700) a translation of the whole *Iliad* (c. 800 B.C.), "if it should please God to give me longer life and moderate health." He added another provision: "that I meet with those encouragements from the public, which may enable me to proceed in my undertaking with some cheerfulness." This is the remark of a public figure—a former poet laureate, author of a stream of plays and published books since the 1600's, a veteran attraction at Will's Coffee House in London.

Poets had not always expected such encouragements. When Donne died in 1631, only four of his poems had been published. Herbert, Marvell, and Traherne saw few or none of their poems in print. Jonson, on the other hand, had offered his work to the public, even inviting ridicule in 1616 by boldly calling his volume *Works*. Like Dryden after him, he had developed a healthy sense of audience in his career as a playwright. He had even more reason to fear an unhappy audience than Dryden, for along with John Marston and George Chapman he had been imprisoned and very nearly mutilated by a gang of Scots retainers of James I whom the trio had outraged by some of their jests in their play *Eastward, Ho!* (1605). Nevertheless, Jonson promised a translation of Horace's *The Art of Poetry*, with no provisions whatsoever, that same year. The fact that he did not deliver the translation until long afterward does not seem to have had anything to do with readers' wishes. Jonson usually conveyed the impression that whatever he had to say amounted to nothing less than a golden opportunity for any sensible reader or listener.

Even if one assumes that Dryden's hope for encouragement may have been only an expression of politeness, that politeness itself signifies a change of relationship with the "public." Most of the poetry written in the time of Donne and Jonson has the quality of being overheard. It is as if the poet is praying, making love, or rebuking a fool, and the reader has just happened to pass by. If the poem is a verse epistle, the reader experiences the uncomfortable feeling that he is reading someone else's mail—and quite often that is so. By 1700 the poet seems conscious of producing a document for public inspection and proceeds accordingly, with all the implications—fortunate and unfortunate—of such a procedure. He will not tax the public with too many difficulties, for some of them—too many, perhaps—will not understand. He had better polish his work, and he had better not be dull. He might produce one of those "overheard" lyrics once in a while, but the chances are that they will yield few excellences not imitative of earlier poets whose circumstances favored that type of poem.

The neoclassical sense of audience would continue, as the neoclassical period would continue, for nearly another century—at least in those poets with access to a public. The poet's public stance would give rise to more fine satire and reflective poems of great majesty and sustained moral power. The knack of lyric would be largely lost, and, when recovered, the lyrics would be romantic. No one would ever write poems like "A Valediction: Forbidding Mourning" or "To His Coy Mistress" again, but poets would offer, in compensation, poems such as *The Dunciad* (1728-1743) and *The Vanity of Human Wishes* (1749).

Robert P. Ellis

THE EIGHTEENTH CENTURY

The eighteenth century in Britain saw the blossoming of seventeenth century poetic modes and the sprouting of modes which would blossom into Romanticism. It was an age of reason and sentiment, of political turbulence, of growing colonialism and wealth, of beautiful landscapes and parks, of gin-addiction and Evangelicalism, of a burgeoning middle class and growing respect for middle-class values, of increasing literacy and decreasing dependence on patronage, and of cantankerous Tories and complacent Whigs. As England became the center of world commerce and power, so, too, it became the center of literary achievement.

John Dryden died in 1700, but his death signaled no dramatic change in poetic style. Poets walked in his footsteps, moving away from Metaphysical conceits—from the style of those poets who glittered "Like twinkling Stars the Miscellanies o'er"—to search for smoothness and a new style of thinking. Symptomatic of the eighteenth century's passion for order and regularization was Alexander Pope's tinkering with the poetry of John Donne: he made Donne's numbers flow melodiously and corrected his versification. Heroic couplets and lampoons and political satires such as Dryden's were written throughout the century. Common Restoration subjects such as the imperious mistress and the cacophony of critics continued to be used.

Dryden named William Congreve his poetical successor, but Pope was his true heir. From the appearance of his *Pastorals* in 1709 until William Wordsworth's *Lyrical Ballads* in 1798, Pope dominated poetry. His influence, for example, pervades Robert Dodsley's *Collection of Poems, by Several Hands* (1748), in William Mason's *Museaus* (1747), in the half dozen other poems concerned chiefly with Pope, and in the many others which refer respectfully to him. If the poets of the latter part of the century did not imitate him, they at least grudgingly admired him while reacting against him.

The "ancients"—Homer and Vergil in particular, but Horace, Pindar, Juvenal, Martial, and Anacreon, too—were devoutly followed. As schoolboys, the poets did countless exercises translating Latin and Greek verse, and, like John Milton before them, poets such as Joseph Addison and Samuel Johnson began by writing Latin verse. In the middle of his career, Pope translated the *Iliad* in 1715-1718 and the *Odyssey* in 1725-1726; he spent his later career writing imitations of Horace. Johnson chose to write imitations of the other great Roman satirist, Juvenal. These imitations were not strict translations; rather, they picked up hints from the classics and made the subject relevant to contemporary life. Even at the end of the century, William Cowper translated Homer (1791), though his style was too heavily Miltonic.

William Shakespeare and other Elizabethans provided a third important example for eighteenth century poets. Both Pope and Johnson edited Shakespeare: Pope's edition was valuable chiefly for restoring "prose" passages to the original blank verse, Johnson's for his criticism founded upon common sense. Joseph and Thomas Warton and other mid-century poets appealed to the example of Shakespeare to free themselves from the classical doctrine of the superiority of judgment and taste to the imagination. Shakespeare helped inspire William Collins' *Ode on the Popular Superstitions of the Highlands of Scotland, Considered as the Subject of Poetry* (1788), and even William Blake was drawn to Elizabethan poetry. For the eighteenth century, Shakespeare represented unlearned genius, and his quality of irregularity, of "great beauties and blemishes" was highly praised.

Although less influential than Shakespeare, Edmund Spenser had his followers. James Thomson's *The Castle of Indolence* (1748) imitated Spenserian melody and descriptive techniques and William Shenstone parodied Spenser in *The Schoolmistress* (1742). James Beattie's *The Minstrel* (1771-1774) was one of the longest and best poems of the century written in Spenserian stanza. Another poet who owed much to Spenser was the tragic Thomas Chatterton. Like Spenser, Chatterton wrote vigorous lyrics and showed much metrical originality.

When eighteenth century poets sat down to write a poem, they did not pour forth images of their souls; they attempted certain genres and looked to the ancients for inspiration and example. Their voices and emotions were public rather than private, and they wrote about the present rather than about their own pasts. The poet was the spokesman for his age and his subject was man as a social creature. The personal did, however, creep into eighteenth century verse: Matthew Prior's best work was personal, if not autobiographical, and Pope used the epistle form to speak personally.

Eighteenth century poets valued elegant ease and noble urbanity. "Decorum" was a key word: the eighteenth century classicists sought to control the abundant energy which characterized earlier English classicists. Augustan poets tried to achieve the effect of apparent casualness of structure with definite coherence under the surface. Their use of noble Roman tone and classical patterns familiar throughout Europe gave them a Continental audience, something the Elizabethans never had.

The most popular genres were epic, ode, satire, elegy, epistle, and song. To show their fealty to Homer and Vergil, nearly every eighteenth century poet at least thought of writing an epic. Pope, for one, was planning an epic on Brutus when he died. None of the plans for writing epics or the epics that were written brought forth anything but sour fruit (Aaron Hill's biblical epic *Gideon*, 1749, is a prime example); however, the mock-epic form in this possibly nonheroic age brought forth delicious fruit, including Pope's *The Rape of the Lock* (1712) and his undelectable but brilliant *The Dunciad* (1728-1743).

Eighteenth century poets had more success writing odes than they did writing epics. In the early years of the century, poets looked to Pindar or to

Horace as models for writing odes. They used Pindaric odes for exalted subjects and Horatian odes for various urbane, personal, and meditative themes. In the seventeenth century Abraham Cowley had popularized irregularities in the Pindaric odes; after Congreve denounced them in his *A Pindarique Ode on the Victorious Progress of Her Majesties Arms* (1706), most poets knew the duty of Pindaric regularity but still preferred the laxness of Cowley's form. Thomas Gray was an important exception: he wrote two Pindaric odes—"The Bard" and "The Progress of Poesy"—in rigidly correct form.

In the second quarter of the century, a new type of ode appeared, inspired by John Milton's "L'Allegro" and "Il Penseroso." The "descriptive and allegorical ode" centered around a personified abstraction, such as pity or simplicity, and treated it in a descriptive or pictorial way. Collins and the Warton brothers did much to popularize this mode in the 1740's.

The eighteenth century was, of course, the golden age of satire. Satirists such as Jonathan Swift and Pope attacked the frivolity of polite society, the corruption of politics, and false values in all the arts. The aim of satire, as Pope explained it, was not wanton destruction: satire "heals with Morals what it hurts with Wit." Satirists, he claimed, nourished the state, promoting its virtue and providing it everlasting fame.

Eighteenth century poetry has been accused of monotony and weak feeling. The zeal of the satirists for truth and virtue, however, blazes through many lines, and the warmth of their compassion for the poor, the sick, the mistreated, and the aged glows through many others. Pope, in the *Moral Essay* (1731-1735), for example, pities the ancient belles of court: "See how the World its Veterans rewards!/ A Youth of Frolicks, an old Age of Cards." The age, particularly the state under the administration of Sir Robert Walpole, may not have been as black as the satirists painted it—it was an age of increasing wealth and progress—but the satirists were obsessed by the precariousness of intellect and of civilization, by the threat of fools and bores and pedants, by the fear of universal darkness burying all. In a world where man's intellect alone keeps society from the disintegration caused by unthinking enthusiasts and passionate pigheads, dullness is morally objectionable—an aspect of vice. Satirists thus became moral crusaders for truth, virtue, and intelligence. They believed in an ancient state of purity which man could not re-create; man could, however, "relume the ancient light" (in Pope's words) for the future.

Elegies in Latin and Greek were composed in elegiac couplets rather than the hexameter lines of the epic and the pastoral. Donne wrote amatory elegies in the seventeenth century, but by the eighteenth century elegies were meditative pieces, often about death. Gray's *Elegy Written in a Country Churchyard* (1751), said by some to be the best poem of the eighteenth century, is an elegy for all "average" and obscure men. It achieves the ideals of its day in its attempt to work in universal terms and in its purity and harmony of diction; it approaches Romanticism in its placid melancholy and rustic setting. In *Elegy to the Memory of an Unfortuante Lady* (1717), the other important elegy of the eighteenth century and one of the only works of Pope which the Romantics could tolerate, Pope laments the mortality of a young suicide victim and his own mortality, stressing the threats to human feeling and the glory of its intensity.

The epistle, or verse letter, an important form in the seventeenth century, reached its height in the epistles of Pope in the 1740's, and continued to be popular until the end of the nineteenth century. Horace provided the classical model for the verse epistle. The familiar form of the epistle allowed poets to seem to speak sincerely and intimately to a close friend while addressing the public about general issues. Almost all epistles were written in heroic couplets, began in a rather rambling way, and finally came to a point about halfway through the poem. Charles Churchill's *Epistle to William Hogarth* (1763), for example, begins with a miscellaneous discussion of satire. The effect of this structure is comic and optimistic: order is brought out of disorder.

Lyric poets used the song to achieve brevity and, at times, elegance. Songs were collected and written throughout the period, but the greatest of the songwriters—Robert Burns—came at the end. He not only composed his own songs but also reconstituted and envigorated old Scottish songs, turning a drinking song into "Auld Lang Syne" and a disreputable ballad into "John Anderson my Jo."

Other popular genres included the epigram, the fable, and verse criticism. The tradition of the epigram, modeled on Martial and on Horace, began in the Renaissance and appealed to the eighteenth century because of its conciseness and the opportunity it provided to display wit. The average epigram was at most six lines long, beginning with something to arouse curiosity or anticipation and closing with humor or surprise. Common topics included love and the characters of people, though some epigrams were obscene. A specialized form of the epigram was the epitaph, which several poets composed for themselves. John Gay's epitaph reads: "Life is a jest, and all things show it/ I thought so once; but now I know it," and Swift's Latin epitaph, roughly translated, says that he is now gone where bitter indignation no longer lacerates his heart.

The fables of the eighteenth century demonstrate the ability of Augustan writers to enrich and vary a genre. The favorite form for the fables was the iambic tetrameter couplet. Gay wrote the best English fables (1727-1738), though Swift, Bernard Mandeville, Prior, Christopher Smart, Cowper, Beattie, and Johnson also wrote them. Far from being childlike, Gay's *Fables* (1727) expressed a disillusioned cynicism toward mankind, particularly emphasizing man's foolish pride. No English fable, however, could measure up to those written in France by Jean de La Fontaine in the seventeenth century.

The critical poem was popular in the Restoration and came into full bloom in the eighteenth century. Following the pattern set by Horace in his *Ars Poetica* (13-8 B.C., *The Art of Poetry*), the Italian poet Girolamo Vida wrote *De Arte Poetica* in 1527 and the French poet Nicholas Boileau wrote *L'Arte poetique* in 1674. In England, John Sheffield's *Essay on Poetry* (1682), Wentworth Dillon, Earl of Roscommon's *Essay on Translated Verse* (1684), and Lord Lansdowne's *Essay upon Unnatural Flights in Poetry* (1701) bore testimony to the increased interest in literary criticism and theory. Pope's *Essay on Criticism* (1711), the zenith of this genre, condensed eighteenth century poetic standards. *Essay on Criticism* is actually a poem on how to judge a poem and on what morals are requisite for a critic. The first requirement is to follow nature, then to follow the ancients who "discov'red" and "Methodiz'd" the rules of nature. The "laws of Nature" to the Augustans meant, roughly, the right principles which every man of common sense and goodwill would follow in his thought and conduct. The French called nature "*la belle nature*," and Pope maintained that it is "the source, and end, and test of Art." The faith that man has in a world of universal human values underlies the concept of nature.

From the *Essay on Criticism* comes such neoclassic advice as: "The Sound must seem an Eccho to the Sense," "Avoid Extreams" (the Augustan ideal of the golden mean), "In all you speak, let Truth and Candor shine," and "Men must be taught as if you taught them not." The poem's merit lies in its compressed phrasing of current standards, not in any originality of thought. Early eighteenth century poets or their audiences were not as much impressed by originality as by memorable expression: Pope said that true wit is "What oft was *Thought*, but ne'er so well *Exprest*," and Joseph Addison in *Spectator 253* wrote that "wit and fine writing doth not consist so much in advancing things that are new, as in giving things that are known agreeable turn."

Eighteenth century poets generally came from good families in much reduced circumstances. Prior, Swift, and Johnson fit this generalization, though Pope was the son of a wealthy linen draper. Poets still sought patrons, praising their parks and estates, but more and more their writings at least partially supported them. Prior, for example, apparently netted four thousand guineas from his *Poems on Several Occasions* (1709). The audience for literature was growing, thanks in large measure to the graduates of charity schools and the newly founded grammar schools. Political preferment also proved lucrative for poets. Addison served as Undersecretary of State and later secretary to the Lord-Lieutenant of Ireland, and Robert Burns collected excise taxes. Samuel Johnson's letter to Lord Chesterfield on his tardy recognition of the *Dictionary of the English Language* (1755) is said to have given the final blow to patronage, though the letter was not printed until near the end of the century.

In the first half of the century, poets aligned themselves according to politics. Addison and Whigs such as Ambrose Philips reigned at Button's coffeehouse. The Tories—Swift, Gay, Thomas Parnell, Pope, and John Arbuthnot— formed the Scriblerus Club and met at Arbuthnot's apartments in St. James's Palace. Thomas Parnell and John Gay both worked closely with Pope and yet remained independent: Parnell published his Miltonic poems chiefly in miscellanies, and Gay became the king of burlesque. Barbs flew back and forth between the Whig and Tory parties, the deadliest of which was Pope's portrait of Addison in *Epistle to Dr. Arbuthnot* (1735).

Though there undoubtedly was venom in these attacks, there was also a good measure of humor written in the early decades of the century. Gay was a chief contributor with *Wine* (1708), a burlesque of Milton and John Philips' *Cyder* (1708) and *Trivia: Or, The Art of Walking the Streets of London* (1716). Swift, Lady Mary Wortley-Montagu, and others helped to popularize "town eclogues." The most delightfully imaginative and amusing of the exposés of society was Pope's mock-heroic *The Rape of the Lock*, with its sylphs and gnomes and diminution of Homeric epic. *The Rape of the Lock* is much more complicated than Dryden's *MacFlecknoe* (1682): Pope reveals the confusion of moral values in society in such catalogs as "Puffs, Powder, Patches, Bibles, Billet-doux." Pope simultaneously laughs at the foibles of society and warns of the fragility of beauty.

Most poets wrote in heroic couplets, a pair of rhyming pentameter lines. In Shakespeare's time, couplets closed sonnets or scenes in blank verse dramas; in the later seventeenth century couplets were adapted to correspond to the elegiac couplet of classical verse and to the heroic, unrhymed Greek and Latin hexameter. Pope was the master of the heroic couplet; he knew how to build two or three couplets, each technically closed, into a unified, easy period. Throughout the century, poets in England and America tried to equal his artistry. By the end of the century, poets such as Cowper still attempted heroic couplets, but with little success. Cowper could achieve the Horatian simplicity admired in the eighteenth century, but his verses lacked Horatian polish and piquancy.

Even in the early part of the century, however, poets such as Swift and Prior ignored heroic couplets in favor of tetrameter couplets. Prior criticized the heroic couplet, complaining that it "cuts off the Sense at the end of every first Line, which must always rhyme to the next following, and consequently produces too frequent an Identity in the Sound, and brings every Couplet to the Point of an Epigram." Short poems and irregular meters, on the whole, were not highly regarded.

The Civil War left deep scars which lasted well into the eighteenth century. Religious and political factions still strained the country, and the atmosphere was at once one of compromise and tolerance and one of skepticism. It was a time when writers questioned and strove to understand the nature of man, his limitations, and the limitations which must be set on his passions. Answers to these questions differed significantly: some optimistic moralists believed in the essential goodness of man, some satirists and cynics bemoaned man's incorrigible pride which would forever keep him from the truth, and some realists insisted that man and the world must be accepted as they are, in all their ugliness.

In *Characteristics of Men, Manners, Opinions, Times* (1711), the Earl of Shaftesbury promulgated a belief in the perfection of the universe and the naturalness of virtue in man. Opposing Thomas Hobbes's belief in the natural selfishness of man, Shaftesbury wrote that it is "impossible to conceive that a rational creature coming first to be tried by rational objects, and receiving into his mind the images or representations of justice, generosity, gratitude, or other virtue, should have no liking of these or dislike of their contraries. . . ." He asserted that unselfishness is as natural to man as selfishness and that man has "social instincts" and "social passions" as well as egotism. Although Shaftesbury had many detractors, including Bernard de Mandeville in his *Fable of the Bees* (1714), his beliefs gained wide acceptance in England, France, and Germany.

Pope's *Essay on Man* (1733-1734), another influential document on these ethical questions, reflects Pope's own attempts to balance optimism and a sense of fact. He describes the "great chain of being" and man's placement in this "isthmus of a middle state,/ A Being darkly wise, and rudely great." He tried to build his rational system of ethics without denying religion but by being independent of it. Thomson, who was influenced by Shaftesbury, anticipated Pope in declaring in *The Seasons* (1730) that that which seems evil is only seen in part because the whole is good, that order may be threatened yet will survive in a larger sense. He did not, however, attack the problems of evil and man's moral responsibility head-on.

A corollary to the question about man's nature was the problem of happiness. As the wealth of the citizenry increased, leisure time, sports, recreation, and the search for happiness became important. "Happiness" replaced "property" as one of the inalienable rights of man. In searching for happiness, man becomes disillusioned, and many a writer from Prior through Johnson to Oliver Goldsmith expressed the pessimism that neither knowledge, riches, pleasure, nor power can avail against the assault of time and human weakness. John Dyer voiced the feeling well in these lines from *Grongar Hill* (1726):

> A little Rule, a little Sway,
> A Sunbeam in a Winter's Day
> Is all the Proud and Mighty have,
> Between the Cradle and the Grave.

This pessimism led Prior to urge men to cherish fleeting joys as the only respite in the human world of suffering and led Edward Young in *Night*

Thoughts (1742-1745) to insist upon the latent divinity of man and his power to fly above worldly claims to the blessed realms of infinity. Gray, in his "Hymn to Adversity" (1742), which Johnson termed both "poetical and rational," cautioned against expecting more of life than life can give. Chastising men for chasing "treacherous phantoms" and deluding themselves with visions of "airy good," Johnson in *The Vanity of Human Wishes* (1749) urged men to study, exertion, and prayer. All these men evince the increasing concern and compassion of the century with the lot of man.

While Pope inherited satire and heroic couplets from Dryden, there was another poetic movement in the eighteenth century whose ancestors were Milton, reflective poetry, and blank verse. Poets increasingly used landscape as material for their poetry and wedded it to philosophical discourse. Thomson's *The Seasons* was both the crowning effort of this movement and a stimulus to its further development. Thomson patterned *Autumn* and *Winter* on the chronological progress of the season and *Summer* on the events of a typical day. The passages alternate between description and meditation, with description being the most innovative. Thomson excelled in the presentation of exuberant motion and tightly packed detail. Pope and Ambrose Philips had written lovely pastorals earlier in the century, and Gay incorporated much folklore and the sights and sounds of the country in his *Rural Sports* (1713) and *The Shepherd's Week* (1714); but Thomson's work differed sharply from the pastoral in its description of nature for its own sake, with human incidents as background rather than nature as background for human drama. *The Seasons* started a tradition of descriptive poetry which at its extreme became a love of what Shenstone called "odd picturesque description." The descriptive poem usurped the place of the epic as the most honored poetic form, and Thomson was invested as the preeminent English poet of nature until Wordsworth succeeded him.

Thomson has been accused of having an overly Latinate style with false ornamentation. His strength lies in his minute observation of nature, in his almost scientific curiosity. A professed deist, Thomson saw in nature a revelation of the attributes of God; other deists and even the more orthodox upheld him in this belief. The scientist in Thomson admired the orderliness of the mathematical universe. Like Pope, Thomson insisted on intelligence and reason; he believed that a study of nature frees men from superstition and ignorance. He, too, reflected on the wants and miseries of human life.

Encouraged by *The Seasons* and the *Essay on Man*, many poets began to write in a moralizing, didactic manner, including William Somerville (*The Chace*, 1735), Henry Brooke (*Universal Beauty*, 1735), Dr. Mark Akenside (*The Pleasures of the Imagination*, 1744), and Edward Young (*Night Thoughts*). Akenside's *The Pleasures of the Imagination*, based on Addison's discussion of the same subject in the *Spectator*, insists on the interconnection of truth, goodness, and beauty. Akenside's training in religion, philosophy, science, and art is evident throughout the poem, which is more a document for a historian of ideas than for an appreciator of poetic beauty.

Night Thoughts is essentially a Christian book of piety, but its appeal lay in its concentration on death and its autobiographical elements. Its main theme is that death's inevitability should sober both the reckless libertine and the complacent deist. Its moral reflections are addressed to a "silken son of pleasure" named Lorenzo, whose "fond heart dances while the siren sings." The pious gloom of *Night Thoughts*, which was mistranslated and misinterpreted, caused a sensation on the Continent and was gradually incorporated into the European tradition of romantic *Weltschmerz*.

Another important movement in the literature of England and the Continent in the first half of the eighteenth century has been named "sensibility." By this is meant an exquisite sensitiveness to the beautiful and the good, a sensitiveness which induces melancholy or sorrow. All that is noble and generous in human conduct was thought to have its source in this exquisite sensitivity, and nature assisted as a moral tonic to the human heart. The pensive mood, even though it induced melancholy, also induced pleasure because it freed the emotions and the imagination from the conventions of civilization and from the vanity and corruption of mankind. Milton's "Il Penseroso" partly influenced this new mode, and Richard Steele promoted melancholy in *Tatler 89*: "That calm and elegant satisfaction which the vulgar call Melancholy, is the true and proper Delight of Men of Knowledge and Virtue." In *Grongar Hill* Dyer employed picturesque ruins and other devices to summon a mood of gentle melancholy, and Shenstone asserted his independence from the satirists and wits, writing that the eighteenth century had "discovered sweets in melancholy which we could not find in mirth." Thomas Warton's celebratory "The Pleasures of Melancholy" (1747) avoided the didacticism of some of Milton's followers and cultivated relaxed and idyllic moods instead. In some ways, sensibility was a natural reaction to the Restoration, to its moral cynicism and its exclusive culture. Sensibility was a movement toward moral feeling and conduct, toward middle-class values, and, politically, toward the Whigs.

The latter half of the century produced no English poet equal to Pope, but it did produce a large number of important writers and did serve as a transition period from concentration on society as the preserver of the best in man to concentration on the nobility and potential of the individual. The beautiful city of Bath was built in the classical style, and the Adam brothers designed and built new streets and squares in Edinburgh. Advances were made in the art of writing history because men had come to believe with Pope that the "proper study of mankind is man." Shaftesbury's doctrine of man's natural goodness coupled with materialistic rationalism had led to optimistic political programs based on the perfectibility of man.

Writers did not rebel overtly against the classical tradition but increasingly began to write about realistic matters of everyday life. Thomas Gray's *Elegy Written in a Country Churchyard* is one of the best examples of this new poetic material. Humble life is treated humorously as well as realistically and much less idyllically. Writers began to claim that absolute standards are impossible and to believe in progress and novelty. With increasing doubts about Pope's assertion that truth is "one clear, unchanged, and universal light," the pendulum swung from fear of individualism and enthusiasm (which had led to civil war) to love of diversity (which, in turn, led to revolutions).

Poets became expressers of mood rather than eloquent preachers of general truths. The poet was exalted as a mysterious and sacred natural force which mere intelligence could not comprehend and training could not bestow. "Genius" supplanted wit as the creative force in the poet's mind. Abbe Yart in his sketch of Pope distinguished between the two: "Wit consists in adorning well-known thoughts, but genius is creative." William Duff in his *Essay on Original Genius* (1767) wrote that genius combines a "plastic and comprehensive imagination" with "an acute intellect, and an exquisite sensibility and refinement of taste." Imagination, the key ingredient in genius, was for Johnson a lively, delightful faculty which objectifies truth, recombines experience, and produces novelty by its varied combinations. For Blake, the imagination was the highest power in man, the organ of morality, art, and spiritual illumination. It had a daemonic power and, indeed, was said to be the voice of Nature herself speaking through the poet's soul. Genius, which was subject only to its own laws, produced "natural" literature of wild irregularity or homely simplicity. Giving a suprarational source to poetic genius eventually created problems, particularly in Blake's works. It served to weaken the poet's powers of self-criticism and control.

Moving away from the Renaissance and neoclassic idea that poetic genius should be learned, mid-eighteenth century audiences believed in "natural" or unlearned genius. Johnson, however, while affirming that "no man ever became great by imitation," insisted that genius must be trained by study. Belief in "natural" genius went hand in hand with a return to folk and national literature. In Germany, Johann Gottfried von Herder developed his famous distinction between *Volkspoesie*, poetry which springs spontaneously from the people, and *Kunstpoesie*, poetry which the educated produce within the traditional culture. In England, Collins' *Ode on the Popular Superstitions of the Highlands of Scotland, Considered as the Subject of Poetry* (1750) used folklore to inspire the poetic imagination and voiced the view that literature should have its source in the indigenous folk culture rather than in Graeco-Roman literary tradition.

The better poets imitated Horatian and French models inexactly. Even the conservative Goldsmith could write *The Deserted Village* (1770) without setting out to write an elegy or a pastoral. In Pope's time imitation was supposed to be creative rather than servile, but by mid-century critics such as Edward

Young were writing that it is the poet's duty and highest possible achievement to be "original." Originality, not to be confused with novelty, meant going back to the originals of things, not going to the "copies" of others. As one newspaper critic wrote, "striking out new Paths" rather than "treading very circumspectly in old ones" is of primary importance (*Daily Gazetteer*, 1741). The classical soil had been tilled out.

In addition to the fertile soil found in humble, everyday life, poets found new material in the Middle Ages, in castles and ruins and anything "Gothic." The Frenchman Paul Henri Mallet and his work *Northern Antiquities* (1770) did more than any other individual to set Europe ablaze with enthusiasm for ancient Germanic mythology and the medieval manners and customs of the North. In England, Horace Walpole built his monument to Gothicism, Strawberry Hill. Thomas Warton, the elder, wrote "A Runic Ode," and Thomas Warton, the younger, wrote three volumes on the history of English poetry from the twelfth to the close of the sixteenth century (1774-1781). Pope earlier in the century had chronicled love pangs in an *Epistle from Eloisa to Abelard* (1717), though this also had its source in Ovidian elegy, Dyer described Welsh ruins in *Grongar Hill*, Thomas Warton set his "The Pleasures of Melancholy" in the yard of a partially ruined Gothic church, and Gray published two odes "from the Norse tongue"—"The Fatal Sister" and "The Descent of Odin"— and some translations of Welsh stories. The poetry of Gray, in fact, provides a useful example of the turn from Graeco-Roman traditions to Northern antiquities: he began his career writing classically correct elegies and odes and finished his career imitating the primitive minstrelsy of the North.

Even though James Macpherson's Ossian tales were not authentic, they were extraordinarily successful, praised by Gray because they were "full of nature and noble wild imagination." The tales of Ossian reveal what eighteenth century audiences thought they saw in medieval writings: primitivism and sentimentalism. The idea of a Centic bard such as Ossian who could rival Homer thrilled Macpherson's contemporaries. They also enjoyed the sententious melancholy they could feel in such tales as that of the warrior Carthon whose father Clessámmoor unknowingly kills him. The sentimentality and melancholy of the tales is increased by double distancing: the tales themselves are supposedly old and the poet Ossian is writing longingly of a time past. Macpherson owed more to the Bible, Homer, Milton, and more recent authors, however, than he did to an oral tradition.

Concurrent with the interest in medievalism came the reawakening interest in the ballad. Popular ballads in the first half of the century include Henry Carey's *Sally in Our Alley*, Gay's *'Twas when the Seas Were Roaring* (1715) and the ballads in his *The Beggar's Opera* (1728), and Henry Fielding's *Roast Beef of Old England* (1731). Even Swift's two saints found broadside ballads plastered on the walls of the cottage of Baucis and Philemon. Many of the ballad songs are narratives. Allan Ramsay, an important publisher of ancient

Scottish ballads, modernized and "improved" the texts. In America, many complaints against the British took the form of ballads.

Considered a rather rude and plebeian amusement, the ballad gained respectability with the publication of Thomas Percy's collection, *Reliques of Ancient Poetry*, in 1765. The ballad's simple style profoundly affected the changing tastes of the writers and public of the eighteenth century. In the latter part of the century, Cowper's "The Diverting History of John Gilpin" had tremendous success; Cowper adapted it from the true story of a wild horseback ride taken by John Beyer, a Cheapside linen draper. Cowper credited the popularity of the ballad to its nationalism (he believed the ballad form was peculiar to England), its flexibility in being used for both humorous and tragic subjects, and its simplicity and ease.

Percy's *Reliques of Ancient Poetry* caught the imagination of its German readers. Addison, Swift, and Pope had had followers in Germany, and, then, Thomson, Milton, and Young. Sentimental verse won approval in the writings of F. G. Klopstock and Ewald Christian von Kleist. H. W. von Gurstenberg, F. F. Kretschmann, and Michael Denis (the translater of Ossian) led the "bardic" movement. It was Percy's collection, however, which directly influenced the poets who in 1772 founded Gottinger Hain, or the Brotherhood of the Grove, and who belonged mainly to the peasant or bourgeois classes.

The same yearnings that the eighteenth century felt for native poetry and nature stimulated the glorification of the "noble savage." Particularly in the latter half of the century, writers expressed longing for a "return to Nature" and brought primitivism into vogue. They contrasted the innocent child of the wilderness with the selfish man of artificial civilization. Urban life and civilization departed from the "natural." Jean Jacques Rousseau, the greatest European supporter of the "Return to Nature," believed that nature had originally made men good and happy but that civilization had made them criminal and miserable. Poets such as Cowper escaped to the countryside for tranquillity, and in those times nature was easily found: one could walk into the country even from central London, the largest of the few large towns in England. Cowper expressed the sentiments of many when he wrote, "God made the country, but man made the town."

The spread of education and the longing for innocence produced another new literary form, literature for children. Before the eighteenth century, poets wrote about children, particularly about their deaths, in hopes of parental patronage, but few poems were written for children. At the beginning of the century, Isaac Watts wrote *Divine Songs and Moral Songs for Children* (1715) and at the end of the century William Blake wrote *Songs of Experience* (1794) specifically for children. Blake did not condescend to children or indulge in humorous play to amuse the adults who read to children. His verses are childlike but never childish. Other writers for children include Ambrose Philips and Matthew Prior. Philips, a writer of pastorals, earned the nickname

"Namby Pamby" for his syrupy children's verses. Much better were Prior's mock-serious verses like the one in which Kitty begged Mama for the chariot and "set the world on fire."

Another new flowering in the eighteenth century was hymn writing. As more and more sects formed in opposition to established churches, new music for worship had to be created. In the first part of the century, Watts was one of the best and most scholarly of the Dissenting writers. His hymns, including "God our help in ages past," expressed the popular view that the universe displays the Almighty's hand. With fresh and independent critical ideas, Watts believed that the cultivation of faith can elevate poetry. Watts's hymns and others in the early part of the century tended to be "congregational" in point of view.

In Germany, pietism revived and left its traces in the sphere of religious poetry. The main emphasis lay in the individual's spiritual experience, not in conformity. A comparable revival in England was Evangelicalism. Just as literature had reacted to excessive cynicism and rationalism by growing in emotional intensity, so religion, both within and without the Anglican Church, reacted to skepticism and deism by emphasizing the passions and conversion of the individual soul. John and Charles Wesley, ordained Anglican ministers, felt forced by the hostile Established Church to break off and form an independent sect of Methodism. Methodism rapidly gained converts, especially among the humble and less educated. It brought them solace for their sorrows, gave them a moral force and feeling of personal importance, and added to the stirrings of democracy within society. The Wesleys themselves wrote hymns, mostly personal in nature. Charles Wesley's most famous hymn is "Jesus, Lover of My Soul." Another famous hymn written at this time is "Rock of Ages, Cleft for Me" by the now unknown writer, Augustus Toplady. Many hymn writers, unfortunately, committed the error of mixing secular metaphor and symbolism, with ludicrous and unsavory results.

William Cowper, *the* poet of the Evangelical revival though still an Anglican, wrote sixty-five *Olney Hymns* (1779) in conjunction with Reverend John Newton, the most famous of which is "Light Shining Out of Darkness" ("God moves in a mysterious way"). For the most part, his hymns express the beauty and serenity of the religious experience, although self-doubts darken "Light Shining Out of Darkness." Cowper was obsessed by the idea that God's grace had been withheld from him and that his eternal damnation had already been decided. His poetry expressed despair and hope and made firm doctrinal assertions which were typical of his day.

The two best poets of the new belief in secular progress were William Collins and Thomas Gray. Both accomplished scholars, they expressed their poetic ideals of liberty and simplicity in historical surveys or "progress poems." Collins excelled in writing odes: his "Ode to Evening" is particularly beautiful in its delicate "dying fall" of cadence. His "Ode Written in the Beginning of the Year 1746" has a delicate and pensive melody. Emotional apostrophes fill Collins' work, making it more exclamatory than reflective and making it less warm and personal. He chiefly appeals with his curious, ornate fantasies and his creation of dim and dreamlike effects.

Even though Gray and Collins resembled each other in temperament and literary principles, Gray was the better and more popular writer. Among the most learned of English poets, Gray read widely in Latin and Greek, in his English predecessors, and in Old Norse and Welsh. His range in various meters was unmatched in his century: he could write ceremonious heroic quatrains in the *Elegy Written in a Country Churchyard*, energetic effluences in his Pindaric odes, and primitive chants in his later period. His poetry dealt with emotions more directly than Collins'. "The Bard" and "The Progress of Poesy," which combine tight organization with wild imaginative flights, approach the sublime as few other attempts at this time did. Gray's fastidiousness and habit of endless revision limited the number of poems he published.

Although the spring and summer of neoclassicism had passed, there still remained the colorful autumn in the writings of Johnson and his friends, writings which insisted on presenting life realistically. The impressive figure of Samuel Johnson dominates the later half of the eighteenth century. The last major Augustan figure, he excelled in writing poetry, essays, and criticism, and in compiling the great *Dictionary of the English Language*. His first major poem, *London* (1738), satirized the city's corruption in imitation of Juvenal's denunciation of Rome. It came out on the same day as Pope's *Epilogue to the Satires* and was thought to compare favorably with it. In 1747 Johnson composed a prologue for the opening of the season at Drury Lane, a poem remarkable for its compressed and intelligent dramatic criticism. His greatest poem, *The Vanity of Human Wishes*, expressed Christian pessimism about man's earthly lot. Johnson opposed the currents of his age in criticizing Milton, the pastoral tradition, and blank verse, and in condemning the elevation of instincts and emotions over reason.

Johnson's friend Oliver Goldsmith displayed a similar range of talent in writing poetry, a novel, essays, and plays. In *The Traveller* (1764), representative of the "survey" convention of eighteenth century verse, he scrutinizes and judges the national temperaments and political constitutions of several European nations. He explains the doctrine of the principle of compensation, yet another eighteenth century exegesis on the idea of happiness: every state has its own particular principle of happiness, which in each may be carried to "mischievous excess." In *The Deserted Village* he chastizes large estate owners for razing country villages and scattering the villagers to increase their holdings. He describes the economic plight of the villagers and warns of the dangers of luxury and "trade's unfeeling train." Both poems, written in heroic couplets, display the gentle humor and kindness of their author.

Another poet who insisted on portraying life realistically was George Crabbe. Crabbe despised the weak idealism of the pastoral and poured his energy into describing the sordid and humble life of the Suffolk villagers of his youth. Crabbe was no devotee of Shaftesbury: he had no sentimental confidence in the goodness of human nature. Unlike earlier classicists, he emphasized individual responsibility rather than societal responsibility for crime and distress.

Charles Churchill, a dissipated clergyman who turned poet in his later years, continued the classical tradition of satire with all the faults of Pope and fewer merits. In his first important poem, *The Rosciad* (1761), he vigorously attacked theatrical personalities (some critics have named this poem the best satire between Pope's *The Dunciad* and Lord Byron's *English Bards, and Scotch Reviewers*, 1809). Churchill's satires have the energy and venom of Pope's satires, but they lack deftness and elegance. Churchill wrote many of his satires in support of his friend John Wilkes. Wilkes had condemned the Scottish people in *The North Briton*, a weekly political periodical; Churchill continued the outcry in *The Prophecy of Famine* (1763). William Hogarth had drawn a caricature of Wilkes in the courtroom; Churchill took revenge on him in *Epistle to William Hogarth*. Wilkes dueled with Samuel Martin; Churchill defended him in *The Duellist* (1763). The fourth Earl of Sandwich was Wilkes's enemy; Churchill attacked his hypocrisy in *The Candidate* (1764). Contemporaries of Pope and Churchill could relish the frequent personal allusions, but to succeeding generations they have meant little.

William Cowper tried to add to the satirical tradition, but he was too gentle and gracious a man to be a great satirist. In "Table Talk" he commented on the poetry of the century; in "Retirement" and "The Progress of Error" he attacked the follies of high life; and in "Expostulation" he condemned patriotic poems, including the lyric "On the Loss of the Royal George."

Cowper could write moving realistic poetry. In *The Task* (1785) he accurately and delightfully sketched country life, recording the sights and sounds and shrewdly portraying human character. *The Task* satisfied the hunger of the eighteenth century for long poems (a hunger which soon began to be satiated), for rambling structure, and for reflective description. "Domestic happiness" and gardening, he rejoiced, give "blest seclusion from a jarring world." Humor at this time was becoming rare and precious in poetry. Cowper wrote *The Task* on the urging of his friend Lady Austen, who wanted him to try blank verse and who told him, when he complained of not having a subject, "Oh, you can never be in want of a subject; you can write upon any—write upon that sofa!"

Cowper's poetry blended and harmonized the new and sometimes disquieting elements of his era: evangelical religion, sensibility, and democratic rumblings. Unlike his predecessors, Cowper seldom philosophized about the abstraction "Nature" when he described and reflected about the landscape.

Unlike his contemporaries, he did not follow the rationalist tradition of placing the "Book of Nature" beside the Bible, although he did believe in creation as "an effect whose cause is God." Unlike the Romantics, he found no strangeness in beauty and felt no intense passion for nature; he was simply and genuinely attached to it.

Unlike Thomson and Young, the other two great descriptive poets of the century, Cowper had a natural fluency and could choose his polysyllables well. He avoided the stereotypical "poetic diction" used for objective detail and wrote easy, graceful blank verse. Although his verse lacks the concentration and intensity of the greatest poetry, it nevertheless remains faithful to reality and does so in natural, nearly conversational diction.

Cowper and Burns were among the late bloomers of the cult of simplicity, writing of rural domesticity and using subjective, autobiographical material. More intimate and emotional than their predecessors, they saw their roles as poets more as individuals speaking to themselves or to small audiences about their own experience than as the loud voice of the public. As such, they were transitional poets. Although less intellectual than Dryden or Pope, Cowper wrote intelligently about prison reform, slavery, and the French Revolution, and Burns wrote cogently about the oppressive Church of Scotland. Unlike Dryden, Swift, or Pope, Cowper never zealously burned for causes, but he did defend George Whitfield, an eminent Methodist who had been slandered.

Like Cowper, Burns wrote satire and realistic verse in natural and spontaneous style. He too was a poet of domestic emotion, but he described his environment not for itself but for the human relationships implied in it. Although he lived among and wrote of the common people of the Scottish lowlands, he was a highly educated man and a worthy inheritor of the ancient tradition of vernacular song and poetry. He wrote about Scottish life and manners in Scottish dialect and used his local Ayrshire neighborhood for inspiration. His manner, though not original, struck his non-Scottish audience as fresh and unusual.

Earlier Scottish poets had been ignored in London. In the cases of Allan Ramsay and Robert Fergusson, this was perhaps understandable; they wrote unpretentiously about their native land. Ramsay's work resembled that of John Gay in many ways: he displayed hearty humor and shrewd observation for vivid rustic detail. Like Gay, he used the pastoral form for realistic ends and attempted a ballad opera, *The Gentle Shepherd* (1728). John Home, the author of *Douglas* (1756), who was known as the "Scottish Shakespeare," and William Wilkie, the author of *The Epigoniad* (1757), who was known as the "Scottish Homer," had also been slighted.

Working with stanzaic types popular with Scottish poets since the Middle Ages, Burns added vigor and musicality to his inheritance. (The stanza of "The Holy Fair," for example, is adapted from the old "Christis Kirk on the Green" stanza.) In his most effective satires—"Holy Willie's Prayer," "The

Holy Fair," and "Address to the Unco Guild"—Burns savagely exposed religious hypocrisy. He wrote at the height of the liberal-minded rebellion against the doctrine of election and the impossibly strict rules of conduct enforced by the orthodox Presbyterian Church and its courts.

Like Cowper, Burns sympathized with the growing democratic tendencies: he believed in the essential worth of a man, whether rich or poor. His mind was free and modern, and his powers of observation accurate and penetrating. His nature poetry was the plain, simple observation of a Scottish farmer, not the reflective scientific musing of a devotee of Thomson. Above all, he was an extraordinarily gifted lyricist. He became the voice and symbol of his people, pleasing non-Scots with his "primitive" and "native" verse and focusing the national feelings of his own people.

The most significant event of the end of the eighteenth century was, of course, the French Revolution. In German literature it was regarded as a warning about the problem of liberty. In English literature it kindled enthusiasm in poets, but their celebratory poetry did not sparkle. Cowper and Burns saw in the revolution a declaration of the worth of all men, a manifesto of the political rights of the people. Beyond this, the revolution generated a millennial movement in English thought and life. William Blake was the greatest of the millennial prophets, imagining a day when a new Jerusalem would arise in England after the reconciliation of Urizen (reason) with Los (imagination) and Luvah (passion).

The classical myths were dead, but the millennial era provided a seedbed for new myths. In *The Book of Thel* (1789), Blake introduced his own myths to symbolize philosophical ideas, which he later expanded in his "Prophetic Books." Against the character Urizen, the spirit of reason, custom, and institutions, Blake could vent all his revolutionary ire.

It is easy to write generalizations about the poetry of a particular period; it is less easy to make the poetry fit the generalizations. One can say, though, that the eighteenth century is a garden of exotic and diverse blooms. (Any century which included Blake, Gray, and Pope would have to be.) With some reservations, one can generalize that the century began with the glories of satire, the desire for improvements in society, and ended with the uncertainties of a new individualism and emerging social order. In between grew the love of description, reflection, and moralizing; an appreciation for everyday life and the common man; a yearning to know man, his native land, his history, and his place in the universe; a burning for feeling as well as reason; and a search for truth and imaginate beauty. The garden was ready to blossom into the fresh colors of Romanticism.

Bibliography
The Age of Johnson: Essays Presented to C. B. Tinker, 1949.
Bate, W. J. *From Classic to Romantic: Premises of Taste in Eighteenth-Century*

England, 1946.

Brown, W. C. *The Triumph of Form: A Study of the Later Masters of the Heroic Couplet*, 1948.

Mack, Maynard. *The Garden and the City*, 1969.

Price, Martin. *To the Palace of Wisdom*, 1964.

Rogers, Pat. *The Augustan Vision*, 1974.

Smith, D. N. *Some Observations on Eighteenth-Century Poetry*, 1937.

Sutherland, James. *A Preface to Eighteenth-Century Poetry*, 1948.

Ann Willardson Engar

THE NINETEENTH CENTURY

Because creativity pays little attention to the calendar as such, a literary century does not necessarily begin and end on schedule nor last precisely one hundred years. The nineteenth century in English and American literature, however, was remarkably well contained, beginning (as many think) in England with William Wordsworth's poetry of 1798 and poetic manifesto of 1800, then halting noticeably with the deaths of Queen Victoria and President McKinley in 1901. Because England dominated American culture throughout most of the nineteenth century—with increasingly formidable influence in the reverse direction, however, this brief essay on a highly complex subject will emphasize interactions between the two literatures.

Despite its geographical separation from England, the east coast of what is now the United States was very strongly British during the eighteenth century, not only politically but also culturally. The American Revolution, which justified itself on grounds derived primarily from British thought, changed nothing in that respect, for though American writers such as John Trumbull, Timothy Dwight, and Philip Freneau soon turned toward American subjects, they continued to see them through British eyes and to imitate British literary models, which were still of the neoclassical type. Neoclassicism was appropriate to a society in which religious and social values were well assured and stability was more evident than change. Yet this stability was vanishing rapidly throughout the latter eighteenth century, in both England and America.

It was an era of revolutions, through which much that has since characterized the West came into being. Not all of these revolutions were sudden or dramatic, but their cumulative force was irresistible. For example, population increased enormously throughout the latter eighteenth century in England and America as better sanitation, nutrition, and medicine increased longevity and reduced infant mortality. This larger and healthier population strained available resources, pressured an outmoded economic system, and gave both countries unusually large numbers of the young, who utilized the increasing availability of books to effect political, agricultural, technological, scientific, and social revolutions on behalf of the abundance and freedom with which their own interests were identified.

Two of the most obvious revolutions were political, as America broke away from England in 1776 and France attempted to discard its outmoded monarchy and religious establishment in 1789. Less precipitously, agriculture was revolutionized by the development of improved plows, crop rotation schemes, selective breeding, and (in England) an improved network of canals and turnpikes that allowed farmers to market specialty crops over greater distances. The superior transportation of the latter eighteenth century was also broadly effective in extending the boundaries of urban culture beyond London to provincial and even rural centers, so that authorship (for example) was more widespread. As mail service improved, men of letters everywhere corresponded more meaningfully, and even American colonials such as Benjamin Franklin were effective participants in the European ferment. Other aspects of technological change were also rapid, as both England and America responded ever more fully to the development of mechanical power. The steam engine, developed by James Watt, inaugurated the first phase of the Industrial Revolution, which would then transform the two countries for a second time during the nineteenth century with the advent of railroads and steamships; these latter inventions made the territorial ambitions of Britain and America feasible. The factory system, with its emphasis on regulated labor and standardized parts, was not only of economic and social importance—it strongly influenced nineteenth century literature and thought as well. Prior to the American Revolution, however, because British law prevented the full development of American manufacture (finished goods had to be imported from England), much colonial ingenuity was devoted instead to improved nautical technology—at which New England quickly became outstanding—and eventually to exploring the resources of the constantly retreating western frontier.

The sea, the frontier, and foreign countries attracted young adventurers who would otherwise have been victimized by the economic inequities of hereditary wealth. Thus, the Industrial Revolution fostered a new entrepreneurial class that gained both economic and social prominence. These aggressive and often uncouth opportunists challenged the increasingly moribund landed aristrocracies of England and America, wresting a larger share of political power and social respectability for themselves. If the eighteenth century was, at its beginning, dominated by hereditary nobility, its internal conflicts gave rise to a nineteenth century in which an aristocracy of talent was more important.

The internal conflicts of the eighteenth century derived in large part from a crosscurrent of ideas known as the Enlightenment, which originated in seventeenth century England with Francis Bacon, John Locke, and Isaac Newton, then spread during the next hundred years to France, where ideals of cosmopolitan urbanity, rational humanism, and religious toleration (if not outright disbelief) were popularized by Voltaire, Denis Diderot, and Jean Jacques Rousseau, all of whom advocated freedom and change. A second eighteenth century center of Enlightenment initiative was Scotland (then experiencing a nationalistic revival), which contributed the skepticism of David Hume, the economic theories of Adam Smith, and an impressive series of historiographic, scientific, technological, and literary achievements. The American phase of the Enlightenment, including Benjamin Franklin, Thomas Jefferson, and James Madison, guided restless colonials toward independence, economic self-sufficiency, and a radically new theory of government. Yet both the Declaration of Independence and the Constitution of the United States were based on Enlightenment ideals that derived in large part from those of Republican Rome.

Nineteenth century minds never forgot their indebtedness to the past, and one of the most reliable characteristics of nineteenth century literature is its historicism. The science of archaeology, for example, arose during the 1740's with sytematic digging at Pompeii and Herculaneum, leading to a revival of visual classicism in architecture, sculpture, and painting. Then the nineteenth century began with French archaeological discoveries in Egypt, including the Rosetta stone. As a result, pyramids recur throughout nineteenth century arts as symbols of death, the sphinx and hieroglyphics appear as mysterious embodiments of knowledge denied to man, and Egypt itself becomes the new symbol (replacing Rome) of antiquarian grandeur. Incremental archaeological enthusiasm soon overwhelmed Europe and its more creative minds with statuary from the Parthenon, winged lions from Assyria, relics from Troy, many now-familiar classical masterpieces, and vast new sites, art forms, and religions from the Americas, Asia, and Africa. During the nineteenth century also, the concept of geological time was established, with all its vast duration and wondrous legacy of vanished giants. Thus, the nineteenth century past no longer began with Adam, as had been accepted for almost two thousand years, but instead an immensely complex progression through incalculable time from uncertain beginnings to the illustrious present. No other century in the history of the West experienced such a readjustment of its time sense as did the nineteenth.

Although overwhelmingly Protestant, nineteenth century writers in England and America were often attracted to the Catholic Middle Ages. Gothic architecture was popularly revived in Britain, and there was a resurgence of medieval craftsmanship in the Pre-Raphaelite movement of Dante Gabriel Rossetti and William Morris, which (together with the aesthetic and social criticism of John Ruskin) did much to reduce the ugliness of overindustrialized Victorian minor arts. Poets likewise returned to the Middle Ages for inspiration, though seldom realistically. For Sir Walter Scott, John Keats, Alfred, Lord Tennyson, James Russell Lowell, William Morris, and other writers, medievalism was a utopian alternative to the deficiencies of the present, but one that the cold scrutiny of history could not fully corroborate.

To some extent, the same disparity characterizes the nineteenth century's image of classical Greece, which overshadowed Rome in cultural prestige and was accepted as a symbol of liberty, whether political, intellectual, or behavioral. For the many Hellenists of the nineteenth century, Greek mythology was a major inspiration. Among the most popular myths was that of Prometheus, which attracted William Blake, Thomas Campbell, Lord Byron, Elizabeth Barrett Browning, Robert Bridges, and especially Percy Bysshe Shelley, for whom Prometheus was the mythological embodiment of enlightened, technological man. In related contexts, Byron died on behalf of Greek independence, and Keats revered its artistic legacy. Mid-Victorian writers, such as Tennyson, valued Greece primarily for its writers, particularly Homer, while later ones such as Matthew Arnold and Thomas Hardy admired the realism of Greek tragedy. Greek lyric poetry found readers throughout the century and influenced A. E. Housman, especially. Combining the lyric and dramatic traditions of classical Greece, Shelley attempted two lyric dramas on Greek subjects, *Prometheus Unbound* (1820) and *Hellas* (1822), which would be imitated later by Arnold (*Empedocles on Etna*, 1852), Algernon Charles Swinburne (*Atalanta in Calydon*, 1865), and Hardy (*The Dynasts*, 1903, 1906, 1908). The pagan, libertarian, and sometimes erotic influence of Greece was taken very seriously.

Nineteenth century writers admired individuality and boldness. They found the heroic age of exploration particularly congenial, as poems about Christopher Columbus (for example) were written by Joel Barlow, Samuel Rogers, William Lisle Bowles, Alfred, Lord Tennyson, Walt Whitman, Joaquin Miller, and James Russell Lowell. Samuel Taylor Coleridge's *The Rime of the Ancient Mariner* (1798) was based upon exploration literature and the voyage of Magellan; Keats mistook Cortez for Balboa; while Bowles and Whitman celebrated Vasco da Gama and the spirit of discovery in general. Other heroes of the century included George Washington, Napoleon Bonaparte, The Duke of Wellington, and Abraham Lincoln. There were also many poems and essays about writers, including Homer, Vergil, Dante, William Shakespeare, Torquato Tasso, John Milton, Johann Wolfgang von Goethe, the British Romantic poets, Ralph Waldo Emerson, and Whitman. Artists of the Italian Renaissance were often extolled for their individuality—the Renaissance as a whole was popular—and various Enlightenment figures (Bacon, Newton, Voltaire, and Rousseau primarily) were either praised or damned, according to the religious preferences of the writer. Surprisingly little was written, however, in praise of religious heroes as such.

Traditional religion was sorely pressed throughout the nineteenth century (its latter half particularly) to retain credibility in the face of pervasive doubts which arose on all sides—from biblical criticism, undermining the literal word; from Enlightenment objections to religious authority and intolerance; from the diversity of religious observance and the insipidity of orthodox spirituality; and from the currently popular philosophies of materialism and utilitarianism, neither of which found much use for the inanities of a debased theological tradition which, during the eighteenth century, had clearly become part of an oppressive church-and-state establishment. One of the most pervasive features of nineteenth century literature, therefore, is religious doubt, which frequently resolved itself in any of several ways: by regarding history as a manifestation of God; by turning from God to man; by abandoning religion in favor of art; or by returning to orthodox belief. Though there were also a number of alternative faiths, including spiritualism, the guiding light of the century was science.

The literary nineteenth century is commonly divided into periods or phases, more or less arbitrarily. There was clearly a Romantic period in England from about 1786 to 1832, however, followed by a more sedate Victorian reaction that itself began to disintegrate after 1860. American literature remained minor and derivative until about 1820, when William Cullen Bryant emerged. While the 1830's were comparable on both sides of the Atlantic, with significant interaction, Romanticism lasted longer in America—to which it was more applicable. The traumatic Civil War of 1861 to 1865, however, soon drew American letters toward the increasing pessimism already common in England. During the last third of the nineteenth century, British and American literature were widely separate, and the uniqueness of American writers was generally acknowledged. This essay will now characterize several aspects of the century, beginning with the English Romantics, who were influential in both England and America.

British Romantics

Neoclassical literature, which dominated the first half of the eighteenth century in England, emphasized practical reason, social conformity, emotional restraint, and submission to the authority of classical literary techniques. It was generally allied to political and religious conservatism as well. As life in eighteenth century England was transformed by political, economic, social, and technological innovations, however, the old manner of literary expression seemed increasingly obsolete to younger and more audacious writers who had absorbed the Enlightenment philosophy of humanism and freedom.

Among the first of these new men in literature was Robert Burns (1759-1796). Though he did not live quite long enough to experience the nineteenth century at first hand, Burns strikingly exemplified a number of its tendencies. Far from apologizing for either his Scottish burr or his rural origins, at a time when both were disparaged in polite society, he appealed to the 1780's as a supposedly untutored genius, a *natural* poet whose verses arose not from the inkwell but from the heart. Beneath his colorful regionalism and earthy rural sensuality there remained a stubborn dignity, an antiaristocratic humanity, and a concentration upon his own emotions that favored meditative and lyric poetry. Burns's carefree morality and religious satire signaled the approaching end of religious orthodoxy in British poetry (it would last longer in America) and effectively countered the turgid morbidity into which so many mid-century versifiers had fallen. In his egalitarian social attitudes ("A man's a man for a' that"), Burns portended the imminent French Revolution of 1789. His literary influence throughout the next century extended to Scott, Tennyson, John Greenleaf Whittier, Lowell, Hardy, and Rudyard Kipling, all of whom profited from Burns's use of dialect in serious literature and from his revolutionary insistence that the right of an individual to worth and dignity is not dependent upon the urbanity of his speech.

If William Blake (1757-1827), of Burns's generation, was not so obviously an outsider as the Scottish poet, he soon became one through the seeming incomprehensibility of his highly individualistic poetry and art. A firm supporter of the American and French revolutions, Blake was also the first important author to sense the underlying dynamism of his times. No other poet, for example, perceived the historical importance of either the Industrial Revolution or the political upheaval in America so clearly. Similarly, no other poet has influenced twentieth century theories of literature so much. Yet Blake was dismissed as a madman in his own times, and his influence on nineteenth century literature became important only toward the end, with Swinburne, Rossetti, James Thomson, and William Butler Yeats. It is now clear, however, that Blake's concerns with innovation, energy, myth, lyric, and sexuality were extremely prescient.

Though William Wordsworth (1770-1850) was more in accord with late eighteenth century restraint than Blake, he effected the most significant theoretical change ever seen in English literature and did more than any other individual to give nineteenth century literature its distinctive character. With its explicit rejection of neoclassicism and the aristocratic tradition in literature, Wordsworth's *Lyrical Ballads* of 1798 (first American edition, 1800), written with Samuel Taylor Coleridge, is often considered the official beginning of the literary nineteenth century. Its famous Preface, added to the English edition of 1800, outlined Wordsworth's new criteria for literature, to which virtually all the significant poets of his century would subscribe. His influence is evident in Coleridge, Byron, Shelley, Keats, Tennyson, Arnold, and Hardy, among major British poets, and in Bryant, Emerson, Henry David Thoreau, Whitman, Henry Wadsworth Longfellow, and Whittier, among American ones. He was the most written-about poet of the century. Wordsworth also had a significant impact upon non-poets such as John Stuart Mill; even Charles Darwin read him. Nineteenth century literature in all its forms is immensely indebted to Wordsworth's preoccupations with rural life, childhood, mental and emotional development, language, history, and nature.

Although Wordsworth's collaborator, Samuel Taylor Coleridge (1772-1834), was also an accomplished poet, his substantial influence on later writers (Emerson in particular) came primarily through his prose. As a poet, however, he influenced Wordsworth, Scott, Shelley, Keats, and Edgar Allan Poe, preceding the latter as a symbolist of sometimes uncanny power. Coleridge was also a foremost theorist and critic of English Romanticism, as well as an effective transmitter of German Romantic thought to both England and America.

Wordsworth and Coleridge now seem far greater poets, but Sir Walter Scott (1771-1832) and George Gordon, Lord Byron (1788-1824), were more immediately popular, not only in Britain and America but also throughout Europe. In his narrative poems and many novels (all too hastily written), Scott further popularized regionalism, historicism, and folk traditions. His novels influenced Washington Irving and James Fenimore Cooper, thus virtually beginning nineteenth century literature in America, and created an immense vogue for historical literature of all kinds; his poetic insistence on a nationalistic muse helped to inspire the Irish harp of Thomas Moore, the Indian one of Bankim Chatterjee, and the "barbaric yawp" of Whitman. Henry Wadsworth Longfellow (1807-1882) was also indebted to Scott's influence for his well-known longer poems on American themes, but went beyond Scott in the amazing cosmopolitanism of his literary sources. In his pseudomedieval manor house at Abbotsford—much copied by his fellow artisans—Scott played the gracious host to innumerable literary visitors, several of them American. Throughout his lifetime, he was the kindest and most accessible major literary figure in Europe.

During the first decade of the nineteenth century, when Britain was preoccupied with its resistance to Napoleon and travel upon the Continent was scarcely possible, Scott was also his country's most popular poet. Byron dominated the following decade, the Regency, when from 1811 to 1820 England was governed by their heir apparent (later George IV), George III having been declared hopelessly insane. Byron's contradictory but forceful verses, cynical and witty as they were, appealed to a disillusioned younger generation that had seen its hopes for political reform quashed by the failure of the French Revolution, and its taste for heroics eradicated by the unnecessary holocaust of the Napoleonic wars. After 1816, however, as England reverted to peacetime reconstruction, Byron's immorality and religious heterodoxy became too much. He was forced into exile on the Continent that year, soon to be followed by Percy Bysshe Shelley (1792-1822), against whom the same charges were leveled, and (primarily for reasons of health) by John Keats (1795-1821), who appeared to some imperceptive critics as nothing more than a sensuously explicit Cockney. These judgments, of course, did not prevail as Byron's influence extended to John Clare, Tennyson, Arthur Hugh Clough, Elizabeth Barrett Browning, Emily Brontë, Poe, Whitman, and Joaquin Miller; Shelley's to Arthur Henry Hallam, Thomas Lovell Beddoes, Tennyson, Browning, Swinburne, Thomson, Hardy, and Yeats; and Keats's to Tennyson, Thomas Hood, Rossetti, Morris, Emily Dickinson, Lowell, Swinburne, and innumerable minor poets. The Byronic hero also became a familiar type in Victorian fiction, Shelley had a major impact upon freethinkers and labor leaders, and Keats became almost a model for both writers and artists during the latter half of the century. Thus, the major English Romantic poets as a group were highly influential in and beyond literature throughout the nineteenth century.

American Transcendentalists

The transcendentalist movement in America during the 1830's and 1840's, centering upon Ralph Waldo Emerson (1803-1882), who disassociated himself from the term, was an awakening of new literary possibilities comparable to, and in part derived from, the literary revolution initiated by Wordsworth and Coleridge. Whereas British Romanticism was often a rebellion against social oppression within the country itself, however, much of its American equivalent was pitted against the tyranny of British literary predominance and European snobbishness generally. William Ellery Channing concluded in 1830 ("Remarks on National Literature") that a truly American literature did not yet exist, and there were many subsequent laments regarding the Yankee failure to achieve cultural independence. "We have listened too long to the courtly muses of Europe," proclaimed Emerson in his famous oration on "The American Scholar" in 1837. Nathaniel Parker Willis, a minor poet from New York, was even more emphatic two years later. "*In literature*," he claimed,

> *we are no longer a nation*. The triumph of Atlantic steam navigation has driven the smaller drop into the larger, and London has become the center. Farewell nationality! The English language now marks the limits of a new literary empire, and America is a suburb.

Like many desperate pronouncements, this one soon proved wrong, but it was by no means clear in 1839 that those then living would witness the remarkable effulgence of American letters that was to come.

The significant American poets whose emergence showed Willis to be a false prophet included Emerson, Thoreau, Jones Very, Poe, Whitman, Dickinson, Longfellow, Whittier, Oliver Wendell Holmes, and Lowell. Emerson himself was a major influence upon contemporary and later American poets, including Thoreau, Very, Whitman, and Dickinson. His essays influenced such remarkable British thinkers as Thomas Carlyle, Arnold, Clough, John Sterling, James Anthony Froude, Herbert Spencer, and John Tyndall. Poe, eventually a force in France, was significant in England only for Swinburne, Rossetti, and Thomson. Whitman appealed to a number of late Victorians, influencing Tennyson (in "Vastness"), Swinburne, William Rossetti, John Addington Symonds, Lionel Johnson, Edward Dowden, and even Robert Louis Stevenson. Those who appreciated his accomplishment were generally fond of Blake and Shelley also. Longfellow became the most popular poet in the English-speaking world around the mid-century, so beloved in Britain and elsewhere that hundreds of his editions appeared, including one of *The Song of Hiawatha* (1855) illustrated by Frederick Remington. Although now considered only a genial minor figure in world literature, Longfellow alone among American poets was accorded by his British admirers a memorial in "Poets' Corner," Westminster Abbey. As for the others, Whittier, Holmes, and Lowell had only moderate international appeal, while Thoreau, Very,

Dickinson, and Herman Melville were virtually unknown. Even so, it could no longer be said that literary influences between England and America ran only in one direction.

Attitudes Toward Nature

From certain Germanic sources, often transmitted through the philosophical prose of Coleridge and Carlyle, Emerson and his associates derived a fundamental conviction that all material facts are emblematic of spiritual truths, which led them to believe that religious revelation was continuous. This openness to factual and spiritual enlightenment prompted American writers to read widely, often in untraditional sources. Thus, classical works of Oriental religion, the *Bhagavad-Gita* and others, were of interest. The Orientalism of Emerson, Thoreau, and Whitman, more serious and better informed than that to be found in the work of earlier English poets such as Thomas Moore (*Lalla Rookh*, 1817), helped them to accept the benevolent impermanence of nature.

Because of their belief in progressive revelation, American transcendentalists were also more able than their British literary counterparts to accept the current findings of natural science—astronomy, geology, and biology— by which many nineteenth century writers were influenced. Though these three sciences were together discrediting the Creation narrative in Genesis (a task virtually completed by 1840), and suggesting the relative insignificance of man in a mechanistic world of vast time and space, the American transcendentalists remained almost sanguine in denying the unique status of any one religious tradition, for they regarded the world of nature (whose cruelty they overlooked) as God's most reliable revelation of Himself and as a corrective to the mythological understanding of all earlier peoples.

Attitudes toward nature remained benign in America well after they had become suspect in Britain, where a skeptical tradition among the unorthodox had been articulated by Shelley and soon reasserted itself through Alfred, Lord Tennyson (1809-1892), who was the official and most influential poet of Victorian England. Yet just after Emerson had published his idealistic, Wordsworthian essay *Nature* (1836), he and Tennyson both read Charles Lyell's *Principles of Geology* (1830-1833), which emphasized the immensity of geological time and raised fundamental questions about the history of life. The book exhilarated Emerson, who regarded it as a demonstration of the pervasiveness of natural law, and hence of morality. Tennyson, however, had still not reconciled himself to the premature death of his friend Arthur Henry Hallam at the age of twenty-two and was led by Lyell into agonizing despair over a seemingly amoral world in which whole species perished routinely.

Tennyson's doubts were eventually assuaged by his reading of Goethe, friendship with Carlyle, and a conviction (reinforced by several naturalists) that life's record in the rocks was purposeful and upward. Yet his literary resolution of the dilemma in *In Memoriam* (1850), the greatest long poem of its time, only temporarily delayed the specter of amoral, indifferent nature that would come to haunt the remaining half of the nineteenth century. In America, on the contrary, the prevailing attitude toward nature long remained that of Thoreau's *Walden* (1854) or even became symbolic of national greatness, as western exploration revealed mountains, rivers, and other scenic wonders unequaled in England; surely they were emblematic of the country and its future. The future that most concerned Americans at mid-century belonged to this life rather than the next, for their nation had been imperiled by issues of slavery and states' rights, despite the glitter of California gold.

Victorian Reforms and Doubts

In general, the first third of the literary nineteenth century in England was preoccupied with political questions, as public concern responded in turn to the French Revolution and its failure; to the subsequent rise, threats, and necessary defeat of Napoleon; to the internal dislocations of the Regency; to the complicated international situation after Waterloo; and especially to needed reforms at home—for inequities between social classes were rife, and England seemed to be on the brink of insurrection. After 1832, however, when the first Reform Bill (enfranchising the middle class) was enacted, it became clear that social betterment would be achieved through legislation and education rather than revolution. Poets such as Ebenezer Elliott, Thomas Hood, Elizabeth Barrett Browning, and (in America) Lydia Huntley Sigourney joined Thomas Carlyle, Charles Dickens, and other writers of prose in depicting the hard lot of the underprivileged, particularly children and the working poor. Black slavery was no longer at issue in Britain because the slave trade had been abolished in 1807 and slavery itself (common only in the West Indies) in 1832. It would last until 1864 in America. There was also feminist agitation, but this was a social revolution for which the Victorian world was not yet prepared; Victoria herself (crowned in 1837) opposed it.

Even so, a remarkable transformation took place within mid-century England as enlightened advocates uncovered inequities old and new. Among the revolutionary bills passed by reforming parliaments were the Factory Act of 1833, regulating child labor; the Poor Law Amendment Act of 1834, regulating workhouses; the Municipal Reform Act of 1835, unifying town governments; an act of 1842 prohibiting the employment of women and children in mines; another in 1843 prohibiting imprisonment for debt; the first public health act in 1848; another factory act, shortening hours and days, in 1850; a second major political reform in 1868; and, finally, the great public schools act of 1870. If there were fewer reforming acts in less-developed America, it was in part because fewer were needed. Whatever the indigenous shortcomings of British industrialism, its problems were taken seriously by both workingmen and writers. One of the few European states to avoid armed revolution during the nineteenth century, Britain was perhaps the most socially advanced nation in the world, as well as the most industrialized, for humanitarianism and progress had become its prevailing creeds.

This humanitarianism increasingly superseded orthodox religion, which had begun to experience severe problems of credibility. The Oxford movement toward a more historical Christianity, less dependent upon the precise text of the Bible, had begun under John Keble in 1833, but this promising doctrinal initiative on the part of the Anglican Church (official in England) lost effectiveness when John Henry Newman, its most persuasive advocate, announced his conversion to Roman Catholicism in 1845. The high road to orthodoxy having proved disastrous, Anglican theology was afterward dominated by the Broad Church movement (to which the poets Coleridge and Clough were important), which scarcely emphasized doctrinal conformity at all. Except for Newman, Christina Rossetti, and Gerard Manley Hopkins, few English poets afer 1850 were orthodoxly religious.

Tennyson's *In Memoriam* managed a dubious immortality for the young skeptic that it commemorated, but other poets of the time were less sure, as Clough and Arnold remained agnostics at best. In *Christmas Eve and Easter Day* (1850) Robert Browning rejected both doctrinal and evangelical Christianity in favor of a theistic religion of love, Arnold implying much the same in "Dover Beach" (1851). While meeting the equivalent American spiritual crisis with more gusto, Whitman observed in *Leaves of Grass* (1855) that "Creeds and schools" were "in abeyance." His own faith derived from all religions and did not include curiosity about God. In a poem of 1871 addressed to Whitman, however, Swinburne admitted that "God is buried and dead to us." Among American poets, Melville and Dickinson became religious seekers; Emerson, Whittier, and Longfellow, among others, remained relatively confident of supernatural goodness throughout the 1850's and 1860's, but their optimism (shared by Tennyson and Browning to some extent) seemed increasingly tenuous to younger readers.

One by one, traditional verities disappeared from English and American literature, and more rapidly in Britain. God was doubtful, Nature cruel, History vindictive, Love impossible, Man animalistic and corrupt. The poet who articulated the new disillusionment most forcefully, Matthew Arnold (1822-1888), saw himself as an isolated wanderer through a post-Christian, postrationalistic wilderness of historical and personal estrangement. Like Shelley's poet in *Alastor* (1816), Arnold sought for love and could not find it; of all men he wrote, "Thou hast been, shalt be, art, alone." Several later Victorian poets, including Browning (*Men and Women*, 1855), D. G. Rossetti, George Meredith, and Coventry Patmore, wrote extensively of their relationships with women, and of the failure of love; others turned from normal eroticism altogether. Compare these works with other long poems of the times which concentrate upon women, including Tennyson, *The Princess* (1847), and "Guinevere," from *Idylls of the King* (1859-1885); Clough, *The Bothie of Tober-na-Vuolich* (1848); Elizabeth Barrett Browning, *Aurora Leigh* (1857); Longfellow, *The Courtship of Miles Standish* (1858); and Morris, *The Defense of Guenevere* (1858).

As for nature, history, and man, all three had become suspect by mid-century and all three coalesced in the theory of natural selection publicized by Darwin's *On the Origin of Species* (1859), which transformed nineteenth century skepticism into disillusioned pessimism and savage exploitation. Darwin himself should not be held uniquely responsible for the capitalistic and imperialistic excesses mistakenly derived from his biological theories; his work inspired a major literary movement called naturalism and certainly ennobled the tragic sense of such powerful, effective poets as Thomas Hardy (1840-1928) and Stephen Crane (1871-1900). In both England and America, Darwin's harsh view of nature was coupled with the reality of war (India, 1857; Charleston, 1861; Havana, 1898). Perhaps even more disillusioning, however, was the incremental recognition in both countries that the optimism of previous decades regarding human nature was implausible. Throughout the last quarter of the nineteenth century authors repeatedly proclaimed, though usually in prose, that man is defiled on the surface and ugly to the core. Though the century could bear its religious losses with stoic fortitude, it could not maintain an essentially optimistic outlook against the pervasive antihumanism of its final years.

Throughout the century literature had been closely allied with art. Much of its descriptive poetry, for example, was based upon painted forebears or similar contemporary work; thus, Wordsworth is often compared with John Constable, Shelley with J. M. W. Turner, Coleridge with German Romantic art, Byron with Eugène Delacroix, and Browning with the Impressionists. Several important writers, including Blake, John Ruskin, Morris, and D. G. Rossetti, were authentic artists in their own right; others combined their verbal work with others' art to collaborate upon illustrated editions. That poets were makers of pictures, as the Roman poet Horace had declared, was assumed throughout the century. They became interpreters of pictures also, as can be seen in Bowles, Wordsworth, and especially Browning. For many later nineteenth century poets, however, the writer was no longer a prophet but a critic, concerned less with cosmic purpose than with man's revelation of himself through art.

It is symptomatic of the times that poetry became more personal, less prestigious, and even private (Dickinson, Hardy, Hopkins) as public utterances turned instead to evaluation of the literary past. Thus, Arnold virtually abandoned poetry for criticism of various kinds, while D. G. Rossetti, Lowell, Swinburne, and William Watson all reveal critical aspirations overtopping creative ones. Major anthologies of the time, edited by Edmund Clarence Stedman and Francis Palgrave, show that poetry appealed to the later nineteenth century more as conventional verbal prettiness than as original thought; a great deal of it was essentially decoration. Fanciful, but not imaginative (in the searching, Romantic sense), late Victorian poetry soon became, with only a few exceptions, a minor art, as statements of intellectual importance tended increasingly to be made in prose.

The Pre-Raphaelite Brotherhood of Dante Gabriel Rossetti (1828-1882) and his circle, which fostered both poetry and art, was a major attempt to defend creative imagination against the economic, social, and intellectual forces that were depressing it, which is to say, against the impersonality of manufacture, the bad taste of the rising middle class, and the unidimensional reality of empirical science. William Michael Rossetti (1829-1919) was, with his brother, largely responsible for bringing Whitman, Joaquin Miller, and Edward Fitzgerald (*The Rubáyat of Omar Khayyám*, 1859) to critical attention, while reviving interest in the work of Blake and Shelley. Only a small coterie in London, however, fully appreciated how desperate the artistic situation had become. From them emerged William Butler Yeats (1865-1939), an Irish cultural nationalist influenced by Thomas Moore and Sir Walter Scott, who based his major poems (mostly twentieth century) upon the bold visions of Blake and Shelley, while rejecting Tennysonian doubt and the depressing outlook of scientific materialism. Tennyson, Browning, Whitman, Arnold, Hardy, and Yeats are now regarded as the most significant poets of the latter part of the nineteenth century, and all have had their impact upon subsequent writers.

Dennis R. Dean

TWENTIETH CENTURY POETRY

Twentieth century poetry has been variously characterized as romantic, antiromantic, impersonal, highly personal, chaotic, orderly, classical, symbolist, wholly untraditional, reasoned and measured, incomprehensible—depending upon the critic whom one reads. This radical diversity suggests a fundamental problem with poetry in the twentieth century: it has no clear path to follow. Finding previous poetry inadequate to deal with the situation in which he finds himself, the modern poet must create anew, must, in Wallace Stevens' phrase, "find out what will suffice." The modern poem is an act of exploration. In the absence of givens, it must carve out its own niche, make its own *raison d'être*.

Not surprisingly, then, twentieth century poetry is marked by astonishing variety. What logic could successfully yoke together Robert Frost and Allen Ginsberg, Philip Larkin and William Carlos Williams, Sylvia Plath and Ezra Pound? None, so long as the category of modern poetry is understood to be a fixed entity; such definitions always aim at closure and exclusion. Nevertheless, it is possible to see all of modern poetry as a piece, and that possibility is what this essay hopes to explore.

Modern poetry began with a sense of discontinuity, a sense that the world of the twentieth century was not merely different as one century always is from another but decisively different, qualitatively different from all the centuries past. This sense of discontinuity was shared by the other arts; it was "on or about December 1910," Virginia Woolf wrote, that "human character changed." This shared conviction of radical change gave rise to the far-flung, loosely defined movement in the arts known as "modernism," characterized in poetry by the fragmented, elliptical, allusive styles of Ezra Pound and T. S. Eliot.

To believe that the poetry of the Pound-Eliot school constitutes the whole of important modern poetry, however, or that modernism was a cohesive, unified movement, is to ignore many of its characteristic elements. As early as the first meetings of the Imagist group, gathered around Ezra Pound in England in 1912, the diversity of talent, ideas, and aesthetics among modernist poets was already clear. Modernism was not a unified movement even in its early stages. Moreover, there were significant poets who did not buy into modernism at all. Against Pound's famous injunction to "compose in the manner of the musical phrase, not the metronome," there is Frost's equally well-known statement that writing free verse is like "playing tennis without a net." Against the heavily idea-laden poetry of Eliot and the New Critic/Fugitive poets—John Crowe Ransom and Allen Tate, in particular—stand William Carlos Williams' "no ideas but in things" and Archibald MacLeish's "a poem should not mean but be." The pillars of what is commonly regarded as modernism, then, found themselves flanked right and left by dissenters, as well as faced by independent thinkers within their camp. Modernist poetry, as commonly construed, represents a fairly limited if important range of the whole of modern poetry. If discussion of that entire range (and the diversity of British and American poetry in this century is staggering) is to go forward, *modern* must be reclaimed from modernist. As distinguished from the self-consciously modernist, "modern poetry" can be understood to be roughly synonymous with twentieth century poetry, excepting the occasional reactionary or nostalgic poet and a few carry-overs from Victorianism.

Influences and Trends

Modern literature is less united in what it stands for than in what it opposes. In a sense, almost all writing in the twentieth century attempts to throw over the nineteenth, particularly those aspects of it generally classified as "Victorian." Both the sociopolitical and the literary elements of Victorianism come under fire from the modern artist, and the combination of targets should not be surprising, since politics and economics combine with literature in the nineteenth century to form what appears to modern eyes to be a uniform culture. While this uniformity may be largely mythical, it nevertheless has become one of the *données* of discussions of Victorianism.

Behind most of the philosophical, social, and political inquiries of the nineteenth century, not merely in England and America but throughout the Western world, lies the idea of progress, of a goal toward which society is moving perceptibly. One of the clearest manifestations of this idea is Karl Marx's *telos*, the goal or endpoint of civilization's quest for utopia. Marxism depends on this idea as on no other; the supposition that one can chart the course of societies with certainty that each will follow the same line of development rests on the unstated assumption that all societies are moving in the same direction, and that therefore there must be some goal toward which all, willingly or not, tend. Marx is not alone, of course, in so thinking. The utilitarianism of Jeremy Bentham and John Stuart Mill, with its emphasis on "the greatest good for the greatest number," builds on similar foundations: that act is best which, since it offers maximum benefits to the most members of society, promotes the greatest social progress. Other progress-centered developments in thought range from American "Manifest Destiny" (and other nations' quest for empire, as well) to Mary Baker Eddy's "Every day in every way things get better and better."

Nor is this phenomenon limited to social thought; the single greatest scientific contribution of the century bears the mark of its time. Charles Darwin's evolutionary theory is every bit as dependent on the notion of *telos* as is Marx's: the result of the fittest surviving to mate with one another is that newer and fitter forms of life constantly come into being. The newest and fittest form, naturally, is man. That Darwinian thought is a logical extension of nineteenth century notions of progress is borne out by the readiness with which evolution was accepted not by biologists, but by social thinkers. Social Darwinism combines evolutionary thought with the already accepted mode of utilitarianism.

Against this concept of progress lies its opposite, and what may even be seen as its necessary complement. A society that is constantly progressing is undergoing constant change, which in turn means that traditional institutions and ways of life must break down. In *The Education of Henry Adams* (1907), Adams expresses this idea in terms of the twin images of virgin and dynamo. The virgin, representative of traditional culture, symbolizes stability and order, a manageable, if static, society. The dynamo, the modern society, spins constantly faster, changing incessantly, leaving its members with a sense of chaos and confusion. While modern society shows progress, it also falls into relativism, since the traditional institutions on which absolutes are based are breaking down. Whereas the idea of progress was a product of mid-nineteenth century thinkers, the time of the Great Exhibition in London, the notion of cultural breakdown achieved its widest circulation late in the nineteenth century and into the twentieth, receiving its fullest development, perhaps, in the work of T. S. Eliot.

Nineteenth century literature, particularly in England, mirrored the development of thought in the period. It should not be surprising, therefore, that the chief poet of High Victorianism, Alfred, Lord Tennyson, was tremendously popular as well as critically acclaimed, and that the same should be true for the novelist Charles Dickens. The artists of mid-century specialized in giving the people what they wanted. Walt Whitman, the nineteenth century poet to whom American moderns so often look, would seem to be an exception. One must remember, of course, that Whitman's work was largely ignored during his lifetime, that he was not a popular poet by any means when his work first appeared, and that the recognized poets of the era, such as John Greenleaf Whittier and Henry Wadsworth Longfellow, worked with the public's desires more firmly in mind. Then, too, even Whitman wrote directly to his audience much more than the typical modern poet (if there be such a thing), does and his great poem, *Leaves of Grass* (1855), is a public celebration of the people.

The late nineteenth century produced the expected countermovement, in which the characteristic poem is much darker, more decadent, suspicious of the openness and health of the High Victorians. Under the influence of the darker Romantics and the French symbolists (who got their own dose of dark Romanticism from Edgar Allan Poe), the late Victorians from the Pre-Raphaelites on demonstrate a tendency toward the sinister and the unhealthy, toward madness and dissipation. Prostitutes, drug addicts, criminals—all those, in short, from the underside of society, from the social strata largely ignored by Tennyson—figure heavily in the work of Dante Gabriel Rossetti and Algernon Charles Swinburne, Ernest Dowson, Lionel Johnson, the early

William Butler Yeats, and, of course, Oscar Wilde. Their fascination with dark subjects and dark treatments shows a suspicion of the methods and beliefs of the earlier Victorians analogous to Adams' suspicion of progress. Their work collectively embodies the fin de siècle sense of impending change, the exhaustion of old modes, the existential ennui of a society in decline. The late Victorian poets were not a new beginning but a clear end, a cry for the new, while in America the cry was silence, the absence of any major poetic talents. On both sides of the Atlantic, poetry in English was a gap waiting to be filled, and awaiting of something as yet unknown.

The early years of the twentieth century produced three separate groups of poetic innovators: the Georgian poets, the Sitwell group, and the Imagists. Although all three failed to sustain movements, each contributed elements to the larger field of modern poetry. The first two groups were decidedly minor, producing little work that has continued to be held in high esteem by the critical or poetic communities. The Georgians are often dismissed as the old guard that the true modernists struggled to overthrow; yet such an easy dismissal overlooks the radical nature of the movement. As Geoffrey Bullough has pointed out in *The Trend of Modern Poetry* (1934), Georgian poetry, while a throwback to Romanticism, represents a break with the Imperial poetry of the same period, and the established poets of the day looked upon it with some horror. Moreover, while the movement itself died down, some of its work in loosening the reins on traditional verse forms has survived, as one can see in the repeated comparisons of Philip Larkin's work with the Georgian poetry of Edward Thomas. The conversational diction and simplicity of their poetry, as Bullough further notes, has become something of a standard feature in certain strains of modern poetry. Similarly, the work of the group gathered around the Sitwells ultimately came to little, yet there is much in that poetry that foreshadows developments in other, more important poets. The spiritual despair, the often forced gaiety, the combination of wit and bleakness of Sitwellian poetry shows up in many other writers' work in the century. Ultimately, their work is for the most part ignored or forgotten because they had very little to say; their poetry had much surface but lacked substance.

Of the three, Imagism is by far the most important school for modern verse at large. The goal of the movement, as the name implies, was to bring to poetry a new emphasis on the image as a structural, rather than an ornamental, element. Growing out of French symbolism and taking techniques, styles, and forms from Japanese haiku, tanka, and hokku; Chinese ideograms; and Classical Greek and Provençal troubadour lyrics, Imagism reflects the diverse interests of its founders and their rather dilettantish nature.

While there were a number of very fine practitioners, among them F. S. Flint, D. H. Lawrence, T. E. Hulme, H. D. (Hilda Doolittle), Richard Aldington, William Carlos Williams, Carl Sandburg, and Amy Lowell, it is

Ezra Pound who stands as the major spokesman and publicist for the group. Pound, along with Aldington and H. D., formulated the three cardinal rules of the movement in "A Retrospect": direct treatment of the thing discussed; absolute economy of diction; and composition "in the sequence of the musical phrase, not in the sequence of the metronome." At various times others from the group expanded upon or modified those three initial rules, yet they stand as the basis for Imagist technique. In fact, they are descriptive of the movement rather than prescriptive; the Imagist group had been meeting in one form or another for several years when Pound formulated these precepts. Much of the philosophical basis for the school comes from Hulme's study of Henri Bergson's thought. Under Hulme's influence the varied interests of the members jelled into a more or less cohesive body of theory, at least for a short time.

The poetry produced by the group, although by no means uniform, shared certain characteristics. First of all, it was an attempt to put the creation of images at the center of the poetic act. The image is a sudden moment of truth, or, as Pound describes it, "an intellectual and emotional complex in an instant of time." It shares a good deal with other modern moments of revelation, from Gerard Manley Hopkins' "inscape" to James Joyce's "epiphany." The brevity of the Imagist poem, another defining characteristic particularly of those produced early in the group's history, is a logical extension of the emphasis on the image. As an attempt to eschew rhetorical and narrative forms and to replace them with the "pure" poetic moment, the Imagist poem, existing almost solely for the creation of the image, completes its mission with the completion of that image. A long poem of the type would simply be a series of discrete images whose relation to one another could only be inferred, since explicative transitions would be a violation of precept. The longer poems produced under the leadership of Lowell evidence a loosening of form and a laxity of craftsmanship. The late Imagist poems are not so much transitional, pointing toward some new development, as they are decadent, indicative of the movement's demise.

That Imagism would be short-lived was almost inevitable. The goals and techniques of the movement were antithetical to sustaining even a poem of any considerable duration, let alone a school. The tiny Imagist poem is much too limiting to allow its creator much variety from one poem to the next. The chance to explore themes, ideas, and beliefs simply does not exist, since that sort of argument-oriented poetry is what Imagism sought to replace. Yet even the proponents of Imagism had larger plans than their espoused methods would allow. Pound, for example, even while he was most closely associated with the group, was working on his plan for the *Cantos* (1925-1972). Nevertheless, even if Imagism lacked the qualities to make it a sustained movement, its methods have been adopted in the great majority of poems written in this century. Of course Imagist techniques appear in Williams' *Paterson* (1946-

1958) and in the *Cantos*, but they also appear in the work of such non-Imagists as Allen Tate, Eliot, Sylvia Plath, and Dylan Thomas, and make possible such later developments as surrealism and the "deep image" poetry of James Wright and Robert Bly.

Imagism, itself a product of diverse influences, is only one of a great many influences on modern poetry. Perhaps the single most important influence has been nineteenth century French symbolism. Ironically, the source of much symbolist theory was Poe, whose work was largely ignored by Anglo-American critics. The French, however, saw in his darkly Romantic speculations, in the bleakness and horror of his work, even in his impulse toward dissipation, the vehicle appropriate to poetry on the modern predicament. In his own country he may have been a Gothic oddity; in France he was a prophet. The work produced by his French followers—Jules Laforgue, Tristan Corbière, Charles Baudelaire, Stéphane Mallarmé, Arthur Rimbaud, and Paul Verlaine—incorporated much from Poe: the darkness, the exploration of life's underside, the penchant for urban landscapes, and, most importantly, the centrality of the symbol.

Certainly symbols have always been used in poetry, and little that the symbolists accomplished with symbols was entirely new. What was fresh and unique, however, was their insistence on the symbol as the structural *raison d'être* of the poem. No longer relegated to the status of ornament or occasional item, the symbol became for these men the goal one actively sought to achieve in the poem. Like so many of their modern followers, they were reacting against the Scylla and Charybdis of loose, discursive verse on the one hand, and didactic, allegorical verse on the other. Also like their followers, they mistrusted language, having seen too much bad poetry turned out by following conventional use of "poetic" language. They therefore felt that the achievement of poetry must lie elsewhere than in the play of words. Their solution was to place heavy emphasis on the poetic moment, the symbol. They attempted to separate radically the symbolic from the allegorical use of imagery, and there is about much symbolist poetry a vagueness that refuses to let the symbol be quite pinned down. In some of the followers of symbolism, particularly in the work of the English poets of the 1890's, that vagueness drifts off into airy realms too thin for habitation.

Symbolism found its way into Anglo-American modern poetry by so many routes that it is nearly impossible to chronicle them all. Nevertheless, a few of the points of entry require mention. The earliest important mention of symbolism is in Arthur Symons' famous book of 1899, *The Symbolist Movement in Literature*. Symons, along with Yeats and other poets of the Rhymers' Club, introduced the work of these Frenchmen to English audiences not only through essays and defenses, but also through original English poetry on symbolist models. Giving as much attention to prose writers as to poets, Symons hailed the new literary wind blowing from Paris as one that did not shrink from neurosis, nightmare, and decadence. Of Mallarmé he says, "All his life he has been haunted by the desire to create, not so much something new in literature, as a literature which should be itself a new art." This sense of newness, of shocking, appalling novelty, was immediately grasped by defenders and vilifiers alike, and symbolism itself became a symbol. Oscar Wilde could not have set the character of Dorian Gray so well in ten pages of description, at least for his immediate audience, as he did by having Dorian reading, at several key points, J. K. Huysmans' *À rebours* (1884, *Against the Grain*). This first wave of enthusiasm, however, was mainly a matter of imitation, and if it largely died out before producing any major works of interest, it was because the writers who experimented in the mode were playing with an exotic toy, not working with an instrument fitted to their own machinery.

The second major attempt at importation, this one aiming for domestication, grew eventually into Imagism. If the work of Symons and Yeats was important because it showed that such a thing as symbolism existed, Imagism's importance lay in the translation of a movement from one century and one place into another movement in another century and another place. Imagism sought to further refine the terms of the symbol; Pound, writing of the aims of Imagism, said that symbolic function was one of the possible uses of the image, but that it should never be so important that the poem is lost on a person for whom "a hawk is simply a hawk."

The third major importer of symbolism into English was T. S. Eliot. He wrote extensively about the symbolists; he copied their style, even to the point of writing in French in some early poems; he openly acknowledged his debt in direct borrowings from their work; and, most important, he produced the most complete example of a symbolist poem in English, *The Waste Land* (1922). In the use of urban landscape, the feverish, nightmarish quality of the imagery, the darkness of the vision, the layering of symbols and images within symbols and images, *The Waste Land* demonstrates its creator's overwhelming debt to the symbolists. The poem's centrality in the modern canon lends further weight to the significance of symbolism for modern Anglo-American poetry. Knowingly or not, every poet who has found himself affected by Eliot's great work has also been affected by Laforgue and Baudelaire.

Symbolism was not, however, the only major influence on modern poetry. Another example of Eliot's importance as an arbiter of poetic taste and style is the resurrection of the English Metaphysical poets as models for modern verse. Long ignored by English critics, the Metaphysicals—John Donne, in particular—offer the modern poet another use of a controlling metaphor. If the symbolists reintroduced the poet to the symbol, Donne and his contemporaries—Andrew Marvell, George Herbert, Henry Vaughan, Richard Crashaw—showed him how to use it in extended forms. The conceit of the

Metaphysical poem, like the symbol of the symbolist poem, is an example of figurative language used not as ornament, but as structural principle. Since the conceit of a Donne poem is used as a way of integrating metaphor with argument, the model served to overcome the limiting element of Imagism and, to a lesser extent, of symbolism itself. Both the latter movements, since they eschewed argument as a poetic method, shut themselves off from the possibility of sustained use. The Metaphysical conceit (and what is the image of the wasteland if not a conceit, a unifying metaphor?) allows Eliot to adapt Imagist and symbolist techniques to a long, elaborately structured poem.

Another, very different model for long poems was found in Walt Whitman's *Leaves of Grass*. Whitman's great contribution is in the area of open form. The sometimes chatty, sometimes oratorial, usually freewheeling style of his poetry has done more than anything else to show the path away from iambic verse. His influence is clear on such poets as Williams, Lawrence, Ginsberg and his fellow Beat poets, and Charles Olson and the Black Mountain poets, yet he also often moves through less obvious channels, and virtually any poet who has experimented with open forms owes him a debt. Even a poet as strongly opposed in principle to the looseness of his verse as Pound accorded Whitman grudging respect.

Against this characteristically American model stands the typically British example of Thomas Hardy. Where Whitman's poetic is antitraditional and iconoclastic, open and rhythmic and boisterous, Hardy's is tight-lipped, satisfied to work within established forms, dour and bleak. Yet Hardy's work was not merely traditional; while he worked within standard forms, he often pushed their limits outward, expressing the modern dissatisfaction with form not by rejecting it but by bending it to suit his needs. Very much Victorian, he still anticipates the modern, standing as a threshold figure for such followers as W. H. Auden, Philip Larkin, Roy Fuller, and perhaps the entirety of the British Movement poets of the 1950's.

Both Whitman and Hardy offer alternatives to the mainstream of modernist poetry as embodied by Pound and Eliot, the Fugitive poets, William Empson, and Geoffrey Hill (to cite a recent embodiment). Contemporary Whitman-esque poetry—such as Olson's *The Maximus Poems* (1960), which also are strongly indebted to the *Cantos*, and Ginsberg's "Howl"—is commonly regarded as avant-garde, that in the Hardy line as reactionary or antimodern, yet to accept such labels is to misunderstand the nature of modern poetry. These three camps represent not so much three separate attitudes toward art or aesthetics, as three attempts at dealing with the world poetically, those attempts being based on regionalism as much as anything else. The poetics of the Eliot-Pound camp are essentially cosmopolitan, the result of ransacking international literary history from the classics and Chinese lyrics to the Provençal poets to the symbolists. The other two schools are much more closely related to place, to national identity. Auden is not less modern than Williams;

he is more British. Moreover, to insist on too clear a dividing line among the camps is to falsify the situation. While the influence of one figure or school of poetry may be more pronounced on some groups or individuals, there is also a general influence on the whole of modern poetry, so that the struggle of a poet such as Larkin to loosen forms may be the result of the undetected (and probably undetectable) influence of Whitman, who has caused a general trend toward openness. On the other hand, if there is a rancor in Ginsberg that is not present in Whitman, it is perhaps that the later poet has picked up the typically modern ambivalence that is present in Hardy. In short, one should not be too hasty in excluding any potential influence, nor in assessing a poet's "modernity."

The foregoing discussion, while it has applicability to the entire century, fails to address some of the significant developments since World War II. Poetry seems to have undergone a mid-century crisis, during which time it made a number of motions that appeared to indicate rejection of the poetry that had immediately preceded it. The Movement in England, the Beats and Black Mountain poets in America, confessional poetry, and surrealist poetry are all symptomatic of change, and the critical tendency has been to read that change as sweeping, as a revolution. There is, however, much evidence to suggest just the contrary—that what has taken place since 1945 has not been revolutionary but domestic: a periodic housecleaning occasioned by changes in fashion and perhaps also by changes in the world around the poet.

It is not entirely unfair to say that modern poetry came into being when the dilettantism of Georgian and Sitwellian and Imagist poetry ran into World War I. The utter inability of those movements to deal effectively with a world in which such a cataclysm was possible forced poets to abandon certain precepts that had failed them. It is no mere coincidence, for example, that Imagism flourished in the years immediately preceding the war when, as Paul Fussell notes in his study *The Great War and Modern Memory* (1975), England was blithely, even determinedly ignorant of impending events, or that it faltered and died during the war years. The Imagist poem did not offer sufficient scope for the creation of a work of "a certain magnitude." Eliot's great contribution, as mentioned earlier, lay in grafting Imagist (and symbolist) technique onto forms that allowed greater expansiveness.

Similarly, the tremendous destruction brought about in World War II caused a shift in attitudes and, by extension, in poetic practices. In World War I, the destruction was limited largely to combatants; battle was a distant thing. By the end of World War II, the bombing of population centers, the unveiling of atomic weaponry, and the revelation of genocide had made warfare both more personal and more terrible. The poetics of impersonality and detachment as sponsored by Eliot suddenly seemed outmoded, and the movement in much of modern poetry since that time has been toward a renewed involvement with the self. Eliot's self is an extension of culture, a member of church, state, and critical school, a representative of agencies and institutions. His concern with the self, from "The Love Song of J. Alfred Prufrock" to the *Four Quartets* (1943), is a curiously impersonal involvement. After the war, however, many poets turned their verse inward, examining the self with all its flaws, hungers, and hidden violence.

Another branch of postwar American and English poetry has been heavily influenced by surrealism. Whereas the early modernists went directly to the symbolists, these postwar poets first encountered symbolism through its later development, surrealism. The French surrealism of André Breton has had comparatively little impact in England, where only a handful of writers, notably David Gascoyne and Dylan Thomas, have employed its techniques with any regularity, and even less in America. Spanish surrealism, on the other hand, has been imported into American poetry through the work of Robert Bly, James Wright, and W. S. Merwin, all prolific translators, and into English poetry in small bits through Charles Tomlinson's association with Octavio Paz. The "deep image" poetry of Bly and Wright, owing much to Federico García Lorca, César Vallejo, and Pablo Neruda, often reads like a symbolist rendering of deep consciousness. The New York school of Kenneth Koch, Frank O'Hara, and John Ashbery also demonstrates its indebtedness to earlier, continental surrealists.

Earlier native poets have been reevaluated in the postwar period as well. Hardy has become even more important to certain strains of British poetry than he was before the war, while the reappraisal of Whitman and the discovery of Emily Dickinson as a poetic resource has led American poets to a new sense of tradition. If Beat poetry would be impossible without Whitman, then confessional poetry would also be impossible, or at least radically different, without Dickinson. Her intense concern with self and soul, her death obsession, her striking use of associative imagery, her use of very simple poetic forms for very complex ideas, all show up in the work of Robert Lowell, Sylvia Plath, Anne Sexton, and John Berryman.

As the interest in Dickinson suggests, the renewed emphasis on the self in postwar poetry leads to a new involvement with Romanticism. Often, though, it is with the darker side of Romanticism that contemporary poets interact— with symbolism, with Lawrence and Dickinson—with those elements, in short, that show the self on the edge of disaster or oblivion. There is, of course, the buoyant optimism of Whitman to counteract this trend, yet even his influence often appears darker than the original. The return to favor of Romanticism might be the sole real break with earlier moderns, with modernism, with Eliot's classicism.

Yet even here such a generalization is dangerous. One must remember that Lawrence, Williams, Wallace Stevens, Dylan Thomas, Robert Graves, and even elements in Eliot's work belie the antiromantic stance usually accepted as a basis for modernism. Similarly, the more positive attitude toward the

Romantics is by no means universal. The Movement poets, for example, adopted a vigorous antiromantic position in their dryly ironic verse, while there is much in Romanticism that even those poets who seem closest to it find unappealing. The modern Romantics, like the modern classicists, select only those elements that fit the modern platform they happen to be building.

Not all influences on recent poetry are domestic. Like the earlier moderns, the postwar poets have made forays into exotic poetics. Indeed, the period of contemporary poetry might be called "the Age of Translation," in which English-language poetry is open to the riches of world poetry as never before. Both Japanese and Chinese poetry have been particularly influential in the postwar years, notably in the work of Kenneth Rexroth and Gary Snyder. In this period there has been a marked trend toward going below the surface of Asian culture to the deep structure of its modes of thought. Snyder, for example, spent several years in a Zen monastery in Kyoto, and while the experience did not turn him away from Western society entirely, it caused him to reexamine more familiar cultural forms in the light of another perspective.

Another distinctive characteristic of modern poetry is its preoccupation with myth and archetype. To be sure, much of the poetry in the Western tradition, from Homer and Ovid to Percy Bysshe Shelley, from Dante to Tennyson, is explicitly concerned with myth, yet the modern sense of the mythic differs from anything that went before. In modern poetry, everyday life is frequently seen as a series of rituals, often acted out unawares, by which mankind expresses its relation to the universal.

In part this distinctively modern awareness of myth and archetype can be attributed to the influence of the new science of anthropology as exemplified in Sir James Frazer's pioneering work *The Golden Bough* (1890-1915). The work of Sigmund Freud and C. G. Jung early in the twentieth century further added to the modern writer's interest in myth. Where Frazer examined mythic patterns as cultural phenomena, Freud and Jung demonstrated the ways in which individuals internalize such patterns. Myth and archetype derive their power, then, from their timeless hold on the individual consciousness.

The result of this thinking was a tremendous explosion of genuinely new literature, of poetry and fiction in which the quotidian acts of ordinary individuals take on meaning beyond their understanding. Among the fruits of this new flowering were the two most important works produced in English in this century, both too significant for subsequent writers to ignore and too awesome to copy. One was the story of a single day in Dublin in 1904, during which the ramblings of an Irish Jew parallel the wanderings chronicled in the *Odyssey* (c. 800 B.C.): James Joyce's *Ulysses* (1922). The other, of course, was the *The Waste Land*. In his essay "*Ulysses*, Order, and Myth," Eliot announced that in place of the traditional narrative method, the modern artist could henceforth use the mythic method, that fiction and poetry would gain power not from their isolated stories, but through the connection of the stories to a universal pattern.

William Butler Yeats, of course, had been working in the field of myth in poetry for a very long time, and had been actively creating his own mythology, through the work surrounding *A Vision* (1925), for several years. Lawrence, too, was a mythmaker, both in his poetry and in his fiction. Yet both of these writers' uses of myth constitute dead ends of sorts, for their mythologies are largely private, unusable by others. The mainstream of poetic use of myth in the twentieth century runs, not through the mythmakers, but through myth-followers. From Eliot and Pound to Sylvia Plath and Seamus Heaney, modern poetry has produced a great deal of work that follows mythic patterns.

A final defining characteristic of modern poetry is its ambivalence. The modern poet seems, on the whole, constitutionally incapable of wholeheartedly loving or hating the world in which he lives. The foremost example of ambivalence is the work of Yeats, in which he simultaneously strives for release from the world and regret at the possibility of release. Indeed, Yeats carries this double attitude further than anyone else, turning it into an elaborate system. Yeats provides an elaborate image of that ambivalence with his "whirling gyres": the interlocking gyres stand for ideas, beliefs, and qualities which, while completely opposed to one another, nevertheless require each other for completion. In Yeats, one idea is never whole; it must have its opposite idea, for only the interlocking pair are completed, as the tower is incomplete without the winding stair (to use his own symbols).

As a result, Yeats is virtually incapable of rendering a wholehearted judgment in his poetry. He sees both good and bad, the positive and the negative, in all things. In his poems about the Irish Civil War, for example, although he supports Irish independence, he can see the destruction brought about by members of the IRA as well as by the British Royal Irish Constabulary. In "Easter 1916," he celebrates the courage of the insurrectionists, yet at the same time questions their wisdom. Even that questioning is edgy, incomplete; he says that perhaps it was unwise, that perhaps it will set back the cause of Ireland; he refuses either to denounce the uprising or to praise it unreservedly. The most famous example of Yeatsian ambivalence, mirroring the pair of gyres, is a pair of interlocking poems about Byzantium. In "Sailing to Byzantium," the speaker is old and world-weary. He seeks the quietude, the tranquillity of the artificial world represented by Byzantium; he speaks longingly of the work of the city's artisans, of escaping out of the world of flesh into the world of pure beauty. In "Byzantium" he finds himself looking back across the ocean, again longingly, at the world of flesh and mire. Here he is weary of the world of timeless beauty, and the imagery of the poem's desires is of living creatures, particularly of the dolphin that could carry him back to the living world.

The Byzantium poems embody a fundamental feature of modern poetry:

the chaos and contingency of the modern world leads the poet to distaste, to a desire for escape, to a retreat into the sheltered world of aesthetics that Edmund Wilson referred to in *Axel's Castle* (1931). Yet contrary to Wilson's contentions, that move is very much an act of engaging the world, every bit as much as Rimbaud's rejection of poetry (the example that Wilson cites as the alternative) for the life of a gunrunner. The characteristic attitude is not rejection but ambivalence; the poet, while wishing to withdraw from the world, is nevertheless caught in it, is a part of it, can never escape from it. His poetry, therefore, while it may attempt to hold the world at arm's length, still remains in contact with it, and is constantly a response to, not an escape from, life.

Yeats and Hardy are models for this attitudinal complex, along with the late Victorians—such as Algernon Charles Swinburne, Ernest Dowson, and Dante Gabriel Rossetti—and the French symbolists. British poetry tends to be dominated by ambivalence more than its American counterpart does; the Beats, for example, seem less ambivalent than the British Movement poets. In general, however, modern poetry may be characterized fairly as the poetry of ambivalence.

In turn, much of the attitudinal bias of the New Criticism—the influential critical movement spawned by modernism—can be explained on the basis of ambivalence: the emphasis on irony, tension, ambiguity, as keys to poetry; the elevation of the Metaphysical poets and the concomitant devaluation of Romantic and Victorian verse; the blindness to poetry that is open or single-minded. Despite its shortcomings, the New Criticism's great contribution was that it taught readers, and still teaches them, how to read modern poetry. That most of the illustrious practitioners of the New Criticism—Tate, Robert Penn Warren, John Crowe Ransom, William Empson—were also poets of considerable accomplishment should come as no surprise. The New Critics, despite the claims of Cleanth Brooks and others, did not read all kinds of poetry equally well, yet their sensitivity to modern poetry remains unequaled, because they were so attuned to the various forms that ambivalence can take in a poem.

The Poem Sequence

Modern poetry—particularly, after *The Waste Land*—is characterized by deliberated discontinuities. Several impulses came together more or less at once to create the disjointed poetics of modern verse. One, of course, was the inheritance of Imagism, the concentration on the intensely poetic moment almost to the exclusion of everything else. More fundamental was the sense of fragmentation in society and in consciousness that many modern writers express, a sense of radical discontinuity with the past. One consequence of this sense of fragmentation was a distrust of language. The ambivalence of the modern writer toward the world leads him to suspect received forms, particularly those forms that suggest continuity and wholeness. Such completeness contradicts his experience of the world, in which things are fragmented, discontinuous, chaotic, intractable. To blithely write long, flowing poems in the manner of Tennyson would be to violate one's own experience of the world and one's own consciousness. Other literary forms come under suspicion as well, but the modern poet is particularly wary of sustained, regular forms. Even such artists as Philip Larkin or Yeats who work in received forms often take great pains to change them, to make them less regular. The corrollary—a suspicion traceable to the symbolists—is that language itself is unreliable, a debased medium encrusted with connotations from previous usage.

These several forces came together to move the modern poem toward disjuncture and discontinuity. Again, in this respect as in so much else, *The Waste Land* was seminal work. The poem leaps from image to image, throwing unconnected and even antithetical elements violently together to produce a work that, although it draws heavily on earlier literature, is like nothing that had gone before. The links between the five main sections of the poem have particularly troubled readers, since they are not related in any immediately identifiable manner. Still, they do cohere, they do move toward some final point as a group that none of them achieves individually. Their cohesiveness is a function of each section's relation to the whole, rather than, as one might expect, the relations between pairs of successive sections.

When the disjunctive poetics of modern verse are practiced in works of large scale, as in *The Waste Land*, traditional forms must necessarily be scrapped. In very short lyrics, of course, there is no problem with the connection between sections, but in longer works the sections must stand together in some logical fashion or risk the outrage heaped on Eliot's work when it first appeared. Even so, a poem can go on piling image upon image without respite for just so long before it breaks down, before the reader becomes hopelessly lost in the morass. To circumvent the problems raised by continuity in a disjunctive poetry, the modern writer has turned to the poem sequence. The sequence has been variously defined, but perhaps it is most satisfactory to think of it as a series of poems that are capable of standing alone but that take on greater significance through their mutual interaction.

Thus, a sequence is a long poem made of shorter poems; the modern poem sequence has its opposite number in what Joanne V. Creighton, in her study *Faulkner's Craft of Revision* (1977), calls the "short-story composite." The composite is a book composed of chapters that are themselves stories; the stories can be read separately, as in an ordinary collection, but they also form a unified whole when read together. She cites Ernest Hemingway's *In Our Time* (1924) and William Faulkner's *Go Down, Moses* (1942) as such works, in which the writer has given as much planning and work to the book's larger structure (as in a novel) as he has to the individual parts (as in a normal short-story collection).

The poem sequence is not the exclusive property of the twentieth century, of course. Many earlier examples can be cited, depending on how one judges such matters: Rimbaud's *Une Saison en Enfer* (1873, *A Season in Hell*), Whitman's *Leaves of Grass*, Rossetti's sonnet sequence *The House of Life* (1869), William Morris' *The Earthly Paradise* (1868-1870), perhaps even Dante's *La Divina Commedia* (c. 1320, *The Divine Comedy*). Yet in almost every case, the premodern sequence attempts to justify its disunity by displaying the unity among its sections, by talking its way through or over the gaps. By contrast, the modern sequence often works through silence, by exploiting the interstices, allowing ambiguity or multiple meanings to slip in through the cracks. The unexplained juxtaposition of elements adds to the possible meanings of the work; the reader must participate in the construction of the sequence.

In the loosest possible sense, any book of poems is a sequence; so, in the twentieth century, sequences come in all denominations. Both Lawrence and Yeats experimented with sequencing fairly informally in their work. Lawrence often collected his poems in a book around a theme or a method of creation, and strung poems together by resonant phrasings, as in the group of poems whose central piece is "The Ship of Death." Yeats, too, carefully arranged the poems in his books, and in his revisions not only changed poems but the order as well. At the other end of the scale stands *The Waste Land*, which is not, strictly speaking, a sequence at all, yet which shares some characteristics of the sequence: fragmentation, separate titles for its sections, length, and scope. Still, it fails to meet one of the criteria: its separate sections cannot stand alone as poems. One cannot dissect the poem without making hash of it. It looks like a sequence, and indeed it is often listed as one, but it is not. It is a long, fragmentary, truly modern poem. To find a real poem sequence in Eliot, one must look to the end, to *Four Quartets*.

The Waste Land owed its striking discontinuity in large measure to the blue pencil of Ezra Pound. Pound's editorial assistance, as in the case of Hemingway's *In Our Time*, nearly always took the form of radical deletion, and in this poem he cut much transitional and explanatory material, resulting in a formal jumpiness that reinforces the cultural and personal neurasthenia. It is to Pound's own work, though, that one must look to find an early example of a poem sequence.

Both *Homage to Sextus Propertius* (1934) and *Hugh Selwyn Mauberley* (1920) are early sequences by Pound, and, while not mere exercises, are trial pieces for his major life sequence, the *Cantos*, which even then he had begun. Both are attempts at sustained works made up of smaller units. The *Homage to Sextus Propertius* is a single poem made up of twelve loose translations or renderings of poems by Propertius, each of which had stood alone in the original. The effect, in Pound, is of a series of more or less autonomous pieces that have an affinity for one another, a common language or flavor, a function in part of the Latinate diction employed by the poet. His *Hugh Selwyn Mauberley* is a more recognizable sequence, unified by the persona of Mauberley. When read as a whole, the poems take on much greater meaning through their collective resonance. The renderings of Propertius' work are loosely affiliated, are similar to one another; the poems in *Hugh Selwyn Mauberley* are parts of a whole.

It is in the *Cantos* that Pound works most concertedly in the poem sequence. Taking Dante's *The Divine Comedy* as its extremely loose model (Pound once said he was writing a *commedia agnostica*), the poem works its way through ancient and modern history, Eastern and Western thought and art, economics, literature, politics, music, architecture, and personal experience. The *Cantos* comprises a record of a modern poet's experience, an epic-scale work of the man of sensibility in the world.

The unity of the sequence is established through purely internal means: echoes, repetitions, thematic and ideological ties. The apparent obscurity of a given canto is a function of the unity of the poet's mind: the obscure utterance will likely be expanded, explained, revised, rearticulated at some later point in the proceedings. Thus the *Cantos* have a hermetic quality that can make reading a single canto difficult, while rewarding a comprehensive reading of the whole. The publication history suggests that the parts of the *Cantos* can be read singly or in groups, coming out as they did by fits and starts over fifty years, but they prove most rewarding when taken as a total work, when read as the epic they were intended to be. They are the Ur-sequence of modern poetry. Allen Tate says of them that they beg for a ceaseless study at the rate of one a year in depth, the whole to be read through every few weeks to maintain perspective. His comments are suggestive of the demands that modern literature makes upon its readers; works such as *Ulysses* and the *Cantos* are pitched away from the popular audience and toward the professional reader who can give them the kind of constant and loving attention they demand.

At about the same time that the first thirty cantos were appearing, Hart Crane was writing another sequence which would become a refutation of the wanderlust and classicism of Pound's work and of the wasteland-mentality of Eliot's. *The Bridge* (1930) is a sequence much closer to Whitman's than to Pound's, celebrating America and the American people, very much a home-grown thing. Where Pound is something of a literary Ulysses, traveling the known world for his materials, Crane relies primarily on native sources, native images, native speech, native treatments. Like most poets of his time, he had wrestled with the influence of Eliot and the symbolists, learning much from them but unwilling to remain in that camp. He found his liberation through Whitman, whose buoyant optimism and sense of universal connectedness countered Eliot's pessimism and exhaustion.

The result of that influence is impressive: if Eliot can connect nothing with nothing, then *The Bridge*, with its emphasis on connections, is the antithesis of Eliotic aesthetics. Crane finds connections everywhere, and the poem's two major symbols, the bridge and the river, are both connectors, uniting distant or separate elements of the country. They are a brilliant pair of symbols, necessary complements. While the river connects one end of the country with another, it also divides it and requires a counter-symbol; the bridge, ridiculous without a river underneath, provides the literally overarching symbol of unification. The poem also strives to unify its disparate elements in ways that neither Eliot's nor Pound's work needs to do. The individual poems in *The Bridge* are much more genuinely separate than the individual cantos, certainly than the sections of *The Waste Land*. They are, for the most part, fully capable of standing alone, poems of unquestionable autonomy. What they lack, when separated from the whole, is the thematic power of Crane's emphasis on unity and wholeness. It is the constant harping on the theme that drives it home for the reader, the continual transformations of the quotidian into the symbolic, the universal. A bridge in New York becomes the symbol of America; a river becomes the Mississippi, which becomes another symbol of the enormous variety and range of experience in the country; a woman becomes Pocahontas, whose presence in the poem leads toward an exploration of American history. Crane shared with his contemporaries Carl Sandburg and John Dos Passos a desire to write works that encompassed the whole of the national experience, which remained open to the promise of America. Dos Passos' novel trilogy, *USA* (1937), has many affinities with *The Bridge* and with William Carlos Williams' *Paterson*.

Two other significant modern poets have sought to capture America in poem sequences, but they have differed from Crane's method in their insistence on the local as the key to the universal. Both Williams' *Paterson* and Charles Olson's *The Maximus Poems* (both of which appeared over a number of years) portray American life by concentrating on individual cities. Neither work shows the kind of boundless enthusiasm and optimism that Crane displays, probably because their very close relationships with the microcosms of Paterson, New Jersey, and Gloucester, Massachusetts, force them to see society with all its warts. Crane's general view, like Whitman's before him, allows him the luxury of not seeing the country close up, of blithely ignoring what does not suit him. Williams, on the other hand, can see all the squalor and pollution of the Passaic River and show them to the reader, but he can also see the falls. His optimism is a greater achievement than Crane's because it is harder won. So too with Olson, who, even while railing against the economic exploitation of nature and what he calls the "perjoracracy" of American society, can still see its possibilities.

While the two works share many similarities, they are also different in many ways. *Paterson* reflects Williams' scientific interest in minutiae, his

Imagist background, his passionate attachment to place. The poem focuses almost entirely on the city of Paterson and environs, scarcely bothering to suggest the ways in which it is representative of the larger society. That connection Williams leaves to the reader to make. He says repeatedly in the poem, "No ideas but in things," and he holds fast to this precept. He makes a collage of newspaper accounts, essays, personal recollection, and direct observation. One of the poem's great innovations, in fact, is Williams' use of unreworked materials, such as newspaper reports, personal letters, and historical accounts. *Paterson* proceeds not by wrenching its materials into poetic form, but by building the poetry around the materials that are evidence of life; it is a genuinely organic work in the most exact sense of its growing out of, and thereby taking its form from, the materials it employs. Williams criticized Eliot for the elitism of his poetry and his criticism; in *Paterson* he demonstrated his commitment to an egalitarian poetry.

Unlike Eliot, he does not shy away from the contingency and chaos of life, does not feel obliged to superimpose an artificial order, but instead is content to live with what order he can discover in the world around him. He is closer to Crane and Whitman than to the method of the *Cantos*.

It is Olson who employs Pound's poetics towards a Whitmanian vision of America. Like *Paterson*, *The Maximus Poems* are grounded in a specific place, but they employ the sweeping style, the cross-cultural borrowing, the often declamatory tone of the *Cantos*. Tate says of Pound's work that despite all the allusions, quotations, and foreign sources, the structure and method of the *Cantos* is simply conversational, the talk of literate men over a wide range of subjects. *The Maximus Poems* are also heavily conversational, relying on a listener for all the speaker's pronouncements. They embody a curious paradox: despite their ostensible epistolary structure (Olson calls the separate poems letters, and even addresses them to various individuals), their principal unit of structure is speech-related.

These poems are the major work exemplifying Olson's theory of "projective verse." In an attempt to break the tyranny of the traditional poetic line and the iambic foot, Olson proposes a system of "composition by field," of thinking in terms larger than the line, of composing by means of, not a formal unit, but a logical one. The line of poetry should reflect the thought it contains and be limited by the breath of the speaker. A line, therefore, is roughly equivalent to an utterance, and should be controlled by it, rather than forcing the thought to conform to the limitations of the line, as in traditional verse. Although few of the other practitioners of projective verse—Robert Duncan, Robert Creeley, Denise Levertov, Edward Dorn—have insisted on a "breath unit" as an essential part of the definition of what they do, Olson does insist on it as the standard for the poetic line, and the result in *The Maximus Poems* is that the letters have a strikingly oral quality. Each poet, Olson believed, must strike his own rhythm in poetry as personal as a signature.

Of course, not all sequences have dealt with issues of such enormous scope. When poetry took a confessional turn in the 1950's, so did the poem sequence. Two of the most notable examples of the genre are Robert Lowell's *Life Studies* (1959) and John Berryman's *The Dream Songs* (1969) both of which employ the techniques of sequencing toward highly personal ends. Lowell's career moved from the highly formal poetry he learned under the influence of Ransom at Kenyon College to a looser style. By the time of *Life Studies*, he was able to include a long prose section, "91 Revere Street," something that would have been unthinkable even a few years before. Since each poem deals with a discrete event or mental state or person from a poet's past, little is lost when individual poems are read out of sequence.

By contrast, Berryman's *The Dream Songs* gain greatly by their association with one another. Forming as they do a more or less unified narrative of the life of their protagonist, Henry, the poems develop as they go along, and to excerpt one or a few is to lose much of the flavor of the whole. Alternately riotous and melancholy, boastful and mournful, the songs careen through moods and events at a furious pace. Even the voices are unstable. Henry uses a variety of ways of talking about himself, sometimes "I," sometimes "Henry," sometimes even "you," and there is even a voice of a heckler, which may or may not be a separate person, who addresses him as Mr. Bones and who speaks in the parlance of nineteenth century minstrel shows. The poems gain a formal tension in the play between the looseness of the story and the rigid structure; while a given song may use multiple voices, employ jumps in logic or time frame, or tinker with silences and double entendre, it will always contain eighteen lines in three six-line stanzas, a form that the poet says he learned from Yeats. The poems, like Lowell's, chronicle the weaknesses, failures, successes, and torments of their creator, although Berryman's are always masked by the story line.

While much of the most interesting work in sequences has been done by American poets, some very fine sequences have come out of England and Ireland, including the work of some recent poets, among them Geoffrey Hill, Ted Hughes, Seamus Heaney, and Charles Tomlinson. Hughes has worked with sequences on several occasions, and the most notable product of those experiments is his *Crow* (1970). The book represents his first effort at creating a mythology, at overthrowing the tired mythology of Christianity. Where Christ is human, loving, gentle, compassionate, soothing, and bloodless, representing the human desire for order and tranquillity, Crow is lusty, violent, animal, raucous, deceitful, cruel, unsympathetic, and, perhaps worst of all, cacophonous. He represents those qualities of disorder and chaos that mankind tries to control with such myths as Christianity, the side that will not be controlled or denied. Yet Crow is not human; he tries at one point to be, but fails, and the closest he comes is in acquiring language. As an effort at wholesale mythmaking, *Crow* is best read as a complete sequence, since the function of Crow himself is often not fully explained by a single poem.

Geoffrey Hill, the maker of several sequences, including "Funeral Music," "The Songbook of Sebastian Arrurruz," "Lachrimae," and "An Apology for the Revival of Christian Architecture in England," has created a figure similar to Crow in his domination of the poetic landscape in King Offa of the *Mercian Hymns* (1971). Offa is the presiding spirit of the West Midlands, the setting of the work, a figure out of medieval history whose presence explains and unifies the poem as Williams' Paterson and Joyce's Finn do in *Paterson* and *Finnegans Wake* (1939), respectively. Whereas *Crow* takes on the whole of Western experience and culture, Hill satisfies himself with the problems of the England he knows. He is deeply rooted in place, in the sense of history and geography of his England, and the mythology he creates is local, as opposed to the universality of the Crow myth.

In the *Mercian Hymns* a series of thirty prose poems (although Hill has objected to the phrase, he has offered nothing in its place) present scenes from past and present English life—especially that of the West Midland region—so juxtaposed that Hill and his grandmother and Offa all appear as figures in the work. Hill draws from literature, history, philosophy, architecture, and anthropology for his materials, weaving them into a tapestry of place. He has been compared to Eliot in his concern for the relation of the modern world to traditional society, the function of belief in personal life, the impulse to withdraw from the world; yet he is unlike Eliot in his insistence on locale, as well as in his distrust of his impulse to reform the world. Hill's verse has a built-in heckler, a questioner of motives and achievements. If he owes much to Eliot (and of that there can be no doubt), he also shares many qualities with Hughes, including the recognition of man's animal side and the ferocity of some of his poetry.

Seamus Heaney also sets his poem sequences in a specific place. Throughout his work, Heaney, an Ulster Catholic, is concerned with the relation of his language and the literary forms in which he works to the history of his people and their current troubles. That concern culminates in *North* (1975), in which he explores the history of Irish oppression through poetic excavation. Probing back into literary history, he settles on a modification of Old English poetics, with its heavy alliteration, its pounding rhythms, and its cacophonous vocabulary, as a means of transporting himself out of contemporary Ireland and back to the beginning of the conquests of the Celts by Germanic, Roman, and English armies. He finds an analogous archaeological situation in the excavation of the bog people in Jutland.

The book is made up of two very loosely structured sequences, within which are smaller and more tightly controlled sequences. The first section of the book is the historical exploration and an attempt to turn the intractable forces of history and politics into a workable personal mythology. The section is framed with poems dealing with Antaeus, the earthbound giant of Greek mythology, and indeed all the poems gather their power as well as much of their material from the land. The poems about the bog people and Heaney's reaction to them lie at the very heart of the section, forming a smaller sequence of their own. The poet is also concerned in this first section, through his interest in the bog people, with the Viking occupation of Ireland, and out of that interest grows a small sequence, "Viking Dublin: Trial Pieces." The poem's six sections carry the poet, by means of an ancient whalebone carved as a child's toy, into the Ireland of the Vikings and into those aspects of culture, the poet's culture, that are remnants of that time.

Having made his peace with the past, Heaney turns in Part Two to present social and political conditions. Like the first, this section is a loose thematic sequence, all of the poems building around the same set of subjects: violence, oppression, and suspicion in occupied Ulster. Within the section is the powerful sequence, "Singing School." The poem takes its title from Yeats's "Sailing to Byzantium," which hints at his ambivalence toward the conditions in his homeland. Like Yeats, he finds himself torn between the desire to escape the mayhem and violence surrounding him and his need to remain attached to the land. The sequence is composed of six poems recounting Heaney's personal encounters with the forces of oppression, with the highly charged emphasis on personal dialect and language, with the frustration that leads to violence and the fear that violence spawns. "Singing School" is one of the few modern poems to rival Yeats in the authentic presentation of emotional and intellectual responses to social turbulence and personal danger.

One of the most interesting efforts at writing a poem sequence in recent years is the collective poem, *Renga* (1971), written by Charles Tomlinson, with Octavio Paz, Jacques Roubaud, and Eduardo Sanguinetti. The *renga* is a traditional Japanese form, a chain poem written collectively, an effort to overcome the ego by blending one's poetry with that of others, sometimes many others. The emphasis is on continuity rather than individual brilliance, and as such is another form of that strain of Oriental thought whose goal is self-effacement. These four Western poets broke with tradition in establishing as the basis of their *renga* a Western form, the sonnet. Each one began a section which was to run for seven sonnets, and each contributed part, a quatrain, a tercet, or a couplet, to each of the first six. The seventh was then to be written by the poet who had begun the series. Sanguinetti declined to write a sonnet at the end of his cycle, declaring that it was complete, so the sonnets total twenty-seven instead of the expected twenty-eight. The multilingual poems, translated into English by Tomlinson, have as their goal the laying aside of ego and personal style for the greater goal of the poem's unity.

The foregoing discussion might give the impression that the poem sequence is the only serious form that poetry has taken in this century. Such is not the case, of course. Not all poets have written sequences or have cared to try; a few modern poets have worked successfully in longer, sustained, traditional forms, among them W. H. Auden and Wallace Stevens. Then, too, the short poem has been the most prevalent form in this age. Nevertheless, the sequence is one of modern poetry's great contributions to literature.

Confessional Poetry

One of the important divergences from the modernist program in the wake of World War II was the turn toward a more personal poetry, even a painfully personal, confessional poetry. No doubt the shift was motivated in part by politics; a number of those writers who had espoused the impersonal theory of art had also veered dangerously close to totalitarian political thought. Eliot had openly proclaimed himself a reactionary in politics and religion, while Pound, institutionalized at St. Elizabeths, provided an irrefutable link between modernism and Fascism. Moreover, the turn toward personal poetry was part of a larger move away from the academic, often obscure verse of Eliot and Pound and toward a more open, more accessible poetry. Among the models for such a move were Whitman and Dickinson, although Whitman's contribution to the proletarianization of poetry was not in confessional but in Beat poetry.

The confessional school was, in its beginnings, a specifically regional movement; indeed, it had deep historical roots in Puritan New England. Puritan literature characteristically revealed the struggle of the soul with belief and with evil; in a world where the Devil was so ominously and constantly present, the soul could never be at rest, and the writings of Edward Taylor and Jonathan Edwards, along with a host of lesser preachers, show the vigilance that the believer must maintain in his war with the powers of darkness. Those highly personal revelations are often public in nature; that is, the purpose for telling of the pits and snares into which one has fallen and out of which one has endeavored to climb is to better equip one's neighbors or one's congregation to fight off the blandishments of the forces of Hell. Yet this is not the only function of such revelations. In the poetry of Anne Bradstreet, the purpose of such personal revelations is much more private, cathartic; she seems to need release from the pressures and torments of her life, and in writing about them she externalizes them. In the frequency with which her poems deal not with salvation and temptation, but fear of death, anxiety for children's well-being, hope, aspirations for the future, and love for her husband, she displays the privacy of her revelations. These are not pulpit-poems, as so many of Taylor's are, not poems of a person who is first of all a citizen of God's City on the Hill, but rather of a woman, mother, and wife.

Another major model for confessionalism was Emily Dickinson. Her poetry, in its patterns of thought, its death-obsession, its simultaneously domestic and violent imagery, its self-absorption, and its veerings toward the insane and the clairvoyant, exemplifies many of the themes and treatments that show up in confessional poetry. Dickinson's fiercely personal verse concerns itself not with the workings of self-in-society, but with the self-in-its-own-society. In poem 465, "I heard a Fly buzz—when I died," for example, she writes not of death as a universal experience nor of the communal effects of death, but of the personal experience of dying. The poem gains its power from the tension between the commonplace of a buzzing fly and the extraordinary circumstance of a dying person's taking notice of it. Certainly death itself is a commonplace, but Dickinson's attempt to portray the workings of the mind of a dying person, or one who is already dead, makes the reader's experience of that death extraordinary. In other poems she makes equally astonishing leaps into madness, despair, delight, grief, solitude, even into closed coffins, and in each of those poems the most remarkable feature is the stark, unmediated sense of reality that she conveys. The states of being in her poems are almost never filtered through the grid of literature; rather, they come directly from her experience, either real or imagined. Like Whitman, she insists on the genuineness of experience and shuns conventions and received forms or modes of expression. Often their very genuineness makes the poems grate on the reader; their cumulative effect can be very nerve-jangling, owing in large measure to her intense rendering of emotion.

It is possible to see the beginnings of contemporary confessional poetry in Pound's *The Pisan Cantos* (1948), which demonstrate a radical departure from the poet's earlier work, focusing much more heavily on personal experience in the nightmare world of his Italian captivity. Yet Pound was never properly speaking a "confessional poet," and perhaps no such thing existed until 1959, when W. D. Snodgrass' *Heart's Needle* and Lowell's *Life Studies* appeared. Lowell has claimed that teaching Snodgrass at the University of Iowa was the greatest single factor in the conversion of his poetry from the intricately formal style of *The Mills of the Kavanaughs* (1951) to that of *Life Studies*. Certainly it was more than coincidence that the two works appeared in the same year and displayed such similarity in their use of personal material.

Yet there are important differences, as well. Snodgrass, even while looking squarely at the events of his life, incorporating them unglossed into his poetry, maintains a cool irony. "Heart's Needle," for example, deals directly with his relationship with his daughter in the wake of his divorce. The sequence is filled with moments of melancholy and pathos, rue and self-recrimination. All the while, though, the poet keeps a certain distance from the Snodgrass who is his subject, or attempts to, for the detachment is in constant danger of breaking down. His concentration on the versification, on the syllabics in which he writes, on ironic self-deprecation, on himself as spectator of a scene in which he is also the principal actor, all wrestle with the impulse to bare his feelings. That impulse is most victorious on the edges of poetry: the ends of verses and the ends of sections, at those interstices where the momentum of the conscious poetic necessarily falters. The effect on the reader is a periodic jarring, as the rhythm of the waltz around Snodgrass' true feelings is tripped up by their sudden appearance, by the protruding foot of honest emotion that refuses to be denied. This struggle between alternating sides of the poet's self is paradigmatic of the inner war that manifests itself in all of the chief confessional poets. In Snodgrass, however, it is more gentle, more intellectualized, perhaps, than in any of the others. One rarely has the sense in reading his work that his struggle is of a self-destructive, violent nature, as it is with the others.

The poems of Lowell's confessional mode, similarly, while they may display a greater urgency of self-revelation, are often gentler in tone than those of Plath, Sexton, or Berryman. Still, it is important to remember that not all of Lowell's work is confessional, not even at the time when he was most closely identified with the movement. Two of the sections of *Life Studies* deal with material that cannot be called confessional, and Part One cannot even be termed personal. Nevertheless, both of those sections show affinities with the work in Part Four, "Life Studies," for which the book is most commonly remembered. In the poem about Ford Madox Ford, for example, the laughing, trivializing reminiscence suddenly gives way in the last sentence to "Ford,/ you were a kind man and you died in want." Like Snodgrass' poems, Lowell's often turn on final switchbacks, reclaiming the poet's memory from the trivial, the quotidian, the petty details of scenes and relatives. Those final moments can be quiet, as in the recollection of his father's last words in "Terminal Days at Beverly Farms." Yet those quiet endings thinly veneer a dangerous, even violent reality trying to break through, as the poet, holding a locked razor in "Waking in the Blue," cannot be trusted any more than the wife in "'To Speak of Woe That Is in Marriage,'" trusts her drunken husband. The madness and violence of Lowell's poetry contends with the understatement and irony he learned from the Fugitives Tate and Ransom. The controlled diction of his verse gives a greater cutting edge, in its implicit denial, to the wild swings of his mental and emotional life.

Not all of the confessional poets attempted to control those swings as did Lowell and Snodgrass. Berryman, for one, actively exploited the extremes of his emotional states for comic and grotesque effects in *The Dream Songs*, and even invented separate voices to accommodate separate levels of consciousness. Henry speaks of himself in both the third and the first person, and goes through periods of wild elation and equally wild despair, through paranoia and delusions of grandeur, and through it all there is the voice of the heckler, the voice of Mr. Bones that undercuts and mocks all other voices. The result is a multilayered narrative in which the various states exist not quite simultaneously but nearly so, on different levels, reflecting the layering of an embattled consciousness. Numerous writers, among them Berryman's first wife, Eileen Simpson, in her book *Poets in Their Youth* (1982), have commented on the wild swings of mood to which Berryman was subject, the turbulence of his personal life, including his alcoholism, his difficulty with his mother, and his extreme, myopic intensity when he was writing. Those various strains find their mythologized way into *The Dream Songs*, and their much more direct way into *Delusions, Etc.*, published shortly before his death in 1972.

Sylvia Plath and Anne Sexton, too, fought their wars much more openly than Lowell, their one-time teacher. Plath in particular dissected her life with a ferocity that, while it is certainly descended from Dickinson's work, is not comparable with any other poet's self-revelation. One of the most disturbing features of the public reception of the work of Berryman, Plath, and Sexton is the morbid fascination with the personal details that their poems reveal. Clearly, Plath fuels such interest; she spares the reader nothing, or virtually nothing, of the pain and despair of her life, yet her poetry is far from the mere raving of a madwoman. She controls, directs, and mythologizes her material rather than remaining its victim. In "Lady Lazarus," from the posthumous *Ariel* (1965), she becomes not simply a woman with suicidal tendencies, but a mythological goddess who dies periodically to rise revivified from the ashes, phoenixlike, to "eat men like air."

In "Daddy" she uses the same material, the pattern of repeated suicide attempts, in the opposite direction. No longer a power-goddess but the victim of abandonment by her father (who died when she was eight), she assumes the role of archetypal victim, a Jewess of the holocaust, casting her father, whom she comes to associate with all Germans, as her Nazi oppressor. Her great ability to find in the world around her the correlatives of her personal suffering, or perhaps her ability to bring the events and cultural institutions around her into focus through the vehicle of her personal disorder, turns her poetry into a striking, if at times repellent, force. One almost certainly will not feel at ease reading her work; one will almost as certainly be impressed with its power, with the force of her imaginative wrestling with her demons. Such poetic revelation of spiritual turbulence is rarely seen in English literature; perhaps not since Gerard Manley Hopkins has a poet bared psychic anguish so totally.

Each of the celebrated confessional poets has produced very impressive work, although not all of it is of a kind, yet the slackness and self-parodic nature of some of Sexton's and Berryman's later work points to a weakness of the genre: the self can be bared only so often, it seems, before the reader has seen quite enough. The profusion of terrible poetry by followers of these writers has suggested its limitations as well as its attractions. It is very easy to write wretched confessional poetry, since the subject matter is always at hand. It is much more difficult to turn that subject matter into art.

This is reactionary poetry, and like most things reactionary it remains on the fringe; it is extremist. There has been a marked movement in poetry after World War II toward personal, autobiographical poetry. Writers as different as Robert Duncan, Allen Ginsberg, Robert Creeley, Stevie Smith (who, although British, most resembles Dickinson), Thom Gunn, and Jon Silkin all make use of material from their own lives. Very few writes now shy away from autobiographical material as Eliot would have them do, and as writers of the first half of the century often did. Confessional poetry, then, although not of the mainstream itself, however much its apologists, such as M. L. Rosenthal in *The New Poets* (1967), may argue for its centrality, has turned the course of poetry toward the personal.

The work of its main practitioners will probably survive despite, not because of, the confessional nature of the poetry. The ironic self-observation of Snodgrass, the wistful, mournful verse of Lowell, with its tension between the trivial and the painful, the hilarious mythologizing of Berryman's *The Dream Songs*, the power and ferocity of Plath's imagery and phrasing will stand with the work of any group of poets of any age. It is well to remember that much poetry remains important *despite* some major component, be it subject matter, thematic treatment, or political orientation. There is much that modern readers find disagreeable, after all, in Geoffrey Chaucer, John Milton, and William Shakespeare.

Beat and Movement Poetry

Confessional poetry provided, if not the answer for modern poetry after World War II, at least an articulation of the problem. During the 1950's two other literary groups sprang up, one in America and one in Britain, both of which were also concerned with the plight of the individual in an intractable world. Beat and Movement poetries are violently dissimilar expressions of similar revulsions to the same world situation. Both react against the formalist art of the modernists, against uptight, bourgeois, philistine society, against the repressive political and cultural institutions of the period. The differences between the two lie more in national attitudes and predispositions than in first principles. Moreover, both show affinities with existentialism.

The Self underwent a series of shocks beginning with World War II, with its death camps, its blitzkriegs, its atomic bombs. The twentieth century is distinguished by a new scale of violence and terror: the virtual destruction or totalitarian suffocation of vast areas, of whole nations or peoples. In the face of that leveling destruction, the individual is quite lost. Furthermore, the prevailing ideologies of the century have not given the individual much room for maneuver. Both Communism and Fascism, of course, are anti-individual in their very orientation, and quite willing to sacrifice the autonomy of the self for the good of the state. Yet free enterprise capitalist democracy has also partaken of its dollop of statism in the modern world, the most outstanding example of which is the McCarthy-era witch hunts, those exercises designed not so much to ferret out saboteurs and seditionists as to enforce conformity and steamroll deviation from the average. As already mentioned, the impersonal theory of poetry put forth by Eliot and his circle coincided historically as well as theoretically with the rise of totalitarian politics, and it was that entire complex that writers of the 1950's sought to overthrow. To see the argument in purely literary terms is to miss a great deal of the significance of the action.

Both the Beats and the Movement poets, then, wrestle with the problem posed by existentialism; namely, how does the individual maintain his autonomy in the face of an overwhelming, repressive society? Their answers, while divergent, displayed certain similarities that can perhaps be understood in terms of various strains of existentialism. The Movement writers leaned more toward despair and quiet rebellion from within the ranks, while the Beats were open insurrectionists, confronting a hostile world with wild romanticism.

Philip Larkin has written of life at Oxford during the war, showing how, at the very moment when students normally developed their grandest ideas of themselves, the privation, uncertainty, and anxiety of wartime undercut their natural tendencies. He suggests that his own self-effacing poetry and that of his contemporaries was in large measure a by-product of Nazi aerial technology, that the blitz and the V-2 rockets reduced the range of options available to the undergraduates, and that he has never broken out of that range. One has the sense in Larkin's work that he is trapped, that society closes in around the individual before he has a chance to stake out his own territory. That sense is shared in the work of many of his contemporaries, although it takes many different forms.

The generation preceding the Movement, including the Auden circle, was at times highly political. Many writers became involved in the urgent issues of the day; many actively sought roles in the Spanish Civil War. William Empson accompanied Mao Tse-tung on the Long March. Most, although by no means all, of the writers of the 1930's embraced leftist politics to some degree, and a great many of them, like Auden himself, later either repudiated or quietly slipped away from their earlier beliefs. The Movement writers, even while sometimes claiming kinship with the writers of the 1930's, particularly Empson, shied away from the grand political gesture, as indeed they seemed to suspect all large gestures.

The Movement poets were in some respects a strikingly homogenous group—much more so than the Beats. All of the principals attended one of the two major English universities: Larkin, Kingsley Amis, Robert Conquest, John Wain, Elizabeth Jennings, and John Holloway went to Oxford, while Donald Davie, D. J. Enright, and Thom Gunn were at Cambridge. They were from, or at least they celebrated in their writings, middle-class or working-class backgrounds. Many had their educations interrupted by the war, and as a result they seemed, in Ted Hughes's analysis, to "have had enough."

The Oxford group, for the most part, emerged from the penumbra of neoromanticism. Larkin, for example, has recorded his struggle to free himself from the influence of Yeats, and, through Vernon Watkins, of Dylan Thomas.

His early poetry is largely a rehash of Yeats's style and imagery, neither of which sounds at all natural coming from Larkin. Not until the privately printed *XX Poems* of 1951 did his true voice begin to assert itself. Similarly, much of Jennings' early work fairly drips with syrup, wending its way through enchanted woods on the trail of unicorns. Like Larkin, and, for that matter, like most of the Oxford writers, she began to find herself only around 1950, although glimmers of her distinctive style had begun to show themselves earlier. The Cambridge three took a more direct route, one that led straight through their studies under F. R. Leavis. As Blake Morrison points out in *The Movement: English Poetry and Fiction of the 1950's* (1980), all three credit Leavis with shaping their thought and, to a great extent, their poetry. His skeptical rationalism served as a natural springboard to the highly rational, un- or even antimetaphorical poetry of the Movement.

The Movement, then, was a cultural and social phenomenon as well as a literary clique. A great many British writers from about the same time, some of whom turned out to be highly averse to the Movement views, have at one time or another been seen as belonging in some sense or other. The Movement was a reactionary school, looking back to Edward Thomas and the Georgians as well as to the writers of the 1930's for its models, looking away from both the modernism of Eliot and Pound and the Romanticism of such 1940's poets as Thomas, David Gascoyne, and Edith Sitwell. It was antiromantic, anti-metaphorical, highly rationalistic, and formally very traditional. It stressed colloquial diction and concreteness against both highly wrought "poetic" diction and the airy abstraction of neo-Romanticism and English surrealism. The tone is often flat, neutral, especially in Larkin, and a chief mode, as one might suspect, is irony. The irony, like the formal precision, is a stay against the isolation and the alienation that lies behind much of this writing.

Nearly everything about the Movement writers points to their alienation as an almost necessary state of young, thinking people of that time. They stood outside the institutions, either looking in the windows or ridiculing those inside, but in either case they were outsiders. Amis' Jim Dixon in *Lucky Jim* (1954) is a textbook case of a movement hero, an outsider who suddenly finds himself on the inside, who is suddenly confronted with the smallness and tackiness and pomposity and arrogance of the powerful and well-heeled. Typically, he causes disaster wherever he goes.

Larkin has lived perhaps closer to the Movement program than any of the others, always isolated, always provincial, always alienated, reeking of spiritual exhaustion and cultural bankruptcy to the point that he can barely bring himself to write at all. (By his own count, he averages three to five short poems a year.) His poetry has also remained closest to the original line; much of his recent work is very similar in spirit and tone, and even technique, to that written in the early 1950's. Its poetic qualities lie in its tight control and its compression rather than in any overtly poetic devices. It crawls rather than leaps, uses reason and intellection rather than surges of spirit. This is a highly Apollonian poetry.

To find the Dionysian poetry of the 1950's, one must leap an ocean and a continent, to San Francisco. If one were to take as a starting point the same basic rejection of values and suspicion of social and cultural institutions that prompted the Movement, and add to it the rejection of values and styles adopted as a makeshift solution by the Movement (and *perhaps* also of the personal, Freudian anguish of the confessional poets), one would be left with approximately the Beat mentality. While the Beats rejected the cozy middle-class complacency of the Eisenhower 1950's, they did so with characteristically American flamboyance, as opposed to the typically British reserve, tightness, and control. The Movement fought by withdrawing; the Beats fought by setting the enemy on his ear.

At its broadest, the Beat generation can be considered to include not only those San Francisco writers (and occasional drop-ins from the East Coast) normally associated with it—Lawrence Ferlinghetti, Gary Snyder, William Everson, Allen Ginsberg, Jack Kerouac, Philip Whalen, Michael McClure, Gregory Corso—but also, as John Clellan Holmes suggests in an essay in Lee Bartlett's *The Beats: Essays in Criticism* (1981), the Black Mountain group of Olson, Duncan, Creeley, Dorn, and Levertov, and perhaps even the New York circle centered around John Ashbery, Kenneth Koch, and Frank O'Hara. Most of these writers share certain attitudes toward literature and toward their audience.

One of the first calls-to-arms was sounded in Olson's 1950 essay "Projective Verse," in which, among other things, he calls for an end to the pedestrian verse line. Olson felt that the tyranny of the accentual-syllabic line, which had ruled since the Renaissance in English prosody, was strangling creativity. He therefore made his plea for an open-form poetic line, a variable line based on the requirements of phrasing and the poet's own natural voice—and on the devices peculiar to the typewritten poem. What Olson really argues for is the primacy of the poet in the poetry. No longer, he says, should the poet wrench his vese around to meet the standards of an exhausted poetics. Rather than making poetry with his head only (and this is perhaps the importance of the breath-unit), the poem must be the result of the effort of the whole person. Olson even gives form to his idea in the essay itself. This is no textbook example of essay-writing; its form is a large part of its function. The reader knows simply by reading it whether he is one of the chosen, for it is designed to call to the loyal and heap confusion on the enemy; it is intended to perplex the sturdy specimens of traditionalism simply by its language. This exclusionary technique became a hallmark of the entire Beat experience.

Certainly the Beat life-style was designed to be "off-putting" to non-hipsters, with its slang, its sexual and drug experimentation, its rootlessness. The poetry itself also challenged its audience, with its free-flowing forms, its often-incantatory rhythms, its wild flights of imagination, its sometimes coarse language. These qualities established themselves very early, so that when Robert Lowell, then a rising young poet with a formidable reputation, went to San Francisco to give readings in 1956, he found the audiences bored with his work because they had already become accustomed to hearing verse best typified by the then still unpublished "Howl" of Allen Ginsberg.

If confessionalism looked to New England for its source, then the Beats looked to Camden, New Jersey. There could have been no Beat poetry without Walt Whitman. The movement followed him not only in the openness of its form and in its attitudes, but also in its declamatory poetic voice. Ginsberg was particularly indebted to Whitman in the matter of a public poetic voice. Whitman was not the only source, of course, although he was the most important one. Others would include William Blake (whose voice, says Ginsberg, came to him in 1948, reciting poems), D. H. Lawrence, Henry Miller, William Carlos Williams, and Kenneth Rexroth. These last three were early champions of the fledgling movement as well as models, and Rexroth especially offered intense verbal support. Williams had said that Eliot set back American poetry twenty years or more, that his highly academic, closed poetry flew in the face of the proletarian, egalitarian verse toward which Whitman pointed. When the twenty years (more or less) were up, the new proletarian uprising made itself felt.

In a movement that is overtly social as well as literary, there are always social as well as literary sources. Black culture, especially jazz, Mexican peasant culture for dress and even behavioral models, Zen Buddhism, Hinduism (and Orientalism in general), were among the origins of the exoticism of Beat life. Yet much of what the Beats adopted they turned upside down. There was a demonic quality about their movement, an urge toward self-immolation, toward willful dissipation and disintegration, that was lacking in the originals. While it could be argued that the fiery urge toward dissolution was a by-product of the jazz influence, that the Beats learned self-destruction from Charlie Parker and Billie Holiday, it seems more likely that such an impulse was a fairly natural outgrowth of the rejection of safe, "straight" values. yet the movement was angelic as well as demonic; "Beat," as Everson reminds the reader, means "Beatific." While Everson may stand closer than any of his compatriots to a traditional Christian mysticism, an ultimate goal of the Beats was a kind of godliness. If they employed the tigers of wrath rather than the horses of instruction, it was nevertheless to arrive at wisdom. It is easy for an outsider to mistake the methods of the Beats for their ends. Certainly there have been many figures both famous and obscure who have used the movement's ideals as a shield for intellectual or moral slovenliness, but just as surely it is a mistake to fail to discern the difference between the pilgrimage and the destination.

Generalizations are dangerous, particularly when dealing with a group of writers so obviously devoted to individualism in life and art, yet there are features common to the generality of Beat poetry. There is a formal openness. The projective verse of Olson and Creeley becomes a wholly subjective form, a totally personal and even unconscious matter in much of Beat writing. Kerouac, who can be considered the discoverer of the movement, since it was he who named it, hated revision, and his version of revision was to remove and expand sections until they became new works. In many of his novels he wrote in a state of semicontrol, surrealistically allowing his material to take over. In like manner, the poetics of "Howl," for example, work very close to the unconscious. Its rhythmic, pulsating regularities, its incantatory insistence, its word and phrase repetitions insinuate themselves into the reader's (or the auditor's) consciousness, almost without requiring intellectual understanding. It is a poem to be felt as much as to be comprehended. In Gary Snyder's work, crumbled and reassembled syntax creates the effect of compression of thoughts and ideas, of puzzles and conundra stumbled onto in the act of creation. While his poems are considerably more ordered than the prose of William Burroughs' cut-up method, they seem to be springing naturally from the psyche, newly freed from the constraints of rationality.

The formal openness of Beat writing, in fact, is a function of its emphasis on the unconscious, on some aspect of humanity divorced from intellection. The Dionysian impulse is always away from reason, from order, from control, and toward those elements that modern society would have mankind erase or submerge under the great weight of orthodoxy. The use of drugs, of primitive cultures, of Christian mysticism, Oriental meditation, and Hasidic prophecy are all aimed at freeing the kernel of preconscious truth from the centuries-old and miles-deep husk of social conformity and "rational" behavior.

Most of the Beats believe, with Snyder, that if the inner being can be liberated and made to speak for itself, society can be changed. In his essay "Buddha and the Coming Revolution," he quotes the World War I slogan, "Forming the new society in the shell of the old," and that slogan can stand as well for the society of one, the primary object of reform for the Beats. Once the individual has learned how to live, the new society can be developed. Only in a society in which people have given up their individuality, where they have willingly immersed their differences in the stagnant waters of conformity, can such a thing as McCarthyism occur. Inevitably, then, the Beats go to the greatest lengths imaginable to assert their individuality. One cannot, after all, write in one's native rhythms unless one knows one's own mind and spirit. The act of writing, then, like living itself, is a political act, and the Beats have been as politically visible as any literary group of the last one hundred years.

Their work has been both important in its own right and tremendously influential. While Ginsberg's *Howl and Other Poems* (1956) and *Kaddish and Other Poems* (1961) and Snyder's *Riprap* (1959), *Myths and Texts* (1960), and

Six Sections from Mountains and Rivers Without End (1965) are probably the best-known works, there are a host of others. Gregory Corso's *The Mutation of the Spirit* (1964) is clearly a major work, a wrestling with important issues, as is much of Everson's work, including the pre-Beat *The Residual Years* (1968). The sheer mass of good poetry by Everson ensures his continued importance in the movement, although none of it has found the audience that Snyder's or Ginsberg's has. Michael McClure, particularly in his drug poems, is a valuable recorder of a phase of experience vital to the movement. It is Ferlinghetti, however, who chronicles the Beat experience and attitude most carefully, who consciously plays the role of Beat poet, sometimes to the point of seemingly losing himself in it. In such books as *A Coney Island of the Mind* (1958) and *The Secret Meaning of Things* (1969), and particularly in such poems as "Autobiography," he captures the essence of Beat life.

Whither?

Literature is always an act of becoming, a dialectical process between the mind of the writer and the literary and social-historical forces around him. Yet modern literature is perhaps uniquely in a state of flux. Its rejection of the past has been so vehement, its condition of upheaval so prolonged, its experimentation so striking, that writers and critics alike have come to look upon it as an arrival, as what literature has become. That constant upheaval within modern poetry, however, suggests that such is not the case. Rather, the overthrows and insurrections point to the extremely transitory nature of the modern experiments. In a body of poetry in which versification changed relatively little from Shakespeare to Rossetti, but in which no school of poetics has held sway for much more than a decade since then, the impermanence of modern poetry can hardly be avoided. It may well be that it has arrived at a state of perpetual dislocation, but that is hardly the same as consensus.

The problem, as suggested at the beginning of this essay, lies as much in the modern world as with the writers themselves. When Stevens says that the modern poem must find out what will suffice, he implies that the traditional givens of poetry will not suffice, and that they will not because the world has changed. After the myth-analysts and the psychoanalysts of the last one hundred years, after the awful destructions of two world wars, after the rise of modern multinational corporate entities, after the end of traditional society, how can poetry be expected to remain where it was? God may or may not be in his Heaven; all is certainly less than right with the world.

So the writing of modern poetry constitutes an incessant quest for form, a struggle to find a form that works in the modern context, that will suffice. The range of attempts can seem utterly baffling, yet it is possible to break them down into several loose categories.

The antimodernist poet recoils from the world around him, refusing also its chaotic poetics, which he often sees as symptomatic. Instead, he retreats into traditional forms. He writes in regular meters and rhyme schemes, in recognizable stanzaic patterns. Included among the ranks of antemodern poets would Robert Frost, A. E. Housman, E. A. Robinson, the Georgian poets, the Movement poets, and some of the poetry of the Fugitives, particularly some of the work of John Crowe Ransom and Donald Davidson. Their tradition is primarily English, looking back through Hardy and the Victorians.

By contrast, the modernist poet is, simultaneously, constantly reminded of the literary past and struggling to use it to create a new work of art, to "make it new." This artist's method is probably best described in T. S. Eliot's essay "Tradition and the Individual Talent," in which he says that a new work of art is not merely added to the collection of existing monuments, that a new work both alters and is informed by those already in existence. Eliot is the preeminent modernist poet. Others would include Ezra Pound, Wallace Stevens, Robert Lowell, Geoffrey Hill, Seamus Heaney, Allen Tate, Robert Penn Warren, W. H. Auden and his circle, Sylvia Plath, John Berryman, and W. S. Merwin. The modernist literary inheritance is much more eclectic, and much more continental, than that of the antimodernists, and looks to France, to the symbolists, for much of its immediate impetus.

The postmodernist poet openly rejects the forms and styles of literary tradition in his attempt to create a radically new poetry to engage the world he finds. He generally chooses open forms, loose structures, and writes out of his own experience. He is a much more personal poet than Eliot's modernist, feeling the world move through him, sensing that the necessary forms can be had through self-knowledge rather than through a study of tradition. On the Continent he has appeared as a Dadaist or a surrealist, and nearly everywhere he is an experimentalist. Early types would include Edith Sitwell (sometimes), D. H. Lawrence, William Carlos Williams, Kenneth Rexroth, Louis Zukofsky, David Gascoyne (also sometimes), and Carl Sandburg, while more recent manifestations can be found in the Beats, Charles Olson's Black Mountain group, Ted Hughes, the Liverpool group, and Robert Bly, James Wright, John Ashbery, and their fellow surrealists.

There is, finally a fourth category, not so much a group as an assortment of leftovers, actually poets whose work is so individual, whose vision is so much their own, that they defy taxonomic classification. William Butler Yeats is such a poet, certainly, and so too are Hart Crane, Dylan Thomas, Galway Kinnell, and perhaps others already located in one group or another, such as Lawrence, Hill, or Merwin. There are those writers who find themselves confronted with a specific social or political situation that forces their poetry in a direction that it might not otherwise have taken. Such is very likely the case with the Irish poets from Yeats and Louis MacNeice to Seamus Heaney, John Montague, Thomas Kinsella, and Tom Paulin. It may also be that their situation is paradigmatic of modern poetry generally: it is not merely that literature is changing in this century, but rather that the context of literature is changing so drastically and so rapidly that writers find themselves in a mad scramble to keep up.

Poetry has not found itself in such turmoil since Western society careened its way out of the Middle Ages and into the Renaissance. Perhaps when and if society once again settles onto some stable course (and modern weapons technology and multinational economics make *that* seem unlikely enough), then the course of poetry may also become more uniform. As things stand, though, both society and poetry appear to be headed for a very protracted period of transition. If that is so, then readers of verse will continue to be blessed, or cursed, with the astonishing variety that has characterized modern poetry.

Bibliography

Bartlett, Lee, ed. *The Beats: Essays in Criticism,* 1981.

Blackmur, R. P. *Form and Value in Modern Literature,* 1952.

Bly, Robert. *Leaping Poetry,* 1975.

Bullough, Geoffrey. *The Trend of Modern Poetry,* 1949.

Faas, Ekbert. *Towards a New American Poetic,* 1979.

Faulkner, Peter. *Modernism,* 1977.

Hoffman, Daniel, ed. *Harvard Guide to Contemporary American Writing,* 1979.

Hough, Graham. *Image and Experience,* 1960.

King, P. R. *Nine Contemporary Poets,* 1979.

Leavis, F. R. *New Bearings in English Poetry,* 1960.

Morrison, Blake. *The Movement: English Poetry and Fiction of the 1950's,* 1980.

Pratt, William C. *The Fugitive Poets,* 1965.

_____ . *The Imagist Poem,* 1963.

Ray, Paul C. *The Surrealist Movement in England,* 1971.

Spender, Stephen. *The Struggle of the Modern,* 1963.

Tate, Allen. *Essays of Four Decades,* 1968.

Thurley, Geoffrey. *The Ironic Harvest: English Poetry in the Twentieth Century,* 1974.

Thwaite, Anthony. *Twentieth Century English Poetry,* 1978.

Wilson, Edmund. *Axel's Castle: A Study in the Imaginative Literature of 1870-1930,* 1931.

Thomas C. Foster

THE AMERICAN SENSIBILITY

If one phrase best defines the American poetic sensibility it must be Ezra Pound's advice to "Make it New." Pound, in 1912, was speaking about Imagism, yet he was also identifying the strong antitraditional, heterogeneous, and individualistic qualities which distinguish the best American verse. Several geographical and cultural reasons contributed to this passion for innovation. When the American poet first attempted to follow the example of English literature—notably in the seventeenth and eighteenth centuries—the isolated and provincial raw land forced accommodations of language and expression upon him. It forced him to define his originality. As Wallace Stevens observes in *Opus Posthumous* (1957), "Nothing could be more inappropriate to American literature than its English source since the Americans are not British in sensibility."

Even so, the "flower of art blooms only where the soil is deep," said Henry James, and at first American poetry needed the nourishment of a thriving culture to develop its own roots. Anne Bradstreet and Edward Taylor, Puritan poets, depended early in their careers on European models, but, after their apprenticeship, discovered their own personal visions of love and grace. Equally noteworthy is the fact that the first poetic voice of America belonged to a woman, clearly an anomaly for the time, but also a sign of future cultural originality. Both Bradstreet and Taylor, however, followed the poetic formula of their age: a plain style used for allegorical purposes to demonstrate how the supernatural impinges upon the natural world. The Puritans frowned upon any fanciful display of delight or beauty for its own sake and relegated the imagination to the service of religious dogma. Yet, remarkably, both poets discovered sufficient breathing space within such a stern aesthetic to create freshness of vision. Bradstreet's "To My Dear and Loving Husband" and "Verses upon the Burning of Our House July 10th, 1666" are unprogrammed and passionate poems; they express an individualism and inquiring spirit suitable to the new land. Taylor, America's first great poet, circumvented Puritan censorship entirely by keeping his work hidden from view. His poems were not published until 1939. They are noted for the ingenious and often brilliant manner in which Taylor correlates commonplace reality with divine revelation. His best works include "The Preface" (who, he asks ingenuously, referring to Creation, could have bowled the sun, except Christ, the bowler?), "Sacred Meditations," and "Huswifery." Taylor's attempt to domesticate the infinite demonstrates a search for correspondences between nature and the spirit—a recurring concern of American poetry, and one which is later addressed by Ralph Waldo Emerson, Emily Dickinson, Robert Frost, and T. S. Eliot.

If the Puritan period provided infertile soil for American poetry, the eighteenth century did no better. Alexander Pope, John Dryden, and Jonathan

Swift eloquently dominated the English literary scene, but in the remote colonies, oppression, revolution, and the new political order destroyed any cultural transfusion, except for pale imitations of neoclassical style. Philip Freneau, frustrated by the imposition of a style unsuitable for a society in transition, complained of the neoclassical tyranny which kept the imagination utilitarian—suitable for satire and elevated discourse—yet quite disdainful of "fancy's sway." How, Freneau seemed to ask, could the verse qualities of harmony, proportion, balance, and restraint be applied to a pluralistic culture whose feelings demanded the opposite? The American sensibility craved not a poetics based on reason and the intellect, on order and propriety, but one created from the emotions and the individual imagination, heeding the rebellious spirit and beauty's lure. Tired of the aesthetic frustrations imposed by Puritanism and neoclassicism, America's poetic voice turned to Romanticism and its first great encounter with originality.

The Romantic spirit is by nature contrary and capricious, asserting its will according to the poet's vision of the world. In the nineteenth century, the American Romantic contemplated the world in two distinctly opposing fashions. One Romantic approach identified the poetic role as that of democratic spokesman for society, an inspirational and trusted public figure such as Walt Whitman and, later, Frost. By contrast, Edgar Allan Poe fits the role of poetic outsider, or *poète maudit*, in Paul Verlaine's phrase, as "accursed" figure, whose sensitivity to beauty and myth makes him a victim of a hostile, indifferent society. Both types, the egalitarian and the *poète maudit*, profoundly influenced the direction of American poetry, until in modern times their distinctive edges begin to blur and blend together. Emerson was the first major nineteenth century poet to consider the artistic consequences of political equality, and hence to set down some general observations on what a poet of a democracy should do. If the democratic state is based upon its citizens' needs, what function does the poet provide beyond the material well-being promised by the state? Emerson's response in his central essays—"The American Scholar," "Self-Reliance," and "The Poet,"—is hortatory: he serves as the seer or source of inspiration to ordinary man, who lives a life of quiet desperation. The poet aids him to "see the sun once more"; that is, a world of freshness and joy, beyond stale conventions and habits. The poet, Emerson believes, is "the sayer, the namer, and represents beauty," and thus truth, beauty, and goodness are equal.

Other important contributions made by Emerson include his assumption that poetic form itself is a means to truth and should not be harnessed to an unsuitable meter. "For it is not meters, but a meter-making argument that makes a poem. . . ." His concern with purifying the language to a new and eloquent speech was also influential. Each generation, he observes, must reexamine its use of words in order to restore its potency and weed out the "rotten diction" of previous ages. Although he was a poet himself ("Merlin" and "Hamatreya" are two of his best works), Emerson's reputation rests upon his enormous influence as an inspirational figure and craftsman. Frost, Stevens, Eliot, and Pound, in their time, have all disdained the "rotten diction" to discover their own new eloquence.

"I was simmering, simmering, simmering," Walt Whitman said, "and Emerson brought me to a boil." He was the perfect embodiment of Emerson's American Scholar, and in his great poems from *Leaves of Grass* (1855)— "Song of Myself," "Out of the Cradle Endlessly Rocking," "The Sleepers," "Crossing Brooklyn Ferry"—exemplifies the great, generous, humanitarian quality of American verse. Whitman dramatizes the self as his subject matter, a poetic device that allows him not only ordinary representation, but also the persona of the democratic self—a sensibility encompassing all of America. This transcendent figure looms over and merges with what it discovers in existence: love, pain, sex, faith, defeat, and death, celebrating them as part of the "procreant urge." *Leaves of Grass* is the American sensibility, vicariously lived through verse, from 1855 (the date of its first publication) to 1891-1892 (when the so-called "deathbed" edition appeared). In all of its various editions, "Song of Myself" remains the centerpiece, the poem Whitman saw as most representative of his work. It is completely American in its epic depiction of democracy, its candid delight in the miracle of life and the senses, and its use of vernacular language and free verse. The fifty-two stanzas exhort, tease, flatter, praise, and provoke the reader into acknowledging the necessity for poetry to define and dignify the average man as democratic hero. Whitman is the seer and Comarado who takes the reader on a psychological and spiritual voyage (while his catalogs capture the sense and sound of city and country), attempting to make him into the ideal Democrat envisioned by Emerson. On the trip, the passenger learns about the joys of nonconformity, the equality of body and soul, the pleasures of sex, and the evils of repression and intimidation. The poem's cheerful didacticism, its faith in mankind's future ("I launch all men and women forward with me into the unknown"), and its glorification of selfhood, all demonstrate how far the egalitarian imagination can take poetry triumphantly into commonplace existence.

By contrast, Edgar Allan Poe's Gothic vision of life emphasizes the nightmare aspects of pain and terror to be found in reality. He has been called a poet of the subconscious and a pioneering aesthetician; both descriptions are accurate. Poe often described his poetry as "dreamwork," suggesting that only by an appeal to the unconscious could the imagination be set free from commonplace reality to seek out the archetypal nature of existence. Life, as most men know it, is too brief and inconclusive to offer him much knowledge and happiness. Many of his poems, therefore, describe the search for supernal beauty in a shadowy, dreamland region, as in "To Helen," or else dramatize the despair of love brought about by doom and change, as in "Annabel Lee" and "Ulalume." Unlike Whitman, who would merge the imagination with reality, Poe sets the two forces in opposition to each other, stressing that one becomes a haven from the other, as the dream is a sanctuary from burdensome reality. Poe's theories were later taken up by the French symbolists, who in turn influenced such American poets as John Crowe Ransom, Eliot, Pound, and Stevens.

Emily Dickinson, along with Whitman, produced the best poetry written in America during the nineteenth century. Yet she had no wish to become an American seer like Whitman; nor does she follow Poe in exhausting the imagination by searching for an unreachable beauty. Instead, her journey is one of self-realization, discovering in the psyche that meticulous, unique viewpoint that renders the commonplace extraordinary. Whether examining nature, deprivation, God, or love and friendship—her favorite subjects— Dickinson's psychological insight and subtlety of expression are so astonishing that the reader is startled into a new and vivid awareness of the world. She wrote 1,775 poems (none longer than fifty lines), and most of them owe their coiled tension to an inherited Calvinistic streak at odds with the romantic idealism of her day. The poetic result is seen in her form, hymnal quatrains often called "fourteeners," and in her unconventional outlook, aptly summed up in her title: "Tell all the Truth but tell it slant." At times, Dickinson appears to be looking at her 1850 Amherst world through the eyes of her favorite Metaphysicals, John Donne and Andrew Marvell, yet with a sufficiently modulated vision to allow her own use of paradox, pun, conceit, and aphorism to appear boldly reinventive. Her use of these devices to create an original approach can be seen in many of her titles: "Much Madness is divinest Sense," "I Felt a Funeral, in my Brain," or "I like a look of Agony."

Dickinson's favorite subject is death (some five hundred poems); two of the most famous on this subject are "Because I could not stop for Death" and "The Bustle in a House." The former poem shows Dickinson's brilliant use of the delayed impact, a poetic ruse in which truth is withheld from the speaker until the final lines, to create a chilling shock of recognition. Here, the situation is ironically amusing because Death is personified as a kindly gentleman whose considerate offer of a carriage-ride masks an awesome truth. During the course of the journey, they pass the various stages of the speaker's life, symbolized in an image or two not fully understood until they reach their destination—the grave. How like life, the poet seems to be saying, to pass by without being noticed! In contrast, the second poem starkly addresses the psychological effects of death upon the living. The necessary adjustments made by the living are so final and irreversible that they appear to match death's own certainty. Despite a certain ornateness of style, Dickinson is close to the modern sensibility because of her genuine wish to be painstakingly herself in poetry, instead of assuming some cosmological guise. Thus her poetry can be regarded as a compulsive need for self-definition, and perhaps it is important that two contemporary poets, Anne Sexton and Sylvia Plath, claiming her as their spiritual sister, carried Dickinson's flirtatious preoccupation with death to a tragic conclusion in suicide.

The failure to "Make it New" in poetry accounts for the eclipse of the minor Romantics, Henry Wadsworth Longfellow and James Russell Lowell. While successful and honored in their lives, they were content to follow traditional versification and decorous poetic diction, and to leave innovation to Whitman, Poe, and Dickinson. As Daniel G. Hoffman comments in *American Poetry and Poetics* (1962), both regarded literature as a continuum with past masterpieces, and, guided by them, "wrote as though they were Englishmen resident in Cambridge, Massachusetts." A lack of inspiration marked the years between the Civil War and the turn of the century. Except for Stephen Crane, whose bitter aphoristic verses were influenced by Dickinson, most poets exploited the commercial vein of sentiment desired by average readers. James Whitcomb Riley, for example, always pleased his audience with such works as "An Old Sweetheart of Mine," and "The Old Swimmin'-Hole." Yet, growing up in isolation from one another, were such masters as Edwin Arlington Robinson, Frost, Stevens, Pound, and Eliot. The poetic revolution called modernism awaited their maturity.

Although Robinson and Frost were not exactly innovators, they provided, at the turn of the century, a reappraisal of traditional values badly needed by a generation of future poets. Robinson, in his great short poems—"Miniver Cheevy," "Richard Cory," and "Bewick Finzer"—laid to rest the romantic optimism of Emerson and Whitman. In a post-Darwinian world, the poet seemed to say, such innocence is fatal. Consequently, his poems document the process of disillusionment as it comes to bewildered dreamers who expect too much from life. In failing to accept a flawed world, they inevitably fail to accept themselves. Frost also separated himself from the Romantic age by adopting a decidedly ambivalent attitude toward nature. Instead of regarding it as a symbol of spiritual rebirth, like Emerson and Whitman, or as a hallowed shrine, like William Cullen Bryant, Frost evoked its terror as well as its beauty. "Stopping by Woods on a Snowy Evening," his most famous poem, captures nature's ambiguity brilliantly, by showing how the still coldness of the snowy woods appeals to man's aesthetic sense as well as his desire for oblivion. Although the poem is often read as an optimistic view of man's ability to meet challenges and to persevere in life, the last quatrain more than hints that after responsibilities have been met, death's winter sleep will be welcome.

Scholars still debate the precise date of the birth of modernism, though all agree that it made an early appearance in the pages of Harriet Monroe's *Poetry* magazine, started in 1912. In an early issue, Pound first stated his Imagist manifesto, declaring an end to the past century's "rotten diction," and asking for a new national poetics that would incorporate greater economy, flexibility of form, and a more precise use of imagery. Here, too, was published the early work of Eliot, Stevens, and William Carlos Williams—all deeply affected by the influence of French symbolism. Their transactions with symbolism provide a good example of how the American sensibility absorbs and finally modifies influences from other traditions. As a movement, French symbolism began with the publication of Charles Baudelaire's *Flowers of Evil* (1857) and stressed the exploration of the inward states of the psyche instead of external reality. Poetry, Baudelaire and his followers believed, should evoke and suggest, transcending the level of objective description to re-create human consciousness by symbol and metaphor rather than by realistic details. Baudelaire was greatly influenced by Poe, whose works he had translated, and he reaffirmed Poe's vision of the poet as the *voyant* and *poète maudit*, a figure whose intensively personal vision of existence contradicted and renounced the beliefs of conventional society. Symbolism, as finally affirmed by Pound and Eliot, became a liberating agent that freed them from the restrictions of conventional versification and also provided them with their dramatic subject: the modern world as a wasteland.

"In the broadest terms," F. O. Matthiessen declares, "most of our later poets could be described as descendents of Whitman or as descendents of Poe." Eliot found in Poe affinities that are recognizable in his two great early collections, *Prufrock and Other Observations* (1917) and *The Waste Land* (1922). Eliot shares Poe's fierce dislike of modern life, his respect for tradition, and his veneration of the imagination and the craft of poetry. It is unlikely, however, that Poe would have comprehended how his descendant transformed these affinities into a revolutionary method of presentation.

In *The Waste Land*, Eliot morally indicts the post-World War I generation, regarding it symbolically as the point of breakdown for an entire civilization. To support his condemnation, the poet juxtaposes the spiritual stagnation of the present age with the enriching myths of the past, using the city as the focal point of entropy. Here, in the modern metropolis, the traditional symbols of regeneration—Christian and Eastern religious practices, fertility rituals, art itself—all appear to fail before pervasive doubt and disbelief. Eliot fleetingly introduces characters who represent the spiritually dead; and as they speak of their agony and yearn for salvation, he interweaves the medieval legend of the Grail, which also tells of a cursed land finally cured by a knight whose purifying ordeals show him the path to wisdom and faith. What is needed, then, Eliot states in his brilliant, conservative jeremiad, is the spiritual determination to move through the Chapel Perilous, and discover in the sinking West the hope of regeneration. The immense erudition of *The Waste Land*, the difficulties of its exegesis, and its abrupt transitions and shifts of mood create problems for the new reader; its total effect, to borrow a pictorial term, resembles a cubist painting by Georges Braque. Fortunately, the thematic outlines are quickly made clear, and each rereading of the poem makes it evident why it is considered the greatest poem of the first half of the century.

Pound, like Eliot, was an expatriate, and preferred to live in England and Italy in order to escape American provincialism. (Eliot became a British subject in 1927 and died there in 1965; Pound, accused of treason for his Fascist leanings in World War II, died in Rapallo, Italy, in 1972.) Of the two men, Pound exerted the greatest influence on modern poetry, although Eliot wrote its most famous poem, *The Waste Land*. Yet even here Pound exerted significant editorial influence, and Eliot's poem is dedicated to him, as "il miglior fabbro," the greater master. Pound was among the first artists to understand how the symbolists (along with Henri Bergson's philosophy, French impressionistic painting, and a score of other influences) had revolutionized poetry into a new, abstract, and cosmopolitan system, with an international vision. *Hugh Selwyn Mauberley* (1920) and the *Cantos* (1925-1972) demonstrate both the strengths and weaknesses of the poet's need to recast the search for beauty in new, expressive forms. *Hugh Selwyn Mauberley* draws a sharply satiric contrast between the poet and his society—especially as epitomized by his London stay from 1912 to 1920—based upon the commercial exploitation of art, and how it is cheapened by the philistine pleasures of the social moment. For the artist to live under such tawdry conditions is to be sentenced to death, and Pound compares this waste of talent with the waste of life in World War I. Both poet and soldier are victims of a decadent civilization, cynically pursuing its pleasures, while what is valuable—life and the transcendent imagination—are lightly sacrificed. In the second sequence of *Hugh Selwyn Mauberley*, Pound projects a horror-image of the artist trapped and surrendering to this sterile environment, all substance and style given up as accommodations to ease and survival. Mauberley, of course, is Pound himself, a persona of the poet-in-exile, whose poetry provides both vindication and encouragement for desertion from the crass world. In addition to the satire, there are sections of *Hugh Selwyn Mauberley* that possess incomparable grace and loveliness, such as "Envoi," which echoes the English poet Edmund Waller, and sings of the endurance of beauty, even in a bad time.

The *Cantos* continue Pound's attack on the philistines, especially their love of usury. Against this money-mania, the poet juxtaposes visions of past glory, offered as hopeful inspiration for society's rebirth. Pound once described this incomplete epic poem as a ragbag, and as the poet offers to the reader numerous historical periods as models for imitation—whether historical Greece, the Italian Renaissance, or John Adams' America—the final effect is haphazard and anticlimactic. Pound employs numerous voices to dramatize his panoramic vision, including Thomas Jefferson, Confucius, Sigismondo Malatesta, and even himself. They all form part of his "ideogrammic" method, a Chinese device used to make his scenes appear presentational. Thus the Jefferson persona would imitate Jefferson's actual speech and actions, along with the gestalt of his age. Central to most of the sections is the figure of

Odysseus, a poet in search of his proper homeland. Numerous references to Ovid's *Metamorphoses* (before A.D. 8) encourage the idea of individual and cultural transformation and imply a theory of history that is finally hopeful, despite man's best efforts to enact one death wish or another. Pound's *Cantos* is a truly heroic work, yet one that also demands a heroic reader, one who understands a dozen languages, has a taste for arcane history, and appreciates numerous non sequiturs.

Hart Crane and Wallace Stevens bring the modernist process closer to home by wedding it to the American Romantic tradition. They attempt to "make it new" by absorbing qualities from both the Poe and Whitman canons, although they are clearly more partial to Whitman's epic vision of America. Crane and Stevens inherited from Poe the desire for a purified poetry, in which the imagination transcends reality, yet they also inherited from Whitman his vision of poetry as the source of spiritual identity and community. When they attempt to resolve these divergent strains, the resulting tension aids in the creation of their best works. *The Bridge* (1930), according to Crane, is an attempt to capture the myth of America, refuting Eliot's accusation in *The Waste Land* that modern life is spiritually sterile. His epic poem addresses the Brooklyn Bridge in much the way that Whitman did in "Crossing Brooklyn Ferry." For Crane and Whitman, the awesome bridge is not only a miracle of engineering and a symbol of great beauty, but also a revelation of God's immanence in man's present experience. The poem introduces figures from the American past, such as Christopher Columbus, Whitman, Poe, and Dickinson, to testify to American greatness, showing its continuity and progress toward greater individual freedom and spiritual self-discovery.

Stevens' central image of the "blue guitar" (after Pablo Picasso's painting entitled "The Old Guitarist"), although less dramatic than Crane's bridge-metaphor, nevertheless conveys even greater claims for poetry. In *Harmonium* (1923) and *The Man with the Blue Guitar* (1937), Stevens identifies the blue guitar with the poetic imagination; its song of fictive music is a way of restoring freshness and purpose to life. The poet thus becomes a modern Orpheus, transforming quotidian reality by his imaginative vision. Although this poetic metamorphosis is an idea acquired from the French symbolists, Stevens daringly extends it to embrace the metaphysical as well. His premise holds that the twentieth century has witnessed the death of all gods because man has failed to sustain them by imaginative faith. Consequently, the poet, as Orphic seer, must discover a secular substitute, a supreme fiction that will satisfy man's need for belief even in this skeptical modern age. Stevens' claims for poetry are the ultimate extension of Emerson's secular humanism noted in "The Poet" and later celebrated by Whitman in "Song of Myself." If, as Emerson states, "Man is but a God in ruins," then Stevens' romantic belief in the imagination's sacred task to redeem life, is the corollary. Stevens develops this theme in many moods and forms: satiric, rhapsodic, consolatory, and philosophical. Such virtuosity has made him, after Eliot, America's greatest modern poet.

In "A High-Toned, Old Christian Woman," Stevens ironically contrasts two visions of heaven, one quite traditional, the other a riot of paganism. Both concepts, the poem satirically affirms, are valid, because both are products of man's imagination. Thus, the "high tones" of the title represent cries of dismay sounded by an affronted orthodoxy. "The Idea of Order at Key West" is a great lyrical poem illustrating how man's search for meaning can order even so chaotic a shape as the sea. It is night on the Caribbean, and the listener, hearing an anonymous girl's song, notes that it merges with the sea sounds, bestowing on the sea an identity formed by the imagination. As the girl knits the sea into her song, so the poet understands how the imagination mediates between sea and reality to create a new transformation. "The Emperor of Ice Cream" is the poet's most disarming work: a surreal approach to the subject of death, in which the plea for a modest acceptance of that dismal state is presented in an extravagance of metaphor. If death is final, the poet asks, then why not present it as a three-ring circus, an action as relevant as the ceremony of mourning.

William Carlos Williams shared with Stevens a belief that there are no poetic ideas except in things themselves. Unlike Stevens, however, who chose to celebrate the "things" or objects of life capable of imaginative transformation, Williams sought out the enduring qualities in existence which supported man and gave him happiness. His greatest praise was reserved for self-reliance, which in an age of overwhelming conformity had to struggle very hard to preserve its integrity. Williams' epic poem, *Paterson* (1946-1951), describes the relationship between man and the city on various realistic and mythic levels upon which the battle for self-survival is fought. As Donald Barlow Stauffer says of *Paterson* in *A Short History of American Poetry* (1974), the poet concerns himself with discovering life's regenerative sources, first through language, and then through the powers of love and sexuality, the desire for beauty, and the dignity of man. The common link is the poet's symbolic use of the Passaic River, once seen as pure, but now fouled by pollution. Similarly, the inhabitants of Paterson have also fallen upon evil times; but they await renewal by a sense of purpose and faith in the self. In Williams' world, nothing is irreversible, not even nature.

The final legacy of the Romantic tradition comes in the urgent form of social activism, most dramatically seen in such black poets of the Harlem Renaissance as Claude McKay in *Harlem Shadows* (1922), and Langston Hughes in his *Selected Poems* (1959). Both poets are less concerned with formal innovation than with a revitalization of theme: the emergence of black racial consciousness and pride. McKay's famous "If We Must Die" pleads for a new black heroism to come forth and defy the white establishment's racism and moral blindness. The poem is ironically cast in the shape of a sonnet to dramatize not the form's usual subject, love, but its opposite, betrayal and the need for revenge. Hughes's "The Negro Speaks of Rivers," by contrast, speaks of the timeless quality of the black experience, as it was formed in ancient African rivers and is still nourished in the present, affirming the vital, enduring life-force through time. The tone resists racial antagonism in favor of the spirit's encouragement, witnessed in patience and survival. Gwendolyn Brooks, the best black poet writing today, has published seven books of poetry, ranging from a poetry of protest to the adoption of a black nationalist posture. *In the Mecca* (1968), her best volume, speaks with a hard-edged clarity about life in the ghettos of the big Northern cities, with its particular vibrancy and tenseness. In the one decayed slum apartment house which is used as a microcosm, Brooks reveals the physical and spiritual blight of her characters, haunted by their deep burden of cultural neglect. Yet Brooks, unlike McKay of an earlier era, never raises her voice, except in irony.

Allen Ginsberg's *Howl* (1956) reveals a different yet strident form of social protest in American poetry. Ginsberg was part of the San Francisco Beat scene which flourished in the 1950's and 1960's. Along with Lawrence Ferlinghetti and Jack Kerouac (who coined the term "beat"), Ginsberg lashed out at President Dwight D. Eisenhower's silent generation, its middle-class conformity, its fear of Communism, and its puritanical distrust of sexual pleasure. Against these restrictions, the Beat movement advocated a countertherapy of individualism, voluntary poverty, and "liberation" through jazz, drugs, and sexual experience. Yet its momentum was dependent upon how effectively it could outrage the middle-class sensibility. Its very name was a challenging code word that sneered at Establishment sanctities by advocating a vagabond life-style and a state of bliss or beatitude, reached by unorthodox means. Ironically, once the Beats had made their cultural point, their effectiveness as a romantic minority group decreased, and they were swallowed up by commercial exploitation; many of them became business partners of the Establishment.

Howl was the vital literary force for the "beat down" way of life, exhorting its readers to renounce injustice and the worship of money in favor of meditation, personal growth, and the understanding of the "holiness" of all life. Yet, despite this distinctly Emersonian point of view, the poem deliberately courts offensiveness with its jubilant use of obscene language, its obsessive sexual references, and its hysterical emotional explosiveness. The publication of *Howl* caused Ginsberg to be prosecuted for obscenity; the poem was defended on the grounds that it possessed redeeming value as a serious criticism of society. The widely reported trial made the poem and its maker famous. Today, the work is safely ensconced in most college anthologies, and it has taken on the dignity of a cultural landmark. In terms of poetic technique, it is interesting to note that the voice of *Howl* is that of Poe's *poète maudit*, whose sharp complaints against his culture are recited in Whitman's free verse and incantatory method.

Thus, the American sensibility in poetry continues to develop, creating and transforming its identity by following the advice of Ezra Pound to make it new.

Edward Guereschi

THE AFRO-AMERICAN SENSIBILITY

The struggle for freedom—social, psychological, and aesthetic—is the distinguishing attribute of Afro-American poetry from its origins during slavery through its pluralistic flowering in the twentieth century. Although the impact of the struggle has only intermittently been simple or direct, it has remained a constant presence both for writers concentrating directly on the continuing oppression of the black community and for those forging highly individualistic poetic voices not primarily concerned with racial issues. Generally, two basic "voices" characterize the Afro-American poetic sensibility. First, black poets attempting to survive in a literary market dominated by white publishers and audiences have felt the need to demonstrate their ability to match the accomplishments of white poets in traditional forms. From the couplets of Phillis Wheatley through the sonnets of Claude McKay to the modernist montages of Robert Hayden, Afro-American poets have mastered the full range of voices associated with the evolving poetic mainstream. Second, black poets have been equally concerned with forging distinctive voices reflecting both their individual sensibilities and the specifically Afro-American cultural tradition. This dual focus within the Afro-American sensibility reflects the presence of what W. E. B. DuBois identified as a "double-consciousness" that forces the black writer to perceive himself as both an "American" and a "Negro." The greatest Afro-American poets—Langston Hughes, Sterling Brown, Gwendolyn Brooks, Robert Hayden, Imamu Amiri Baraka—draw on this tension as a source of both formal and thematic power, helping them to construct a poetry that is at once unmistakably black and universally resonant.

From the beginning, Afro-American poets have continually adjusted to and rebelled against the fact of double consciousness. To be sure, this rebellion and adjustment has varied in form with changing social circumstances. Nevertheless, Baraka's statement in his poetic drama "Bloodrites" that the aware black artist has always been concerned with helping his community attain "Identity, Purpose, Direction" seems accurate. Over a period of time, the precise emphasis has shifted between the terms, but the specific direction and purpose inevitably reflect the individual's or the era's conception of identity. To some extent, this raises the issue of whether the emphasis in "Afro-American" belongs on "Afro" or on "American." Some poets, such as Baraka during his nationalist period, emphasize the African heritage and tend toward assertive and frequently separatist visions of purpose and direction. Others, such as Jean Toomer in his late period, emphasize some version of the "American" ideal and embrace a variety of strategies for the purpose of reaching a truly integrated society.

Phillis Wheatley, the first important Afro-American poet, was forced to confront this tension between African and American identities. Brought to

America at an early age, she experienced only a mild form of slavery in the north. Although her poem "On Being Brought from Africa to America" views slavery as a "mercy" since it led her from "pagan" darkness to Christian light, she was never accepted as a poet on her own merits. Rather, her work was advertised as the product of a "sable muse" and she was presented as a curiosity rather than as a poet as accomplished as her white contemporaries. Other early writers, such as George Moses Horton and Frances Watkins Harper, shared a common purpose in their antislavery poetry but rarely escaped the confines of themes acceptable to the abolitionist journals that published their work. The pressures on the Afro-American poet became even more oppressive during the post-Reconstruction era as the South "reconquered" the black man, in part by establishing control over the literary image of slavery. The "Plantation Tradition" portrayed contented slaves and benevolent masters living in pastoral harmony. Paul Laurence Dunbar attained wide popularity in the late nineteenth and early twentieth centuries, but only by acquiescing partially in the white audience's stereotypical preconceptions concerning the proper style (dialect) and tones (humor or pathos) for poetry dealing with black characters.

Spearheading the first open poetic rebellion against imposed stereotypes, James Weldon Johnson rejected Dunbar's dialect in his "Preface" to *The Book of American Negro Poetry* (1922), which issued a call for "a form that will express the racial spirit by symbols from within rather than by symbols from without." This call was heeded by the poets of the "Harlem Renaissance," who took advantage of the development of large black population centers in the north during the Great Migration of blacks from the rural south to the urban north during the 1910's and 1920's. Where earlier poets lived either among largely illiterate slave populations or in white communities, the "New Negroes," as Alain Locke, one of the first major black critics, labeled the writers of the movement, seized the opportunity to establish a sense of identity for a sizable black audience. Locke viewed the work of poets such as McKay, Countée Cullen, and Jean Toomer as a clear indication that blacks were preparing for a full entry into the American cultural mainstream. The support given Harlem Renaissance writers by such white artists and patrons as Carl Van Vechten and Nancy Cunard, however, considerably complicated the era's achievement. On the one hand, it appeared to herald the merging predicted by Locke. On the other, it pressured individual black writers to validate the exoticism frequently associated with black life by the white onlookers. Cullen's "Heritage," with its well-known refrain, "What is Africa to me?" reflects the sometimes arbitrarily enforced consciousness of Africa that pervades the decade. Afro-American artists confronted with white statements such as Eugene O'Neill's "All God's Chillun Got Wings" could not help remaining acutely aware that they, like Wheatley 150 years earlier, were viewed as much as primitive curiosities as sophisticated artists.

The first flowering of Harlem as an artistic center came to an end with the depression of the 1930's, which redirected Afro-American creative energies toward political concerns. The end of prosperity brought a return of hard times to the Afro-American community and put an end to the relatively easy access to print for aspiring black writers. If the Harlem Renaissance was largely concerned with questions of identity, the writing in Hughes's *A New Song* (1938) and Brown's *Southern Road* (1932) reflect a new concern with the purpose and direction of both black artists and black masses. Where many of the Harlem Renaissance writers had accepted DuBois' vision of a "talented tenth" which would lead the community out of cultural bondage, the 1930's writers revitalized the Afro-American tradition which perceived the source of power—poetic and political—in traditions of the "folk" community. Margaret Walker's "For My People" expresses the ideal community "pulsing in our spirits and our blood." This emphasis sometimes coincided or overlapped with the proletarian and leftist orientation that dominated Afro-American fiction of the period. Again external events, this time World War II and the "sell-out" of blacks by the American Communist Party, brought an end to an artistic era.

The post-World War II period of Afro-American poetry is more difficult to define in clear-cut terms. Many more poets have been active, especially during the 1960's and 1970's, and poets such as Hughes and Brown, who began their careers earlier, continued as active forces. Nevertheless, it is generally accurate to refer to the period from the late 1940's through the early 1960's as one of universalism and integration and that of the mid-1960's through the mid-1970's as one of self-assertion and separatism. The return of prosperity, landmark court decisions, and the decline of legal segregation in the face of nonviolent protest movements created the feeling during the early postwar period that Afro-American culture might finally be admitted into the American mainstream on an equal footing. Poets such as Brooks, who became the first black to win the Pulitzer Prize for Poetry—for *Annie Allen* (1950)—and Hayden, who later became the first black Library of Congress poet, wrote poetry that was designed to communicate to any reader, no matter what his racial background and experience. Neither poet abandoned black materials or traditions, but neither presented a surface texture which would present difficulties for an attentive white reader. Brooks's poem "Mentors" typifies the dominant style of the "universalist" period. It can be read with equal validity as a meditation on death, a comment on the influence of artistic predecessors, a commitment to remember the suffering of the slave community, or a character study of a soldier returning home from war. The universalist period also marked the first major assertion of modernism in black poetry. Although both Hughes and Toomer had earlier used modernist devices, neither was perceived as part of the mainstream of experimental writing, another manifestation of the critical ignorance that has haunted black poets since Wheatley. Hayden and Melvin B. Tolson adopted the radical prosody of T. S. Eliot and Ezra Pound, while Baraka, Bob Kaufman, and Ted Joans joined white poets in New York and San Francisco in forging a multiplicity of postmodernist styles, many of them rooted in Afro-American culture, especially jazz.

As in the 1920's, however, the association of black poets with their white counterparts during the 1950's and 1960's generated mixed results. Again, numerous black writers felt that they were accepted primarily as exotics and that the reception of their work was racially biased. With the development of a strong black nationalist political movement, exemplified by Malcolm X (who was to become the subject of more poems by Afro-American writers than any other individual), many of the universalist poets turned their attention to a poetry that would directly address the Afro-American community's concerns in a specifically black voice. Jones changed his name to Imamu Amiri Baraka, Brooks announced her conversion to a pan-Africanist philosophy, and community arts movements sprang up in cities throughout the United States. A major movement of young black poets, variously referred to as the New Black Renaissance and the Black Arts Movement, rejected involvement with Euro-American culture and sought to create a new "black aesthetic" that would provide a specifically black identity, purpose, and direction. Poets such as Haki R. Madhubuti (Don L. Lee), Sonia Sanchez, Nikki Giovanni, and Etheridge Knight perceived their work primarily in relation to a black audience, publishing with black houses such as Broadside Press of Detroit and Third World Press of Chicago. Most poets of the Black Arts Movement have remained active since the relative decline of the black nationalist impulse in the late 1970's and 1980's, but, with such notable exceptions as Madhubuti, their tone has become generally more subdued. They have been joined in prominence by a group of poets, many of whom also began writing in the 1960's, who have strong affinities with the modernist wing of the universalist period. If Madhubuti, Knight, and Giovanni are largely populist and political in sensibility, poets such as Michael Harper, Ai, and Jay Wright are more academic and aesthetic in orientation. Although their sensibilities differ markedly, all of these poets assert the strength of both the Afro-American tradition and the individual voice.

This recent pluralism attests to the persistence of several basic values in the Afro-American sensibility: survival, literacy, and freedom. Even highly idiosyncratic poets, such as Toomer in "Blue Meridian" and Ishmael Reed in his "neo-hoo-doo" poems, endorse these basic values, all of which originate in the experience of slavery. In his book *From Behind the Veil: A Study of Afro-American Narrative* (1979), Robert B. Stepto identifies the central heroic figure of the Afro-American tradition as the "articulate survivor," who completes a symbolic ascent from slavery to a limited freedom, and the "articulate kinsman," who completes a symbolic immersion into his cultural roots. The articulate survivor must attain "literacy" as defined by the dominant white society; the articulate kinsman must attain "tribal literacy" as defined by the black community. Literacy, frequently illegal under the slave codes, both increases the chance of survival and makes freedom meaningful. Tribal literacy protects the individual's racial identity against submersion in a society perceived as inhumane and corrupt. To a large extent, black poets writing in traditional forms establish their "literacy" as part of a survival strategy in the white literary world. Those concerned with developing black forms demonstrate their respect for, and kinship with, the culturally literate Afro-American community.

Against this complex of values and pressures, folk traditions assume a central importance in the development of the Afro-American sensibility. Embodying the "tribal" wisdom concerning survival tactics and the meaning of freedom, they provide both formal and thematic inspiration for many black poets. Afro-American poets have become extremely adept at manipulating various masks. Originating with the trickster figures of African folklore and Afro-American heroes such as Brer Rabbit, these masks provide survival strategies based on intellectual, rather than physical, strength. Existing in a situation during slavery where open rebellion could easily result in death, the slave community capitalized on the intimate knowledge of white psychology encouraged by the need to anticipate the master's wishes. The white community, conditioned not to see or take into account black needs and desires, possessed no equivalent knowledge of black psychology. Lacking knowledge, whites typically turned to comfortable stereotypes—the loyal mammy, the singing darkie, the tragic mulatto, the black beast—for their interpretation of black behavior. The observant slave found it both easy and rewarding to manipulate white perceptions of reality by appearing to correspond to a stereotypical role while quietly maneuvering for either personal or community gain. The nature of the mask, which exploits a phenomenon of double consciousness by controlling the discrepancy between black and white perspectives, is such that the true goal must always remain hidden from the white viewer, who must always feel that he is making the "real" decisions. Brer Rabbit asks *not* to be thrown in the briar patch; he will be allowed to escape, however, only if Brer Bear, the symbolic white man, believes that Brer Rabbit's mask is his true face.

This folk tradition of masking adds a specifically Afro-American dimension to the standard poetic manipulation of persona. Afro-American poets frequently adopt personae which, when viewed by white audiences, seem transparent incarnations of familiar stereotypes. Dunbar's dialect poetry and Hughes's Harlem street poems, for example, have been both accepted and dismissed by white readers as straightforward, realistic portraits of black life. An awareness of the complex ironies inherent in the Afro-American folk traditions, that each drew on, however, uncovers increasingly complex levels of awareness in their work. Dunbar's melodious dialect songs of plantation life contrast sharply with his complaint against a world that forced him to sing "a jingle in a broken tongue." Similarly, his classic poem "We Wear the Mask" expresses the anguish of a people forced to adopt evasive presentations of self in a nation theoretically committed to pluralism and self-fulfillment. Less agonized than Dunbar, Hughes manipulates the surfaces of his poems, offering and refusing stereotypical images with dazzling speed. "Dream Boogie" first connects the image of the "dream deferred" with the marching feet of an army of the dispossessed, only to resume the mask of the smiling darkie in the sardonic concluding lines: "*What did I say?/* Sure,/ I'm happy!/ Take it away!/ *Hey, pop!/ Re-bop!/* Mop!/ Y-e-a-h!" The critical record gives strong evidence that Hughes is frequently taken at "face" value. His mask serves to affirm the existence of a black self in control of the rhythm of experience, as well as to satirize the limitations of the white perception.

Throughout the history of Afro-American poetry, poets choosing to address the black political experience without intricate masks have been plagued by the assumption that their relevance was limited by their concentration on racial subject matter. Particularly in the twentieth century, a new stereotype—that of the "angry black" writer—has developed. The conditions of black life frequently do, in fact, generate anger and protest. Afro-American poets, from Wheatley through Alberry Whitman in the late nineteenth century to Cullen and Giovanni, frequently protest against the oppression of blacks. McKay's sonnet "If We Must Die" embodies the basic impulse of this tradition, concluding with the exhortation: "Like men we'll face the murderous, cowardly pack,/ Pressed to the wall, dying, but fighting back!" Far from being limited by its origins in the Afro-American experience, such poetry embraces a universal human drive for freedom. Winston Churchill quoted lines from the poem (ironically written partially in response to British exploitation of McKay's native Jamaica) during the early days of World War II. The stereotype of the angry black, while based on a limited reality, becomes oppressive at precisely the point that it is confused with or substituted for the full human complexity of the individual poet. Giovanni, at times one of the angriest poets of the Black Arts Movement, pinpoints the problem in her poem "Nikki-Rosa":

> I really hope no white person ever has cause to write about me
> because they never understand Black love is Black wealth and they'll
> probably talk about my hard childhood and never understand that
> all the while I was quite happy.

The drive for freedom transcends any single tone or mode. While frequently connected with the protest against specific conditions limiting social, psychological, or artistic freedom, the impulse modifies a wide range of poetic voices. At one extreme, explicitly political poems such as Baraka's "Black Art" call for "Poems that shoot/ guns." Even Baraka's less assertive poems, such as the early "For Hettie" or the more recent "Three Modes of History and Culture," seek to envision a world free from oppression. At another extreme, the drive for freedom lends emotional power to "apolitical" poems such as Dunbar's "Sympathy," with its refrain, "I know why the caged bird sings." Although the poem does not explicitly address racial issues, the intense feeling of entrapment certainly reflects Dunbar's position as a black poet subject to the stereotypes of white society. Similar in theme, but more direct in confronting racial pressures, Cullen's sonnet "Yet Do I Marvel," a masterpiece of irony, accepts the apparent injustices of creation, concluding: "Yet do I marvel at this curious thing/ To make a poet black, and bid him sing." Hughes's "Mother to Son," and "I, Too" with their determination to keep moving, reflect a more optimistic vision. Despite the hardships of life in a country which forces even the "beautiful" black man to "eat in the kitchen," Hughes's characters struggle successfully against despair. Significantly, many of Hughes's poems are very popular in the Third World. "I, Too," for example, has become a kind of anthem in Latin America, which honors Hughes as a major poet in the Walt Whitman tradition.

Where Hughes and Walker frequently treat freedom optimistically, Sterling Brown's "Memphis Blues" provides a stark warning of the ultimate destruction awaiting a society that fails to live up to its ideals. McKay's sonnet "America," with its echoes of Percy Bysshe Shelley's "Ozymandias," strikes a similar note, envisioning the nation's "priceless treasures sinking in the sand." Perhaps Robert Hayden best embodies the basic impulse in his brilliant "Runagate Runagate," which employs a complex modernist voice to celebrate the mutually nourishing relationship between the anonymous fugitive slaves and the heroic figure of Harriet Tubman, who articulates and perpetuates their drive for freedom. Blending the voices of slavemasters, runaway slaves, the spirituals, and American mythology, Hayden weaves a tapestry that culminates in the insistent refrain, "Mean mean mean to be free."

Hayden's use of the anonymous voice of the runaway slave with the voice of the spirituals underscores both the drive for freedom and the nature of the individual hero who embodies the aspirations of the entire community. It exemplifies the importance of folk traditions as formal points of reference for the Afro-American poetic sensibility. Poets seeking to assert a specifically black voice within the context of the Euro-American mainstream repeatedly turn to the rhythms and imagery of folk forms such as spirituals and sermons. During the twentieth century, the blues and jazz assume equal importance. As Stephen Henderson observes in *Understanding the New Black Poetry* (1973), these folk traditions provide both thematic and formal inspiration. Hayden's "Homage to the Empress of the Blues," Brown's "Ma Rainey," Brooks's "Queen of the Blues," and poems addressed to John Coltrane by Harper ("Dear John, Dear Coltrane," "A Love Supreme,"), Madhubuti

("Don't Cry, Scream"), and Sanchez ("A Coltrane Poem") are only a few of countless Afro-American poems invoking black musicians as cultural heroes. Bluesmen such as Robert Johnson (who wrote such haunting lyrics as "Cross-roads," "Stones in My Passageway," and "If I Had Possession over Judgement Day") and singers such as Bessie Smith frequently assume the stature of folk heroes themselves. At their best they can legitimately be seen as true poets working with the vast reservoir of imagery inherent in Afro-American folk life. DuBois endorsed the idea by montaging passages of Afro-American music with selections of Euro-American poetry at the start of each chapter of *The Souls of Black Folk* (1903). Similarly, Johnson's poem "O Black and Unknown Bards" credits the anonymous composers of the spirituals with a cultural achievement equivalent to that of Ludwig van Beethoven and Richard Wagner.

These folk and musical traditions have suggested a great range of poetic forms to Afro-American poets. Johnson echoed the rhythms of black preach-ing in his powerful volume *God's Trombones: Seven Negro Sermons in Verse* (1927), which includes such classic "sermons" as "The Creation" and "Go Down Death—A Funeral Sermon." Hughes and Brown used their intricate knowledge of black musical forms in structuring their poetry. Early in his career, Hughes was content simply to imitate the structure of the blues stanza in poems such as "Suicide." As he matured, however, he developed more subtle strategies for capturing the blues impact in "The Weary Blues," which establishes a dramatic frame for several blues stanzas, and "Song for Billie." The latter mimics the subtle shifts in emphasis of the blues line by altering the order of prepositions in the stanza:

> What can purge my heart
> of the song
> and the sadness?
> What can purge my heart
> But the song
> of the sadness?
> What can purge my heart
> of the sadness
> of the song?

The persona moves from a stance of distance to one of identification and acceptance of the blues feeling. In merging emotionally with the singer, he provides a paradigm for the ideal relationship between artist and audience in the Afro-American tradition.

Brown's blues poem "Ma Rainey" incorporates this "call and response" aspect of the blues experience into its frame story. Ma Rainey attains heroic stature because her voice and vision echo those of the audience that gathers from throughout the Mississippi delta to hear its experience authenticated.

Brown's attempt to forge a voice that combines call and response points to what may be the central formal quest of Afro-American poetry. Such an ideal voice seeks to inspire the community by providing a strong sense of identity, purpose, and direction. Simultaneously, it validates the individual experience of the poet by providing a sense of social connection in the face of what Ralph Ellison refers to as the "brutal experience" underlying the blues impulse. Both Ellison and Hughes, two of the most profound critics of the blues as a literary form, emphasize the mixture of tragic and comic world views in the blues. Hughes's definition of the blues attitude as "laughing to keep from crying" accurately reflects the emotional complexity of much blues poetry.

Like the blues, jazz plays a significant formal role in Afro-American poetry. Poets frequently attempt to capture jazz rhythms in their prosody. Ambiguous stress patterns and intricate internal rhyme schemes make Brooks's "We Real Cool" and "The Blackstone Rangers" two of the most successful poems in this mode. Brown's "Cabaret" and Hughes's "Jazzonia" employ jazz rhythms to describe jazz performances. On occasion, poets such as Joans ("Jazz Must Be a Woman") and Baraka ("Africa Africa Africa") create "poems" which, like jazz charts, sketch a basic rhythmic or imagistic structure that provides a basis for improvisation during oral performance. Jazz may be most important to Afro-American poetry, however, because of its implicit cultural pluralism. In his critical volume *Shadow and Act* (1964), Ellison suggests a profound affinity between the aesthetics of Afro-American music and Euro-American modernism: "At least as early as T. S. Eliot's creation of a new aesthetic for poetry through the artful juxtapositioning of earlier styles, Louis Armstrong, way down the river in New Orleans, was working out a similar technique for jazz." As Ellison suggests, jazz provides an indigenous source for an Afro-American modernism incorporating voices from diverse cultural and intellectual sources. In effect, this enables the Afro-American poet to transform the burden of double consciousness, as manifested in the traditions of masking and ironic voicing, into sources of aesthetic power.

Many of the masterworks of Afro-American poetry, such as Hughes's "Montage for a Dream Deferred," Brooks's "In the Mecca," Hayden's "Middle Passage," and Jay Wright's "Dimensions of History," accomplish precisely this transformation. Choosing from the techniques and perceptions of both Euro- and Afro-American traditions, these works incorporate the dreams and realities of the American tradition in all its diversity. Aware of the anguish resulting from external denial of self and heritage, the Afro-American tradition recognizes the potential inherent in all fully lived experience. Hughes's vision of individuals living out a multiplicity of dreams within the American dream testifies to his profound respect and love for the dispossessed.

Focusing on concrete human experience rather than on abstract universals, the Afro-American sensibility distrusts the grandiose rhetoric which has too frequently glossed over the materialism, racism, and solipsism that disfigure the American democratic ideal. The Afro-American tradition seeks to provide a sense of identity, purpose, and direction connecting the visions of Frederick Douglass and Malcolm X with those of Thomas Jefferson and Walt Whitman. Drawing on folk roots and forging a complex pluralism, it reaffirms the values of universal survival, literacy, and freedom.

Bibliography
Brown, Sterling. *Negro Poetry and Drama*, 1969.
Gayle, Addison, Jr., ed. *Black Expression*, 1969.
Gibson, Donald. *Modern Black Poets: A Collection of Critical Essays*, 1973.
Harper, Michael, and Robert B. Stepto. *Chant of Saints*, 1979.
Henderson, Stephen. *Understanding the New Black Poetry*, 1973.
Kent, George. *Blackness and the Adventure of Western Culture*, 1972.
Levine, Lawrence. *Black Culture and Black Consciousness*, 1977.
Wagner, Jean. *Black Poets of the United States*, 1972.

Craig Werner

SOCIOLOGICAL CRITICISM

Of the major critical approaches to reading poetry, the sociological is the least clearly defined. Not a monolithic critical system or even a coherent body of criticism, the sociological approach consists of various methods and objectives. The traditional emphases of sociological criticism are politics and economics and their relation to literature. The definition of the term "sociological" can be expanded to include historical, philosophical, and psychological emphases as well, but then it becomes a component of intellectual history and loses its functional meaning as a critical approach. The essential difference between intellectual history and sociological criticism rests not in methodology or necessarily in objective but in the selection and focusing of materials. Regardless of definition, the sociological criticism of poetry resists easy classification, and its more tempered eclecticism, which is perhaps its most marked characteristic, is clearly seen in such diverse works as Christopher Caudwell's *Illusion and Reality: A Study of the Sources of Poetry* (1937), F. W. Bateson's *English Poetry: A Critical Introduction* (1950), John F. Danby's *Poets on Fortune's Hill* (1952), Raymond Williams' *The Country and the City* (1973), and T. S. Eliot's "The Social Function of Poetry." All of these works, as different as they are in content, value, interest, and purpose, are legitimate expositions of the sociological approach to poetry.

All literature is a social phenomenon, and poetry no less than drama and fiction relates to its cultural milieu and is in some measure a product of it, but the nature of that relationship is less explicit in the case of poetry. Poetry is more than a repository of a people's manners, customs, and public history. F. W. Bateson argues in *English Poetry: A Critical Introduction* that "the subject-matter of poetry is not 'things,' but conflicting moods and attitudes, *human nature in its social relations*," and he cautions against identifying the social content of poetry with "the concrete particulars of everyday life." "The imprint of the social order must be looked for at a higher level of abstraction." According to Harry Levin in "Literature as an Institution," all literature, not only poetry, refracts life instead of reflecting it. The critic's task, Levin believes, "is to determine the angle of refraction." This is never easy because the angle, which "depends upon the density of the medium," is always changing. The task is further complicated by the reciprocal nature of the relationship between literature and society: "Literature is not only the effect of social causes; it is also the cause of social effects." If criticism forgets that literature often distorts the world, it takes us into a region of its own creation, "where everything is clear and cool, logical and literal, and more surrealistic than real."

Poetry, perhaps because it is a denser medium—to use Levin's term—than fiction and drama, is less susceptible to sociological treatment than other genres. To establish the ways that Robert Browning's *The Ring and the Book*

(1868-1869) manifests a Victorian climate of values would be a more demanding task, for example, than to do the same thing with William Thackeray's *Vanity Fair* (1847-1848). With the more personal types of poetry, the problem of fleshing out the forms of social relevance is especially formidable, although René Wellek and Austin Warren point out in *Theory of Literature* (1949) the possibility of linking "even lyric poetry with love conventions, religious preconceptions, and conceptions of nature." They are quick to add, however, that such relationships "may be devious and oblique." The greater resistance of poetry to sociological criticism is reflected in the exhaustive bibliography in Hugh Duncan's *Language and Literature in Society* (1953), where no more than ten percent of the studies listed are devoted to poetry.

The sociological criticism of poetry can focus on the social background of the poet, the social content of the poetry per se, the influence of the poet on society, and the extent to which poetry "is actually determined by or dependent on its social setting, on social change and development." In English criticism the social background of the poet has been all but ignored. Raymond Williams' chapter on "The Social History of English Writers" in *The Long Revolution* (1961) seeks to analyze the complex correlations between literature and society by examining several hundred writers born between 1470 and 1920 in terms of social origin, education, and vocation. He finds that Romantic poetry "shows no consistent relation with the social history of its creators," and he reaches the general conclusions that the "good writer may be born anywhere," that "the pattern of his social development can be very varied, and that there may be danger in attempting to standardize it."

The social content of poetry itself, together with its effect on society, have been the areas of main concern of sociological criticism and the exclusive preoccupation of Marxist criticism. Certain poems and kinds of poetry that are immersed in their milieus in special ways require the clarifying mediation of sociological scholarship for a fuller understanding. A knowledge of the social ferment of later fourteenth century England is necessary for an informed reading of William Langland's *The Vision of William, Concerning Piers the Plowman* (1362, c. 1377, c. 1393) just as some understanding of the Courtly Love tradition is required for an intelligent response to Geoffrey Chaucer's *Troilus and Criseyde* (1382). Poems of social protest and political and social satires are not likely to exert their full effects without some grasp of the accompanying background. John Dryden's highly topical *Absalom and Achitophel* (1681) and Alexander Pope's *The Dunciad* (1728-1743) demand a rather extensive knowledge of their social contexts, while Lord Byron's *The Vision of Judgment* (1822) requires considerably less. Bernard de Mandeville's *The Fable of the Bees* (1714) is a social poem that deals explicitly with the problems of governance and social organization, and a knowledge of the political theory that underlies it is essential. To regard this poem as a self-contained linguistic organism with a completely intrinsic meaning in the manner of the New

Criticism would be to place theory before reality, and to ignore much that is important in the poem. In many cases sociological criticism is necessary to gain a full understanding of a poem. W. Witte in "The Sociological Approach to Literature" cites William Wordsworth's sonnets and odes collected under the heading *Poems Dedicated to National Independence and Liberty* (1897) as a case where "the influence of social, economic, and political factors" is particularly strong, requiring a sociological approach. The English and Scottish popular ballads, according to Witte, are also poems that fall "into a definite social pattern" and can best be treated within a sociological context.

Ideally, sociological criticism, in the words of David Daiches, helps us "to avoid making mistakes about the nature of the work of literature we have before us, by throwing light on its function or on the conventions with reference to which certain aspects of it are to be understood." Witte emphasizes a twofold value of the sociological approach: the uncovering of "those elements in a work of literature which are merely of the time" and the revealing of "universal values and significances" of a literary work that transcend its historical period. In either case, the sociological approach makes a significant descriptive contribution by preparing the way for informed critical evaluation. Understood in this way, the sociological approach is an important adjunct of evaluative criticism rather than an end in itself. Taken merely by itself, it ceases to be literary criticism and becomes political or social history or, at worst, an instrument of political propaganda.

The sociological criticism of poetry has its origins in the eighteenth century, in the writings of such men as Johann Herder and the Schlegels, and the magazines and journals of the period contain articles describing literature as the expression of national characteristics of various kinds. Edmund Wilson in *The Triple Thinkers* (1938) traces the sociological approach to poetry to Giambattista Vico's *La Scienza Nuova* (1725, *The New Science*) quoting a lengthy passage from that work that analyzes the *Iliad* (c. 800 B.C.) as reflective of a young Greece "burning with sublime passions such as pride, anger and vengeance" and the *Odyssey* (c. 800 B.C.) as a much later work composed when Homer was old, reflecting a different Greece, one whose passions were "somewhat cooled by reflection." A hundred years later G. F. W. Hegel was lecturing on national literatures as expressive of their societies as part of his general view of history. It was not, however, until the appearance of the French critic Hippolyte Taine that the sociological criticism of literature came into its own. Taine's *History of English Literature* (1863) is the first attempt to apply systematically to a large body of literature a fully elaborated theory of literature's historical and sociological origins.

Taine's theoretical conception of literature, as set forth in his Introduction to the *History of English Literature*, is extremely mechanistic. A poem bears the imprint of its creator as a fossil bears that of the once living animal. Complex civilizations derive "from certain simple spiritual forms," just as "in mineralogy the crystals, however diverse, spring from certain simple physical forms." The great motive forces for all human creations are "the *race*, the *surroundings* and the *epoch*" of the creator, by which are meant, respectively, "the innate and hereditary dispositions" of a people, a kind of national character and consciousness; the physical environment, social conditions and form of government, in fact "all external powers which shape human matter, and by which the external acts on the internal"; and "the acquired momentum," the "ground on which marks are already impressed," the historical seedbed of growth, development, and decay. Every result of human creativity has as its direct cause "a moral disposition, or a combination of moral dispositions: the cause given, they appear; the cause withdrawn, they vanish."

Taine's mechanistic determinism now seems antiquated and simplistic. Wilson writes that Taine thought of himself as a scientist examining literature in the same way that a chemist experiments with chemical compounds in the laboratory. Since literature is not subject to such controlled conditions, the critic must be content to analyze results which have already occurred. Taine, in Wilson's words, pretends "to set the stage for the experiment by describing the moment, the race and the milieu, and then to say: 'Such a situation demands such and such a kind of writer.'" After describing the kind of writer demanded by the situation, he produces a William Shakespeare, a John Milton, a Byron, or "whoever the great figure is—who turns out to prove the accuracy" of his prognosis "by precisely living up to the description." Actually, Taine's criticism of individual writers is not as procrustean as Wilson's description suggests. Levin remarks that Taine's theory is more "a manifesto than a methodology" and that the "history does not adhere to the rigorous principles of the theory." Taine's pages are filled with vivid, memorable portraits of poets and evaluations of their poems—Shakespeare, Jonathan Swift, and Byron immediately come to mind—and to a large extent the history is more a celebration of personality than of the quasi-Hegelianism of the Introduction. If after more than a century many of Taine's judgments, particularly of the poetry of his own time, are no longer credible his criticism retains more than an archaelogical value. It is the work of a man who loved literature, and is a triumph of practice over theory.

One of the more interesting sociological approaches to poetry of modern criticism is Bateson's *English Poetry: A Critical Introduction*, which creates a structure for sociological interpretation more elaborate in many ways than Taine's. For Bateson, the individual poem, and by extension poetry, has an absolute meaning which "is the meaning that it had for the ideal representative of those contemporaries of the poet to whom the poem, implicitly or explicitly, was originally addressed." This meaning can only be recovered by the critic-historian through an understanding of the poem's words and their social implications. He must, through a kind of intellectual metamorphosis, become the "ideal representative" of the poet's contemporaries to whom the poem was at first directed. Impressionism is viewed as the great enemy of critical understanding, and the emphasis on analysis throughout the book—to the point of redundancy—reflects the measure of Bateson's scorn for the "lotus-eating" concept of reading poetry.

Convinced that English poetry constitutes too vast a field "for profitable historical treatment," Bateson divides it into six consecutive schools: Anglo-French, Chaucerian, Renaissance, Augustan, Romantic, and Modern. The parameters he establishes for each defy the conventional wisdom: "the last genuinely Renaissance poem of any merit is perhaps Congreve's 'On Mrs. Arabella Hunt Singing' (c. 1692)" and "the only surviving Romantic poet of any distinction is de la Mare (b. 1873), whose last collection of poems came out in 1945." Bateson hypothesizes that each poetic school covers approximately five generations, each lasting about thirty-five years, and each generation is seen as a distinct stage of poetic development, beginning with "the Experimental Initiators," proceeding to "the Assured Masters" and ending with "the Decadents." Parallel with the six schools, Bateson sets up "six distinguishable social orders whose basic incentives will provide a poetic content in the central line of evolution of each school." These are the Period of Lawyers' Feudalism, the Local Democracy of the Yeomanry, the Centralized Absolutism of the Prince's Servants, the Oligarchy of the Landed Interests, the Plutocracy of Business, and the Managerial State.

The second half of Bateson's book is devoted to the analysis of individual poems within the framework of the social orders. The approach is signified by such chapter headings as "The Yeoman Democracy and Chaucer's 'Miller's Tale'" and "The Money-Lender's Son: 'L'Allegro' and 'Il Penseroso.'" Bateson's readings, while interesting and original, do not always establish compelling relationships between the poems and the social formulations. Though it is not possible in a short space to reproduce the intricacies of his analysis of Thomas Gray's *Elegy Written in a Country Churchyard* (1751), Bateson's conclusion that the poem is in large measure a protest against the "arrogant oligarchy" of mid-eighteenth century England is highly conjectural, and his interpretation of Jonathan Swift's "A Description of the Morning" as an attack on "the *laissez-faire* individualism of urban capitalism" is not entirely convincing.

In "The Quickest Way out of Manchester: Four Romantic Odes" Bateson argues that the upper middle class in nineteenth century England suffered from a suppressed sense of guilt over the plight of the poor caused by laissez-faire capitalism that resulted in a splitting of the individual psyche, and that it is precisely this conflict "between the personality integrated in a social environment and the anti-social 'split man' (Dr. Jekyll and Mr. Hyde), that is mirrored in Romantic poetry." The argument that "Ode: Intimations of Immortality from Recollections of Early Childhood," "Dejection: An Ode," "Ode to the West Wind," and "Ode on a Grecian Urn" reflect this Romantic disintegration, though fascinating, is simply not persuasive. Bateson asserts that William Wordsworth and Samuel Taylor Coleridge were suffering from the "disease" of Romanticism. They are seen as "among the first victims of that *mal du siècle* which derived from the attempt to prolong adolescence artificially." The interest of their two odes rests in the different ways they "react to what is fundamentally the same phenomenon." The weakness of this argument is that the "attempt to prolong adolescence artificially" is not related to the guilt resulting from the heartless competitiveness of laissez-faire economics, supposedly the root cause of Romantic guilt and dissociation. Despite such shortcomings as these, Bateson's approach is worthwhile in that it forces readers to reexamine traditional poems from radically new perspectives.

No discussion of the sociological approach to poetry would be complete without some attention being given to Marxist criticism, which is considerably more uniform in its objectives and methods than other sociological approaches. Flourishing in the 1930's, it frequently sought to impose a greater correlation between literature and life than Karl Marx himself thought existed, severely distorting both in the process. In its classic form, it holds that dialectical materialism is the fountainhead of all human activity, including literature, which is valued only to the extent that it expresses Marxist ideas. In its reduction of the ends of literature to service to the state, Marxist criticism displays as myopic a didacticism as Leo Tolstoy's *What Is Art?* (1896), which values literature only as an expression of evangelical Christianity. Bourgeois literature is dismissed as "decadent" and out of harmony with the inevitable tide of history.

Granville Hicks's *Figures of Transition: A Study of British Literature at the End of the Nineteenth Century* (1939) is one of the better works to come out of the tradition. More temperate and better written than most Marxist criticism, it contains perceptive chapters on "Socialism and William Morris," "The Pessimism of Thomas Hardy," and especially "Oscar Wilde and the Cult of Art." Hicks argues that in the Victorian period a new industrial class was able to consolidate its political power to rule the nation and that in the course of its rise it gave birth to or received "sets of ideas adapted to the process of its growth—ideas loosely organized in utilitarianism and evangelicalism." These ideas became established as a significant "part of the intellectual world of the Victorian authors." How the major writers grappled with them is the real subject of the book. Hicks's method is largely biographical and broadly analytical and his evaluations are for the most part evenhanded. Even as he is aware that people read poets for their poetry, not their politics, Hicks clarifies "why the great Victorians stood in a curiously complicated relationship to the dominant ideas and attitudes of their period" by examining the rise of the middle class and the progress of industrial capitalism during the period.

Christopher Caudwell's ambitious *Illusion and Reality: A Study of the Sources of Poetry* undertakes to analyze the origin and future of poetry as well as the development of English poetry from the mid-sixteenth century to the 1930's within the context of doctrinaire Marxism. For Caudwell, "Art is the product of society, as the pearl is the product of the oyster," and "Poetry is clotted social history, the emotional sweat of man's struggle with Nature." Caudwell's theory that poetry grew out of the necessity of bringing in the harvest is intriguing, and his idea that the rhythm of poetry puts people in touch with one another in a particular physiological and emotional way, creating "a special herd commonness that is distinct from the commonness of seeing each other in the same real world of perceptual experience," is especially acute in view of the psychology of Woodstock; but his assertion that free verse "reflects the final anarchic bourgeois attempt to abandon all social relations in a blind negation of them, because man has completely lost control of his social relationships" illustrates the degree to which his belief in the irrefutable power of dialectical materialism dominates his thinking, leading him into oversimplifications and procrustean distortions.

These weaknesses are especially evident in the three chapters on "English Poets," which purport to trace the development of English poetry through eleven movements beginning with what Caudwell calls "Primitive Accumulation, 1550-1600" and ending with "The Final Capitalistic Crisis, 1930—?" Intermediate movements are "The Bourgeois Revolt, 1625-1650," "The Era of Mercantilism and Manufacture, 1688-1750," "The Decline of British Capitalism, 1825-1900," and so on. In a schema more detailed than Bateson's, each period of transition is characterized by "General Characteristics" and "Technical Characteristics." The "Period of Primitive Accumulation" encompass the Elizabethan age, which is seen to be informed by the triumph of individuality with the characteristic hero of the "absolute prince." The iambic rhythm of Elizabethan poetry is thought to indicate "the free and boundless development of the personal will." On the other hand, the poetry of the Restoration, which occurred in the movement of "The Counter-Puritan Reaction, 1650-1688," "forgets its noble sentiments and becomes cynical, measured or rational." There is an alliance of the bourgeoisie and the aristocracy "and the court returns, but no longer in the form of the absolute prince." The formal rules of Restoration poetry are designed "to restrain the 'spirit' whose violence has proved dangerous. Poetry indicates its readiness to compromise by moving within the bounds of the heroic couplet."

Caudwell's method is mainly one of categorical pronouncement uninformed by close reading. There is virtually no citation of texts. Individual poets and poems are made to fit preestablished categories, resulting in the grossest deformations. Thus, Shakespeare "is an official of the court or of the bourgeois nobility" and his writing "is not in its form individualistic: it is still collective." *In Memoriam* (1850) is "the most genuinely pessimistic poem in English up to this date" and it alone of Alfred, Lord Tennyson's poems "in any way successfully mirrors contemporary problems in contemporary terms." Various other examples of such fallacious interpretation might easily be adduced.

The final chapter of Caudwell's book is entitled "The Future of Poetry," but it is mainly an analysis of the coming collapse of the bourgeoisie state and the inevitable triumph of Communism when the State, no longer necessary, will "wither away." Caudwell predicts that under Communism poetry will become more individual:

> The change of values, the de-vulgarisation of life, the growth of collective freedom and the release of individual consciousness which take place in communism, means the return of these social values, regenerated and ennobled, to the palette of the artist.

Caudwell is remarkably short on specifics, and the history of the Soviet Union in the almost fifty years since his book appeared has not borne out either his political or literary prophecies. *Illusion and Reality: A Study of the Sources of Poetry*, as ambitious as it is, collapses under the weight of its own theory.

This is clearly not the case with Raymond Williams' *The Country and the City*. This book, published in 1973, may well be the finest work yet to emerge from the general tradition of Marxist criticism. Characterized by an encyclopedic grasp of detail and a profound understanding of the mechanisms of historical change, *The Country and the City* is an analysis of the ideas of the country and the city in English literature within the broad context of economic history. Williams believes that from the very beginning "of the capitalist mode of production, our powerful images of country and city have been ways of responding to a whole social development." The ideas of the country and the city are necessarily complex because they have at the same time "specific contents and histories" and "forms of isolation and identification of more general processes." What makes Williams' book particularly valuable is his dramatization of this complexity through the acute analysis of literary texts, largely poems, always buttressed by ample citation, together with an equally perceptive analysis of social and economic forces pressing through in the literature. Such stereotypes as "wicked town," "innocent country," and "good old days" are dispelled, and new readings of poets as diverse as Ben Jonson and Wordsworth are given. Especially enlightening are Williams' discussions of the intricacies of the pastoral tradition, of the ways in which the country-house poems of the seventeenth century relate to transformations of the social order, and of how the "agrarian confidence of the eighteenth century" is tempered by "feelings of loss and melancholy and regret: from the ambivalence of Thomson to the despair of Goldsmith."

The final chapters of *The Country and the City* are devoted to an analysis of the forms and consequences of capitalist exploitation at the local, national, and international levels. Though Williams is not a blind follower of Marxist doctrine, he does assert that "the active powers of minority capital, in all its possible forms, are our most active enemies, and they will have to be not just persuaded but defeated and superseded." The book, concluding with the hope that the dehumanizing division of labor can be overcome by "new forms of cooperative effort," is a triumph in the skillful use of diverse materials, modified by a guiding vision, to produce a coherent view of the interrelations of literature and the changing social world.

The sociological criticism of poetry derives its strength from its eclecticism. It is most effective when it is not tied too closely to theory and when it leads to educated critical evaluation. It occupies a central place in the study of literature, illuminating what many in the great classical tradition of criticism, beginning with Aristotle and progressing through Sir Philip Sidney and Percy Bysshe Shelley to Matthew Arnold and T. S. Eliot, consider central: the humanizing and ultimately socializing power of poetry.

Bibliography

Bateson, F. W. *English Poetry: A Critical Introduction*, 1950.

Caudwell, Christopher. *Illusion and Reality: A Study of the Sources of Poetry*, 1937.

Danby, John F. *Poets on Fortune's Hill*, 1952.

Daiches, David. *Critical Approaches to Literature*, 1956.

Duncan, Hugh Dalziel. *Language and Literature in Society*, 1953.

Eliot, T. S. "The Social Function of Poetry," in *On Poetry and Poets*, 1957.

Hicks, Granville. *Figures of Transition: A Study of British Literature at the End of the Nineteenth Century*, 1939.

Levin, Harry. "Literature as an Institution," in *Accent*. VI (Spring, 1946), pp. 159-168.

Taine, H. A. *History of English Literature*, 1863.

Wellek, René, and Austin Warren. *Theory of Literature*, 1949.

Williams, Raymond. *The Country and the City*, 1973.

_____ . *The Long Revolution*, 1961.

Wilson, Edmund. *The Triple Thinkers*, 1938.

Witte, W. "The Sociological Approach to Literature," in *Modern Language Review*. XXXVI (January, 1941), pp. 86-94.

Robert G. Blake

ARCHETYPAL AND PSYCHOLOGICAL CRITICISM

Historically, an archetypal approach to poetry is derived from Sir James Frazer's work in comparative anthropology, *The Golden Bough* (1890-1915), and from the depth psychology of Carl G. Jung. Frazer discovered certain repetitive cultural patterns which transcended time and place appearing in widely different myths and literatures. Jung posited the existence of a collective unconscious within each individual, a racial memory which held a variety of archetypes. The archetypes or recurrent patterns and images had to do with birth, death, rebirth, marriage, childhood, old men, and magnanimous mothers, heroes and villains, male and female, love and revenge, and countless others. A type of person, a type of action, a type of relationship was so embedded within a man's history that any new appearance was imbued with the force and richness of every past occurrence. When literature possesses such archetypes, its potency is magnified.

An archetypal critic of poetry can employ a Jungian psychology as an extraliterary body of knowledge, in contrast to the archetypal criticism represented by Northrop Frye, in which archetypes do not refer to anything outside literature but to a larger unifying category within literature itself. Even though the term "archetypal" is relevant to both Jung and Frye, their critical intentions differ. A Jungian approach to poetry seeks to wrest meaning from the poem by referring specific images, persons, and patterns to broader, richer archetypes. A Frye approach assumes that there is a totality of structure to literature represented by a variety of common literary archetypes. It is the critic's job to connect individual works to the total structure of literature by way of the recognition of archetypes. Thus, one archetypal approach, Jungian, involves content and meaning, and the other, derived from Frye, involves systematic literary form.

It is only the Jungian variety of archetypal criticism that has relevance for a distinctively "psychological" approach to literature. A Jungian archetype is an inherited racial pattern or disposition residing in a layer of the unconscious which all persons share. It is brought to light by the poet's imaginative transformation of the archetype into a symbol, a symbol which appears in the poem. All depth psychologies, which postulate the existence of an unconscious, are predicated on the notion that a symbol emerging from an unconscious level may manifest itself in a poem. Freudians, however, do not interpret man's psychological base as the collective unconscious; their symbols emerge from the personal unconscious and therefore have no connection with archetypes. Within the psychoanalytic group, there are a number of schools and therefore a number of psychological approaches to poetry. After discussing the Jungian approach (which is both archetypal and psychological), Frye's approach, and the varieties of psychoanalytic approaches, the phenomenological approach, which owes nothing to archetype or symbol, will be discussed.

A Jungian Approach to Poetry

Carl G. Jung deals specifically with literature in the following essays: "The Type Problem in Poetry," "The Phenomenology of the Spirit in Fairytales," "On the Relation of Analytical Psychology to Poetry," and "Psychology and Literature." What ties Jung's discussion of literature to psychology is the symbol. The inexplicable part of the symbol is, according to Jung, a manifestation of certain "inherited" structural elements of the human psyche. These elements or "archetypes" are revealed in dreams, visions, or fantasies and are analogous to the figures one finds in mythology, sagas, and fairytales.

In "Psychology and Literature," Jung mentions those "visionary artists" who seem to allow us "a glimpse into the unfathomed abyss of what has not yet become." Beyond Jung's specific focus on symbol as revealed in literature as a basis for certain hypotheses and finally for an entire depth psychology which may be applied in turn to literature itself, Jung's study of the nature of symbol gives him an especially perceptive understanding of the nature of literature. Jung has no concern for the specific form, the presentation of symbols in literature; it is not possible to distinguish the symbolic processes of the poet from those of anyone else. The symbolic richness of a work as illuminated by the Jungian approach, therefore, does not itself make the work successful. A Jungian methodology, however, can be said to reinforce the notion of a symbolic unity of a work in the sense that it can make explicit certain image-patterns which may be obscure.

The Freudian attacks upon Jung's view of art are strident and somewhat muddled. Frederick Crews believes that invoking the Jungian system is contradictory—a view presented at length in Edward Glover's *Freud or Jung* (1950). For Jung, art represents necessary contact with the personal unconscious, as in the case of psychological art, and with the collective unconscious, as in the case of visionary art. While Sigmund Freud's artist is a man who turns from the real world to a fantasy life that permits him to express his erotic wishes, Jung's artist is not driven to art because of such unfulfilled desires but achieves his art through a natural encountering of energies existing on two levels of the unconscious and through a manifestation of archetypal energy by means of unique symbols.

With Freud, no universal, inherited archetypes exist; therefore no continuum of comparable symbols can be traced in literature except those that refer to the personal unconscious and specifically to repressed energy therein. Symbols in Freud's view represent instinctual needs and are always defined within a limited model of the human personality—one in which no real growth beyond childhood takes place. On the other hand, Jung's consideration of archetype and symbol as emerging from a nonpathological relationship between consciousness and two levels of the unconscious goes beyond Freud's notion that all art is the sublimation of repressed drives.

The Jungian approach has been criticized for reducing the artist to a mere instrument of the archetype. This criticism, however, is based on a confusion between the archetype and the symbol, the observable image representing the archetype; it is an image which cannot be fully grasped and which does not fully realize the archetype. The archetype may be considered autonomous, since it does not depend on the conscious mind. The symbol that the imagination grasps, however, is manifested in accord with the volitions of the conscious mind. Actual pictorial and verbal images owe their aesthetic aspects not to the uncontrollable forces of the archetype but to the forming disposition of the conscious mind. A Jungian approach to literature casts light on the symbolic aura of a literary work as well as on the creative process itself. Such revelation in turn, from a psychological view, acquaints us with unconscious levels that we ourselves cannot reach and encourages a continuation of our own growth. As in Norman Holland's reader-response approach, the Jungian critic-reader possesses a personality which develops through literature, although the literary text in the Jungian view is certainly a repository for symbols which transcend the personal.

A Jungian Approach to "The Sick Rose" by William Blake

> O Rose, thou art sick!
> The invisible worm
> That flies in the night,
> In the howling storm,
>
> Has found out thy bed
> Of crimson joy,
> And his dark secret love
> Does thy life destroy.

The design accompanying the poem pictures the worm in human form. Two other human figures are pictured in lamenting postures. A Jungian interpretation of this poem brings in archetypes of Anima and Animus and Shadow. In Jung's view, the human male must assimilate his contrasexual self, his female Anima, and the human female must assimilate her contrasexual self, her male Animus. The totally individuated person is androgynous on the psychic level and is able to utilize energies from male and female contrasexual portions of the psyche. In this poem, the worm is the rose's Animus and she is his Anima. Both are clearly divided, obdurate in their own sexual identities. Divided so, there is no mutual sexual interaction, no sexual dynamic. Instead, the rose has a "bed of crimson joy" which obviously must have been hidden, since the worm has to journey to find it. The Shadow archetype is formed in the personal unconscious by repressed desires. In this poem, the rose has clearly repressed sexual desire since she hides from her male counterpart and thus allows him but one entrance—as a ravager. His love is dark and secret from the perspective of the rose. He is indeed a shadow figure emerging from the night, a shadow of the rose's own unconscious.

Northrop Frye's Archetypal Criticism

Frye's archetypes connect "one poem with another and thereby [help] to unify and integrate our literary experience" (*Anatomy of Criticism*, 1957). Literature, in Frye's view, is an expression of man's imaginative transformation of his experiences. Ritual and myth were the first creative expression, beginning as stories about a god and developing into "a structural principle of story-telling" (*The Educated Imagination*, 1964). Essential mythic patterns or archetypes manifested themselves in literature. Writers in various periods drew upon these archetypes, modifying them in accordance with the conventions of their own day and the force of their own personalities.

The archetypal literary critic views the entire body of literature as a self-contained universe of these archetypes, an autonomous and self-perpetuating universe which is not effectively interpreted by extraliterary analogues. Frye believes that by confining criticism to an exploration of essential archetypes recurring throughout literature, he is developing a "science" of literary criticism, a science which recognizes that literature, like all art, is self-referential and that the function of criticism is to bring past imaginative transformations of human experiences into the present and to explore the parameters of present transformations. According to Frye, the critic is scientific in his study of literature, although his mission is not to proclaim literature as science but to make man's imaginative transformations of his experience, his literature, "a part of the emancipated and humane community of culture."

Frye discerned four basic types of imaginative transformations of experience in literature. These types first developed as mythic patterns expressing man's attempt to humanize the world around him. The imagination fuses the rhythms of human life with the cycle of nature and then invests the whole with variable emotional import. The fused natural-human cycle is one in which a youthful spring declines into winter and death. Frye then relates literature to the following mythic structure: romance is synonymous with dawn, spring, and birth; comedy is synonymous with the zenith, summer, and marriage; tragedy is synonymous with sunset, autumn, and death; satire is synonymous with darkness, winter, and dissolution.

Frye defines commentary as "the translating of as much as possible of a poem's meaning into discursive meaning" ("Literary Criticism"). Such allegorical commentary, however, is not the aim of *criticism*, which, in Frye's view, is to identify the poem. Like a cultural anthropologist, the literary critic places the poem within its proper literary context. The first context is the total canon produced by the poet under consideration. The second context is historical. For example, John Keats's poetry must be understood within the broader context of Romanticism. Beyond considering the poet's historical context, the critic must consider the genre. Tragedy, Frye says, is a "kind of literary structure," a genre exemplified throughout literary history. The critic must also pay attention to the allusions within the poem itself. John Milton's "Lycidas" for example, reveals historical ties both in its form—pastoral elegy—and in its imagery. These ties are within literature itself. Allusions in a poem by Milton are to a poem by Vergil.

Poems in Frye's Romantic mode possess a vision of the heroic, either religious or secular, with which the poet himself is identified. Gerard Manley Hopkins' "The Windhover" presents a view of Jesus as hero, while Walt Whitman's *Passage to India* (1871) presents the poet as hero. The poet of the romantic mode seeks the imaginative transformation of the natural world, as do Andrew Marvell in "The Garden" and William Butler Yeats in "Sailing to Byzantium." The poets in the comic mode, however, are satisfied with the world as it is, as in Keats's major odes. The tragic mode involves loss and reconciliation through some effort to make sense out of loss, as in Milton's "Lycidas," Percy Bysshe Shelley's *Adonais* (1821), and Hopkins' "The Wreck of the *Deutschland*." The ironic poet does not achieve imaginative transformation of the world through supernatural help but rather achieves a vision of a shattered world. Emily Dickinson's poetry, T. S. Eliot's *The Waste Land* (1922), and Robert Frost's "Stopping by Woods on a Snowy Evening" are examples.

In Frye's criticism, mythic images were the first and clearest expressions of a relationship between man and his world. Literature is thus a "direct descendant of mythology," and biblical and classical mythologies are central myths in Western literature. What the poetry critic of archetypal persuasion ultimately does is to explore archetypal connections, recurrent patterns, in literature. As criticism continues to explore the structure of literature rather than its content, it eventually encompasses literature as a whole as its content. Once this is achieved—when criticism has a hold on literature as a whole— questions regarding the purpose of literature, its relationship to society, and its connections with discursive literature can be tackled.

Frye has been criticized for ignoring the critic's task of evaluation, for separating literature from life, for ignoring the individuality of a work by emphasizing its archetypal relations with other literature, and for creating, in *Anatomy of Criticism*, a literary work rather than a critical theory which has practical applications. Frye is criticized for assuming that literary discourse and poetic vision are unique and separable from all modes of "extraliterary" thought and discourse. Frye's views here are traced to the German idealist tradition, in which the words of the poet are somehow autonomous, free of referential meaning. Frye's view of literature is criticized because literature is seen as the ultimate goal of culture, as superior to the objective world because it transcends it by way of the imagination. The liberally educated person has replaced an unsatisfying world with its imaginative transformation—literature. What is celebrated in Frye "is a fantastical, utopian alternative to the perception of a degraded social existence: a human discoursing free of all contingency, independent of all external forces, a discoursing empowered by unconditioned human desire" (Frank Lentricchia).

A Frye Approach to "The Sick Rose"

In Frye's essay "Blake's Treatment of the Archetype," he comments on Blake's powerfully integrated theory of art and of the unity of symbol and archetype in Blake's work. Frye places Blake in the anagogic phase of symbolic meaning, in which the total ritual of man, the total dream of man is represented. Blake's "The Sick Rose" is interlocked with Blake's entire canon; in itself it re-creates the "total form of verbal expression" of Blake's work ("Levels of Meaning in Literature"). Blake's symbols are anagogic symbols, symbols which turn outward toward the macrocosm of Blake's entire myth and inward toward any individual work (in this case "The Sick Rose") which expresses the unity of desire and reality, of dream and ritual.

Only religious myths have achieved this combination of personal dream or desire and reality or ritual. Romance, a phase just below the anagogic phase, reflects a conflict rather than a unity of desire and reality. It also employs archetypes which do not have a limitless range of reference as do the "monads" of the anagogic phase. If "The Sick Rose" is placed within a mythical rather than anagogic phase of symbolic meaning, the rose and the worm would have correspondences to other roses and worms in literature but would not be true representations of the visionary apocalyptic kind of poetry that Blake's is. The location of the poem within Frye's anatomy depends upon a proper location of Blake's entire work within that anatomy. All the richness of the proper fit can be brought to bear on "The Sick Rose." Thus, finding the proper niche for the poem rather than interpreting it as a unique, unconnected entity is the task of Frye's critical anthropologist.

Psychoanalytic Approaches to Poetry—Freud

Sigmund Freud's views of the relationship between art and psychoanalysis were presented in his "Delusion and Dreams in Jensen's *Gradiva*" and in "The Relationship of the Poet to Daydreaming." The forbidden wishes of dream, associated with the psychosexual stages (oral, anal, phallic, and genital), appear in the literary work but are disguised by distracting aspects of aesthetic form. The superegos of both reader and author are circumvented, and art serves to release unconscious forces which might otherwise overwhelm the ego. The critic's job is to delve below the surface of a distracting literary façade and point out the lurking fantasies. Freud himself began, in his book on Leonardo da Vinci, a stage of psychoanalytic criticism which has been termed "genetic reductionism," or the discussion of a work in terms of the author's neurosis.

Genetic reductionism has been and remains a primary focus of psychoanalytic criticism in spite of a general recognition that the danger for psychoanalysis is the lure of a simplistic and mechanistic interpretation. The dispute here is between those who hold that literature is autonomous, existing independently of a creator's emotional disposition, and those who hold that a psychoanalytic critic can "show how a writer's public intention was evidently deflected by a private obsession" (Frederick Crews). A psychoanalytic examination of the author's wishes and anxieties, in the view of antipsychoanalytic criticism, ignores the variety and ontology of literature. Crews argues, nevertheless, that there does exist a certain range of problems which psychoanalytic assumptions illuminate.

Freud also initiated a psychoanalytic interpretation of particular characters in his work on Wilhelm Jensen's *Gradiva* (1918) and in his discussion of oedipal complexes displayed by certain characters in Sophocles' *Oedipus Tyrannus* (c. 429 B.C.) and William Shakespeare's *Hamlet* (1600-1601). While most contemporary psychoanalytic critics deplore genetic reductionism, there is debate regarding the treatment of characters as real people. Critics on one side of the spectrum tend to put a character on the analyst's couch, talk about the character's childhood, and totally neglect other aspects of the literary work. Opposing critics contend that while readers do indeed experience characters as human beings, the critic must use psychoanalysis so as to understand fully the character in relation to other aspects of the work.

In Freud's view, literature was like dream—a symbolic expression of the unconscious whose original meaning could be interpreted. This interest in the relationship between the writer and his work, in the creative process itself and its importance in interpreting a work, remains an interest of contemporary psychoanalysts and psychoanalytic critics. Freud's original view of creativity has been refashioned in various ways and psychoanalytic critics now fall into various camps. Freud's view of the work of literature as a product of the author's sublimated desires has been challenged by an emphasis upon the literary work as "the potential space between the individual and the environment," by an emphasis upon the reader whose own "identity theme" fashions meaning from a work of art, and by an emphasis on preconscious and conscious involvement with literary creation (Donald W. Winnicott). These views have been termed, respectively, Object-Relations, Reader-Response (based on the work of Norman Holland), and Ego Psychology. The psychoanalyst Jacques Lacan has also created a unique approach to literature.

The Classic, Freudian Approach to "The Sick Rose"

The focus in this approach is immediately upon the poet. The question is: What "dark secret" repressed by the poet has found release in this poem?

The poem is a mere symptom of the poet's neurotic desires. The rose can be viewed as a female whose "bed of crimson joy" is "found out." This is no healthy, natural sexual act, however, because the "worm" or phallus "flies in the night," in a "howling storm," and destroys his beloved with "his dark secret love." At the root of the poem, therefore, is the incestuous desire of the poet. The secret love of the poet is his mother.

Psychoanalytic Approach to Poetry—Ego Psychology

Freud's view of literature-as-symptom emerging from the id is modified by ego psychologists who recognize creativity as a function of the ego. For the ego psychologists, literature in the service of the ego reflects the ego's mission of mediating between self and others, between id and super-ego. Symbols from the id are therefore shaped in literature so as to be communicable beyond the intrapsychic level. The movement in ego psychology is away from literature as raw wish fulfillment of the author and toward the literary text as a manifestation of id instinct and ego-monitoring. Literary critics utilizing ego psychology seek in the text not the disguised wish or wishes of the author but their transformation by the ego in the direction of something beyond the personality of the author, something of thematic import, communicable and succeeding or not succeeding depending upon the author's gifts or skills.

The ego psychoanalyst analyzing poetry emphasizes ego functions rather than id impulses. In what ways, this critic asks, does the poem display the ego's assertion of control by allowing repressed instincts an outlet? A discovery of what instincts are latent does not lead the critic into the entire poem, but a study of the poem as a manifestation of an ego directing the release of repressed instincts does.

The Ego Psychologist's Approach to "The Sick Rose"

For the critic applying the theories of ego psychology, incest may remain the repressed desire of the poem, but the ways in which the conscious ego expresses that hidden desire in the form of the poem itself is the proper subject matter of the critic. The poet distances himself from the poem by adopting a censorious tone. The directness and clarity of poetic style also reveal the wise perceptiveness of the poet with regard to the sexual plight of rose and worm. Thus, both tone and style point to the ego's mastery over a repressed desire of the id, and a search for such ego mastery results in an analysis of the poem. The poet's perceptiveness does not lie in the core fantasy of incest but in his view of love which must be invisible, which must emerge only at night. The poet's perceptiveness lies in his understanding that a covert sexuality injures and ultimately destroys both sexual partners. His censoriousness lies in his view that such clandestine sexuality is "unethical," that it works against humanity and the individual human life. The instinctual base remains incest but it has been controlled by the ego's fashioning of the poem, making the poem something other than the wish which inspired it.

Psychoanalytic Approach to Poetry—Reader-Response

Norman Holland, in *The Dynamics of Literary Response* (1968), emphasizes the instinctual drives of the id rather than the monitoring, controlling powers of the ego, although, unlike early Freudian interpreters of literature, he posits an ego which mediates between the id and the superego and whose mediation is the form of the work itself. The form of a literary work is indeed comparable to the ego defenses against the assault of the id, but it is this assault which is the hidden, determining root of the work. A core fantasy is the base of every literary work and the writer, through form, defends against it, tries to shape it in the direction of redeemable social, moral, and intellectual value. The eye of the critic, in Holland's view, is on the core fantasy, on the id, while the eye of the ego psychologist-critic is on the ego's manipulation of the id through literary form. The core fantasy critic seeks out the core fantasy and demonstrates the author's artistry in shaping and disguising it. The reader accepts both the core fantasy, which he or she may share, and the devices employed to contain the fantasy. Thus, the reader achieves pleasure by possession of the fantasy as well as by having it controlled. The reader, in the view of the ego psychologist-critic, attains pleasure primarily through the pattern of ego control expressed in the literary work.

In Holland's later work (*Poems in Persons, Five Readers Reading*, both 1975), he places the pertinent core fantasy in the mind of the reader rather than in the text. The reader extracts meaning from the text in accordance with his "identity theme." The reader may be directed by his own desires to seek them in the text he reads. Finding them, he may deal with them as he does in his own life. He may also attend the author in transforming a core fantasy into something socially acceptable or intellectually significant. Holland believes that through the literary text the reader confronts himself, engaging in an act of self-discovery by analyzing what he as a reader has said about a text. Throughout the three faces of psychoanalysis which Holland identifies— psychology of the unconscious (id), of the ego, and of the self—readers have always been structuring the text by means of their own intentions. A realization of this fact enables readers to make use of literature as an opportunity to gain self-knowledge.

A critical approach to poetry based on Holland's later work would begin with a description of the critic-reader's own responses to the poem. These responses, determined by the critic-reader's "identity theme," direct an analysis of the poem. A dialectic then takes place between the objective reality of the poem, a common store of sharable realities, and the critic.

The Reader-Response Critic's Approach to "The Sick Rose"

The reader-response critic approaches the poem by focusing on those personal connections made in the poem. Such an interpretation is not necessarily the same thing as a literal interpretation, for example, that the poem is about the perils of gardening. From the reader-response view, this poem would be seen as a poem only about gardening by a gardener. It is quite possible in the first line of the poem, "O Rose, thou art sick," for a reader to think of someone named Rose, perhaps a mother or a sister or a lover, who was or is or may be sick. The "invisible worm" becomes a disease, such as cancer, that has struck the reader-critic's beloved suddenly, perhaps in the full bloom of life, in bed of "crimson joy." Now, this cancer slowly destroys the beloved.

Given this personal reading, what can the poem do to assert its own existence? The reader-critic must first be willing to entertain the notion that perhaps the poem is not about Rose's bout with cancer. The poet has used the word "love." The poem asserts itself, if given a chance, by its words, and the word here is "love." This "love" "flies in the night" "in the howling storm"—it emerges from Nature. Thus, in spite of the apparent ludicrousness of such a subjective beginning, the reader-critic is led toward an acceptance of this "love" as natural. It is in the nature of things to die, or to love sexually. Neither death nor sexuality can be repressed wisely. In this instance, the path of subjectivity is modified by the poem itself. As this dialectic continues, the original subjectivity of the reader-critic is modified, and the interpretation becomes more "objective" though determined by the identity theme of the reader-critic. What the poem is connects with what the reader is and the result is a thoroughly human form of comprehension.

Psychoanalytic Approaches to Poetry—Object-Relations

Object-relations theory does not hold, as do traditional psychological and ego psychological theories, that a literary work is the product of psychic conflict. It holds, rather, that a literary work is the place where the writer's wishes and the culture around him meet. Rather than emphasizing the literary work as narcissistic wish fulfillment, object-relations critics emphasize those aspects of a literary work which are not the author's self, which lead toward a world outside the writer. This outside world of convention and tradition is transformed by the writer, he having accepted what is outside his own self. The literary work as an object is an extension of the writer somewhat as a teddy bear is an extension of a child. Both teddy bear and literary work are invested with illusions; yet they are objects in the world. In the case of the child, the teddy bear is something like the mother's breast, although significantly it is another object. Similarly, the literary work is wish fulfillment and yet an object which is not pure wish fulfillment but a place where wishes and world meet, an object representing a "collective love affair with the world."

A critical approach to poetry based on an object-relations theory would not focus on the poem as an expression of intrapsychic conflict but as the ground in which the poet's wishes and the outside world meet. In what ways does the poem signify what the internal desires of the poet are? In what ways does it stand as a transformation of those desires into what is outside the poet? The meeting of internal and external is the poem.

The Object-Relations Critic's Approach to "The Sick Rose"

The object-relations critic views the poem as a meeting ground of the poet's fantasies and the surrounding environment—in this case, late eighteenth century England. If incest is on the unconscious mind of the poet, he has presented it as nothing more specific than "dark secret love," a phrase that has meaning in the context of an England in which hypocrisy with regard to sexuality was increasing. If the poet were really expressing a desire to unite sexually with his mother, then the poem would serve as an illusionary connection between himself and his mother. The poem as object, however, is clearly a transitional object rather than a complete illusion of the poet. The poem is a transition between the poet's desire for uncensored sexuality and the moral prohibitions against sexuality that were prevalent in the poet's day.

Psychoanalytic Approaches to Poetry—Jacques Lacan

Lacanian psychoanalysis once again resurrects the sole supremacy of the id in the creative process. Indeed, the unconscious itself is structured as a language and therefore both the conscious and the unconscious are identically rooted. Literary discourse, like ordinary discourse, is symbolical and subjective. Rather than the id being a source of instinctual drives which appear disguised in literature, specifically in the language of literature, the Lacanian id is a reservoir of words which determine perceptions.

Lacanian literary interpretation depends upon tracing literary language to a constitutive language of the unconscious. It depends upon relating significant words in the literary text to words signified in the unconscious. The unconscious is structured not according to innate laws but originally according to the image of another, someone whom the child is dependent upon (usually the mother). This desire to remain secure is fulfilled when the child constructs his unconscious in accordance with the significant other. The "discourse" of the other becomes the discourse of the child's unconscious, which is fictional insofar as it is not the child's but another's.

In Lacan's view, the ego is composed of a *moi*, which is unconscious, overriding the other but determined by it, and the *je*, which is identified with spoken language and culture. The discourse of the *moi* permeates the discourse of the *je*. The symbolic, subjective *moi* permeates the apparent logical discourse of the *je*. The Lacanian literary critic seeks to go from the discourse of the *je* to the discourse of the *moi*, from a symbolical consciousness to a symbolical unconsciousness. The discourse of the *moi*, of the unconscious, is weakly and elusively manifest in the surface of the literary text. Both signifiers and signifieds are available in the surface of the text, and the act of literary interpretation attempts to reconstruct, wherever possible, the connection between signifiers and signifieds. It is an act which seeks to uncover what unconscious desires determine the details of the literary text.

A Lacanian Approach to "The Sick Rose"

A Lacanian interpretation attempts to break through the language of the *je* and reach the symbolical unconscious of the *moi*. The literal language of the *je* in this poem has to do with gardening, with the destruction of a rose by a worm which is invisible to the naked eye. When readers probe more deeply, they discover that the poem is really "talking" about human sexuality. The poet, Blake, clearly reveals his symbolic intent in his depiction of human figures in the design accompanying the poem. A Lacanian analysis probes below the level of the language of the *je* in poems apparently not symbolical and not intended to be symbolical by the poet, whose surface language seems to mean no more than it says. The "invisible worm" as a phallus signifies a flaccid phallus. The erect, firm phallus *lies* not *flies* in the night. The "dark secret love" cannot be consummated with the flaccid phallus and thus the *moi*, formed by a desire to please the mother, describes in this poem the fulfillment in words of a desire the reality of which the words themselves belie.

Psychoanalytic Approaches to Poetry—A Critical Overview

Alan Roland and Frederick Crews, among others, have provided criticism of various psychoanalytic approaches to literature. Roland objects to the correlation of literary work and daydream. The literary work, in his view, goes far beyond the author's fantasies and the imagery of dream. Poetic metaphor and the structure of paradox are essential components of the literary work but not of dream. According to Roland, literary form must be freed from the notion that it is synonomous with the ego's defenses. Defense is viewed as only part of form. Object-relations critics do not limit the author's fantasies to those of a psychosexual stage, but they fail, in Roland's view, to integrate their exploration of fantasies with what the work may mean on its highest level. In opposition to Holland's view of the reader, Roland feels that, besides a core fantasy, a literary work possesses an abstract meaning, a total vision formally created. The relationship between these two levels should be described by the critic. In Roland's view, the core fantasy within the reader's mind is apparently affected by the critic's efforts.

Frederick Crews sees as reductionistic the views that Holland expresses in *The Dynamics of Literary Response*, although he admits that Holland is sensitive to literary form and very cautious about making "armchair diagnosis of authors." Holland's reductionism lies in his view of literature as subterfuge for forbidden thoughts. Crews also maintains that no one goes to criticism to discover the "identity theme" of the critic but rather to learn more about literature as a meaning-creating enterprise.

In the final analysis, according to Crews, Holland's focus on the reader is yet another example of academic objectivity being attacked by subjectivists, by those who argue that the interpretation of literature is a private affair. Crews finds no real remedy for contemporary psychoanalytic criticism, not even ego psychology. Eventually, all psychoanalytic critics realize that their interpretations say more about themselves than about the text, that "they have reduced literature to the rigid and narrow outlines of their own personalities." A psychoanalytic critic, according to Crews, must bear in mind that his method is reductive and that there are many aspects of a work excluded from his approach.

In an essay entitled "Anaesthetic Criticism," Crews goes beyond a discussion of the dangers of reductionism in psychoanalytic criticism and defends it against antideterministic critics. He considers the "informal taboo" placed on extraliterary theories by many academic critics. Northrop Frye, the most influential antideterministic critic, in Crews's view, advocates an inductive survey of literary works, in which no external conceptual framework is considered. Literature, in Frye's archetypal view, is its own progenitor; although Crews terms such a belief "a common fantasy among writers, a wish that art could be self-fathered, self-nurturing, self-referential, purified of its actual origins in discontent." Such a "fantasy," of course, is no less common among critics than among writers. In essence, critics who deplore the search for causes and effects are antiintellectual, preferring a literary approach in which references to extraliterary analogues are at once disclaimed. Finally, in Crews's view, criticism which ignores the affective element of literature and accentuates the role of form over chaos, of genre conventions and the like, is anaesthetic criticism. Crews concludes that regardless of the dangers of reductionism in the application of psychoanalysis to literature, the approach is more efficacious than that of such antideterministic critics as Frye.

A Phenomenological Psychological Approach to Poetry

In the case of a phenomenological psychology, a delineation of a *Lebenswelt*, or human life-world of a character, a speaker in a poem, or an author, is in each case a delineation of consciousness. The phenomenologist's desire is to return to lived experiences and "bracket," or set aside, presuppositions. Such experiences are not understood by an examination of external behavior but by an examination of psychic reality, or consciousness. Since consciousness is always consciousness of something, intentionality with regard to external reality being always implicit, a focus on a person in literature or on the author himself, on various self-revelations, reveals the *Lebenswelt*. To the phenomenological psychologist, literary accounts—poetry, drama, or fiction—are personal records, descriptions of psychic reality which aid in achieving a psychological understanding of both behavior and phenomenal experience. Through a phenomenological approach to poetry, which emphasizes various portrayals of self by both poetic speakers and the poet (portrayals of others, of objects and time), it is possible both to define and to reveal meaning in the poem as a whole.

The poetic consciousness involves the poet's own intentions, which are tied to his own human life-world and his own particular arrangement of phenomena. Although such an arrangement is unique to each poet, a patterning presided over by his own poetic consciousness, such consciousness, by virtue of its intentionality, is directed to and tied to objects comprising the reader's natural universe. The very process of poetic construction and patterning reveals the experiential foundation of the reader's world and illuminates rather than mirrors disparate objects and impressions. The critic of poetry has little interest in poetry as a source of phenomenal experience, as an exploration of psychic-subjective reality. Rather, he utilizes the phenomenological perspective to define the relationship between intentionality and aesthetic patterning or form.

The relationship between intentionality and form cannot be defined until the *Lebenswelt* of each speaker or persona in the poem is defined, leaving the poet's own *Lebenswelt* discernible. Thus, the phenomenological perspective enables the critic to analyze speakers and personae by means of their perceptions of the world and eventually to distinguish aspects of the poem which are derived from intentions not of any speaker or persona but of the poet. Nothing less than the entire poem is revealed.

A Phenomenological Psychological Approach to "The Sick Rose"

In "The Sick Rose" it is possible to discern two "characters" almost immediately—worm and rose. It is also possible to discern a speaker, who may or may not be the poet, and, somewhere behind it all, the poet. Neither worm nor rose are true characters since they do not reveal their own perceptions. Focus must be placed on the speaker of the poem who reveals himself in his revelation regarding the worm and the rose. In spite of the conventional perception that a rose is beautiful, the speaker finds, in the very first line, that this rose is sick. She is sick because her life is being destroyed by the dark secret love of an invisible worm. In the mind of the speaker of the poem, the worm is "the" and not "a" worm; in the mind of the speaker of the poem, the worm is obviously someone or some specific thing. If "someone" is first considered, it is someone up to no good, someone evil. That evil has been created not through hate but through love, albeit a dark secret love. A bright, open love is a love which can be displayed in society without fear of censure. A dark, secret love is that sexual love which must go on behind closed doors, which cannot be lawfully witnessed. The worm in this speaker's mind is a diabolical figure bringing death through sexuality to the rose. When one begins to separate poet from speaker, it is clear that the speaker himself is "sick."

The poet's *Lebenswelt* is not restricted to this one poem. In the case of Blake, it is revealed in the totality of the work he has entitled *The Songs of Innocence and of Experience* (1794). "The Sick Rose" is a song of Experience. Most often the speakers within poems of Experience are themselves victims of what Blake considered to be the "evils" of Experience. In the phenomenological approach, critics employ what is known of the poet as revealed in his other work as a gloss on the poem under consideration. Biographical information becomes important so that the *Lebenswelt* of the poet can be defined. The reader-critic's intention is to know enough about the poet's mode of perception to be able to distinguish the poet from speakers or personae in his poems. The richness of the poem is then revealed as a rhetorical juxtaposition of victimized speaker and critical poet.

In another Experience poem entitled "The Garden of Love," a speaker returns to the garden of love, which previously bore so many sweet flowers, and discovers that it is filled with graves, that priests have bound with briars the speaker's joys and desires. This bound speaker is the speaker of "The Sick Rose." In the poet's view, "the" worm may be a priest, or he may be conventional religion's notion of god. The rose of perfect beauty, in its bed of crimson joy, is destroyed by a priest's or a conventionally perceived god's repressive dark secret love—a love which binds the speaker's joys and desires, a love which is fatal. A dark secret love makes love dark and secret. Only man victimized as this speaker is victimized can construct a god for himself who binds and shackles and is then considered loving because of those acts. The love of an institutionalized religion's god, a god outside man himself, is, in this poet's view, not love but death.

Bibliography

Crews, Frederick. *Out of My System: Psychoanalysis, Ideology and Critical Method*, 1975.
_____ , ed. *Psychoanalysis and Literary Process*, 1970.
Kaplan, Morton and Robert Kloss. *The Unspoken Motive: A Guide to Psychoanalytic Criticism*, 1973.
Paris, Bernard J. *A Psychological Approach to Fiction*, 1974.
Psychology and Literature: Some Contemporary Directions. XII, no. 1 (1980), special issue of *New Literary History*.
Roland, Alan, ed. *Psychoanalysis, Creativity and Literature*, 1978.
Strelka, Joseph, ed. *Literary Criticism and Psychology*, 1976.
Tennenhouse, Leonard, ed. *The Practice of Psychoanalytic Criticism*, 1976.

Joseph Natoli

FORMALISTIC CRITICISM

The formalist approach to poetry was the one most influential in American criticism during the 1940's, 1950's, and 1960's, and it is still the one most often practiced in literature courses in American colleges and universities. Its popularity was not limited to American literary criticism. In France, formalism has long been employed as a pedagogical exercise in reading literature in the universities and in the lycées. In England in the 1940's and in the 1950's, formalism was associated with an influential group of critics writing for a significant critical periodical, *Scrutiny*, the most prominent of whom was F. R. Leavis. There was also a notable formalist movement in the Soviet Union in the 1920's, and, although championed by René Wellek in the United States, its influence at that time was primarily limited to Slavic countries.

The formalist approach in America was popularized by John Crowe Ransom, Allen Tate, Robert Penn Warren, and Cleanth Brooks, all four Southerners, all graduates of Vanderbilt University, and all, in varying degrees, receptive to the indirections and complexities of the modernism of T. S. Eliot, James Joyce, and William Butler Yeats, which their critical method—known as the "New Criticism"—was, in part, developed to explicate. A fifth critic, not directly associated with the Vanderbilt group, R. P. Blackmur, made important contributions to the formalist reading of poetry in *The Double Agent* (1935) and in essays in other books. He did not, however, develop a distinctive formalist method.

Formalism in the History of Literary Criticism

Formalism is clearly a twentieth century critical phenomenon in its emphasis on close reading of the literary text, dissociated from extrinsic references to the author or to his or her society. There had been formalist tendencies before in the history of literary criticism, but it did not, as in twentieth century formalism, approach exclusivity in its emphasis on the structure of the work itself. Aristotle's analysis in the *Poetics* (written sometime between 370 and 322 B.C.) of the complex tragic plot as having a tripartite division of reversal, recognition, and catastrophe is one of the most valuable formalist analyses of the structure of tragedy ever made. That Aristotle's approach to poetics was not intrinsic but extrinsic, however, has been made clear by his twentieth century followers, the Chicago Neo-Aristotelians, Ronald S. Crane and Elder Olson. They have been the harshest critics of what they regard as the limited critical perspective of modern formalists, pointing out that an Aristotelian analysis was characteristically in terms of four causes. These were the formal cause (the form that the work imitates), the material cause (the materials out of which the work is made), the efficient cause (the maker), and the final cause (the effect on the reader or audience). Crane charged in *Critics and Criticism: Ancient and Modern* (1952) that the New Criticism is concerned with only one of these causes, language, in order to distinguish poetic from scientific and everyday uses of language without being able to distinguish among the various kinds of poetry. It is true that formalism is largely concerned with literature as a verbal art. This single-mindedness has been its strength in explication as well as its weakness as a critical theory.

Two key concepts in the literary theory of the English Romantic period may have been influential on twentieth century formalism. Although the New Critics were professedly anti-Romantic following T. S. Eliot's call for impersonality in modern poetry, their stress on the meaning of the total poem rather than finding the meaning centered in a specific part probably owes something to the concept of organic form, assumed by most Romantics and stated explicitly by Samuel Taylor Coleridge in his defense of William Shakespeare. This is the concept that a poem grows like a living organism, its parts interrelated, its form and content inseparable; the total work is thus greater than the sum of its parts. This concept was assumed by all the New Critics except Ransom, who viewed "texture" as separate from structure.

The formalist view of creativity is of a "rage" brought to "order" through submission to the discipline of form. A good poem is characterized by tensions that are usually reconciled. The most detailed statement of this view by a New Critic is in Robert Penn Warren's essay "Pure and Impure Poetry," in which Warren gives a long list of resistances or "tensions" in a good poem. The origin of this idea lies in Romantic critical theory. Warren's statements, as well as Allen Tate's discussion of tension in his essay "Tension in Poetry," undoubtedly owe much to Chapter 14 of Coleridge's *Biographia Literaria* (1817), in which he describes the distinctive quality of the creative imagination of the poet as revealing itself "in the balance or reconciliation of opposite or discordant qualities."

The strongest twentieth century influences on formalism in America and in England were the early essays of T. S. Eliot, especially those in *The Sacred Wood* (1920), and two books by I. A. Richards, *Principles of Literary Criticism* (1924) and *Practical Criticism* (1929). Eliot, influenced by the anti-Romanticism of T. E. Hulme in *Speculations* (1924), called for a theory of the impersonal in the modernist view of poetry to rectify the personality cults of Romantic and Victorian poetry, and he even detailed how to impersonalize personal emotions through the use of "objective correlatives." Eliot's intention was to redirect critical attention from the poet to the work of art, which he declared to be "autotelic," self-contained, a fictive world in itself. It was this pronouncement of Eliot's, more than any statement in his essays in the 1920's, which had the strongest influence on the development of formalist criticism.

Eliot also devised his own version of a Cartesian "split" between logic and untrustworthy feelings, his theory that a dissociation of sensibility took place in English poetry in the late seventeenth century. John Donne had a unified sensibility capable of devouring any kind of experience. In the Metaphysical poets "there is a direct sensuous apprehension of thought": they could think feelings and feel thoughts. The New Critics were to develop a formalist approach to poetry that could show this kind of sensibility at work. To a formalist such as Cleanth Brooks in *Modern Poetry and the Tradition* (1939), Metaphysical poetry was the proper tradition in which to fit modern poetry, and critical techniques were needed in order to explicate the complexities of poetry in the tradition. He provided a model for formalist explication in a brilliant analysis of parallelisms and ironic contrasts utilized functionally by Eliot in *The Waste Land* (1922).

The Formalist Defense of Poetry

Formalism in America and England may have evolved in reaction to nineteenth century literary thought and practice as a method of understanding a modernist literature that was indirect, impersonal, complex, and "autotelic." As far as the New Critics were concerned, their formalism was a defense of poetry in an age of science. Their criticism can quite properly be regarded as an "apology" for poetry in the tradition of Sir Philip Sidney and Percy Bysshe Shelley. An "apology" is a formal defense of poetry in an age thought to be hostile to the poetry of its own time. Sidney "apologized" for poetry at a time when Puritans were attacking drama and voicing suspicions as to whether poetry could and did advance morality. Shelley defended the value of poetry in an age that was beginning to turn to prose, assuming that the golden age of poetry was over. In this tradition the New Critics "apologized" for poetry in an age of logical positivism, when scientific method was regarded as the sole means to truth and poetry was being limited to mere emotive effects.

In his *Principles of Literary Criticism*, I. A. Richards sought to find a place for poetry in an age of science by emphasizing the psychological effects of poetry on the personality of the reader. In *Practical Criticism* he documented the helplessness of his graduate students when confronted with an unidentified poem to explicate, and made a case for a literary criticism that specialized in explicating the text. Richards seemed, however, at least in the earlier book, to be in agreement with the positivistic view that poetry was a purely emotive use of language in contrast to science, which was the language of factual assertion. Although influenced by Richards, the New Critics attempted to counter his apparent denial of a cognitive dimension of poetry. They did this through their formalism, staying inside the poem in their explications and declaring it characteristic of the poet's use of language to direct the reader to meanings back inside the poem rather than to referents outside the poem.

Cleanth Brooks contended that poets actually block too direct a pinpointing to everyday referents outside the poem and that the meanings of a poem cannot be wrenched outside the context of the poem without serious distortions. He was making a case for meaning in the poem and at the same time was keeping poetry out of direct competition with science. In a poem, he asserted, apparently referential statements are qualified by ambiguities, paradoxes, and ironies so that the knowledge offered cannot stand as a direct proposition apart from the poem itself. This is why it does not matter that John Keats in a famous sonnet credits Hernando Cortes, not Vasco de Balboa, with the first sighting by a European of the Pacific Ocean. What Keats writes is true to the poem, not to historical fact, and he does not intend a truth claim to be taken outside the poem and examined for factual accuracy. Murray Krieger has argued quite plausibly in the *New Apologists for Poetry* (1956) that the New Critics might be called "contextualists" because of their insistence on getting meaning from and in the context.

Each major New Critic was in his own way trying to establish that poetry offers a special kind of knowledge and does not compete with the more referential knowledge that Richards found characteristic of scientific assertions. Their "apology" for poetry committed them to formalism, to directing critical attention intrinsically to the structure of the poem rather than extrinsically to referents outside. Ransom, *The World's Body* (1938) and *The New Criticism* (1941), even departed from the concept of organic form to argue that the main difference between scientific and poetic language was that while both had "structure," only the latter had "texture," details that are interesting in themselves. Through his "texture" the poet expresses his revulsion against the inclination of science to abstract and to categorize by giving his reader the particulars of the world, the "sensuous apprehension of thought" that Eliot had admired in the Metaphysical poets. To Ransom, this was knowledge of "the world's body." Ransom's single most important contribution to formalism was his often anthologized essay, "Poetry—A Note on Ontology."

The most philosophically inclined of the New Critics, Allen Tate, also made a specific claim that literature offers a special kind of knowledge, more complete than the knowledge of science; it is experiential knowledge rather than the abstracted, shorthand version of experience given by science. Tate argued that a special characteristic of poetic language is the creation of "tension," a kind of balance between the extremes of too much denotation and literalness and too much connotation and suggestiveness. A good poem possesses both a wealth of suggestiveness and a firm denotative base. In his essay "Tension in Poetry," he provided examples of tension as a kind of touchstone for critical judgments.

In "Pure and Impure Poetry," Robert Penn Warren presented his own version of the concept of "tension," one closer to Coleridge's than Tate's was. He was also influenced by Richards' concept of a "poetry of inclusion" (in turn derived from Coleridge), a poetry that contains its own oppositions. Warren believed that such an "impure" poet writing today must "come to terms with Mercutio," that is, use irony to qualify direct propositions, much as William Shakespeare used the realistic, bawdy jests of Mercutio to counter the sentimental love poetry in *Romeo and Juliet* (1954-1596). Such irony is accessible only through formalist analysis of the poem itself, a close reading of the text. As a formalist, Warren believed, as the other New Critics did, in a less assessible meaning beyond the usual public meaning.

The Practice of Formalism

Cleanth Brooks was the most consistent practicing formalist and the most influential as well, whether in collaboration with Robert Penn Warren, in their popular textbooks, *Understanding Poetry* (1946) and *Understanding Fiction* (1943) or in his own studies in formalism, *Modern Poetry and the Tradition* and *The Well Wrought Urn* (1947). In *Modern Poetry and the Tradition*, Brooks extended Eliot's concept of tradition to a selective history of poetry from seventeenth century Metaphysical poetry to twentieth century modernism. The proper tradition for the modern poet was the Metaphysical tradition because "hard" Metaphysical conceits conveyed both thought and feeling and maintained a proper balance, in contrast to the excessive emotion in much Romantic poetry and the excessive rationalism in much neoclassical poetry. Brooks wrote the book to show the relationship between Metaphysical and modern poetry and to explain modern poetry to readers whose understanding of poetry was primarily based on Romantic poetry.

His next book, *The Well Wrought Urn*, was slightly revisionist, expanding the tradition to include some of the best works of Romantic and Victorian poetry, and even a major poem of the neoclassical period, Alexander Pope's *The Rape of the Lock* (1712). The test for admission to the tradition is again a careful formalist analysis, revealing, in unexpected places, tensions and paradoxes—although the formalist technique has been refined and even expanded. Brooks contended that poetry is "the language of paradox," evident even in a poem such as William Wordworth's "Composed upon Westminster Bridge." The paradox central to the structure of the poem is that a city, London, is enabled to "wear the beauty of the morning," a privilege that Wordsworth usually reserves for nature. The city is also paradoxically most alive with this surprising beauty when it is asleep, as it is on this occasion. Brooks conceded that Wordsworth's employment of paradox might have been unconscious, something he was driven to by "the nature of his instrument," but paradox can also be conscious technique, as it was in John Donne's "The Canonization."

Brooks's analysis of "The Canonization" is a model of formalist method, as his analysis of Eliot's *The Waste Land* had been in his previous volume. The poem is complex but unified, an argument dramatically presented but a treatise on the important subject of divine and profane love as well. The tone, an important element of meaning, is complex, scornful, ironic, and yet quite serious. Also central in the poem is the "love metaphor," and basic to its development is the paradox of treating profane love as if it were divine love. Such a treatment permits the culminating paradox in the speaker's argument for his love: "The lovers in rejecting life actually win to the most intense life." In this poem, technique has shaped content: the only way in which the poet could say what the poem says is by means of paradox.

Brooks made another major contribution to formalist practice in *The Well Wrought Urn*. He demonstrated the importance of the dramatic context as the intrinsic referent for meaning in a poem. Even the simplest lyric has some of the drama of a play. There are within a poem a speaker, an occasion, sometimes an audience, and a conflict—in a lyric usually a conflict of attitudes. Brooks declared in "The Problem of Belief and the Problem of Cognition" that a poem should not be judged by the truth or falsity "of the idea which it incorporates, but rather by its character as drama. . . ." The formalist as New Critic, most fully represented by an explication according to Brooks's formula, is concerned with this drama in the poem, with how the conflict of attitudes is resolved, with paradox and how it is central to argument in poetry, with metaphor and how it may be the only permissible way of developing the thought of the poem. He is concerned with technique in a verbal art, and these techniques make possible the poetic communication of what becomes the content.

Ranking with *The Well Wrought Urn* as a major formalist document is René Wellek and Austin Warren's *Theory of Literature* (1949). When it was published, the intention of the book was to argue for the use of intrinsic approaches to literature, drawing on the New Criticism, Russian Formalism, and even phenomenology, in conjunction with literary history and the history of ideas, then the dominant approaches. Its value today is as a source book of formalist theory, just as Brooks's *The Well Wrought Urn* is a source book of formalist practice. Wellek and Warren make the distinction between the scientific use of language, ideally purely denotative, and the literary use of language, not merely referential but expressive and highly connotative, conveying the tone and attitude of speaker and writer. Form and content are regarded as inseparable: technique determines content. Reference to the Russian Formalists reinforces the New Critics on this point. Meter, alliteration, sounds, imagery, and metaphor are all functional in a poem. Poetry is referential but the references are intrinsic, directed back inside the fictive world that is being created.

The Decline of Formalism

The influence of formalism reached its peak in the 1950's and began to decline in the 1960's. In England, *Scrutiny* suspended publication; although F. R. Leavis continued to publish, his criticism became less formalistic and more Arnoldian. In America, the New Critics also became less formalistic, and their formalism was taken over by followers who lacked the explicative genius of Ransom, Tate, Brooks, and Warren.

Warren had always published less formal criticism than his colleagues, and in the 1960's he turned his attention even more to fiction and, especially, to writing poetry. Allen Tate, never as fond as the others of critical explications, continued to write essays of social and moral significance, moving in and out of Catholicism and the influence of Jacques Maritain. His best critical explication remained that of his own poem, "Ode to the Confederate Dead," an exploration of the creative process as well as a formalistic analysis. He died in 1979. Ransom continued to edit the most important new critical journal, the *Kenyon Review* until his retirement from Kenyon College; then he returned to something he had put aside for many years—his poetry. In the few essays that he wrote in the years just before his death in 1974, his Kantian interests preoccupied him more and more. Cleanth Brooks wrote one more book that might be called formalistic, *A Shaping Joy* (1971), but he turned most of his attention to his two major books on William Faulkner, *William Faulkner: The Yoknapatawpha Country* (1963) and *Toward Yoknapatawpha and Beyond* (1978). In these works, Brooks brilliantly discusses Faulkner's novels, but it is clear that his interest is more in the relationship of Faulkner's fiction to his Southern society than in formalist analysis.

Newer critical approaches appeared, none of which was content to remain within the structure of the poem itself—the archetypal criticism of Northrop Frye, the phenomenological criticism of Georges Poulet and Hillis Miller, the structuralism of Roland Barthes and the deconstruction of Jacques Derrida. The latter are influential, but more concerned with the modes of literary discourse than with the explication of texts, and better with fiction than with poetry. During the protest movement of the later 1960's, formalism fell into disrepute because of its lack of concern for the social and political backgrounds of literary works. Ironically, the New Critics were accused of empiricism and scienticism in the analysis of literature.

Nevertheless, twentieth century formalism has had a seemingly permanent influence on the teaching of literature in the United States, just as it has in France. *Understanding Poetry* has stayed in print, and the only widely used introductions to literature are mostly formalistic in their approaches.

The New Critics taught a generation of students the art of close reading of the text. They warned readers against fallacies and heresies in reading and teaching poetry, and the lessons seem to have been widely learned. Although they used paraphrase masterfully themselves, they warned against "the heresy of paraphase." The prose statement should not be regarded as the equivalent of the meaning of the poem. They attacked and seemingly permanently damaged the positivistic view that would limit poetry to the emotions only—what they called "The affective fallacy." As Brooks declared in *The Well Wrought Urn*: "Poetry is not merely emotive . . . but cognitive. It gives us truth. . . ."
Formalism did not prevent, but did restrict, practice of the biographical fal-

lacy, studying the man instead of his works.

The most controversial fallacy exposed by the New Critics was the intentional fallacy, against which all the formalists warned. Monroe C. Beardsley and William K. Wimsatt, who stated (in *The Verbal Icon*, 1954) what was implicit in formalism all along, may have gone too far in seeming to exclude the poet from throwing any light at all on the meaning of his poem; they did, however, warn against finding the meaning of a work in some prose statement by the author before or after he wrote it. Formalism has made the point that the actual intention of a poem can be determined only from an explication of the poem itself. Few literary critics today would regard the poem as a fictive world that is sufficient unto itself. Poems have thematic and psychological contexts as well as verbal and dramatic contexts. Formalist analyses were too innocent of the linguistic structures of the language that poetry used. Nevertheless, no modern critical approach has revealed more of the richness of meaning potentially available within a poem.

Bibliography

Brooks, Cleanth, and William K. Wimsatt, Jr. *Literary Criticism: A Short History*, 1957.

Crane, Ronald S., ed. *Critics and Criticism: Ancient and Modern*, 1952.

Eliot, T. S. *Selected Essays: 1917-1932*, 1932.

Krieger, Murray. *The New Apologist for Poetry*, 1956.

O'Connor, William Van. *An Age of Criticism, 1900-1950*, 1966.

Simpson, Lewis P., ed. *The Possibilities of Order: Cleanth Brooks and His Work*, 1976.

Stewart, John L. *The Burden of Time*, 1965.

Sutton, Walter. *Modern American Criticism*, 1963.

Wimsatt, William K., and Monroe C. Beardsley. *The Verbal Icon*, 1954.

Richard J. Calhoun

STRUCTURALIST AND POSTSTRUCTURALIST CRITICISM

Space and spatial form traditionally bear directly upon the visual arts, and only metaphorically, by virtue of the tradition of the Sister Arts (*Ut pictura poesis*), upon literature; the language of literary criticism is rich in spatially metaphorical terms such as "background," "foreground," "local color," "form," "structure," "imagery," and "representation." The opposition of literal and metaphorical spatiality in literature could be accounted for as a residual effect of Gotthold Lessing's classic and influential attack in the eighteenth century on the *Ut pictura poesis* tradition.

Lessing maintained an absolute distinction between the verbal and visual arts based on a belief that an essential difference between poetry and painting is the divergent perceptions of their signs: the proper domain of language is temporal since its signs are sequential, unfolding one by one in linear fashion along a time line; whereas the proper domain of painting, whose signs are simultaneous images juxtaposed in space, is spatial.

The twentieth century mind, nurtured in Einsteinian physics, would have no trouble collapsing the mutual exclusivity of Lessing's categorization by way of the notion of space-time, in which the description of an object consists not merely of length, width, and height, but also of duration. The fourth dimension is the inclusion of change and motion; space is defined in relation to a moving point of reference.

If time and space are not viewed as mutually exclusive, then Lessing's categories cannot maintain the absolute distinction he desired to establish between the verbal/temporal and the visual/spatial arts. A painting, in fact, is simply not perceived as a whole instantaneously; rather the eye moves across the picture plane, assimilating and decoding in a process not unlike that of reading, which likewise entails movement over spatial form: the words written on the page. Given this interpretation of space and time, literary criticism of the second half of the twentieth century has radically redefined the nature of the relationship between the Sister Arts.

The seminal theoretical work in Anglo-American studies on literature as a spatial art is Joseph Frank's essay "Spatial Form in Modern Literature" (1945). Frank asserts that in the literature of modernism (Gustave Flaubert, James Joyce, T. S. Eliot, Ezra Pound), spatial juxtaposition is favored over normal linear chronology, marking the evolution toward a radical dislocation of the theory that language is intrinsically sequential. The formal method of modern literature is architectonic-spatial rather than linear-temporal, in that meaning is seen to arise *ex post facto* from the contiguous relation among portions of a work, rather than simply being represented in a temporal and progressive unfolding. The theory that the *modern* text has its own space by virtue of the simultaneous configuration of its elements—words, signs, sentences—in temporal disposition, is then extended to language in general in the model of meaning predominant in the critical movement known as structuralism.

Structuralism is a method of investigation which gained popularity in the 1960's in Paris and in the 1970's in the United States through the writings of the anthropologist Claude Lévi-Strauss, the social historian and philosopher Michel Foucault, the critic Roland Barthes, and the psychoanalyst Jacques Lacan, among others. The diversity of the list is accounted for by the fact that structuralism grew out of structural linguistics, whose methods were considered applicable to several disciplines. Analysis is structuralist when the meaning of the object under consideration is seen to be based on the configuration of its parts, that is, on the way the elements are structured, contextually linked.

The linguistic theory grounding structuralism, and, by extension, literary criticism in the structuralist vein, is that of Ferdinand de Saussure (1857-1913). Saussurian linguistics considers the basic unit in the production of meaning to be the sign, an entity conceived of as a relationship between two parts; the *signified* or mental, conceptual component, lies behind the *signifier*, or phonetic, acoustical component. The signifier is a material manifestation of what is signified, of a meaning. Any given sign will be conceived of spatially, inasmuch as it always occupies a particular semantic and phonetic territory whose boundaries mark the limits of that space, thus allowing meaning to *take place*; that is, allowing the sign to function. For example, the phonetic space within which "tap" remains operable is always relative to a limit beyond which it would no longer differ from "top" or "tape." Likewise, its semantic space would be defined in terms of differentiation from other signs verging on "tap" semantically, such as "strike," "knock," "hit," and "collide." Thus, the value of the sign is neither essential nor self-contained but rather is contingent upon its situation in a field of differential relations, in the absence of which meaning would not arise.

Comparable to Frank's attribution of spatial form to modern literature by virtue of its atemporality, Saussurian linguistics renders language spatial in promoting synchrony over diachrony as its procedural method. The synchronic study of language, whose basic working hypothesis is that there exists an underlying system structuring every linguistic event, would reconstruct language as a functional, systematic whole at a particular moment in time, in contrast to the diachronic method of nineteenth century linguisticians interested in etymologies, the evolution of language over the course of time. Space becomes a linguistic activity in structural linguistics through investigation under ahistorical conditions of the synchronic structures governing the language system and through the notion of the sign as constitutive of a space of differential relations. Applied to the analysis of poetic texts, this theoretical groundwork accords the written work a space of its own in which meaning is produced. The pervasive influence of structural linguistics, specifically in the analysis of poetic texts, might be traced to the investigation in the early 1960's by Roman Jakobson of what he termed the *poetic function* of language.

Jakobson designates the poetic function (one of six possible functions fulfilled by any utterance) as "the focus on the message for its own sake"; it is distinct from the referential or mimetic function dominating in normal linguistic usage where the meaning to which signs refer is directly conveyed (represented) by virtue of a univocal rapport between signifier (sound) and signified (meaning). The exchange of signs (communication) is not problematic. Whereas referential or mimetic language would focus on an exterior referent, the nature of the poetic function is introversion. The poetic function reaches its apex in poetry, according to Jakobson: "a complex and indivisible totality where everything becomes significant, reciprocal, converse, correspondent . . . in a perpetual interplay of sound and meaning."

The poetic text is characterized by a high degree of patterning; its principal technique of organization is parallel structure: patterns of similarity are repeated at each level of the text (phonetic, phonological, syntactic, semantic, and so on), such that the grammatical structure is seen as coextensive with the level of meaning or signification. In his analysis of William Blake's "Infant Sorrow," for example, Jakobson uncovers a network of ten nouns contained in the poem—evenly divided into five animates and five inanimates, and distributed among the couplets of the poem's two quatrains according to a principle of asymmetry:

Anterior couplets:	3 animates	2 inanimates
Outer couplets:	3 animates	2 inanimates
Posterior couplets:	2 animates	3 inanimates
Inner couplets:	2 animates	3 inanimates

Recalling "a remarkable analogy between the role of grammar in poetry and the painter's composition," Jakobson compares what he terms the manifestly spatial treatment opposing animates and inanimates in the poem to the converging lines of a background in pictoral perspective. The tension in the grammatical structure between animate and inanimate nouns underscores the tension between birth and the subsequent experience of the world on the poem's semantic level.

This type of structural analysis is characterized by the codification and systematization of the structural patterns grounding textual space, resulting in an immanent rather than transcendent reading of that space, one which reconstructs the rules governing the production of meaning rather than uncovering an essential meaning of that text. The tendency is toward all-encompassing systematic accountability in which every detail supplies information. The poem is interpreted as a highly structured network of interacting parts; it is a space closed off from "normal" language, a polysemic discourse whose semiotic play eventuates meaning within its borders, and not by virtue of an exterior referent or *a priori* idea that the poem is to convey. Structuralism thus implies the rejection of a purely phenomenological approach to language as expression, as denotation. As Vincent Descombes remarks in *Modern French Philosophy* (1980),

> . . . if a poetic utterance presents the construction that it does, this is not at all that some lived state (regret, desire) has elicited this particular form of expression in which to speak its meaning. . . . The poet listens not so much to the stirrings of his heart as to the prescriptions of the French language, whose resources and limitations engender a poetics which governs the poem.

The poem as productive textual space signals the dissolution of the notion of the author as a univocal source of meaning and intentionality situated outside the text and, thus, marks a radical shift away from critical analysis that would determine meaning as controlled by authorial intent or ultimately by the sociological, historical, and/or psychological influences structuring that intent.

A tendency in literary criticism of the 1970's to examine the unquestioned assumptions of structuralism has come to be labeled deconstruction, or poststructuralism. It is largely influenced by the writings of Jacques Derrida, whose examination of the Western concept of representation (of language as referential, mimetic) is responsible in large part for the highly philosophical bent of poststructuralist criticism.

Poststructuralism does not offer an alternate comprehensive system of textual analysis as a replacement for structuralist methodology; it supplements tenets of structuralism. It is not a system, but rather a particular use of language which recognizes the involvement of any discourse, itself included, in paradoxes which may be repressed but cannot be resolved. Whereas structuralism tends to view textual space in the final analysis as the configuration of a unified and stable semantic space—a system actualized by its structure in which every detail is functional—for the poststructuralist a fully coherent and adequate system is impossible. The system in which all coheres depends on exclusion: the repression of elements which will not fit. For example, in the analysis of "Infant Sorrow" on the basis of grammatical categories, Jakobson is able to ignore the *pronoun* "I" in his discussion of animate and inanimate *nouns*. Taken into account, "I" alters Jakobson's numeric scheme, undermining the specific nature of the parallel structures claimed to function in the poem.

When textual space is made to function systematically, it is only by the synthesis or exclusion of elements otherwise disruptive of the system. Such unified totality and closure are illusory from a poststructuralist point of view, which sees textual space effecting a meaning that is always at least double, marked by unresolvable tension between what a discourse would appear to assert and the implications of the terms in which the assertions are couched. Inscription, the writing per se, is thereby not seen as a neutral form at the service of meaning, but a signifying force threatening the determination of signification. In its attention to the graphic force of a word, its "letteral" meaning, poststructuralism would not pass off writing as mere transcription of the spoken word. In some sense dealing with any discourse as if it were concrete poetry, it recognizes the participation of the medium—the letter, the word as plastic form—in its own definition. Signification would be seen to be constantly displaced along a multiplicity of signifying trajectories whose transformations "anagrammatically" engender new possibilities: a signifier might verge on another, perhaps contradictory, signifier that it resembles phonetically or graphically; it may disengage other signifiers by way of semantic similarity; the visual impact of the word or letter on the page might cut a significant figure; signifying combinations might arise from mere juxtaposition of elements without any other apparent connection.

No longer conceived as the transparent carrier of a message, the signifier/word/inscription menaces the establishment of ultimate signification. Poststructuralism thus supplements the structuralist attack on the authority of the writing subject to include the dissolution of the illusion of mastery on the part of the critic. To the poststructuralist, the text is a space of semantic dispersal, a space of dissemination forever in flux, never to be completely controlled and mastered. From this standpoint, structuralist methodology is thought to be overly reductionist in its resolution of the text into a set of structuring components, too akin to the effort of Archetypal criticism, or to Romantic notions of the work as an organic whole, albeit in structuralism an architectural one. Although it might be said in defense of structuralism that the analysis of structure is purely formal, that an essence (meaning, nature of being) is not ascribed to particular structures, structuralist readings imply essentiality by the air of puzzle-solving involved in their uncovering of the semiotic unity of a work, its essential governing principles. Structures are implicitly privileged with the status of eschatological presence; language's suggestive power, the disruptive force of its inscription, is attenuated for the sake of form; that is, of defining the system.

Poststructuralism would regard, for example, structuralist linguistics' emphasis on synchrony as an attempt to exclude linguistic force and change that might undermine the fixity of systematic analysis. Following the implications of structuralism's principle of difference, of meaning produced by virtue of relational differences, one cannot escape the conclusion that the practice of language is implicitly diachronic, temporal, historical, since the principle is undeniably one of combination, selection, and exclusion. If meaning for the structuralist is the product of relational differences rather than derivative of an intrinsic permanent value attached to a word in itself, then it can never be fully present all at once at a given moment; no single word/

gesture/expression/signifier is in and of itself capable of initiating the difference necessary for significance to operate. Like motion, meaning cannot be completely grasped in a present moment that would exclude a past and a future moment, and thus the structuralist principle of difference implies a paradoxically double movement at the "origin" of meaning which is repressed in favor of the oneness and synchrony establishing textual space as an unproblematic domain of simultaneous, systematic relationships.

The structuralist concept of textual space does attribute spatiality to language and not merely to a particular use of it ("modern literature"). It establishes a synchronic stable space containing the movement of signification guaranteeing that the text will be something other than nonsense. Language is dealt with as a spatial phenomenon, but to the exclusion of temporal movement and flux which might trigger disorder or nonsense. In other words, a protest against Lessing's separation of the verbal and visual arts by way of structuralism seems only to reverse the categories of space and time and thus remain within the mode of oppositional thinking: language is synchronic when diachronicity is ignored, spatial when temporal movement is repressed. In an effort to exceed the limitations of oppositional thinking, poststructuralism supplements the principle of difference with what Jacques Derrida terms the "différance" operative in the textual dissemination of signification.

Différance is a neologism whose graphic play—in French—combines the meaning of "différ*ance*" (difference), with which it is exactly equivalent phonetically, and "deferring." It articulates meaning as a complex configuration incorporating both a passive state of differences and the activity of differing and deferring which produces those differences. *Différance* is consequently inconceivable in terms of binary opposition: like motion, it is neither simply absent nor present, neither spatial (differing in space) nor temporal (deferring in time). "Espacement" (spacing), a comparable Derridean term, indicates both the passive condition of a particular configuration or disposition of elements, and the gesture effecting the configuration, of distributing the elements in a pattern.

Like the Einsteinian concept of space-time, *différance* and spacing (articulated along the bar of binary opposition that would separate space and time, active and passive,) disrupt the comfort of thinking within a purely oppositional mode. Derrida demonstrates such lack of guarantees in his reading of "hymen" in the poetry of Stéphane Mallarmé. An undecidable signifier whose meaning cannot be mastered, hymen is both marriage and the vaginal membrane of a virgin. Whereas hymen as virginity is hymen without hymen/marriage, hymen as marriage is hymen without hymen/virginity. Hymen, then, articulates both difference (between the interior and exterior of a virgin, between desire and its consummation), and, at the same time, the abolition of difference in the consummation of marriage; it is the trace of a paradoxical abolition of difference between difference and nondifference.

Within a structuralist framework, meaning produced by textual space, albeit ambiguous or polysemic, is in the final analysis recuperable. Ambiguity is controlled as the various strands of meaning are enumerated and accounted for. Poststructuralism views the implications of such practice as problematic. On the one hand, meaning is claimed to be the product of semiotic play governed by a principle of difference (signaling the dissolution of the control of the writing subject) that implicates a definition of the sign in which meaning floats among signifiers rather than existing *a priori* as an essence—the signified. On the other hand, by enclosing this textual play within the boundaries of the "poetic" and seeking out and privileging structures informing that play, a very classical definition of the sign is implied in which the signifier serves ultimately as a vehicle representing an eschatological presence: an ultimate signified which arrested play and closes off the movement of signification. Dissemination, *différance*, and spacing would splay the fixed borders that characterize criticism's structuring of the movement of signifiers within poetic space so as to explicate texts.

Sign, like symbol, ultimately refers back to a single source, a signified assuring of the determination of meaning; with the poststructuralist gloss on signifier as signifying trace, there can be no return to a simple origin. Signifying trace would articulate an effect of meaning without the illusion of understanding provided by binary opposition. Trace (again, like motion), cannot be determined as simply either present or absent. Giving evidence of an absent thing which passed by, trace "in itself" contains its other which it is not (the absent thing). It paradoxically "is" what it is not, inasmuch as its presence (its identity) depends on alluding to an absence (its nonidentity to the absent thing leaving the trace) from which it distinguishes itself. Its meaning or identity is thus split from the beginning, already always involved in a paradoxical movement of *différance*. The origin of meaning or identity is then not single; the first trace of anything is first only in deferring to a second in relation to which it becomes first—and in that sense it is more of a third. The poststructuralist endeavor is a recognition of the intractable paradox of the nonsingle point of origin of the difference which inaugurates any signifying system. *Différance* is, then, not so much a concept as an opening onto the possibility of conceptualization.

A recapitualization of Ezra Pound's theory of the Image as a generative and dislocating force in Joseph Riddel's "Decentering the Image" is a useful gloss on *différance*. Like spacing, which is both configuration and the gesture effecting that configuration, Pound's Image is both a visual representation (form) and a displacement or trope (force); it is a cluster of figures in a space of relational differences and a transformative machine articulating movement across the differential field. The Image is not an idea, not the mere signifier of a signified, but rather a constellation of radical differences, a vortex whose form as radiating force resists the synthesis and collapse of differences into oneness and unity. Whereas formalist, archetypal, and structuralist criticism tends to privilege implicitly master structures assuring a totalization of the poem's fragments, Pound's vortex would disrupt the assurance of an originating signified in its refusal to be resolved into the unity of presence, to be fully present at a given moment. As the signifying trace is always already split at its origin, constituted in a present moment/space by absence, so too is Pound's vortex always already an image; that is, a field of relations, originally a text, the reinscription of a past into a present text, a vector, a force always already multiple and temporalizing.

There is, then, no continuity between origin and image as there is with symbol and the conventional sign. A poem is not recuperable in synthesizing totality and must be read somewhat in the manner of a rebus, whose play of signifiers annuls/refuses a simple reading, provoking, instead, reinterpretations and reopenings.

The poststructuralist critique of the frame that structuralism would draw around poetic discourse provokes reinterpretation of structuralist discourse. Since the principle of difference provides for theoretically unlimited play of the sign within the textual space, what prevents that movement from exceeding its borders, that force from spilling out of its form? How can one unproblematically draw borders around different language functions, keeping the play of the poetic—that introverted self-referential "focus on the message for its own sake"—framed off from the mimetic referential space of common linguistic usage?

The controversy between structuralism and poststructuralism indicated by such questioning is not a simple dispute over methodological technique in the analysis of poetry. Deconstruction of structuralist discourse betrays the ideological move involved in fixed framing: the strategy of setting up distinctions to shelter "rational" discourse from the vagueries of the poetic.

Relegation of textual play to the poetic seemingly protects the language of critical discourse from irrational forces, guarantees it the possibility of lucidity, of the impression that language is under control—mastered by the critic. Meaning as *différance*/spacing dissolves the illusion of the possibility of purely logical discourse unfettered by the anomolies of the poetic, of a purely literal language unhampered by figural machinations. Furthermore, *différance* annuls the very distinction classically affirmed between literal and figurative. Signification would be neither purely literal nor metaphoric; there would be no literal truth represented by a sign because the very possibility of representation depends on metaphor: in representing an absent in a present, in transferring the literal reference signified, the sign "tropes" and metaphorizes (*metapherein*—to carry over, transfer). Likewise, if purely metaphoric meaning were possible, then there would be a literal meaning of metaphor to which metaphor would refer metaphorically.

Whereas for structuralism, space structures meaning, delineating its borders and giving it form, poststructuralism demonstrates that closure of meaning is illusory. Meaning as spacing/*différance* is neither fixed nor absolute but kept in motion by the figural, the figural both as metaphor usurping the position of the sign's would-be literal referant, and as inscription, whose graphic impact on the page engenders disruptive anagrammatic combinations. Poststructuralism traces the catachresis at play in the space of discourse, be it poetic, philosophic, or critical. The signifying traces at play in the text are catachretic in their deconstruction of the illusion of literal terms whose eschatological presence would stop the movement of signification. Catachresis—the metaphor created when there is not literal term available (such as the foot of the table)—is traditionally considered a form of abuse and misapplication. Poststructuralism demonstrates such misapplication as the condition of language: the sign necessarily fails to hit the mark, the signifier is always something other than its signified in order that language might operate.

Bibliography
Culler, Jonathan. "Jacques Derrida" in *Structuralism and Since*, 1980. Edited by John Sturrock.
——————— . *The Pursuit of Signs*, 1981.
——————— . *Structuralist Poetics*, 1975.
De Man, Paul. "Hypogram and Inscription: Michel Riffaterre's Poetics of Reading," in *Textual Strategies*, 1979. Edited by Josué V. Harari.
Descombes, Vincent. *Modern French Philosophy*, 1980.
Harari, Josué V., ed. *Textual Strategies: Perspectives in Post-Structuralist Criticism*, 1979.
Issacharoff, Michael. *L'Espace et la nouvelle* (*Space and the Novella*), 1976.
Jakobson, Roman. "On the Verbal Art of William Blake and Other Poet-Painters," in *Linguistic Inquiry*. I (1970), pp. 3-23.
——————— . "A Postscript to the Discussion on Grammar of Poetry," in *Diacritics*. Spring, 1980, pp. 22-35.
Mitchell, W. J. T. "Spatial Form in Literature: Toward a General Theory," in *The Language of Images*, 1974. Edited by W. J. T. Mitchell.
Riddel, Joseph. "Decentering the Image: The 'Project' of 'American' Poetics?," in *Textual Strategies*, 1979. Edited by Josué V. Harari.
Said, Edward W. "*Abecedarium Culturae*: Structuralism, Absence, Writing," in *Modern French Criticism*, 1972. Edited by John K. Simon.
Spencer, Sharon. *Space, Time and Structure in the Modern Novel*, 1971.
Sturrock, John. *Structuralism and Since*, 1980.

Nancy Weigel Rodman

LINGUISTIC CRITICISM

American structural linguistics, the principles and research program for which were laid down by Leonard Bloomfield in his *Language* (1933), was concerned with establishing the structure—phonological, morphological, syntactical, and semantic—of languages conceived as systematic wholes. It dealt with what the *Cours de linguistique generale* (1916, *Course in General Linguistics*) of Ferdinand de Saussure (the great French theorist whose posthumously published work has been the point of departure for all modern structuralism, not only in linguistics but also in anthropology and other disciplines as well) called the *langue*, the system of a limited repertoire of sounds, on whose differentiation differences of meaning depend, and of a limited number of kinds of sentence elements that can be combined in certain orders and hierarchical relationships, as distinguished from *parole*, particular utterances. To elicit these elements and rules of combination for a given language, linguists depended primarily on speech rather than on written texts. Furthermore, Bloomfieldian linguists tended to concentrate their efforts on the description of exotic languages rather than of English. Meanwhile, literary critics focused their attention on particular written texts, deemed literary, and were concerned with the interpretation and evaluation of these works of individual writers.

Poems and other literary works are, of course, works of verbal art whose medium is language, and this fact suggested to some linguists a potential for the application of linguistics to the study of literature. The techniques developed by linguistics for the analysis of language could be applied to the language of literary texts. The linguist could bring to bear on these texts an expertise which the literary critic did not have. Much of the work that has been done involving the application of linguistics to the study of literary texts falls under the heading of "stylistics," the study of literary style. Early contributions in linguistic stylistics tended to carry the animus of bringing a new objectivity to a field that had hitherto been merely impressionistic in its methods; however, later work has generally recognized both the inevitability and the value of a subjective component in stylistic analysis. While the interest of literary criticism and, for the most part, stylistics, is in particular literary texts, modern poetics, which traces its roots to Russian formalism (a movement in literary scholarship originating in Russia around 1915 and suppressed there about 1930) is interested rather in the question of the nature of literariness or poeticity. Poetics has a close relation to linguistics (see the discussion below of Roman Jakobson's famous paper on "Linguistics and Poetics").

Besides application of the specific techniques and categories of one or another kind of linguistics for studying the language of literary texts, another kind of application of linguistics to the study of literature has been of great importance: linguistics has been taken as a model for the study of literary structures, such as narrative, that are not intrinsically linguistic but are translatable into other media, and students of literature have identified constituents of such structures and formalized descriptive rules for their combination by analogy with linguists' descriptions of the structure of a language (*langue*). In thus adopting the structuralist approach derived from Saussure, literary critics have participated in a transdisciplinary movement affecting all the human sciences. A discussion of structuralism in literary studies, however, is outside the scope of this survey of linguistic approaches to poetry, which will be limited to applications of the techniques and categories of linguistic analysis to the language of poetic texts. Even within these limits, this survey does not purport to cover all the significant work. The contributions discussed below—which include both general, programmatic pieces and specific, descriptive studies—do not by any means represent all the important figures in the field or even the full range of relevant work by those cited; they are simply examples of various linguistic approaches to poetry from the early 1950's to the early 1980's.

When, in 1951, the linguists George L. Trager and Henry Lee Smith, Jr., published *An Outline of English Structure*, a description of English phonetics, morphology, and syntax such as had been made of many exotic languages, the linguist Harold Whitehall immediately saw the possibility of application to the study of English literature, and went so far as to say that "no criticism can go beyond its linguistics." Specifically, he saw that Trager and Smith's account of stress, pitch, and juncture as each having four functionally distinguishable levels in English would be valuable to students of meter and rhythm of English verse. The rhythm of lines could presumably be much more precisely described in terms of four levels of stress rather than in the two normally recognized in traditional metrics. Such an application of Trager and Smith's findings for modern American speech to the study of verse in English was actually made by Edmund L. Epstein and Terence Hawkes, who found in a body of iambic pentameter verse a vast number of different stress-patterns according to the four-level system. The question of the relevance of such descriptive analysis to the meaning and aesthetic value of the poetry in question was not raised in these early applications of linguistics to literature.

Archibald A. Hill, who did practical work in the application of linguistics to literature in the 1950's, saw linguistic analysis of a text in terms of such factors as word-order and stress as operating on a preliterary level, but considered them to be a useful preliminary to analysis in terms of literary categories such as images. Not unlike the New Critics, he approached a poem as a structured whole and sought to interpret it with minimal reference to outside knowledge such as biographical information, but he differed from the New Critics in thinking it best to begin with specifically linguistic formal details. In a 1955 analysis of Gerard Manley Hopkins' "The Windhover," he took an analysis of Hopkins' stress and word-order, considered in relation to general

English usage, as the basis for resolving ambiguities and determining emphases at particular points—thus, as an aid to interpretation of at least local meaning.

In 1958 a Conference on Style was held at Indiana University, in which a group of linguists, literary critics, and psychologists presented and discussed papers on issues relevant to the matter of style in language. This conference, the papers of which were published in 1960 in a collection entitled *Style in Language*, edited by Thomas A. Sebeok, proved to be something of a watershed for the application of linguistics to the study of poetry. Roman Jakobson's presentation on the relation of linguistics to poetics still remains a point of reference for work on the language of poetry. While the focus of the New Critics and some linguists working on literature was on the individual poem considered as an autonomous structured whole, the concern of poetics, as Jakobson sets it forth, is with the differentiating characteristics of poetic language. He argues that inasmuch as poetics deals with problems of verbal structure, it lies wholly within the field of linguistics, "the global science of verbal structure." He offers a functional definition of poetic language in terms of the constitutive factors of any act of verbal communication, enumerating six such factors—the addresser, the message, the addressee, the context, the contact between addresser and addressee, and the code (the rules of the language, also of a certain register, dialect, and so on) in accord with which the message is constructed. In any given utterance or text, focus will be on one of these factors primarily, though to a lesser extent on others, and the predominant function of the utterance or text can be defined accordingly. Jakobson defines the poetic function of language as "focus on the message for its own sake," stressing that the poetic function is not confined to poetry (appearing also, for example, in political slogans and advertising jingles) and that poetry involves functions of language other than the poetic; different genres, for example, are partially characterized by the relative importance of the referential, emotive, or conative (focus on the addressee) functions.

Contending that "the verbal structure of a message depends predominantly on [its] predominant function," Jakobson then studies the effect of the poetic function on the linguistic structure of a text. His famous account of the differentiating feature of language in which the poetic function predominates over the other functions depends on the fact that making an utterance or constructing a text always involves two operations: (1) *selection* from among a series of items that are syntactically and semantically equivalent and (2) the *combination* of the selected items into a meaningful sequence of words. "The poetic function," runs Jakobson's formulation, "projects the principle of equivalence from the axis of selection into the axis of combination." In verse, for example, every syllable becomes equivalent to every other syllable, every stress to every other stress, as units of measure. A passage of verse is characterized by the repetition of equivalent units.

Jakobson goes on to cite some of the kinds and operations of equivalence in a broad range of poetry of many different languages, in the process providing what amounts to a program for research on poetic language. All metrical systems, he says, use "at least one (or more than one) binary contrast of a relatively high and relatively low prominence"; he gives examples of meters "based only on the opposition of syllabic peaks and slopes (syllabic verse)," meters based "on the relative levels of the peaks (accentual verse)," and meters based "on the relative length of the syllabic peaks or entire syllables (quantitative verse)." Besides features invariably present in lines in a given meter, there will be optional features likely to occur, and these, Jakobson maintains, form part of the metrical system to be described by the linguist. A full description should not, as traditional descriptions of meters typically do, exclude any linguistic feature of the verse design. Jakobson cites, as an example of a feature that ought not to be ignored, the "constitutive value of intonation in English meters," "the normal coincidence of syntactic pause and pausal intonation" with line-ending, such that, even when frequent, enjambment is felt as a variation. Word boundaries and grammatical boundaries may also be among the defining characteristics of a line in a given verse tradition, even if such boundaries are not marked by any distinguishable phonetic features. (He does not specify a method for ascertaining that the enumeration of relevant features has been exhaustive.) What have generally been treated as deviations from a metrical pattern should, according to Jakobson, form part of the description of the pattern, for they are variations allowed by the rules of the given meter.

For rhyme as well as meter Jakobson emphasizes that linguistic analysis should not be limited to sound alone. The similarity of sound between rhyme words throws into relief their grammatical and semantic relations. Whether rhyme words are of the same or different grammatical classes, whether their syntactical functions are the same or different, whether they have a semantic relationship of similarity or antithesis, are all questions relevant to the operation of rhyme in the poetry in question. Poets and schools of poetry that use rhyme differ in favoring or opposing rhyming words of the same grammatical class and function, and grammatical rhymes operate differently from anti-grammatical ones.

While repetition is an important aspect of the sound of poetry, a sound can be important, Jakobson points out, without being repeated: a sound with a single occurrence in a prominent position against a contrasting background and in a thematically important word should not be neglected. Analysis of the sound in poetry must take into account both the phonological structure of the language in question and which of the distinctive features of phonemes (voiced/voiceless, nasal/oral, and so on) are taken into account in the particular verse convention. Besides meter, rhyme, alliteration, and other forms of reiteration that are primarily of sound, though also involving syntactic and semantic aspects, poetic language is characterized by other forms of parallelism. For example, lines may be grammatically parallel, inviting semantic comparison between words in corresponding positions, which may be perceived as having a metaphorical or quasimetaphorical relationship. Concentration on lexical tropes to the exclusion of the syntactical aspect of poetic language is, according to Jakobson, not warranted: "The poetic resources concealed in the morphological and syntactic structure of language, briefly the poetry of grammar, and its literary product, the grammar of poetry, have been seldom known to critics and mostly disregarded by linguists but skillfully mastered by creative writers."

Jakobson asserted "the right and duty of linguistics to direct the investigation of verbal art in all its compass and extent," and provided a program for such research. At about the same time, Michael Riffaterre was concerning himself with the problem that a linguistic analysis of a poetic text could provide only a linguistic description of it and could not distinguish which of the features isolated were operative as part of the poem's style. In a 1959 paper, "Criteria for Style Analysis," he endeavored to supply a technique for distinguishing stylistic features of a text from merely linguistic features without stylistic function.

Riffaterre's argument is based on the dual assumption—diametrically opposed to Jakobson's notion of the nature of poetic language—that the literary artist works to ensure the communication of his meaning, and that this end can be achieved through reduction of the predictability of elements, so that the reader's natural tendency to interpolate elements that seem predictable from the context will be frustrated, and he will be held up and forced to attend to unpredictable elements. The linguistic elements that are to be taken into account in the stylistic analysis of a literary work are precisely these unpredictable elements, which Riffaterre calls "stylistic devices" or "SD's." While he is apparently confident of the efficacy of this means for getting reader-attention, at least one investigator of style in poetry (Anne Cluysenaar) cites an instance where readers failed to notice an unpredictable phrase, simply substituting what they would have expected for what was actually there in the text. Not content that the analyst of style should rely simply on his own subjective impressions as to the location of stylistic devices in a literary text, Riffaterre recommends the use of informants, readers of the text in question, including critics and editors of the text as well as lay readers. In using informants' responses, the analyst of style should, according to Riffaterre, empty them of such content as value judgments and take them as mere indicators of possible sites of stylistic devices. The resultant enumeration should then be verified, by checking whether the points identified coincide with points where a pattern established by a preceding stretch of text has been broken; if so, they are stylistic devices and should be submitted to linguistic analysis by the stylistician.

In choosing to compare parts of a given text with each other, Riffaterre departed from the practice, become common at the time, of taking "ordinary language"—a very vague entity—as a norm with which to compare the text. His examples show, however, that he has not been able to dispense altogether with reference to language usage outside the text in question, for items can be interpreted as unpredictable in a given context only with respect to knowledge or experience of usage in similar context elsewhere. Besides the fact of departure from a pattern established by a preceding stretch of text, another phenomenon can, according to Riffaterre, help confirm the identification of a stylistic device: this is the presence of a cluster of independent stylistic devices, which together highlight a particular passage.

In a well-known paper published in *Yale French Studies* in 1966, Riffaterre assesses an analysis by Jakobson and Claude Lévi-Strauss of the poem "Les Chats" of Charles Baudelaire. Jakobson and Lévi-Strauss had scanned the text on several levels—meter, phonology, grammar, and meaning—discovering equivalences of various kinds, which they took as constitutive of several simultaneous structural divisions of the poem. Riffaterre contends that many of the linguistic equivalences they identify cannot be taken as stylistic features, as elements of the poetic structure, because they would not be perceived in the process of reading. Only such equivalences as would be perceptible should be taken as pertaining to the poetic structure of the text. Equivalences on one level alone generally will not be perceived as correspondences; grammatical parallelism, for example, will need to be reinforced by correspondence in metrical position.

With the development of transformational-generative grammar by Noam Chomsky and others, beginning with Chomsky's 1957 book *Syntactic Structures*, came new kinds of linguistic approaches to literature. The theory of transformational-generative grammar is based on the assumption that native speakers of a language internalize grammatical rules for their language such that they are able to produce unlimited numbers of grammatical sentences they have never heard before and judge a given sentence as grammatical or ungrammatical (or as more or less grammatical, more or less complex). There is the further assumption that the grammar should reflect native speaker intuitions of relation between superficially different sentences, as between a given declarative sentence in the active voice and its passivization, and of ambiguity as to the construction of certain sentences: in the former case, the superficially different sentences are taken as having the same "deep structure"; in the latter, the surface structure of the given sentence is taken as able to have been reached by two or more different routes, from two or more different deep structures. A transformational-generative grammar of a given language ideally consists of an ordered set of rules for the generation of all possible grammatical sentences in the language; besides phrase-structure rules, it includes ordered series of obligatory and optional transformational rules that transform an underlying "kernel sentence" or set of kernel sentences into a surface structure.

The surface structure/deep structure distinction was taken, in early efforts at the application of transformational-generative grammar to the study of literary texts such as Richard Ohmann's, as a confirmation and clarification of the traditional distinction between form and content. A writer's style could be accounted for by the nature of the optional transformations he chose. Ohmann adheres to the position of early transformational-generative theory that different surface structures produced by the choice of different optional transformations have the same content, but he contradicts himself when he says that each writer will make characteristic choices and that these choices correlate with the writer's way of looking at experience. Likewise, regarding deviance in poetic language from usage restrictions on categories of words, he holds that the kinds of deviance employed by a poet will reflect his vision; the kinds of deviance found in Dylan Thomas' poetry, Ohmann suggests, reflect his sense of nature as personal, the world as process.

One of the first linguists to apply transformational-generative grammar to the study of style in poetry was Samuel Levin. Levin was interested in the fact that poetry contains sentences and phrases that a native speaker might consider ungrammatical or semigrammatical. In a 1965 paper called "Internal and External Deviation in Poetry," he takes external deviation in syntax, that is, deviation from a norm of syntactical usage lying outside the text in question, as ungrammaticality; in other words, he assumes that it involves sentences that the grammar of the language in question would not generate. Among such sentences he recognizes degrees of deviance or (un-)grammaticality. He does not find the notion of the probability of a given element at a given point in the text (transitional probability) helpful in rationalizing this sense of degrees of deviance because of the unfeasibility of calculating transitional probabilities for the occurrence of a given word after a given sequence of preceding words. His approach is to determine what kinds of changes would have to be made in the rules of the grammar to make it generate the deviant sentences or phrases, assuming that it does not do so. These would be deemed more or less grammatical depending on the number of ungrammatical sentences that the changes entailed would generate.

In the case of a phrase such as E. E. Cummings' "a pretty how town," the number would be large, since either "how" would have to be added to the class of adjectives, or adverbs would have to be allowed to occur in the place of the second adjective in the sequence determiner plus adjective plus adjective plus noun, changes involving large classes. In the case of Dylan Thomas' phrase, "Rage me back," however, "rage" would simply have to be added to the subclass of transitive verbs taking "back" (mostly verbs of motion). Hence, the Cummings example is less grammatical than the Thomas. In like manner, the Thomas example produces a sense of richness through the conflation of the verb "rage" with notions of transitivity and motion, while Cummings' phrase leaves a sense of diffuseness because what is added to "how" is so unspecific. Levin notes that the former kind of ungrammaticality occurs more frequently than the latter in poetry, and considers it akin to metaphor in its operation.

J. P. Thorne shares Levin's interest in the occurrence in poetry of sentences that would not be generated by the grammar; indeed, he says at one point that such sentences form the subject matter of stylistics. Where Levin takes single sentences and phrases from poetry and considers how the grammar would have to be modified to generate each sentence, however, Thorne proposes taking whole poems and constructing a grammar for the language of each poem. The grammar for a poem should be constructed on the same principles as the grammar for the language as a whole, the point being to compare the two and discover how the one differs from the other. A good poet, in Thorne's view, will invent a new language, differing from the standard language not (or not primarily) in surface structure, but in deep structure, that is, on the level of meaning. The poet will invent a new language in order to be able to say things that cannot be said in the standard language. In reading a good poem, the reader learns a new language. The grammar that one constructs for this new language will make explicit one's intuitions about its structure. One must decide what features of the poem's language are features of that language and what are features merely of the sample, when the sample (the poem) is all of the language there is. One's assignments of words to categories in this grammar and formulation of selection rules for their cooccurrence will reflect one's interpretation of the poem.

In a 1965 paper, "Stylistics and Generative Grammars," Thorne sketches a grammar for Cummings' poem, "anyone lived in a pretty how town." He also suggests that it may be illuminating to construct grammars for poems in which the language does not seem so manifestly ungrammatical, such as John Donne's "Nocturnal upon St. Lucy's Day," where animate subjects have verbs normally selected by inanimate subjects, and inanimate subjects have verbs normally selected only by animate subjects. In a 1970 paper, "Generative Grammar and Stylistic Analysis," he finds a similar deviation from the selection rules for Standard English in Theodore Roethke's poem "Dolour," where there are constructions such as "the sadness of pencils," which attach to concrete, inanimate nouns adjectives that normally select animate nouns or a subcategory of abstract nouns including "experience" and "occasion"; he points out that the decision whether to assimilate "pencils" and the other nouns so used in the poem to the category of animate nouns or to the particular subcategory of abstract nouns will depend on how one reads the poem.

Early efforts at applying transformational-generative grammar to literature have been recognized as limited by (1) the theory's separation of syntax from semantics (that is, of consideration of sentence structure from questions of meaning); (2) the assumption in early versions of the theory that the transformations that produced different surface structures from a single underlying structure did not affect the meaning; (3) the failure to extend analysis beyond the level of the sentence; and (4) the treatment of literary (especially poetic) language as characterized by ungrammatical constructions, deviations from the supposed norm of everyday speech. With these limitations, transformational-generative grammar could not illuminate the relation between form and content in poetry or relate formal description to interpretation. It did not offer a means of discussing the connections within and cohesiveness of a text as a whole. It had nothing to say about poetry in which the language was not in any sense ungrammatical. Much of the irritation of literary critics with early applications of transformational-generative grammar to literature is attributable to limitations in the applications resulting from limitations in the early versions of the theory.

Besides transformational-generative grammar, other modes of syntactical analysis developed by modern linguistics have been used in approaches to poetry. One of these is category-scale grammar, developed by M. A. K. Halliday and set forth in his 1961 paper "Categories of the Theory of Grammar." Category-scale grammar analyzes English syntax in terms of a hierarchically ordered enumeration or "rank-scale" of units: sentence, clause, group, word, morpheme. Halliday introduces the notion of "rank-shift" to refer to cases where a unit operates as a structural member of a unit of the same or lower rank; for example, a clause can be part of another clause or of a group (phrase). Category-scale grammar has been commended to students of literary style as making possible a clear and accurate description of the infrastructuring of the language and helping to discover and specify where the structural complexity of a text resides. Halliday himself has advocated the linguistic study of literary texts, arguing that this should be a comparative study and that it is not enough to discover, say, the kinds of clause structures in a given text, but that their relative frequencies in that text should then be compared with those in other texts, other samples of the language.

In a 1964 paper, he illustrates the sort of treatment he recommends with a discussion of two features of the language of William Butler Yeats's "Leda and the Swan"—the use of "the" and the forms and nature of the verbs. "The" is a deictic (a word that points to or identifies); its particular function is to identify a specific subset, by reference to the context (either of the text itself or of the situation of its utterance), to elements of the rest of the modifier or of the qualifier of the noun it modifies, or to the noun modified itself. In nominal groups where there are other modifying elements preceding the noun or a qualifier following it, "the" usually (in samples of modern English prose referred to by Halliday) specifies by reference to the rest of the modifier or the qualifier. While "Leda and the Swan" has a high proportion of such nominal groups in comparison with another Yeats poem, in only one of them does "the" function in the usual way; in all the rest it specifies by reference not to anything else in the nominal group, but to the title. "Leda and the Swan" is also found to differ markedly in the handling of verbs from both another Yeats poem and a poem by Alfred, Lord Tennyson. A high proportion of verbs, including especially the lexically more powerful, are "deverbalized" by occurring as participles in bound or rank-shifted clauses or as modifiers of a noun (rather than as finite verbs in free clauses).

John McH. Sinclair's 1966 paper, "Taking a Poem to Pieces," is the sort of analysis recommended by Halliday. Further, it represents an effort to remedy linguists' neglect of poetry in which the language is not describable as ungrammatical or deviant. Sinclair hypothesizes that even in poetry where the language is apparently unremarkable, grammatical and other linguistic patterns are operating in a more complex way than could be described—or even perceived—with traditional terms. He uses the terms of category-scale grammar to describe the language of a short poem by Philip Larkin called "First Sight."

Beginning with the highest unit of syntax, the sentence, Sinclair sets forth the syntactical structure of Larkin's text: first the sentence structure (the nature and arrangement of the constituent clauses), then the clause structure (the nature and arrangement of the constituent groups and rank-shifted clauses), then the structure of the groups (the arrangement and relations of the constituent words and rank-shifted higher structures). He shows that the language of Larkin's poems represents a restricted selection from among the wide range of possibilities afforded by the language. Its stylistic character can be in part accounted for by the persistent selection of certain constructions normally occurring with lower frequency.

It is on the level of the clausal constitution of its sentences that Larkin finds the particular quality of the language of "First Sight" to lie. In what he calls "everyday English," in sentences that contain a free clause and a bound clause, the most common arrangement is an uninterrupted free clause followed by a bound clause; discontinuous structure (that is, a free clause interrupted by a bound clause) and the sequence of bound clause followed by free clause are both less common. Of the four sentences in Larkin's poem, only the last has the generally most common arrangement of free clause followed by bound clause. Thus, while this poem's language is not deviant in such a way as to require a special grammar to describe it, it is distinguished by the relative frequency of certain otherwise unremarkable structures.

In a 1972 paper, "Lines About 'Lines,'" Sinclair attempts to integrate stylistic description with interpretation and develop theoretical principles and a methodology for stylistic analysis. He assumes that the analyst must *begin* with a critical understanding of the text; then look for patterns at successive levels; in each case where a pattern is found, relate it to the meaning; and finally synthesize the findings of form-meaning relationships. Sinclair hypothesizes that there will be "intersection points" of form and meaning, and adopts the term "focusing categories" or "focats" for such points. The focats found in the analysis of a given text will be initially taken as pertaining to that text alone, but assumed to be general if subsequently encountered in numerous texts.

In this case, Sinclair takes as his example for analysis William Wordsworth's famous "Lines Composed a Few Miles Above Tintern Abbey." He finds two focats operative in the poem. One, the introduction of an optional element in a syntactical structure not yet complete, he calls "arrest." The other, which he calls "extension," is essentially the continuation of a potentially completed structure by an element not syntactically predictable from any of the preceding elements. Sinclair argues convincingly that arrest and extension do indeed represent instances of significant interrelation of formal structure and meaning in "Tintern Abbey." These two focats also seem to be likely candidates for generality (occurence in numerous texts).

Many of the examples of linguistic approaches to poetry so far considered here have been studies of the language, especially the syntax, of individual poems. Besides focusing on individual texts, however, linguists have also addressed themselves to more general phenomena of poetic language, such as meter and metaphor.

Beginning with a 1966 paper by Morris Halle and Samuel Jay Keyser, a so-called "generative metrics" has been developed, devoted almost exclusively to accentual-syllabic verse, principally iambic pentameter. Halle and Keyser draw an analogy between the native speaker of a language, who has internalized a set of logically ordered rules in accord with which he produces grammatical sentences, and the poet, whom they assume to have similarly internalized a set of rules in accord with which he produces metrical lines. Generative metrics does away with the notion of the metrical foot and replaces the hodgepodge of rules and exceptions of traditional metrics with a brief and ordered sequence of systematically related rules. This sequence of rules governs the realization of an abstract pattern in an actual text. The pattern is represented as consisting of positions rather than feet, each position corresponding to a single syllable. The rules for actualization of the pattern are presented as alternatives arranged in an order from least to greatest metrical "complexity" (greatest to least strictness).

A very different approach to metrics has been taken by the British linguist David Crystal, who, in a 1971 paper, proposed a model for the description of English verse that is supposed to encompass both accentual-syllabic and free verse and to distinguish both from prose. He takes the line, rather than the syllable or the foot, as the basic unit of verse, and hypothesizes that the line normally consists, in performance, of a single complete "tone-unit." A tone-unit is the basic unit of organization of intonation in an utterance; since intonation functions in part to signal syntactical relations, tone-unit boundaries coincide with syntactical—generally clause—boundaries.

Transformationalists have approaches metaphor as deviance through violation of selection restriction rules (rules formalizing acceptable collocations; for example, that for verbs with certain semantic features the subject must be animate). One interprets metaphors, according to this view (espoused, for example, by Robert J. Matthews in a 1971 paper), by deemphasizing those semantic features entailed in the selection restriction violation.

In recent years there has been growing recognition that properties such as metaphoricity, previously assumed to be peculiar to literary language, pertain as well to conversational usage; also, it has been recognized that not only the formal features of a text, but also the situational context and the speaker-hearer (or writer-reader) relationship, are relevant to its operation. Growing interest in speech-act theory (developed by J. L. Austin and John Searle) is a reflection of a concern for context-sensitive analysis of utterances or texts. According to speech-act theory, besides performing a locutionary act (that is, producing a grammatical utterance), a speaker will perform one or another kind of illocutionary act (such as asserting, ordering, promising) and possibly a perlocutionary act (that is, bringing about a certain state in the hearer). Besides being grammatical or ungrammatical, an utterance will be appropriate or inappropriate in the given situation; appropriateness conditions—internalized rules of language use that speakers assume to be in force—can be formulated.

While the Austinian treatment of appropriateness conditions is to define them in relation to particular speech acts in particular contexts, H. Paul Grice has generalized the notion of appropriateness, developing rules intended to apply to all discourse. His "Cooperative Principle," which a participant in a speech exchange supposedly will normally assume his interlocutor to know and to be trying to observe and expecting him to observe also, is: "Make your conversational contribution such as is required, at the stage at which it occurs, by the accepted purpose or direction of the talk-exchange in which you are engaged." At the same time, linguists have been extending the purview of their discipline in ways that bring it into close accord with speech-act philosophy. Since 1968, post-Chomskyan generative semantics (as developed by George Lakoff, Robin Lakoff, Charles Fillmore, and others) has extended the notion of speaker competence to embrace the ability to perform appropriate speech acts in particular situations, as well as phonology and syntax. In addition, sociolinguists are concerned with language *use*.

How do these developments in linguistics and allied fields relate to the study of literature, particularly poetry? Mary Louise Pratt claims (*Toward a Speech Act Theory of Literary Discourse*, 1977) that, with these developments, linguistics is for the first time able to describe literary discourse in terms of the literary speech situation, to define it in terms of use rather than of intrinsic features, and to relate it to other kinds of language use. She cites studies showing that features assumed by poeticians to be exclusively attributes of literary discourse occur in conversation as well; specifically, structural and stylistic features such as are found in fiction also occur in "natural narratives." These formal similarities, she thinks, can be in part explained by the fact that with both natural narratives and literary works, the speech exchange situation is one in which the hearer or reader is a voluntary, nonparticipant audience. She also considers it important to take into account that the reader normally knows that a literary work was, and was intended to be, published, and assumes it was composed in writing with an opportunity for deliberation, hence that it is more likely to be worthwhile than casual utterances; because of these assumptions on the part of the reader, a literary work can get away with being "difficult," and with making considerable demands on its audience.

Pratt attempts to adapt the categories of speech act theorists to accommodate literary discourse and relate it to other kinds of speech acts. She considers that many, if not all, literary works, together with exclamations and natural narratives, fall into the class of speech acts that have been characterized as thought-producing (as opposed to action-producing), representative (representing a state of affairs), or world-describing (as opposed to world-changing). She sees exclamations, natural narratives, and literary works together as constituting a subclass of representative speech acts that are characterized by "tellability," that is, by the unlikelihood and/or problematicalness of the state of affairs represented (whether fictional or not). This characteristic she holds to pertain as much to lyric poetry as to novels and short stories. The subclass is further characterized by (1) detachability from any immediate speech context (this is obvious for literary works, which generally have no immediate relation to the situation in which the reader happens to find himself) and (2) a tendency to elaborate on the state of affairs represented. Indeed, elaborating on the state of affairs they posit, may be taken, Pratt suggests, as what literary works chiefly do.

Roger Fowler, a British linguist, has been advocating and practicing the application of linguistics to the study of literary texts since the 1960's; his early work in this field includes a paper (published in the 1966 collection, *Essays on Style and Language*, which he edited) showing, with a rich variety of examples, that verse of a given meter can have very different rhythmical movements, depending on the relationships of the grammatical units with the lineation. In his most recent work (collected in his 1981 volume *Literature as Social Discourse: The Practice of Linguistic Criticism*), Fowler argues that linguistic description of literary texts should concern itself with the sociocultural context. He exemplifies the sort of description, essentially sociolinguistic, that he advocates in a treatment (in the same volume) of Wordsworth's poem "Yew-Trees."

Fowler's treatment is in answer to a reading of this poem by Michael Riffaterre. Riffaterre concentrates on the lexical aspect of the poem's language, showing that it consists basically of variations on "yew-tree" through translation of certain of its semantic components from "tree-code" into other codes—for example, "snake-code" in the lines, "Huge trunks! and each particular trunk a growth/ Of intertwisted fibres serpentine/ Upcoiling, and inveterately convolved." Fowler contends that by neglecting the matters of register (and what it implies of the activity of the speaker of the poem vis-à-vis an addressee) and of the reader's sequential experience of the text, Riffaterre has failed to give sufficient weight to the shift from a geographical guide register to Miltonic loftiness in these lines. This and other shifts of register in the poem are, he contends, significant, central to its meaning.

Besides speech-act theory and sociolinguistics, recent work on the development of a linguistic theory of discourse is promising for application to literature. Teun van Dijk, for example, has done preliminary work on a grammar taking the text, rather than the sentence, as the structure to be described, and including a "pragmatic" component that would specify appropriateness conditions for discourses.

Bibliography

Babb, Howard S., ed. *Essays in Stylistic Analysis*, 1972.

Chatman, Seymour. *A Theory of Meter*, 1964.

_____ , ed. and tr. *Literary Style: A Symposium*, 1971.

Chatman, Seymour, and Samuel R. Levin, eds. *Essays on the Language of Literature*, 1967.

Crystal, David. "Intonation and Metrical Theory," in *Transactions of the Philological Society*. (1971), pp. 1-33.

Culler, Jonathan. *Structuralist Poetics: Structuralism, Linguistics, and the Study of Literature*, 1975.

Enkvist, Nils Erik. *Linguistic Stylistics*, 1964.

Epstein, Edmund L., and Terence Hawkes. *Studies in Linguistics (Linguistics and English Prosody)*, 1959.

Fowler, Roger. *The Languages of Literature: Some Linguistic Contributions to Criticism*, 1971.

_____ . *Literature as Social Discourse: The Practice of Linguistic Criticism*, 1981.

_____ , ed. *Essays on Style and Language: Linguistic and Critical Approaches to Literary Style*, 1970.

_____ , ed. *Style and Structure in Literature: Essays in the New Stylistics*, 1975.

Freeman, D. C., ed. *Linguistics and Literary Style*, 1970.

Halle, Morris, and Samuel Jay Keyser. "Chaucer and the Study of Prosody," in *College English*. XXVIII (1966), pp. 187-219.

_____ . *English Stress: Its Form, Its Growth, and Its Role in Verse*, 1971.

Hendricks, W. O. "The Relation Between Linguistics and Literary Studies," in *Poetics*. No. 11 (1974), pp. 5-21.

Hill, Archibald A. *Constituent and Pattern in Poetry*, 1976.

Kachru, Braj B., and Herbert F. W. Stahlke, eds. *Current Trends in Stylistics*, 1972.

Leech, Geoffry N. *A Linguistic Guide to English Poetry*, 1969.

Levin, Samuel R. *Linguistic Structures in Poetry*, 1962.

_____ . *The Semantics of Metaphor*, 1977.

Lyons, John, ed. *New Horizons in Linguistics*, 1970.

Pratt, Mary Louise. *Toward a Speech Act Theory of Literary Discourse*, 1977.

Riffaterre, Michael. "Criteria for Style Analysis," in *Word*. XV (1960), pp. 154-174.

Sebeok, Thomas A., ed. *Style in Language*, 1960.

Spencer, John, ed. *Linguistics and Style*, 1964.

Strelka, Joseph, ed. *Patterns of Literary Style*, 1970.

Traugott, E. C., and M. L. Pratt. *Linguistics for Students of Literature*, 1980.

Eleanor von Auw Berry

GREAT CRITICS OF POETRY

The criticism of poetry has always played an influential role in the development of poetry in Western civilization, from the time of the ancient Greeks and Romans up through the Renaissance, neoclassic, and Romantic periods and into the twentieth century. By articulating the general aims and ideals of poetry and by interpreting and evaluating the works of particular poets, critics throughout the ages have helped to shape the development of poetry. Poets, for their part, have often attempted to meet—or to react against—the stated aims and ideals of the prevailing critical theories. Some poets—notably in England—have also formulated and practiced the criticism of poetry, producing a closer and more vital relationship between criticism and poetry. For the student, the study of poetic theory and criticism can be not only an interesting and fruitful study in itself, but also a valuable aid in the attempt to understand the historical development of poetry.

The following review of the great critics of poetry is organized chronologically and is divided into four main sections: Classical Critics; Renaissance and Neoclassic Critics; Romantic Critics; and Victorian and Modern Critics. The focus is primarily on English critics, though the ancient Greeks and Romans are necessarily included because they represent the classical tradition inherited and built upon by the English. Significant American contributors to the mainstream of poetic theory and criticism are, with the exception of Edgar Allan Poe, restricted to the twentieth century. In this essay, T. S. Eliot is the only American critic treated in depth, though even his contributions are seen as a continuation of the English tradition.

Criticism of poetry can appear in many different forms, and one of the purposes of this essay is to make clear as many of those forms as possible. For the time being, however, the following distinctions should be sufficient. Theoretical criticism, or poetic theory, is the articulation of general principles and tenets of poetry, usually regarding the nature, aims, and ideals of poetry, but also covering techniques and methods. Practical criticism, on the other hand, is the application of these principles and tenets to the tasks of interpreting and evaluating particular works of poetry. Both theoretical and practical criticism can be focused on any of four different aspects of poetry: first, the poem itself; second, the relationship of the poem to that which it imitates; third, the poet's relationship to the poem; and finally, the relationship of the poem to the audience. M. H. Abrams has designated these four types of criticism as objective, mimetic (after the Greek work *mimesis*, for imitation), expressive, and pragmatic. A recognition of the critic's orientation as being either theoretical or practical and as being objective, mimetic, expressive, or pragmatic can help the student of criticism to comprehend the contribution of the critic to the history of criticism.

Classical Critics

Four works of poetic theory by ancient Greek and Roman theorists have had a profound influence on the course of Western literature in general and English poetry in particular: Plato's *Republic*, Aristotle's *Poetics*, Horace's *Ars Poetica* (13-8 B.C., *The Art of Poetry*), and Longinus' *Peri Hypsous* (*On the Sublime*). In these four works are found many critical theories that make up the classical tradition inherited by the English. The two most important of these theories address the relationship of poetry to that which it imitates and the relationship of poetry to its audience. The central Greek concept of poetry is that of *mimesis*: poetry, like all forms of art, imitates nature. By nature, the Greeks meant all of reality, including human life, and they conceived of nature as essentially well-ordered and harmonious and as moving toward the ideal. Hence, poetry seeks to imitate the order and harmony of nature. Of equal importance to the mimetic concept of poetry is the Greek belief that poetry has a moral or formative effect on its audience. Poetry achieves this effect by making the reader more aware of reality and thereby more aware of his own nature and purpose. The Roman theorists, in turn, accepted these basic concepts of poetry. Neither the Greeks nor the Romans were very interested, however, in the expressive relationship between the poet and the poem (involving such questions as what takes place in the poet during the creative act of writing poetry), though they do make occasional comments on this aspect of poetry.

In Book X of the *Republic*, Plato (427 B.C.-347 B.C.), the great Greek philosopher, discusses the role of poets and poetry in the ideal society. His ideas regarding poetry are valuable, not because they clarify poetic issues, but because they raise serious objections to poetry that later critics are forced to answer. Indeed, Plato states that poets and poetry should be banished from the ideal society for two reasons: poetry represents an inferior degree of truth, and poetry encourages the audience to indulge its emotions rather than to control them. The *Republic* is written in the form of a dialogue, and in Book X Socrates (speaking for Plato) convinces Glaucon of these two objections to poetry. He arrives at the first objection by arguing that poetry, like painting, is an imitation of an imperfect copy of reality, and therefore is twice removed from ultimate truth. Reality, or ultimate truth, Plato believed, exists in universal ideas or eternal forms and not in the particular concrete objects of this world of matter. A table or a bed, for example, is a concrete but imperfect copy of the eternal form of the table or the bed. A painter who paints a picture of the particular table or bed is thus imitating, not the reality (the eternal form), but an imperfect copy of the eternal form. The poet, in writing a poem about the table or the bed—or about any other imperfect concrete manifestation of reality—is also removed from reality, and therefore his poem represents an inferior degree of truth.

The second objection to poetry raised by Plato stems from his belief that human lives should be governed by reason rather than by emotions. Poetry, Plato believed, encourages the audience to let emotions rule over reason. As an example, Socrates cites the fact that those who listen to tragic passages of poetry "delight in giving way to sympathy, and are in raptures at the excellence of the poet who stirs [their] feelings most" (translated by Benjamin Jowett). Yet, if similar tragic events took place in their own lives, they would strive to be stoical and would be ashamed to be so emotional.

Plato's objections to poetry raise serious questions: Does poetry represent an inferior degree of truth? Does it have a harmful social or moral effect? More generally, and in a sense more important, his objections raise the question of whether or not poetry can be interpreted and evaluated on grounds other than the philosophical, moral, and social grounds he uses. In other words, can poetry be interpreted and evaluated on poetic grounds? Later critics, beginning with Aristotle, argue that it is possible to construct a general theory by which to interpret and evaluate poetry on poetic grounds.

The *Poetics* of Aristotle (384 B.C.-322 B.C.), as W. J. Bate has remarked, stands out not only as the most important critical commentary of the classical period but also as the most influential work of literary criticism in the entire period of Western civilization. Thus it is essential for the student of poetic theory and criticism to have a grasp of Aristotle's basic ideas concerning poetry, especially those that refute Plato's objections and those that help to establish a general theory by which poetry can be interpreted and evaluated on poetic grounds.

The title *Poetics* means a theory or science of poetry, and accordingly Aristotle begins in a scientific manner:

> I propose to treat of Poetry in itself and of its various kinds, noting the essential quality of each; to inquire into the structure of the plot as requisite to a good poem; into the number and nature of the parts of which a poem is composed; and similarly into whatever else falls within the same inquiry. (This and following quotations of the *Poetics* are translations by S. H. Butcher.)

It is important to note that the word "poetry" (the Greek word is *poiesis*, which means "making") is used by Aristotle in a generic sense, to refer to all forms of imaginative literature, including drama, and not in the specific sense in which it is used today to refer to a form of literature distinct from drama and fiction. Unfortunately, the *Poetics* is not complete (either Aristotle never finished it or part of it was lost). As it now stands, the work contains an extensive analysis of tragedy, an account of the sources and history of poetry, and scattered remarks on comedy, epic poetry, style, and language. It also contains an evaluative comparison of tragedy and epic poetry and a discussion of critical difficulties in poetry. Yet, despite its incompleteness and its lack of any discussion of lyric poetry, the *Poetics* is an extremely important document of poetic theory.

First of all, the *Poetics* is important because it refutes Plato's objections to poetry, though it is uncertain whether Aristotle considered the *Poetics* to be a direct reply to Plato. (As a student of Plato at Athens, he must have been aware of Plato's objections, but the *Poetics* may have been written long after Plato's death and therefore not intended as a direct reply.) The key to Aristotle's refutation of Plato's first objection—that poetry represents an inferior degree of truth—is in his interpretation of the Greek concept that poetry is an imitation of nature. It is known from Aristotle's philosophical works that he believed that reality exists, not solely in universal ideas or eternal forms (as Plato believed), but rather in the process by which universal ideas work through and give form and meaning to concrete matter. For example, the reality of a table for Aristotle is not in the universal idea of a table but in the process by which the idea of a table gives form to the wood that goes into the particular table. Hence, in observing the process of nature the poet observes reality, not an inferior copy of it. Furthermore, the poet's act of imitation, for Aristotle, is not mere slavish copying, as it seems to be for Plato. (Plato implies that the poet is concerned with making realistic copies of the objects of the world of matter rather than with representing universal ideas.) Rather, Aristotle apparently saw the act of poetic imitation as a duplication of the process of nature or reality. That is, poetry is an imitation of the process of universal ideas or forms working through concrete matter. For example, a universal idea of human suffering gives shape to language, characters, and action in a tragic poem.

Poetry for Aristotle is both *poiesis* and *mimesis*, making and imitating. Hazard Adams, in *The Interests of Criticism* (1969), explains it in this way:

> To Aristotle, then, there is no contradiction between poet, or maker, and imitator. The two words, in fact, define each other. The poet is a maker of plots, and these plots are imitations of actions. To imitate actions is not to mirror or copy things in nature but to make something in a way that nature makes something—that is, to have imitated nature.

As for Plato's second objection to poetry—that it encourages emotional and irrational responses—Aristotle's theory of catharsis provides a means of refutation. Catharsis (*katharsis*), a term used by the Greeks in both medicine and religion to mean a purgation or cleansing, is apparently used by Aristotle (there is some disagreement) to mean a process that the audience of a tragedy undergoes. Tragedy excites the emotions of pity and fear in the audience and then, through the structure of the play, purges, refines, and quiets these emotions, leaving the audience morally better for the experience. While Aristotle's comments on catharsis are restricted to tragedy, they seem to be applicable to various kinds of literature. Poetry, Aristotle's ideas suggest, does not simply encourage its audience to indulge their emotions, as Plato contended, but rather it engages their emotions in order that they may be directed and refined, thus making the audience better human beings.

The *Poetics*, then, is a significant document in the history of poetic theory because it refutes the specific objections to poetry raised by Plato. It has another significance, however, just as important and closely related to the first: it demonstrates the possibility of establishing a general theory by which poetry can be analyzed and evaluated on poetic grounds, rather than on the philosophical, moral, or social grounds used by Plato. Aristotle's analysis of tragedy, his evaluative comparison of tragedy and epic poetry, and his discussion of critical difficulties in poetry all contribute to establishing such a general theory of poetry.

In his analysis of tragedy, which takes up the better part of the *Poetics*, Aristotle enumerates the parts of tragedy (plot, character, thought, diction, song, and spectacle), ranks them in importance, and analyzes each (though he devotes most of his discussion to plot, which he calls "the soul of a tragedy"). In addition to breaking down the parts of a tragedy, he explains how the parts must interrelate with one another and form a unified whole, "the structural union of the parts being such that, if any one of them is displaced or removed, the whole will be disjointed and disturbed." While his structural analysis is largely restricted to tragedy (he touches on epic poetry), it has the far-reaching effect of demonstrating that every form of literature, including all types of poetry, is made up of parts that ideally should interrelate with one another and form a harmonious and unified whole that is aesthetically pleasing to the audience.

In comparing tragedy with epic poetry, Aristotle concludes that tragedy is the higher art because it is more vivid, more concentrated, and better unified than epic poetry, and that it "fulfills its specific function better as an art—for each art ought to produce, not any chance pleasure, but the pleasure proper to it." Aristotle thus demonstrates, in making this judgment, that poetry can be judged by its poetic elements (such as vividness, concentration, and unity) and its aesthetic effects (the pleasure proper to it).

In one of the last sections of the *Poetics*, Aristotle discusses five sources of critical objections to artistic works, including poetry. Works of art are censured for containing things that are (1) impossible, (2) irrational, (3) morally hurtful, (4) contradictory, and (5) contrary to artistic correctness. Aristotle shows that each of the critical objections can be answered, either by refuting the objection or by justifying the presence of the source of the objection. In several cases the refutation or justification is made on aesthetic grounds. For example, he says that the artist or poet may describe the impossible if the desired artistic effect is achieved. Here also, then, Aristotle shows that poetry can be analyzed and judged as poetry according to a general theory of poetry.

In summary, the *Poetics* of Aristotle is of primary importance in the history of criticism because it answers Plato's charges against poetry and because it demonstrates to later critics how a general theory of poetry can be established.

The greatest Roman contribution to the history of poetic theory is a work by the poet Horace (65 B.C.-8 B.C.), usually entitled *Ars Poetica* (*The Art of Poetry*) but known originally as *Epistle to the Pisos* because it was written as a verse letter to members of the Piso family. Perhaps because it was written in the form of a letter, Horace's work lacks the systematic approach and profundity of Aristotle's treatise and the vigorous thought of Plato's dialogue. Despite these differences, as well as a lack of originality (Horace was restating—perhaps actually copying from an earlier treatise—already accepted poetic principles and tenets), *The Art of Poetry* is valuable for its influence on later ages, in particular the Renaissance and the neoclassic age. Poets and critics of those times found in Horace's graceful verse letter many of the classical poetic aims and ideals, such as simplicity, order, urbanity, decorum, good sense, correctness, good taste, and respect for tradition. In addition, Horace's urbane style and witty tone provided his admirers with a writing model.

Horace comments on a wide variety of literary concerns, ranging from the civilizing effect of poetry to the poet's need for study and training as well as genius and natural ability, though he does not explore any of these in appreciable depth. Some of the concerns are specific to drama (for example, a play should have five acts), but others relate to poetry in general. The most famous statement in *The Art of Poetry* is that "[t]he aim of the poet is to inform or delight, or to combine together, in what he says, both pleasure and applicability to life. . . . He who combines the useful and the pleasing wins out by both instructing and delighting the reader" (translated by W. J. Bate). This idea that poetry is both pleasing and formative extends back to the Greeks and has retained a central position in poetic theory through the ages. Another important concept that pervades Horace's letter is that of decorum, which is defined as the quality of fitness or propriety in a literary work. All elements in the work should be fitted to one another: character to genre, speech and action to character, style of language to genre, and so on. Horace's statements on decorum, the separation of poetic genres, the use of past models for imitation, and the formative effect of poetry became cornerstones of neoclassic theory in the seventeenth and eighteenth centuries.

The fourth classical work to have an important influence on English poetry and criticism is *Peri Hypsous*, usually translated as *On the Sublime*, a fragmentary treatise generally attributed to Longinus, a Greek philosopher and rhetorician of the third century, A.D. The work, however, shows evidence of having been written in the first half of the first century, A.D. (though the oldest extant manuscript is from the tenth century, A.D.), and therefore the authorship is questionable. While the work is mostly a treatise on the principles of rhetoric, it does contain passages of poetic theory.

The author lists five sources of the "sublime," which Bate defines as an "elevation of style, or that which lifts literary style above the ordinary and commonplace to the highest excellence" (*Criticism: The Major Texts*, 1970). The effect of the sublime on the audience are characteristics possessed by the poet: "the power of forming great conceptions" and "vehement and inspired passion" (translated by W. Rhys Roberts). The other three sources are poetic techniques, which the poet must practice and execute: figurative language, noble diction, and the dignified and elevated arrangement of words.

On the Sublime was first published in the sixteenth century by an Italian critic and its popularity among poets and critics of Europe and England reached a peak in the later half of the eighteenth century. Commentators attribute the popularity of *On the Sublime* to its combined appeal to the traditional classical interests and to the emerging romantic interests of the eighteenth century. That is, the author of *On the Sublime* stresses, on the one hand, the classical values of studying and practicing the techniques of writing poetry, of imitating past models, and of creating balanced and unified works of poetry, while on the other hand he stresses the Romantic values of inspiration, imagination, and emotion, both in the poet who creates the poetry and in the reader who is emotionally transported by sublime passages.

Renaissance and Neoclassic Critics

During the Middle Ages scholars had little interest in the literary elements of poetry and valued it, if at all, for its religious and philosophical meanings. Even the great Italian poets of the late Middle Ages—Dante, Petrarch, and Giovanni Boccaccio—state in their critical works that the value of poetry is in its religious and moral teachings. With the Renaissance, however, there came a renewed interest in the literary qualities of poetry. At first, the interest was restricted to studies of technical matters, such as meter, rhyme, and the classification of figures. These studies did not, however, solve what J. E. Spingarn, in *A History of Literary Criticism in the Renaissance* (1899), calls "the fundamental problem of Renaissance criticism": the justification of poetry on aesthetic or literary grounds. The solution to the problem, of course, was contained in classical literary theory, so that, with the rediscovery of Aristotle's *Poetics* (it had been lost to Western Europe during the Middle Ages) and with the study of Horace's *The Art of Poetry*, Renaissance critics were able to formulate a theory that justified poetry on literary grounds and that demonstrated its value for society. In Italy, this theory was developed by such critics as Antonio Minturno, Bernardino Daniello, and Francesco Robortelli. In England, it was most eloquently and persuasively articulated in the late sixteenth century by Sir Philip Sidney in the *Defence of Poesie* (1595), which Bate calls "the most rounded and comprehensive synthesis we have of the Renaissance conception of the aim and function of literature" (*Criticism: The Major Texts*).

Sir Philip Sidney (1554-1586) was neither a full-time poet nor a full-time critic; nevertheless, he is recognized as the first great English poet-critic. The

Defence of Poesie, written in the early 1580's and published posthumously, is Sidney's sole piece of sustained literary criticism, but it so well provided the needed aesthetic defense of poetry that Sidney's reputation as the foremost English critic of the Renaissance rests securely on it. The essay is an impressive reflection of Sidney's classical education in both its structure and style and in its ideas. The structure, as Kenneth Myrick (*Sir Philip Sidney as a Literary Craftsman*, 1935) has pointed out, is that of a classical oration, and the graceful and persuasive style is adapted perfectly to the structure. The ideas, while shaped by Sidney's mind, are derived from the great classical theorists: Aristotle, Plato, and Horace. In addition, the essay shows the influence of Italian literary criticism and contemporary Christian religious thought.

The *Defence of Poesie* (also published as *Apologie for Poetry*) is a justification of poetry in the generic sense, that is, of all imaginative literature, and was occasioned by various puritanical attacks on poetry, such as Stephen Gosson's *The School of Abuse* (1579), which was dedicated to Sidney. Not only does Sidney refute the puritanical charges against poetry, but also he argues that poetry is the most effective tool of all human learning in leading mankind to virtuous action. His essay is devoted to establishing proof for this thesis.

Sidney begins to line up his proof by presenting a historical view of poetry, in which he asserts that poetry is the most ancient and esteemed form of all learning. Poetry, he says, was "the first light-giver to ignorance, and first nurse, whose milk by little and little enabled [peoples] to feed afterwards of tougher knowledges." The first books were books of poetry, and these led to other kinds of books, such as history, philosophy, and science. Hence, poetry is the great educator. Accordingly, poets have enjoyed a place of esteem in most civilizations throughout history. The names given to poets (such as the Roman name *vates*, meaning prophet or diviner) is further proof of the honor accorded poets and poetry.

Following his historical view, Sidney offers a definition of poetry and an analysis of the nature and function of poetry—all of which is designed to buttress his argument that poetry, more than any other kind of learning, leads mankind to virtuous action. It is important to notice in this part of Sidney's argument that he is making a direct connection between the aesthetic quality of poetry and its moral effect—a connection that has its origin in classical theory.

With obvious debts to Aristotle and Horace, Sidney defines poetry as "an art of imitation . . . that is to say, a representing, counterfeiting, or figuring forth—to speak metaphorically, a speaking picture; with this end, to teach and delight." In imitating, Sidney says, the poet is not restricted to nature. He may "mak[e] things either better than Nature bringeth forth, or, quite anew, forms such as never were in Nature," such as demigods and other fantastic creatures. The result is that the poet creates a "golden" world, whereas nature's world is of brass. Poetry, in other words, creates an ideal world and, thereby, "maketh us know what perfection is." In giving us a "speaking picture" of perfection, poetry moves us to virtuous action. The various genres of poetry—epic, satire, elegy, pastoral, comedy, and so on—present various versions of the ideal.

Neither history nor philosophy, according to Sidney, is equal to poetry in its ability to move mankind to virtuous action. History is tied to the actual, "the particular truth of things" or "what is," and philosophy, conversely, is concerned with the universal or the ideal, "the general reason of things" or "what should be." Hence, history fails to show mankind a universal truth or ideal for which to aspire, and philosophy, while possessing the universal truth or ideal, presents it in abstract and general terms, rather than in concrete and particular terms, and thus fails to reach most of mankind. Poetry, on the other hand, "coupleth the general notion with the particular example," that is to say, embodies the universal truth in a concrete image or situation, and, in so doing, affects its readers emotionally as well as intellectually and moves them to virtuous action.

After establishing proof for his thesis that poetry is the most effective tool of human knowledge in leading mankind to virtuous action, Sidney turns to a refutation of the charges against poetry. He lists four specific charges: first, that there are "more fruitful knowledges" than poetry; second, that poetry is "the mother of lies"; third, that poetry is "the nurse of abuse, infecting us with many pestilent desires"; and fourth, that "Plato banished [poets] out of his Commonwealth." Sidney overturns the first charge by stating that, since no knowledge "can both teach and move [mankind to virtue] so much as Poetry," then none can be as fruitful as poetry. As for the second charge, that poetry lies, Sidney states that the poet does not lie because he does not affirm anything that is false to be true. By this, Sidney means that the poet does not attempt to deceive his audience into believing that what his poetry presents is actual or real. Rather, he offers his poem as an imaginary picture of the ideal, or "what should be." Sidney refutes the third charge, the puritanical charge that poetry is harmful because it increases sinful desires, by asserting that the fault lies, not in poetry itself, but in the abuse of poetry. When poetry is abused, it is harmful; but, used rightly, it is beneficial. In refuting the fourth charge, that Plato banished the poets, Sidney argues that Plato was "banishing the abuse, not the thing"; that is, Plato was upset by the mistreatment of gods in poetry. In *Ion*, Sidney claims, Plato gave "high and rightly divine commendation to Poetry."

The *Defence of Poesie* also expresses many of the neoclassic ideas and concerns that were to be treated more fully by critics in the seventeenth and eighteenth centuries; the separation and ranking of genres; the need for decorum in poetry; and the use of ancient classical models and critical authorities. It is, however, in the defense and justification of literature on aesthetic as well as moral grounds that Sidney's essay deserves its high place in the history of criticism.

In the two centuries following Sidney's *Defence of Poesie*, neoclassic poetic theory flourished in England. During this period, and especially from the mid-seventeenth to the late eighteenth century, England produced a number of able exponents of neoclassicism. Some of these critics, following the lead of French critics, insisted on a rather strict form of neoclassic theory and critical practice, turning the ancient classical principles into hard-and-fast rules. The two greatest critics of this period, however, rose above this rule-mongering and inflexibility, so that their criticism has been of permanent value. They are John Dryden and Samuel Johnson.

John Dryden (1631-1700) is known as "the father of English criticism," an honorary title given to him by Samuel Johnson because he was the first English critic to produce a large body of significant literary criticism. Almost all of it, however, is practical criticism, that is, criticism that examines particular literary works and particular problems in literary technique and construction. (Dryden often wrote about his own poems and plays.) Dryden rarely, if ever, treated in depth the larger theoretical issues of literature, such as the aims and ideals of literature, the nature of imitation, the creative process, and the moral and aesthetic effects of literature on the audience. He did write on these issues, but in passing rather than in depth. Furthermore, in no one piece of criticism did Dryden develop a general theory of literature (as Aristotle and Sidney did) as a standard by which to investigate particular works of literature.

Some literary historians are repelled by Dryden's lack of an explicitly stated general theory of literature, especially because his scattered remarks on theoretical issues are sometimes inconsistent or even contradictory. For example, on the matter of the ends of poetry, he says several times that delight is the most important end. This statement from *A Defence of An Essay of Dramatic Poesy* (1668) is typical: "for delight is the chief, if not the only, end of poesy: instruction can be admitted but in second place, for poesy instructs as it delights." In other pieces, however, he expresses a different opinion: "Let profit [instruction] have the pre-eminence of honour, in the end of poetry" ("A Discourse Concerning the Original and Progress of Satire," 1693); and "The chief design of Poetry is to instruct" ("A Parallel of Poetry and Painting," 1695). In still other pieces, Dryden merges the two ends: "To instruct delightfully is the general end of all poetry," he states in "Preface to *Troilus and Cressida* Containing the Grounds of Criticism in Tragedy" (1679).

While some commentators see Dryden's lack of an explicitly stated general theory of literature to be a weakness that results in inconsistent statements and judgments, others see it as a strength that affords him flexibility and allows him to evaluate individual pieces of literature on their own merits rather than against a theoretical standard. These latter commentators point out that much questionable neoclassic criticism resulted from an inflexible adherence to general principles and rules.

Most of Dryden's criticism, as well as being practical rather than theoretical, pertains to drama rather than to poetry and is, therefore, outside the purview of this essay. His best and most famous piece, for example, is *An Essay of Dramatic Poesy* (1668), a comparative analysis of ancient, modern, French, and English drama, examined in the light of neoclassical dramatic principles and rules by four different speakers. It might be argued that it is his criticism of drama that gives Dryden his high ranking among literary critics; nevertheless, he is also at times an astute reader and judge of poetry.

Preface to Fables, Ancient and Modern (1700) is Dryden's best-known commentary on poetry. Written in an informal, discursive style that Dryden perfected, the essay serves as an introduction to Dryden's translations of fables by Homer, Ovid, Boccaccio, and Geoffrey Chaucer. Dryden's method is largely comparative: he compares Homer to Vergil, Ovid to Chaucer, and Chaucer to Boccaccio, revealing the characteristics of the poets and the beauties of their poems. In addition, Dryden comments on the history and the development of poetry, pointing out relationships among various poets, such as Dante, Petrarch, Edmund Spenser, and John Milton, as well as those mentioned above. In doing all of this, Dryden gives a sense of the achievement of poetry in general and of Chaucer in particular. Chaucer, Dryden says, is "the father of English poetry." He was "a perpetual fountain of good sense," and he "follow'd Nature everywhere." In examining *The Canterbury Tales* (1387-1400), Dryden finds a rich variety of characters representing "the whole English nation." It is to Chaucer's magnificent cast of characters that Dryden applies the proverb: "Here is God's plenty."

Although it is impossible to summarize Dryden's critical position because it frequently shifted and because it was not explicitly stated, it is possible to summarize his critical concerns and to list the characteristics he values as a critic of poetry. First, he was concerned more with the practice of poetry than with theory. He liked to examine particular poems and specific literary problems. Second, in examining particular poems he felt that the critic's business is not "to find fault," but "to observe those excellencies which should delight a reasonable reader" ("The Author's Apology for Heroic Poetry and Heroic Licence," 1677). Third, he was interested in genres—satire, epic poetry, and so on. He considered, as did most neoclassic critics, heroic (epic) poetry to be the highest type of poetry (partially because of the mistaken neoclassic notion that Aristotle ranked epic over tragedy). In "The Author's Apology for Heroic Poetry and Heroic Licence," an essay greatly influenced by Longinus' *On the Sublime*, Dryden calls heroic poetry "the greatest work of human nature."

The characteristics that Dryden values as a critic of poetry are unity, simplicity, decorum, wit, grace, urbanity, good sense, and the like. As a poet, he often embodied these characteristics in his own poetry. Thus, in both his poetry and his criticism Dryden stands out as the preeminent model of neoclassic poetic theory of the seventeenth century.

Between Dryden and Samuel Johnson, there were two English critics who, though not of the first rank, deserve mention. Joseph Addison (1672-1719) contributed to English neoclassic criticism through the essays he wrote for popular periodicals of his day, such as *The Tatler* (1709-1710) and *The Spectator* (1711-1712, 1714), which he published with Richard Steele. Addison wrote both theoretical pieces on such poetic matters as wit, taste, and imagination, and pieces of practical criticism on such poems as Milton's epic, *Paradise Lost* (1667), and the medieval ballad "Chevy Chase." As a body, the essays express the prevailing notions of English neoclassic criticism.

Alexander Pope (1688-1744), a poet of the first rank, is the author of *Essay on Criticism* (1711), a verse essay written in heroic couplets and modeled on Horace's *The Art of Poetry* and such contemporary pieces as *L'Art poétique* (1674), by the French critic Nicolas Boileau-Despréaux. Pope's essay contains no new critical ideas, nor does it explore traditional ideas in any appreciable depth. It is, however, commendable for its expression of the prevailing neoclassic principles and tenets and for its liberal interpretation. Pope's couplet on wit is a good example of his ability to express ideas succinctly: "True wit is Nature to advantage dress'd;/ What oft' was thought, but ne'er so well express'd." His discussion ranges from the characteristics and skills needed by the critic to various critical methods and principles. A reading of Pope's essay is an excellent introduction to English neoclassic criticism.

Samuel Johnson (1709-1784) has been called the "Great Cham" of eighteenth century English literary criticism. If to Sidney belongs the honor of writing the first great piece of English literary criticism, and to Dryden that of being the first great practicing English critic, then to Johnson belongs the honor of being the first "complete" English literary critic. Johnson was expert in all forms of literary criticism: he formulated and explained literary theory; he edited texts and practiced the principles of sound textual criticism (criticism that seeks to date texts, to settle questions of authorship, and to establish the author's intended text, free from errors and unauthorized changes); he explained the historical development of poetry; he examined and evaluated particular literary works in relation to genre and in terms of literary aims and ideals; and he wrote literary biography. Johnson's criticism appears in a variety of sources, ranging from the monumental *Lives of the Poets* (1779-1781) to the *Preface to Shakespeare* (1765), from the narrative *The History of Rasselas, Prince of Abyssinia* (1759) to the essays in *The Rambler* (1750-1752) and *The Idler* (1758-1760), two periodicals he published. In addition to his critical work, he wrote poetry, a play (*Irene: A Tragedy*, 1749), a long narrative referred to above, and a great many moral and social essays and meditative works; he also compiled a dictionary of the English language and edited a collection of Shakespeare's works.

Johnson believed firmly in the classical idea that poetry is an imitation of nature, having as its ends instruction and delight. The nature that the poet imitates, however, should be "general nature." In the *Preface to Shakespeare*, he states: "Nothing can please many, and please long, but just representations of general nature." By general nature, Johnson means what is universal and permanent, that is, what is true for all people in all ages. In *Rasselas*, the philosopher Imlac explains:

> The business of a poet . . . is to examine, not the individual, but the species; to remark general properties and large appearances; he does not number the streaks of the tulip, or describe the different shades in the verdure of the forest. He is to exhibit in his portraits of nature such prominent and striking features, as recall the original to every mind. . . . [He] must disregard present laws and opinions, and rise to general and transcendental truths, which will always be the same.

By imitating general nature, the poet instructs and delights the audience. Johnson believed that instruction, or what Bate calls "the mental and moral enlargement of man," was the more important end of poetry, but he realized that poetry could best instruct by delighting. Hence, he repeatedly makes such statements as that "the end of poetry is to instruct by pleasing" (*Preface to Shakespeare*).

As a practicing critic, Johnson examined and evaluated poetry primarily in the light of this principle that poetry is an imitation of general nature with the purpose of instructing and delighting. He also investigated poetry in terms of the prevailing neoclassic notions regarding the conventions and techniques of the various genres. He believed, however, that "there is always an appeal open from criticism to nature" (*Preface to Shakespeare*), so that he never approved of conventions and techniques for their own sakes. In fact, he frequently rejected the rigid neoclassic rules as being in violation of the laws of nature. The poet's duty, he felt, was to imitate nature and life, not to follow critical rules. It was on this principle that Johnson rejected Milton's "Lycidas," a pastoral elegy. The pastoral elements, he felt, divorced the poem from nature, truth, and life. Finally, as a practicing critic Johnson strove for impartiality, seeking to discover "the faults and defects" of a poem, as well as its "excellencies." By giving a balanced and impartial account of a poet's work, Johnson established credibility as a critic.

Lives of the Poets is a set of fifty-two critical biographies of English poets, varying greatly in length and written as prefaces to the works of these poets collected and published by a group of London booksellers. The poets are all from the seventeenth and eighteenth centuries and range from Abraham Cowley to Thomas Gray, Johnson's contemporary. Johnson's general method is to sketch the poet's life and character, analyze his works, and estimate his achievement; but he also discusses a variety of poetic issues, such as diction, wit, and the conventions of genre, and by covering the poets of more than a century he effectively establishes the history of English poetry from the mid-seventeenth to the mid-eighteenth century. A review of several of the more famous biographies will give an idea of Johnson's methods and critical prowess.

In the biographical account of Pope in *Life of Pope*, Johnson includes a description of Pope's method of composition. It serves as a description of the quintessential neoclassic poet (and may be compared to that of the Romantic poet found in various pieces of Romantic criticism). Johnson says that Pope's method of poetic composition "was to write his first thoughts in his first words, and gradually to amplify, decorate, rectify, and refine them." Pope's nearly exclusive use of the heroic couplet resulted in "readiness and dexterity," and his "perpetual practice" led to a "systematical arrangement" of language in his mind. Johnson recounts the rumor that, before sending a poem to be published, Pope would keep it "under his inspection" for two years, and that he always "suffered the tumult of imagination to subside, and the novelties of invention to grow familiar." Johnson's description of Pope emphasizes the neoclassic poet's belief in the importance of practice, labor, revision, and the use of reason over imagination.

Johnson devotes a great part of his *Life of Milton* to a long analysis of *Paradise Lost*, Milton's epic. In neoclassic fashion, he examines the poem in light of the requirements of the epic genre: moral instruction, fable or plot, significance of subject matter, characters, use of the probable and marvelous, machinery, episodes, integrity of design, sentiments, and diction. His judgment is that, in terms of fulfilling the requirements of an epic, *Paradise Lost* ranks extremely high. There are faults in the poem, however, the chief one being "that it comprises neither human actions nor human manners. The man and woman [Adam and Eve] who act and suffer are in a state which no other man or woman can ever know." The result is that the reader cannot identify with the characters or the actions, so that the poem lacks "human interest." Nevertheless, *Paradise Lost*, in Johnson's final judgment, "is not the greatest of heroick poems, only because it is not the first."

In the *Life of Cowley*, Johnson gives an account of the seventeenth century "Metaphysical poets," a term he is credited with coining. His account of them is to a great extent denigrating: they "will, without great wrong, lose their right to the name of poets, for they cannot be said to have imitated anything; they neither copied nature nor life." They were, however, men of learning and wit, and this admission leads Johnson to a penetrating examination of the essence of wit. After rejecting Pope's definition of wit ("What oft' was thought, but ne'er so well express'd") because it "reduces [wit] from strength of thought to happiness of language," Johnson offers his own definition as that "which is at once natural and new" and "though not obvious . . . acknowledged to be just." He finds, though, that the Metaphysical poets do not possess wit defined as such. Rather, their wit is "a kind of *discordia concors*; a combination of dissimilar images, or discovery of occult resemblances in things apparently unlike. . . . The most hetrogeneous ideas are yoked by violence together." It is a tribute to Johnson's critical powers that this definition of Metaphysical wit continues to be applied, despite the fact that his general estimate of Metaphysical poetry is no longer accepted.

Johnson is the last—and arguably the greatest—of neoclassic critics of poetry. In another sense, though, he is apart from them. By appealing to nature and reason and common sense—in other words, by returning to classical literary principles—he almost singlehandedly overturned the tendencies of extreme neoclassic critics to codify and regularize all aspects of literature. Johnson is, in effect, a great proponent of the classical view of poetry.

Romantic Critics

Romantic criticism represents a sharp movement away from the concerns and values of neoclassic criticism. Whereas the neoclassic critic is concerned with the mimetic relationship of poetry to the nature or reality that it imitates and with the pragmatic relationship of poetry to its audience, the Romantic critic focuses primarily on the expressive relationship of the poet to poetry. The neoclassic critic sees poetry as an imitation of nature designed to instruct and delight; the Romantic critic sees poetry as an expression of the creative imagination. In examining poetry, the neoclassic critic turns to matters of genre, techniques, conventions, and effects of poetry; the Romantic turns back to the poet, the imagination, and the creative process. When the Romantic critic does turn to the mimetic relationship, he focuses on the organic and beneficient qualities of nature, and when he looks at the pragmatic relationship, he is especially interested in the connection between feelings and moral response.

In 1798, William Wordsworth (1770-1850) published, with Samuel Taylor Coleridge, a volume of poetry entitled *Lyrical Ballads*. For many literary historians, this publication is the watershed between neoclassicism and Romanticism, and the Preface that Wordsworth wrote for the second edition (1800) of *Lyrical Ballads* is the manifesto of the English Romantic Movement. In this Preface, Wordsworth presents definitions and descriptions of the poet, the creative process, and poetry. He also discusses, among other things, the differences between poetry and prose and the effect of poetry on its readers.

Wordsworth defines the poet as "a man speaking to men," suggesting by this phrase that the poet does not differ in kind from others. He does, however, differ in degree: he has "a more lively sensibility, . . . a greater knowledge of human nature, . . . a greater promptness to think and feel without immediate external excitement, and a greater power in expressing such thoughts and feelings as are produced in him in that manner." In short, the poet is, for Wordsworth, one who responds to life and nature with intense feelings and thoughts and is capable of expressing his feelings and thoughts poetically.

"[A]ll good poetry," Wordsworth says, "is the spontaneous overflow of powerful feelings," a definition that, at first glance, seems to be the very antithesis of the neoclassical view that poetry is the expression of restrained emotion and clear thought and the result of labor and revision. This definition of poetry is, however, sharply qualified by Wordsworth's description of the creative process. The poet, he says, does not compose poetry spontaneously upon the occasion of having an emotional experience. Rather, the emotional experience of the poet must first resolve itself into tranquillity, during which the poet reflects on his emotional experience:

> the emotion is contemplated till, by a species of reaction, the tranquility gradually disappears, and an emotion, kindred to that which was before the subject of contemplation, is gradually produced, and does itself actually exist in the mind. In this mood successful composition generally begins.

In other words, raw emotion is not enough for poetic composition. The emotion must be refined in a period of tranquillity by thoughts, which themselves are the representatives of past feelings. When the tranquillity modulates back into emotion, composition can begin.

Though Wordsworth does not make it explicit in this passage on the creative process, it can be inferred from the passage and from statements he makes in his poems that the faculty by which the poet creates poetry is the imagination. Like the other Romantics, Wordsworth exalts imagination over reason (itself exalted by the neoclassics) and assigns to it a variety of functions, which Bate sums up in his Introduction to Wordsworth in *Criticism: The Major Texts*:

> We have, then, in the imagination, an ability to draw upon all the resources of the mind: to centralize and unify sense impressions, to combine them with intuitions of form and value, and with realizations won from past experience.

In *The Prelude* (1850), his long, autobiographical poem, Wordsworth says that the imagination "Is but another name for absolute power/ And clearest insight, amplitude of mind/ And Reason in her most exalted mood."

One of Wordsworth's principal aims in the Preface to *Lyrical Ballads* is to explain the poetic and philosophical bases for the kind of poems he had written. The purpose, he says, "was to choose incidents and situations from common life, and to relate or describe them . . . in a selection of language really used by men." The incidents would be made interesting by "a certain coloring of imagination, whereby ordinary things should be presented to the mind in an unusual aspect" and "by tracing in them . . . the primary laws of our nature." He goes on to say that he chose to depict "[h]umble and rustic life" in his poems because those who live in such circumstances are closer to nature and its formative and beneficial influences. Their feelings and passions reach a maturity from being "incorporated with the beautiful and permanent forms of nature," and their language is purified because they "hourly communicate with the best objects [that is, those of nature] from which the best part of language is originally derived." The effect of reading such poetry as Wordsworth has prescribed is that "the understanding of the Reader must necessarily be in some degrees enlightened, and his affections strengthened and purified." This poetic and philosophical notion—that poetry should imitate the purified language and the beautiful passions and feelings of those who live simple lives in a close relationship to nature—is known as Romantic Naturalism. Wordsworth's idea that a poetry of Romantic Naturalism will have a profound moral effect on its readers is a central tenet of Romantic poetics.

Wordsworth's poetry of "[h]umble and rustic life" is in opposition to the eighteenth century poetry that depicted a polite, urban society. His espousal of a "language really used by men" is in opposition to the language of eighteenth century poets, known as "poetic diction." Poetic diction is marked by personification, periphrasis, Latinisms, archaisms, invocations, and the like, and is based on the notion that, as Thomas Gray put it, "the language of the age is never the language of poetry." Wordsworth sought, in his poetry and in his Preface, to break down the prevailing distinction between the language of poetry and the language of everyday life because he believed that an artificial poetic language prevents the poet from capturing "the essential passions of the heart." For Wordsworth, "the language of a large portion of every good poem, even of the most elevated character, must necessarily, except with reference to the metre, in no respect differ from that of good prose." This idea, in turn, leads him to the controversial notion that meter and rhyme are superadditions to the poem. They are added by the poet in order to increase the reader's pleasure and to balance the emotional excitement produced by imagery and language with the calmness produced by the regularity of meter and rhyme. This notion that meter and rhyme are superadditions to a poem conflicts, however, with the more accepted concept that all elements of a poem are essential to forming a unified whole.

Wordsworth's importance as a literary critic does not go much beyond the contribution of the Preface to *Lyrical Ballads*. Nevertheless, the role that this document played in the Romantic movement and the importance that it has in the total body of Romantic criticism are great indeed.

Samuel Taylor Coleridge (1772-1834) is, by far, the greatest of the Romantic critics of poetry: he wrote more theory and practical criticism; he ranged farther across critical terrain; and he pondered critical problems more deeply than did the other Romantic critics. It is also true, however, that he is not always clear about his ideas, that some of his ideas are left incomplete, and that he borrowed some concepts from critics and philosophers, especially the

Germans, without proper attribution. The fact that his literary ideas frequently move into philosophical areas also makes it difficult for the student of literature to grasp fully his literary positions. His key literary concepts appear in a variety of publications, the major ones being *Biographia Literaria* (1817) and his lectures on William Shakespeare.

Like the other Romantic critics, Coleridge is interested less in the rules and conventions of poetry than in the nature of the poet, the imagination, and the creative process. He is also deeply interested in the question of what makes a poem a poem.

Poetry for Coleridge is the product of the creative imagination of the poet. He makes this clear when he states in Chapter XIV of *Biographia Literaria* that the question "What is poetry? is so nearly the same question with, what is a poet? that the answer to the one is involved in the solution to the other." He then describes the poet, not by what he *is*, but by what he *does*:

> The poet, described in *ideal* perfection, brings the whole soul of man into activity, with the subordination of its faculties to each other, according to their relative worth and dignity. He diffuses a tone and spirit of unity, that blends, and (as it were) *fuses*, each into each, by that synthetic and magical power, to which we have exclusively appropriated the name of imagination.

Coleridge has thus moved from poetry back to the poet and then to the imagination.

Coleridge spent a great deal of critical effort in attempts to define the imagination because he felt that a concept of the imagination was central to his poetic theory. Some of his key statements, besides the one quoted above, are that the imagination is the "reconciling and mediatory power" that joins reason to sense impressions and thereby "gives birth to a system of symbols" (*Stateman's Manual*, 1816); that it is "that sublime faculty by which a great mind becomes that on which it meditates" (Shakespeare as a Poet Generally"); and that it "reveals itself in the balance or reconciliation of opposite or discordant qualities" (*Biographia Literaria*, Chapter XIV). He also distinguishes between the primary and secondary imagination in Chapter XIII of *Biographia Literaria*. The primary imagination is "the living Power and prime Agent of all human Perception, and as a repetition in the finite mind of the eternal act of creation in the infinite I AM." By this latter phrase, he apparently means that the imagination is godlike in its ability to create. The secondary imagination, he explains, differs in degree but not in kind from the primary imagination. Essentially, Coleridge seems to say that the imagination is creative, emphathetic, perceptive, harmonizing, synthesizing, symbolizing, and reconciling.

One of Coleridge's key literary concepts that has been fully embraced by modern critics is that of organic form. Although the theory is not original with Coleridge (Aristotle advocated it), he was the first important English critic to elaborate on it. In one of his Shakespeare lectures, Coleridge distinguishes between "organic" form and "mechanic" form:

> The form is mechanic, when on any given material we impress a pre-determined form, not necessarily arising out of the properties of the material; as when to a mass of wet clay we give whatever shape we wish it to retain when hardened. The organic form, on the other hand, is innate; it shapes, as it develops, itself from within, and the fulness of its development is one and the same with perfection of its outward form. Such as the life is, such is the form. ("Shakespeare's Judgment Equal to His Genius")

Nature, for Coleridge (as for Aristotle), is the model of organic form. Poetry imitates nature's organic process of giving unifying form to all of its diverse elements. A poem, for Coleridge, is like a plant, a living organism, synthesizing all of its diverse elements—imagery, rhythm, language, and so on—into a harmonious and organic whole.

Coleridge also wrote a great amount of criticism on particular poets— Dante, Shakespeare, John Donne, Milton, Wordsworth, and many others. The greater part of it, however, is on Shakespeare and Wordsworth. Much of his criticism on Wordsworth is negative. He objects (in *Biographia Literaria*) to Wordsworth's Preface, in particular to what he sees as Wordsworth's attempt to present his poetic theory as applicable to all poetry rather than to a particular kind. Despite his objections, Coleridge considers that his fellow Romantic poet ranks just behind Shakespeare and Milton in greatness.

Coleridge's investigations of particular poets are almost always interesting, but his greatness as a critic lies in his contributions to the theories of the creative imagination and the organic nature of poetry.

The poetic theories of Percy Bysshe Shelley (1792-1822) are contained, for the most part, in his essay *A Defence of Poetry* (1840), which he wrote in response to Thomas Love Peacock's satirical attack on poetry in an essay entitled "The Four Ages of Poetry." Shelley's essay shows the influence of Neoplatonism combined with Romantic notions of the organic character of nature, and it bears a resemblance to Sidney's *Defence of Poesie*, especially in its defense of poetry on moral and aesthetic grounds. Although the greater part of the essay is given over to a descriptive history of poetry, it is typically Romantic in its discussion of the nature of the poet, the poetic process, the creative imagination, and the importance of sympathy and feeling in the development of the moral faculty.

Shelley's claims for the poet are very grand: "A poet participates in the eternal, the infinite, and the one." The poet unites the two vocations of legislator and prophet, not in the sense of making social laws and foretelling the future, but in the sense that the poet "beholds intensely the present as it is, . . . [and] beholds the future in the present." Hence, "[A] poem is the very image of life expressed in its eternal truth."

The faculty by which the poet discovers these Platonic laws that govern nature is not reason (which Plato championed) but imagination. Reason, for Shelley, is the "principle of analysis" that dissects, divides, enumerates, and distinguishes objects of nature, whereas imagination is the "principle of synthesis" that grasps the totality of nature in all of its organic character and perceives its value and quality. Poetry, for Shelley, is "the expression of the imagination"; it is not "produced by labour and study," as it was for the neoclassicists. The poet cannot create poetry at will, "for the mind in creation is as a fading coal," which is blown into "transitory brightness" by a power within the poet that comes and goes without warning. Even as the poet is composing, his inspiration is waning, and because inspiration is so fleeting, "the most glorious poetry . . . is probably a feeble shadow of the original conceptions of the poet." This Romantic notion—that the conception is perfect and the execution or composition is imperfect according to its distance from the conception—is the very opposite of the neoclassic notion that the poet approaches perfection through labor and revision.

The effect of poetry on the reader is, according to Shelley, morally formative, not because poetry is or should be didactic, but because it engages the reader's emotions. Shelley echoes the other Romantic critics, especially William Hazlitt, when he states that "[t]he great instrument of moral good is the imagination." The imagination—strengthened and enlarged by reading poetry—enables the reader to move away from his own selfish concerns and sympathetically identify with others, thus developing his moral faculty.

John Keats (1795-1821) was not a professional critic nor did he set down his critical ideas about poetry in a systematic fashion, as did Wordsworth, Coleridge, and Shelley. He expressed his poetical ideas—which are profound and suggestive—sporadically in his personal letters to family and friends. In a letter concerning a personal matter, he would suddenly express his ideas about poetry, the poet, the creative imagination, and other related issues in which he was passionately interested.

Keats describes the nature of the poet to his friend Richard Woodhouse, in a letter of October 27, 1818. The poet, he says, "has no Identity"; rather, he is always "filling some other Body," that is, identifying with someone or something else with which he is poetically engaged—a character, a tree, the sun, a bird, autumn. The poet, for Keats, is like the chameleon: he changes his color to adjust to his environment. Keats distinguishes this sort of poet from "the Wordsworthian or egotistical sublime," by which he seems to mean the poet who is intent on projecting his own feelings onto other things, instead of entering into the nature of other things.

The power by which the poet is capable of sympathetically identifying with other people and things is labeled by Keats "negative capability." At its simplest, negative capability allows the poet to negate his own personality in order to identify with and understand another person or thing. The understanding, however, is not one of reason but of feeling. Keats says that negative capability is at work "when a man is capable of being in uncertainties, Mysteries, doubts, without any irritable reaching after fact & reason" (December 21 or 27, 1817). Stated another way (in the same leter): "With a great poet the sense of Beauty overcomes every other consideration."

Beauty and truth are the chief aims of art and poetry, according to Keats. He says that "[t]he excellence of every Art is its intensity, capable of making all disagreeables evaporate, from their being in close relationship with Beauty and Truth" (December 21 or 27, 1817). Another function of the imagination for Keats (besides that of negative capability) is that of apprehending beauty and translating it into truth. In a letter of November 22, 1817, he states that "What the imagination seizes as Beauty must be truth." Abstract truth—truth gained through "consequitive reasoning"—is not as valuable for Keats as truth embodied in the concrete forms of beauty and experienced with the senses and emotions. This belief that truth must be concretely experienced leads Keats to state that if poetry "is not so fine a thing as philosophy—[it is] For the same reason that an eagle is not so fine a thing as a truth" (March 19, 1819).

Several other Romantic critics deserve mention, though there is not space to describe their contributions in detail. In England William Hazlitt wrote widely on literary matters and promulgated many of the ideas that make up the Romantic theory of poetry. In Germany A. W. von Schlegel and his brother Friedrich articulated the aims and accomplishments of German Romanticism. Edgar Allan Poe is recognized as the leading American Romantic critic, though there is substantial disagreement about the real value of his critical ideas. His most famous critical work is "The Poetic Principle" (1848), which urges that beauty, and not truth, is the proper aim of poetry.

Victorian and Modern Critics

Criticism of poetry in the last century and a half has been extremely diverse. In the last half of the nineteenth century, it ranged from the classical, moral, and humanist interests of Matthew Arnold to the impressionistic, "art for art's sake" theories of Walter Pater and Oscar Wilde and the historical, sociological, and biographical methods of the French critics Hippolyte Taine and Charles Sainte-Beuve. The diversity has increased in the twentieth century, as critics have applied methods and terminology from a variety of other disciplines to the history and interpretation of literature. This diversity makes it difficult to identify the "great" critics of poetry in the Victorian and modern periods, but certainly two in particular stand out: Matthew Arnold and T. S. Eliot.

Matthew Arnold (1822-1888) is the major literary critic of the last half of the nineteenth century. He was a poet, a professor of poetry at Oxford, and an inspector of schools. Furthermore, he perceived his role as critic as extending far beyond literary matters into social, educational, moral, and religious areas, so that he is, in effect, a critic of culture in a broad sense. For this reason, it is imperative to understand his ideas about culture in order to understand his ideas about poetry and criticism.

In "Sweetness and Light" (a chapter from *Culture and Anarchy*, 1869), Arnold defines culture as "a study of perfection, and of harmonious perfection, general perfection, and perfection which consists in becoming something rather than in having something, in an inward condition of the mind and spirit, not in an outward set of circumstances." In other words, culture is not, as it is often thought of today, the possession of certain knowledge or information; rather, it is a condition or habit of being that can be applied to everyday life. Arnold equates the "pursuit of perfection," which is the goal of culture, with the "pursuit of sweetness and light," metaphors for beauty and truth.

The way to culture's goal of perfection, to beauty and truth, is "to know the best which has been thought and said in the world." (Arnold repeats this phrase with some variations in different essays.) When Thomas Huxley, a scientist, accused Arnold of limiting the sources of culture to literature (Huxley believed that scientific knowledge is as effective as literary knowledge in attaining culture), Arnold responded in "Literature and Science" (1882) by stating that all literature—including scientific, social, political, as well as imaginative—contributes to the pursuit of culture. Nevertheless, Arnold goes on to say, a literary education is in fact superior to a scientific education. There is a need in life, Arnold says, for knowledge, and science satisfies this need by providing one with facts about man and nature. There is also, however, a great need to relate knowledge to "our sense for conduct" and "our sense for beauty," and this, Arnold contends, science cannot do. Literature, on the other hand, does have the power of relating new knowledge to people's senses of conduct and beauty. Arnold means that literature, because it unites the universal with the particular and because it affects the emotions as well as the intellect, can show people how to apply new ideas morally in their conduct and aesthetically in the way they perceive the world.

Arnold's most famous definition of literature is that it is "a criticism of life," a definition that he repeatedly uses in his critical works and consistently applies to poetry under his inspection. Arnold means by this phrase that poetry should address the moral question of "how to live." It should provide an ideal by which people can measure their own lives. In another famous phrase that Arnold uses in various essays, he says that great poetry is "the noble and profound application of ideas to life." The purpose of poetry, he says in "The Study of Poetry" (1880), is "to interpret life for us, to console us, to sustain us," a function that he likens to that of religion. Indeed, to an age in which religious faith had been badly shaken by the findings of science, Arnold solemnly offered poetry as a source of consolation and sustenance.

Criticism, as well as poetry, plays a central role in Arnold's concept of culture. In "The Function of Criticism at the Present Time" (1864), Arnold defines criticism as "a disinterested endeavor to learn and propagate the best that is known and thought in the world, and thus to establish a current of fresh and true ideas." Arnold is speaking here of all types of criticism, not only literary criticism, and the ideas generated by disinterested criticism will be ideas relating to all fields of knowledge and will contribute to the attainment of culture. The task in every critical endeavor, according to Arnold, is "to see the object as in itself it really is," and in evaluating new ideas the duty of the critic is "to be perpetually dissatisfied . . . while they fall short of a high and perfect ideal."

Arnold's method as a practicing critic of poetry is seen in a number of essays. The most famous—and most controversial—of these is "The Study of Poetry," an introduction to a collection of English poetry. In the essay, Arnold rejects two traditional methods of evaluating poetry: the "historic estimate," which judges a poem by its historical context, and the "personal estimate," which relies on a critic's personal taste and preferences to judge a poem. In place of these, Arnold proposes the "touchstone" method: the critic compares lines of the poem under consideration with "lines and expressions of the great masters"—Homer, Dante, Shakespeare, Milton. Such lines, which the critic should keep stored in his mind, will serve as "an infallible touchstone for detecting the presence or absence of high poetic quality, and also the degree of this quality, in all other poetry which we may place beside them."

The chief objection raised to Arnold's "touchstone" method is that it appears to place more value on the individual parts (lines) than on the inter-relationship of the parts and the total design and unity of the poem. This may not, in fact, have been Arnold's intention. In other critical works, he emphasizes the importance of total design and unity. For example, in his Preface to *Poems* (1853), he praises the quality of total design in poems, and he disparages "poems which seem to exist merely for the sake of single lines and passages; not for the sake of producing any total-impression." He cites Keats's *Isabella* (1820) as a poem without total design. In *Matthew Arnold: A Survey of His Poetry and Prose* (1971), Douglas Bush suggests that Arnold may have meant that "a line or two [the touchstone] may recall the texture and total character of a long poem—which he assumes that his readers know," so that in effect the critic using the touchstone method is not comparing individual lines but complete poems.

"The Study of Poetry" is also controversial in some of its judgments of English poets. In the latter half of the essay, Arnold uses the touchstone method to evaluate most of the major English poets from Chaucer to Robert Burns. In examining each poet, Arnold looks for "high seriousness," a quality he does not define but which is obviously related to his notion that poetry should be "a criticism of life." Shakespeare and Milton, in Arnold's view, are classics of English poetry because they possess "high seriousness." Chaucer, on the other hand, is not a classic of English poetry because he lacks "high seriousness." This judgment conflicts with past judgments of Chaucer (such as Dryden's), and it is all the more controversial in the light of the fact that Arnold judges Thomas Gray to be a classic poet with "high seriousness." Also controversial is Arnold's judgment that Dryden and Pope are not classics of English poetry. Instead, "they are classics of our prose" because they possess the qualities of great prose: "regularity, uniformity, precision, balance."

The survey of English poetry in "The Study of Poetry" stops with Burns (who falls short of being judged a classic), but Arnold makes judgments of later English poets in other essays, most of which can be found in the two volumes of *Essays in Criticism* (1865 and 1888). He ranks Wordsworth directly behind Shakespeare and Milton in poetical greatness because Wordsworth "deals with more of *life* than [other poets] do; he deals with *life*, as a whole, more powerfully" ("Wordsworth"). Lord Byron, in Arnold's opinion, ranks right behind Wordsworth. The strengths of Byron are his "splendid and puissant personality, . . . his astounding power and passion . . . and deep sense for what is beautiful in nature, and for what is beautiful in human action and suffering." Byron lacks, however, the "great artist's profound and patient skill in combining an action or in developing a character." This and his other faults—such as "his vulgarity, his affectation"—keep him from achieving in his poetry "a profound criticism of life" ("Byron").

Of Keats's poetry, Arnold's opinion is that it "is abundantly and enchantingly sensuous" and possesses "natural magic" equal to that of Shakespeare. He lacks, on the other hand, the "faculty of moral interpretation" and "high architectonics" (by which Arnold means the ability to create a total design) necessary for the great poet. Had Keats not died early, he might, in Arnold's view, have developed into a great poet because he undoubtedly had the "elements of high character" ("Keats"). Arnold's essay on Shelley is a review of a recent biography of the Romantic poet. Arnold rejects the biographer's unqualified veneration of Shelley and "propose[s] to mark firmly what is ridiculous and odious in . . . Shelley . . . and then to show that our former beautiful and lovable Shelley nevertheless survives." He concludes the essay by repeating his now-famous description of Shelley (first used in his essay on Byron): Shelley is "a beautiful *and ineffectual* angel, beating in the void his luminous wings in vain" ("Shelley").

Arnold's literary interests extended beyond English poetry. He also wrote about Celtic literature, the poetry of Homer, of Heinrich Heine and Johann Wolfgang von Goethe, and the works of Count Leo Tolstoy, as well as about many other authors and literary topics. Through all of his critical writings, Arnold maintained the position of the classicist, asserting the broad moral value of humane arts and letters in a world in which proponents of science, on the one hand, and proponents of the "art for art's sake" movement, on the other, were threatening to eclipse classical literary ideals.

T. S. Eliot (1888-1965) deserves the title of "great critic" because of the range and depth of his criticism. A gifted poet and playwright who gave up his American citizenship to become a naturalized British subject, Eliot wrote on a diversity of literary topics. Because of this diversity, his critical work is very difficult to summarize. Rather than attempting to encompass all of his views regarding poetry and criticism, the following discussion presents a rough classification of his critical works and a detailed explanation of several of his key poetic concepts. If Eliot's critical works on drama and dramatists and those dealing with topics other than literature, such as culture and religion, are excluded, most of the remaining works can be classified into three groups: first, works dealing with the nature of criticism; second, works dealing with the nature of poetry; and third, works dealing with individual poets.

The first group includes such works as "The Perfect Critic" and "Imperfect Critics" (both from *The Sacred Wood*, 1920), "The Function of Criticism" (1923), and *The Use of Poetry and the Use of Criticism* (1933). One of the purposes of the latter work is to explore "the relation of criticism to poetry" from the Elizabethan age to the modern period, and it includes essays on many of the great critics of poetry. Eliot's ideas about the criticism of poetry are many and diverse, but on the whole they contributed greatly to modern formalistic or New Criticism by insisting on the primacy of the poem itself. In the Introduction to *The Use of Poetry and the Use of Criticism*, Eliot states that criticism addresses two questions: "What is poetry?" and "Is this a good poem?" At a time when literary critics were often concerned with historical and biographical aspects, Eliot's statement served to remind critics that poetry itself should be the primary concern of the critic.

The second group of critical works includes such essays as "The Social Function of Poetry," "The Music of Poetry," and "The Three Voices of Poetry" (all contained in the first section of *On Poetry and Poets*, 1957). As with the first group, Eliot's range in this group is wide. Almost any aspect of poetry interests him—relatively small matters such as the use of blank verse to larger issues such as the difference between "classic" and "romantic." Probably the two most influential essays in the group are "Tradition and the Individual Talent" and "The Metaphysical Poets" (both in *Selected Essays*, 1932, 1950).

The English poets about whom Eliot writes in the third group of critical works include Andrew Marvell, Milton, Dryden, William Blake, Byron, Algernon Charles Swinburne, and William Butler Yeats, as well as many more. Especially noticeable in these works is Eliot's extensive use of quotations from the poetry to illustrate his observations. This practice is in keeping with his idea that the critic should focus on the poetry. Also noticeable is Eliot's attempts to reshape the reigning view of English poets (especially to downgrade Milton and to elevate the Metaphysical poets and Dryden). Eliot believed that one of the ends of criticism is "the correction of taste."

Several of Eliot's poetic concepts have become very important in modern poetics and therefore deserve special attention. These concepts concern the nature of the poet and the poetic process, the nature of poetry, and the idea of tradition. Eliot developed these ideas throughout several works, the most important of which are "Tradition and the Individual Talent" and "The Metaphysical Poets."

In "Tradition and the Individual Talent" Eliot says that "[t]he poet's mind is in fact a receptacle for seizing and storing up numberless feelings, phrases, images, which remain there until all the particles which can unite to form a new compound are present together." The difference between a poet and an ordinary person, Eliot explains, is that the poet has the ability to form these chaotic elements into a unified whole:

> When a poet's mind is perfectly equipped for its work, it is contantly amalgamating disparate experience; the ordinary man's experience is chaotic, irregular, fragmentary. The latter falls in love, or reads Spinoza, and these experiences have nothing to do with each other, or with the noise of the typewriter or the smell of cooking; in the mind of the poet these experiences are always forming new wholes. ("The Metaphysical Poets")

To explain the actual creative process of composing poetry, Eliot uses a scientific analogy, which has the effect of emphasizing the objectivity and intensity of the process. He compares the creative act of composing poetry to the scientific act of forming sulphurous acid:

> When the two gases previously mentioned [oxygen and sulphur dioxide] are mixed in the presence of a filament of platinum, they form sulphurous acid. This combination takes place only if the platinum is present; nevertheless the newly formed acid contains no trace of platinum, and the platinum itself is apparently unaffected; has remained inert, neutral, and unchanged. ("Tradition and the Individual Talent")

The two gases represent the emotions and feelings and other experiences that the poet has stored up. The filament of platinum represents his mind or creative faculty, and the sulphurous acid is the poem. The objectivity of the process is stressed in the fact that the poem (the sulphurous acid) shows "no trace" of the poet's mind (the platinum) and that his mind is "unchanged" by the experience of writing the poem. Eliot further emphasizes this objectivity (called "aesthetic distance" by formalistic critics) in his statement, following the analogy that "the more perfect the artist, the more completely separate in him will be the man who suffers and the mind which creates."

Eliot calls this process of composing poetry the "process of depersonalization" because it deemphasizes the poet's personality and personal emotions. "Poetry," he states in "Tradition and the Individual Talent," "is not a turning loose of emotion, but an escape from emotion; it is not the expression of personality, but an escape from personality." This does not mean, however, that poetry for Eliot is not intense. There is intensity involved, but "is is not the 'greatness,' the intensity, of the emotions, the components, but the intensity of the artistic process, the pressure, so to speak, under which the fusion takes place, that counts." The result of such an intense artistic process is an impersonal aesthetic emotion, that is, an "emotion which has its life in the poem and not in the history of the poet." Eliot expounds on this idea of an impersonal aesthetic emotion in his essay "Hamlet and His Problems":

> The only way of expressing emotion in the form of art is by finding an "objective cor-relative"; in other words, a set of objects, a situation, a chain of events which shall be the formula of that *particular* emotion; such that when the external facts, which must terminate in sensory experience, are given, the emotion is immediately evoked.

The ideal poet for Eliot, then, is one who keeps his creative self separate from his personal self and who creates an impersonal artistic emotion in his poetry through the "objective correlative" formula. In order to be such a poet, it is necessary for him to "surrender . . . himself . . . to something which is more valuable," that is, to tradition. Tradition, for Eliot, involves the "historical sense," that is, "a perception, not only of the pastness of the past, but of its presence." The historical sense gives the poet a feeling for the "simultaneous existence" and "simultaneous order" of all literature from Homer on, and it will make clear to him how his own work must fit into this literary tradition while at the same time expressing his "individual talent."

With regard to the English literary tradition, Eliot worked to overturn the prevailing opinion that the line of great English poets extended from Shakespeare to Milton to Wordsworth and excluded the Metaphysical poets (Donne, Marvell, and others) and the neoclassic poets, especially Dryden. (Arnold was the critic most responsible for the prevailing opinion, especially by his designation of Dryden and Pope as "classics of prose" and not of poetry and his praise of Wordsworth, but Johnson's view that the Metaphysical poets were more "wits" than poets had stuck through the nineteenth century and contributed to the prevailing opinion.) Eliot argues that the Metaphysical poets "were the direct and normal development of the precedent age," that is the Elizabethan age, and not "a digression from the main current" of English poetry. These poets, like their Elizabethan predecessors, "possessed a mechanism of sensibility which could devour any kind of experience." They had the ability to unite thought and feeling, so that in their poetry "there is a direct sensuous apprehension of thought, or a recreation of thought into feeling." After the Metaphysical poets, "a dissociation of sensibility set in, from which we have never recovered" ("The Metaphysical Poets").

This "dissociation of sensibility"—the separation of thought and feeling in poetry—was "aggravated," Eliot says, by Milton and Dryden. Milton perfected an impassioned language but dispensed with wit, whereas Dryden developed an intellectual wit lacking an emotional element. Both were fine poets, but their followers lacked their poetic qualities and only "thought and felt by fits, unbalanced." Eliot touches on this thesis again in his essays on Milton, Dryden, and Marvell, but he does not develop it further in his essays on the Romantic poets. Nevertheless, his theory of poetic sensibility has become one of the leading theories regarding the historical development of English poetry.

Other modern critics of poetry perhaps deserve to be ranked as great critics, but it is fitting to end this essay with Eliot because he is the latest in a long line of great English critics who are also poets. It is not essential, of course, that a critic also be able to write poetry, but the fact that so many of the great English critics—from Sidney to Eliot—have also been poets has undoubtedly increased the perception, sensitivity, range, and flexibility of English criticism.

Michael L. Storey

SCIENCE AND POETRY

Whether science and poetry are compatible or antagonistic is partly a matter of definition and partly of theoretical commitment, but poets throughout the history of Western literature have versified the scientific knowledge of their times and even considered poetry unusually well suited to scientific discourse. This was particularly true in classical Greece, where early rationalists such as Hesiod, Xenophanes, Empedocles, and Parmenides all considered that thoughts and observations were ennobled when made public through poetry— most of which, unfortunately, has been lost. Among the poets of ancient Rome, Vergil, Ovid, Gratius, Manilius, Callimachus, Aratus, Nicander, and (at the very end of the Empire) Oppian devoted major literary works to science. The greatest and most influential scientific poet of classical times, however, was Lucretius (96-55 B.C.), the author of *De rerum natura* (*On the Nature of Things*), an incomplete long poem in six books that attempted to free mankind from the fears and superstitions of religion by proving that worldly vicissitudes are wholly material in origin.

For a time, in northern Europe especially, much of this classical legacy was lost. The earliest scientific poems in English literature, therefore, present a view of nature totally different from that of Lucretius. For European poets of the Middle Ages, the material world was important not primarily for itself but for the spiritual truths that it embodied as a manifestation of God. Some of the earliest poems, such as the Anglo-Saxon "Wyrta" (perhaps c. A.D. 1000) are half medical and half magical, listing in this case nine plants believed efficacious against poison, snakebite, infirmities, and demons. The Bestiary tradition, derived from allegorical reinterpretation of the Roman author Pliny the Elder's often fanciful assertions about animals, resulted in several poems, one of which, preserved fragmentarily in the Exeter Book, deals with only three animals, the panther, the whale, and the partridge. A longer but otherwise similar poem from the same manuscript deals solely with allegorical interpretations of the phoenix. By the twelfth century, when Anglo-Norman had become the literary language of England, this tradition would appear more elaborately in Philippe de Thaon's "Le Livre des Créatures," an orderly verse survey including the signs of the Zodiac, the allegorical significance of each Zodiacal animal, and the astronomical origin of the calendar. Philippe de Thaon's other major scientific poem, *Bestiaire* (c. 1121, *The Bestiary*), explains the lion, one-horned monoceros, panther, crocodile, stag, centaur, beaver, hyena, elephant, and other creatures, including sea-serpent and siren, all of which exist as reminders of scriptural truths. Other celebrations of the world and its inhabitants appear in early English metrical lives of saints. For this bestiary literature, see *Popular Treatises on Science Written During the Middle Ages, in Anglo-Saxon, Anglo-Norman, and English* (1841, Thomas Wright, editor).

A later but still pre-Chaucerian development was the encyclopedic poem, of which a major example is the northern dialect *Cursor Mundi* (c. 1300, *World Survey*), of nearly twenty-four thousand lines, which divides the history of God's work into seven ages, beginning with the Creation and ending with the Last Judgment. Long poems with scientific passages were also being written on the Continent, especially in France, but the most impressive of them all for modern readers is *La Divina Commedia* (c. 1320, *The Divine Comedy*) of Dante Alighieri, famous for its use of medieval, geocentric astronomy. As a general discussion of the medieval outlook, C. S. Lewis' *The Discarded Image* (1964) is outstanding.

Geoffrey Chaucer (c. 1343-1400), who was broadly familiar with both English and Continental literature, frequently utilized the sciences of his time in verse, as Walter Clyde Currey has pointed out (*Chaucer and the Medieval Sciences*, 1926). These sciences included natural and celestial physiognomy, metroscopy, geomancy, astrology, alchemy, medicine, and psychology. Thus, in *The Canterbury Tales* (1387-1400) there are complicated references to medieval medicine in the Prologue's description of the Doctor of Physic; the Summoner and the Cook are medical cases themselves; and the Pardoner, Reeve, and Miller likewise reveal themselves through physiognomic clues. The Wife of Bath is lusty, she explains, because of her horoscope. Even more replete with astrological references are the Knight's and Man of Law's tales. That of the Nun's Priest includes dream lore and the Canon Yeoman's has some alchemy. *Troilus and Criseyde* (1382), Chaucer's second masterpiece, which has been dated on the basis of an unusual astronomical observation in Book III, goes beyond routine astrology to consider basic problems of free will and destiny. Passages dealing with medieval sciences can also be found in the works of John Gower (1330?-1408) and John Lydgate (1370?-1451?).

From the fourteenth century to the beginning of the seventeenth (despite Copernicus in 1543), European writers generally utilized a fairly consistent body of knowledge, including belief in the historicity of Genesis, a round earth central to concentric planetary spheres, a further sphere of equidistant stars, astrological influences (which inclined but did not impel), alchemical transformations, four elements, and four humors in man, who was a microcosm of the cosmos as a whole. This pervasive series of assumptions—most of which were challenged at various times, until all of them eventually collapsed—has been well described by Robert W. Ackerman (*Backgrounds to Medieval English Literature*, 1966) and E. M. W. Tillyard (*The Elizabethan World Picture*, 1943). Studies of Shakespearean psychology, such as Theodore Spencer's *Shakespeare and the Nature of Man* (1942), and editions of his plays also usually outline many ideas, pointing out herb lore, earthquake theory, fanciful potions, humors, and astrology in such plays as *Romeo and Juliet* (1595-1596), *Hamlet* (1600-1601), *King Lear* (1605), and *The Tempest* (1611) especially. Other English playwrights contemporary with William Shakespeare also dramatized traditional science (Christopher Marlowe's *The Tragedy of Doctor Faustus*, 1592; Ben Jonson's *The Alchemist*, 1610); but only George Chapman foresaw, in plays and poems, that the medieval view of nature was being destroyed by astronomical discoveries.

Among the nondramatic poets between Chaucer and Shakespeare, few are household names today, and those who wrote scientific verse are even less well-known. (They have been listed for scholars by Robert M. Schuler in *PBSA*, 1975). One of the more impressive is George Ripley's *Compound of Alchemy* (1591), composed in 1471; he also wrote scientific poems in Latin. Thomas Norton's *The Ordinall of Alchimy*, written in 1477, was published two hundred years later. *Sidrac and Boctus* (fifteenth century), translated from a French original by Hugh of Campedene, continued the verse encyclopedia tradition, answering 362 questions on theology, morality, and medicine. In 1557, William Bloomfield's *Blossoms* further popularized alchemy in eighty-four stanzas of rhyme royal, and Thomas Charnock did much the same in his versified *Breviary of Naturall Philosophy* (also 1557). Medical poems by William Bullein appeared during the next few years, as did Barnabe Googe's verse translation of Palingenius' *Zodiac of Life* (1560-1565). Thoughtful considerations of nature and its mutability were common at the end of the sixteenth century (which had seen the worst of the Reformation). Among poetic ones are the Mutability cantos of Edmund Spenser's *The Faerie Queene* (1590-1596); the sonnets of Shakespeare and others; two long poems by Sir John Davies, *Orchestra* (1596) and *Nosce Teipsum* (1599); and John Norden, *Vicissitudo Rerum* (*On the Change of Things*, 1600), "an Elegiacall Poem, of the interchangeable courses and varieties of things in this world." Much of this literature on mutability was inspired by the *Metamorphoses* (before A.D. 8) of Ovid, whose works were translated frequently throughout the later sixteenth century, most notably by Arthur Golding (1565, 1567). Another source of inspiration came from on high.

By the final years of the sixteenth century, changes of every kind were apparent to Elizabethan writers, even in the supposedly immutable realm of the fixed stars. In 1572, a new star (supernova) appeared in Cassiopeia and continued to shine brightly for two years. An exceptionally bright comet in 1577, earthquakes in 1580, and—incredibly enough—a further supernova in 1604 further convinced Europeans that a fundamental reassessment of their traditional cosmology was required. Astrologers were full of dire predictions, but three great astronomers (Tycho Brahe, Johannes Kepler, and Galileo Galilei) instead helped to create a new, and ultimately less theological, cosmos. Poets, too, heeded the astronomers and their theories.

The new cosmos affected almost every major English poet (and an American one) throughout the seventeenth century, including Chapman, George Herbert, Edward Taylor, Henry Vaughan, and Thomas Traherne, but hardly any were so thoughtful as John Donne (1572-1631), for whom see Charles

Coffin, *John Donne and the New Philosophy* (1937). Much is known about Donne's familiarity with recent science—including Copernicus, Kepler, Galileo, and William Gilbert—from a prose tract of his satirizing the Jesuits (*Ignatius His Conclave*, 1611), but he is most famous for his "First Anniversary," a poem written in 1610 to commemorate the death a year earlier of Elizabeth Drury. In lines that have often been quoted, Donne there affirmed that the traditional universe believed in for so long had been shattered and that the new cosmos was a melancholy one of chaos and decay. This pessimistic view of nature prevailed throughout the earlier seventeenth century and led to much unpleasant speculation about the perversity of human nature as well. Besides the decay of the world (described by Victor Harris in *All Coherence Gone*, 1949, the title quoting Donne), other scientific themes common in earlier seventeenth century poetry include the motion of the earth, the immensity of the universe, the telescope and its revelations, the habitability of other worlds, and the possibility of space travel. Together with Francis R. Johnson's *Astronomical Thought in Renaissance England* (1937), two books by Marjorie Hope Nicolson, *The Breaking of the Circle* (1960) and *Voyages to the Moon* (1948) are helpful guides to these broader trends. Kitty Scoular's *Natural Magic: Studies in the Presentation of Nature in English Poetry from Spenser to Marvell* (1965) is introductory.

Poems affirming more traditional world views, however, continued to appear throughout the seventeenth century. Thus, Robert Chester complacently surveyed Britain's plants, animals, and stones in *Love's Martyr* (1601), while Edward Pond more ominously described the four elements, humors, and diseases in his *Almanac* for 1604. John Taylor, the Water Poet, wrote poems on astrology (1612) and the causes of weather (1637). Both Taylor and George Wither described the fearful plague of 1625 in lengthy verse. Of many seventeenth century poems inspired by the study of anatomy, Phineas Fletcher's *The Purple Island* (1633) is the most fulsome. William Lilly, the astrologer, wrote minor poems about his celestial knowledge for more than thirty years. Poems on human psychology (often influenced by Robert Burton's prose *The Anatomy of Melancholy*, 1621) continued throughout the century; Henry More's, of the 1640's, include astronomical theories also. Elias Ashmole, *Theatrum Chemicum Britannicum* (1652), and John Collop, *Poesis Rediviva* (1656), are major anthologies of alchemical and medical poems, respectively. Finally, Henry Vaughan translated several Latin scientific poems into English verse for Thomas Powell's *Humane Industry* (1661), which appeared the year that the Royal Society of London was founded, and six years before the last and greatest synthesis of outmoded knowledge.

Influenced by such predecessors as Homer, Vergil, Lucretius, Ovid, Dante, Spenser, and Guillaume de Salluste Du Bartas (the latter being the author of an encyclopedic sixteenth century poem on the Creation), John Milton's *Paradise Lost* (1667), the story of Adam's transgression in Eden, subsumed amazing quantities of biblical exegesis, history, geography, psychology, and natural science, so that study of the poem and its background soon becomes a veritable study of seventeenth century thought as a whole. This, at least, was the approach taken by Kester Svendsen (*Milton and Science*, 1956), who compared passages from Milton's works with others from contemporary encyclopedias and biblical commentaries. Though he wrote knowledgeably about all aspects of God's creation, Milton is best known for his magnificent cosmology (including an imaginative grasp of the immensity of space unprecedented in English literature); he accepted the centrality of the earth, for example, as being at least theologically and poetically true, even if dubious in fact. Thus, in Book VIII of *Paradise Lost*, Adam discusses competing astronomical systems—geocentric and heliocentric—with the archangel Raphael and is told to regard the matter with indifference. Milton (who probably met Galileo in Italy) was the last major poet in English to exemplify the traditional outlook of Christian humanism.

Before about 1650, scientific research north of the Alps was fairly unusual; after that time, however, the precepts of Sir Francis Bacon (*The Advancement of Learning*, 1605; *The New Atlantis*, 1627) became increasingly popular, finally resulting in the formation of the Royal Society for the Promotion of National Knowledge in 1661. (The best background studies are Richard Foster Jones's *Ancients and Moderns*, 1961, and Dorothy Stimson's *Scientists and Amateurs*, 1948.) Abraham Cowley, who wrote a number of scientific poems, praised the new society in a poem attached to Thomas Sprat's *History of the Royal Society* (1667), an important book that urged poets to use natural imagery derived from fact rather than classical myth. The chief publication of the Society, however, was its *Transactions* (1665-present), which disseminated scientific discoveries and opinion throughout the world, with very significant influence upon both literature and art. Inevitably, the *Transactions* also proved a target for scoffers, including the many religiously conservative men of letters who abhorred the skeptical, Lucretian materialism of modern science (which had now come into being) and welcomed opportunities to ridicule the supposed credulity of its practitioners. Some famous satires were Samuel Butler's poem "The Elephant in the Moon" (1670?, published in 1759, a mouse in the telescope); Thomas Shadwell's play, *The Virtuoso* (1676), directed against old phonies; John Gay, Alexander Pope, and John Arbuthnot's *Three Hours After Marriage* (1717), ridiculing the antiquarian and geologist John Woodward; and Book III of Jonathan Swift's *Gulliver's Travels* (1726). Even in the later part of the eighteenth century, suspicions about the soundness and implications of science were voiced by several poets, including Chistopher Smart, William Cowper, and especially William Blake, but all three were simply dismissed as mad, for science by then had become extremely popular.

As Marjorie Hope Nicolson (*Newton Demands the Muse*, 1946) and others have shown, Isaac Newton was the first scientist to become a literary symbol in his own right. There were tributes to him throughout the eighteenth century by many poets, including James Thomson, Pope, Mark Akenside, and William Wordsworth. Blake's responses to Newton—a satirical portrait of him in watercolors and many poetic references—were complex and ultimately profound; they have been traced brilliantly by Donald Ault in *Visionary Physics: Blake's Response to Newton* (1974). Nicolson and other literary scholars have also discussed Blake's opinion of science.

Of the many poems written in praise of Newton, Thomson's "To the Memory of Sir Isaac Newton" (1727, the year of Newton's death) most fully presents the usual eighteenth century image of the great scientist, who was cherished as the supreme example of the heights to which the human intellect might aspire. His *Philosophiae Naturalis Principia Mathematica* (1687, *The Mathematical Principles of Natural Philosophy*), gave poets new metaphors of gravitation, planetary attraction, and lunar influence upon the tides while proving by irrefutable mathematics that heliocentricity was after all correct; as further results, mythological references to natural phenomena, and much traditional poetic imagery, became unfashionable. There were religious implications also, for it was becoming clear that the literal meaning of the Bible (as in Joshua's making the sun stand still) could not be reconciled with the findings of modern science. Newton's second book, written in English rather than Latin and much easier to understand, was the *Treatise on Optics* (1704), in which it was shown that white light was composed of all colors; thus, Newton demystified the rainbow and brought prismatic hues into artistic fashion. Some speculative "Queries" added to the *Treatise on Optics* in its various editions encouraged scientific endeavor throughout the eighteenth century. Not until Benjamin Franklin became famous for his experiments with electricity would another name challenge the popular scientific eminence of Newton's.

Perhaps because Newton had said little about it, natural history flourished throughout the eighteenth century, particularly among amateurs spurred on by such discoveries as the microscope (seventeenth century), the real nature of fossils, ecological relationships, and less primitive systems of zoological classification; Robert Hooke, John Ray, Carl Linnaeus, and Georges Buffon are among the important names. At first most of the investigations were closely associated with the Church; in the earlier eighteenth century, science was still restricted in many quarters to natural theology, or the confirmation of God and His attributes through evidence from nature. Some characteristically long expository poems embodying this point of view are Richard Blackmore's *The Creation* (1712), Thomson's *The Seasons* (1726-1730), David Mallet's *The Excursion* (1728), James Ralph's *Night* (1727, by an American), and Richard Savage's *The Wanderer* (1729), with many later examples, including (in his way) Wordsworth, until the whole tradition was finally rejected by Alfred, Lord Tennyson in *In Memoriam* (1850). Two very helpful surveys of eighteenth century scientific verse are Dwight L. Durling's *The Georgic Tradition* (1964) and William P. Jones's *The Rhetoric of Science* (1966). Nicolson's *Mountain Gloom and Mountain Glory* (1956) deals particularly with landscape poetry and geology.

As depicted by Mallet and Savage, the natural world is full of earthquakes and volcanic eruptions—more violent than what Blackmore and Thomson had described. Following important earthquakes in New England (1729) and London (1750) and the famous Lisbon earthquake of 1755, which nearly flattened a major city, many poets in England and America found it impossible to believe that nature's God was always mild and benevolent. Though Alexander Pope had foreseen the problem of natural disasters in his *Essay on Man* (1733-1734), others could not agree that natural violence and death were necessary to the well-being of humanity (see Voltaire's poem on the Lisbon earthquake and his short novel *Candide*, 1759). Later poets such as Smart, Blake, and even Wordsworth necessarily regarded the power of nature as part of the grandeur of God. For others, however, the seismic disasters proved that nature was an amoral force, to be given purpose and direction by the human mind.

This was the general outlook of what became the Industrial Revolution, and of its most explicit poetic advocate, Erasmus Darwin (1791-1802) whose works were popular in both England and America during the 1790's. Combining the heroic couplet of Pope with the skeptical materialism of Lucretius, the deism of his century, and a personal gusto for the life of the senses, Darwin capitalized on the popularity of natural history in writing voluminous but energetic poems explaining current knowledge and technology in clever ways, with encyclopedic notes attached. His two major scientific poems, *The Botanic Garden* (1789-1791) and *The Temple of Nature* (1803), influenced both naturalists and poets. Most important, Darwin advocated a voluntaristic theory of biological evolution that eventually came to the attention of his grandson Charles, author of *On the Origin of Species* (1859). Erasmus Darwin awoke Romantic minds to the imaginative possibilities of science and furnished some new metaphors (the upas tree and the simoom, for example) that quickly became common property. His influence was strong on Blake, Wordsworth, Samuel Taylor Coleridge, Robert Southey, Lord Byron, and Percy Bysshe Shelley. Desmond King-Hele has discussed Erasmus Darwin's scientific ideas (occasionally bizarre) and their literary influence in a series of sometimes repetitive books.

Of all the Romantic poets, none was more closely associated with science than Shelley, whose references to it in verse have been traced by King-Hele and Carl Grabo. Shelley's devotion to science is apparent in his long poems *Queen Mab* (1813, with extensive notes), *Mont Blanc* (1817), and especially *Prometheus Unbound* (1820). Though strongly indebted to Darwin and some earlier scientific poets, Shelley transcends all of them in the splendor of his natural imagery. Guided equally by Lucretius and the French Enlightenment, he regarded science as the rational understanding of natural forces that would free mankind from the burden of religion; his poem *Mont Blanc*, therefore, derives an unexpected lesson from nature.

A large number of minor Romantic poets also followed Erasmus Darwin's lead in versifying their contemporary science. Though seldom read now, and virtually unknown to most literary historians, this essentially factual poetry was surprisingly acceptable to readers and critics alike during the earlier nineteenth century—so much so that the more imaginative poets often felt threatened by the commonplace demand that their imagery be scientifically accurate. There had been explicit critical commentary regarding science and poetry (broadly speaking) since antiquity, but the modern conflict began in 1667 when Sprat criticized earlier poets for their stale, repetitive imagery. As historian of the Royal Society he looked forward to new and fresher nature poetry based on current knowledge. Poets throughout the eighteenth century attempted to fulfill his expectations, not only with new poems but also by translating and updating the classics (Jones, in *The Rhetoric of Science*, gives examples). Though "scientific" speculations, usually fantastic, were often satirized, genuine new facts were widely respected, and many poets at least grudgingly acknowledged the necessity of accurate observation. Thomas Gray and George Crabbe, among other poets, were authentic naturalists themselves, and many primarily scientific investigators (the chemist Humphry Davy, for example) wrote verses on the side. Throughout the eighteenth century and beyond, then, poets and naturalists usually regarded their divergent tasks as complementary.

At first, only the mad or tragic poets, such as Smart, Cowper, Thomas Chatterton, and Blake, questioned this supposed compatibility. During the Romantic period in Britain, however, the relationship of science and poetry came increasingly to be regarded as antagonistic, until John Keats in December, 1817, drank "confusion to Newton and his mathematics" and three years later in *Lamia* accused the great scientist of having destroyed the poetry of the rainbow. Among the more important critical documents relevant to this pervasive debate (several of them poems) are Sprat's *History of the Royal Society* (1667); John Dryden's *An Essay of Dramatic Poesy* (1668); Mark Akenside's *The Pleasures of Imagination* (1744); Samuel Johnson's *Rasselas* (1759); John Aikin's *An Essay on the Application of Natural History of Poetry* (1777); Erasmus Darwin's Preface to *The Botanic Garden* (1791); Blake's *Europe* (1794); Wordsworth's Preface to *Lyrical Ballads* (1800, but the remarks on science—extremely famous—were added in 1802); Thomas Love Peacock's "The Four Ages of Poetry" (1820); Shelley's *A Defence of Poetry* (unpublished until 1840); Keats's *Lamia* (1820); Thomas Campbell's "To the Rainbow" (1820); Thomas Babington Macaulay's "Milton" (1825); Tennyson's "Timbuctoo" (1829); Edgar Allan Poe's "To Science" (1829); Ralph Waldo

Emerson's *Nature* (1836) and "The Poet" (1841); Charles Dickens' *Hard Times* (1854); and Walt Whitman's "Song of Myself" and "When I Heard the Learn'd Astronomer" (1855). Perhaps the height of Victorian concern with the factuality of poetic images was reached with Robert Newell's *Zoology of the English Poets, Corrected by the Writings of Modern Naturalists* (1845), from which one learns that "The plays of Shakespeare are a storehouse of incorrect zoology." Whatever one thinks of Newell as a literary critic, it is nevertheless true that zoological fables were uncommon in the poetry of his time as references to nature became increasingly exact. A very large number of books promoting natural history and science appeared throughout the nineteenth century, and several were concerned specifically with how to observe, a theme elaborated by John Ruskin on behalf of both science and art.

A nineteenth century poet especially noteworthy for his command of natural history, his concern for factual accuracy, and his sometimes distraught appraisal of modern science was Tennyson (1809-1892), perhaps the greatest versifier of scientific knowledge since Lucretius. To about the same extent that astronomy and alchemy had dominated scientific poetry in the seventeenth century and physics and natural history in the eighteenth, scientific poetry of the earlier nineteenth century (prior to Charles Darwin's *On the Origin of Species* in 1859) was preoccupied with geology and astronomy, the two sciences that most actively engaged Tennyson, especially in *The Princess* (1847) and *In Memoriam*. Essays on Victorian literary astronomy and geology by Jacob Korg and Dennis R. Dean, respectively, in *Victorian Science and Victorian Values* (1981), correct a number of misconceptions about this period. In American literature, Emerson's use of science has been noticed by several commentators, but there is no general survey equivalent to Joseph Beaver's *Walt Whitman, Poet of Science* (1951).

The nineteenth century brought an increasing awareness of nature's cruelty and indifference; concern centered upon the vast sweep of history rather than on sporadic disasters such as earthquakes and volcanoes; Tennyson's *In Memoriam* is the most famous example, with Keats's "Epistle to Reynolds" (1818) an important precursor. Nature grew even more grim-visaged for Victorians after 1859, when Darwin's *On the Origin of Species* appeared. Darwin's influence on literature has been studied by several scholars, including Georg Roppen (*Evolution and Poetic Belief*, 1956); Lionel Stevenson (*Darwin Among the Poets*, 1963); and S. C. Dodge (*Use of Evolutionary Theory by American Poets, 1900-1950*, 1958). The major poets involved include Tennyson, Robert Browning, Matthew Arnold, A. C. Swinburne, George Meredith, Thomas Hardy, Stephen Crane, Robert Bridges, and John Davidson.

Despite these prominent writers, and many other minor ones, fewer long poems by serious poets of the late nineteenth and early twentieth centuries have seriously attempted to versify scientific discoveries or theories in the

Lucretian way. Erasmus Darwin and the American naturalist C. S. Rafinesque were probably the last writers to present significant new scientific theories to the public in verse, a procedure that seems highly eccentric now, but only because the role of poetry has changed. Similarly, few poets since Tennyson have devoted long passages of verse to the explication of prevailing theories—or of their artistic application (Robert Bridges' *The Testament of Beauty*, 1929, was among the last). A long twentieth century poem devoted to the history of science, *The Torch-Bearers* (1922-1930) by Alfred Noyes, despite the influence of Tennyson and Meredith, is not thought to be distinguished. Though some very major poets, such as William Butler Yeats, who was influenced by Blake, have specifically rejected science as a literary influence, many others have simply ignored it. Thus, the theories of Albert Einstein have given rise to very few twentieth century poems, though the theories of Sigmund Freud have been influential in prose (see Frederick J. Hoffman's *Freudianism and the Literary Mind*, 1959). A large number of recent poets, it is true, have been concerned about and influenced by science. Among them, most notably, are Robert Frost, Karl Shapiro, Archibald MacLeish, Edith Sitwell (*The Shadow of Cain*, 1947), Robinson Jeffers, W. H. Auden, Kenneth Rexroth, May Swenson, Gary Snyder, and A. R. Ammons. A relevant study by H. H. Waggoner, *The Heel of Elohim* (1950), deals with modern American poets; there is no British equivalent. In general, recent poets have been increasingly willing to use the facts of current science as metaphors, and some of them (such as Snyder and Ammons) are impressively knowledgeable, but there are fewer long poems or passages devoted to science and its problems.

The literature concerning science and poetry in recent years has been almost entirely critical or historical rather than poetic. Tennyson, for example, was the first modern literary figure to be studied as a poet of science (especially by Norman Lockyer, an astronomer, in 1910). The first broad survey of science and literature was by C. S. Duncan in 1913. Alfred North Whitehead's *Science and the Modern World* (1925) then inaugurated the study of science and Romanticism. C. P. Snow's polemic *The Two Cultures and the Scientific Revolution* (1959) excited a good deal of controversy at one time, some of it meaningful. Other significant books (all of them now dated) include I. A. Richards' *Science and Poetry* (1926); Ralph B. Crum's *Scientific Thought in Poetry* (1931); Douglas Bush's *Science and English Poetry* (1950); B. Ifor Evans's *Literature and Science* (1954); and Aldous Huxley's *Literature and Science* (1963).

Dennis R. Dean

THE ARTS AND POETRY

Various art forms require different critical approaches because each procedural language has different grammatical or syntactical requirements. Despite the differences, the fine arts have many things in common. Each is able to shape the attention span, to organize and determine the temporal span whether on a visual, verbal, or aural level. The attention span is not a level phenomenon: it grows and fluctuates depending on its exposure to a stimulus. The art work provides the stimulus and manipulates the response of the audience. This response has predictable elements that the artist studies while learning the specific technique. Though each approach to art, whether painting, poetry, or music, has its peculiar technical requirements, the fundamental similarity is the psychological anticipation of the audience response. As the artist articulates the event on the canvas, in the poem, or in the musical score, so is the audience response articulated or defined.

To reduce the arts to mere subject matter obscures the very heart of the artistic process. Aestheticians often think that because poetry and prose use words to convey their messages, the visual and auditory arts stand outside the realm of the verbal. Others recognize that the verbal often carries distinct subject matter indications, and argue that this aspect of imitation places visual art beyond even the verbal arts. What both fail to see is that the visual, auditory, and verbal arts all share a language-related approach that, though peculiar to each individual art, functions in similar ways on both verbal and nonverbal levels. Whatever message is involved is an adjunct of the overall artistic entity.

The difficulty of ascertaining and defining relationships among the arts is somewhat like attempting to translate a joke or witticism from one language to another. Words may be found that create a parallel situation, puns may be constructed on a similar principle, the degree of absurdity between the punchline and the preceding situation may be approximated; still, the joke must frequently be explained in some verbal context outside the frame of the joke itself so that the original meaning may be made clear. What often results is a metaphorical relationship through which the listener or audience is led to infer the original impact of the joke in its "foreign" setting.

The joke offers a direct analogy to the art work. The timing of the joke, like the articulation of artistic response, may be more important than the words, the context or the subject matter. The success of the joke or the work is dependent on the syntax or the relationships between the words. Whereas the words may be translatable, the timing may be altered unless the joke is reconceived in the new syntax.

Terminological differences are less of a problem than terminological overlap. Critics have heightened the confusion by translating certain of the artist's terms in order to use them in more than one area. Artistic terms frequently creep into journalistic writing and this deepens the misunderstandings. A politician may be said to have "orchestrated" a particular move in his political career. A more accurate term, and just as colorful, might be "choreographed." In orchestration, most instruments have customary places and duties that are determined by their musical function. Political choreography would be a more encompassing process in which the "performers" are moved about because of and in reaction to certain moves made by the choreographers as well as the other dancers. Whereas orchestration is an arranging process that produces effective combinations of instruments to convey the notes of a composition, choreography determines the entire work in all its facets, though it still allows each individual performer his particular range of expressiveness that may be determined by his personality or style of movement.

Generally, each art area is said to have its own expressive media, that is, visual art has paint, watercolor, crayon, ink; sculpture has bronze, marble, terra cotta, and the like. At the same time, each art area may be considered a medium through which the creative process realizes itself and by which its particular approach to materials is determined. Through this analogy, the visual art work is to the creative process as painting is to visual art.

Although there are certain intrinsic elements shared by all of the fine arts, many terms have slightly different connotations in separate media. Still, they may be listed as organizing principles much as nouns, verbs, and prepositions. These include rhythm, balance, line, volume, texture, perspective, dynamics, color, to name only a few. The degree of translation or analogy from one medium to another will depend on structural as well as metaphorical similarities.

In painting, rhythm may be a matter of repetition, of similarity of diagonals or horizontals, or of a color that is repeated, intensified, or enhanced in different areas of the canvas. The use of rhythm in poetry shares similarities with rhythm of music: there may be a local rhythm based on a moment-to-moment metrical pattern, a larger phrase rhythm, and an even large formal or sectional rhythm. There may also be counter rhythms, syncopations (reversed accents), and changing or modulating rhythms. Because of the simultaneous nature of the visual arts, the rhythm may be on a more figurative level. While the eye is capable of taking in the picture as a whole, there is also a temporal quality involved in the act of perception. The eye sees both whole and part, but since one element takes visual precedence over another, the eye moves from place to place. Therefore, painting has a focal point that begins the journey and recalls the eye again and again, creating a rhythm that functions as a cross rhythm to the patterns, colors, lines or other rhythmic elements.

In a poem, there is often a governing metaphor or extended figure of speech tha furnishes a mental focal point. It may be present throughout a short poem (for example, Robert Graves's "A Civil Servant" or Emily Dickinson's "A

Narrow Fellow in the Grass"). The metaphor may interweave throughout the work, as in Edmund Spenser's *The Faerie Queene* (1590-1596), where the underlying meaning forms a pattern that, in its successive stages, appears to control more and more of the allegory.

In an abstract painting or in architecture, the focal point may work like the poetic metaphor, as an ordering process or a system of tensions and releases. In an Alexander Calder mobile, the controlling image is the fulcrum from which the work emanates or is suspended. Though ultimately controlling the balance and preventing the sculpture from pulling itself down to the ground, this fulcrum represents a syntax of balances that allows the changing shapes to move in and out of various degrees of tension. The moving parts focus the attention as they verge on colliding with one another, and the tensions dissolve and regroup according to the configurations that are created by the fulcrum. The mind's eye forgets the metaphor, the tonic repose, the balancing act itself, but returns to this totality as a counter rhythm to the patterns or altering shapes.

In Archibald MacLeish's poem "The End of the World," the opening lines appear to contradict the serious title, making it slightly melodramatic, since the poem appears at first to be about the circus. The suggestions of danger (lions biting ladies, matches being lit from precarious positions) hardly disturb the air of frivolity. In the midst of the apparent contradiction, the opening words return to make the entire circus scene parenthetical. "Quite unexpectedly," the point has been, after all, to say, "Quite unexpectedly the top blew off." The framing device of the repeated words is inconsistent with the formal sonnet requirements as is the conversational approach to the meter. The repetition causes the reader to move closer to the once chatty, now more ominous tone of the poem.

The second section heralds a warning with a total change in approach: the narrative, on-going, fast-moving sentence construction of the first half suddenly becomes an act of verbal suspension that echoes the imagistic suspension of the situation. The repetition of the word "there," holds the reader, the persistent commas slow the act of reading, and the parallel construction begins again and again to accentuate the breathless quality of the scene, the quick breathing of excitement and danger, and the need to breathe in the act of reading aloud.

The framing device of the first half, which seemed an overstatement at the opening, suddenly takes on an air of heightened expectation. The rhyme scheme in the second half dissolves "unexpectedly" into a couplet, making the poem into the sonnet that was not necessarily indicated by the first half. The counter phrase rhythm of the parallel phrase construction in the middle four lines (second half) does not at first contradict the expectation that the second half will balance the first half. It also implies a new start or a new element, as the repeated "there" of the first line becomes a phrase within the counter phrase. The middle four lines work as a unit, and the first line is followed by a mutation into a smaller unit of three: The second line, "Those thousands," is echoed in "There in the starless . . . There with vast wings . . . There in the sudden. . . ."

Because of the implication of greater complexity that requires space or time to resolve itself, the cutting short is at once formal and figurative. The drum roll in the first half of the poem (the only aural image in an otherwise strongly visual poem) also inserts a counter-rhythm and points aurally, visually, even temporally to the colon that ends the section. The interruption of the narrative that divides the phrase after "while the drum/ pointed," emphasizes the dual aural-visual. Like the drum that punctuates the silence, the colon signals the event that must necessarily follow. The couplet cuts into the rhyme scheme as well as into the not yet completed drum roll. The repetitions that have held the reader "poised," suddenly, like the image, let him drop.

This distinctly musical effect casts aspersions on the generally accepted aesthetic division between spatial and temporal modes of art. The imagery, spatially present to the mind's eye, is totally dependent on a narrative, there-fore sequential, presentation. The suspense is one of intensity rather than of actual duration. The effect makes the picture grow larger, closer to the experience, until it becomes almost tangible or visible, only to be snatched away into the ending: "Of nothing, nothing, nothing—nothing at all." MacLeish subtly uses the rhetorical devices as a foil to the traditional structural patterns of the poem.

This poetic technique has historical analogues in the musical device known as "word painting." From the sixteenth century (dubious examples have also been noted earlier in the Gregorian period) to the present day, composers of liturgical compositions frequently matched the music to words in the text. Hence, on the word "Deus," the music might soar into a high register, or might proceed stepwise so that the loftiness is combined with the sensation of moving upward. The "Lux Aeterna" of a mass will commonly begin quietly in the higher range in long-sustained tones, so that the aural focus is on the harmonic resonance, an often glittering (lux) effect, which is enhanced by the careful placement of upper parts in relation to the overtones produced by the lower parts. Though the effect on the listener is only the suggestive impression of this shimmering light, a closer awareness of the technical procedure reveals a reflection of overtones—the tones produced acoustically by the lower notes that are made to sound fuller because of the mathematical placement of the upper parts.

A visual counterpart to the word painting is produced by the hidden window that Bernini (1598-1680) incorporates into the *Ecstasy of St. Theresa*, in the church of the Santa Maria della Vittoria. In this case, the gilt metal rays reflect the actual light, and against the dark marble of the chapel, the illu-mination seems to pull the figures upward. The space that the sculptor/architect leaves between the figures, the illusory fresco on the ceiling and the surrounding floor space, creates an almost tangible separation between the real domain of the observers (echoed in the presence of a sculpted audience seated around the work) and the domain of St. Teresa, who is drawn into the otherness of space above. The actual light is reflected on the metal beams so that they appear to create the light, and the resulting aura creates a space of its own in the process. This play between the actual or technical and the supposed or rhetorical suggests a direct relationship with the poetic and musical examples presented.

These two examples indicate the presence of the intrinsic similarity among the arts throughout history. One complication involved in comparisons among work from different eras is that the different artistic settings produce works that necessitate a closer examination of poetic or philosophical factors that affect stylistic considerations, both in the creation and interpretation of the art work.

In order to clear away the webs of interferences that hide the functional or intrinsic aspect of the artistic process, it is valuable to study all of the arts from a chronological standpoint. By attempting to understand the methodologies and the mind sets behind the period concept, each time frame serves as precisely that—a frame that separates the work and provides a certain boundary through which the work may be seen. It is important to realize that what is being studied is not the art work itself but the culture, technical developments, and expressive influences. It becomes clearer through the widening perspective of history that the theorizing comes always after the fact, and consequently these theories are only an attempt at explaining the cultural climate. The historical settings, like the theorizing, may be seen as an ever multiplying complex of influences that are reflected in philosophy, religion, politics, economy, and science as well as the arts and finally all human endeavor. With this awareness, it becomes clearer that the basic constructs inherent in all the arts maintain this language aspect despite the transient encroachments of place, time, and theory.

Historically speaking, the labels of Renaissance and Enlightenment lead to a more mature overview of the arts. The cultural dressing of each segment of history may provide the same extrinsic dissonance as that produced by a programmatic approach that links art works, but not if the distinction is made between the frame or theory and the art work or organism. The pockets of influences, though they may frequently be reduced to mere fashion, need not obscure the intrinsic formational elements; they may, in fact, help to reveal them. By concentrating on the separation of setting and specimen, the evidence is overwhelming that the creative process has certain fundamental similarities no matter what cultural and temporal factors intrude, but it is necessary to know how cultural and temporal factors work in order to get to the foundations of the artistic function.

In Paul Klee's (1879-1940) pen, ink, and watercolor drawing *The Twittering Machine*, the initial impression is of a mechanical contraption that appears, from its flat surface, nonperspectival presentation, to work by the simple turning of a handle. This constitutes the distance or first impression—the childlike invention is a bird machine that may be made to twitter. The immediate visual catch in this interpretation is the contrast between the messy smudges on the picture and the stylized bird heads that make up the primitive machine, versus the delicate color scheme, the sensitive line drawing, and the mathematical balance created by the space in the top right against the weight of the bird grouping in the lower left.

The placement that seems both calculated and careless combines with the sense of arrested movement as if the birds had been bobbing up and down just before the viewer happened to glance in their direction. On closer inspection, while the birds appear to represent distinctly different characteristics or personalities, the pared-down system of cues suggests both bird heads and lures used for fishing. The overall effect is that of a mechanical frivolity—even if it works, it works to no purpose. The circus quality of "The End of the World" may be recalled here: the trivial as a foil to the serious.

Like a pun that pokes fun at man's faith in the machine age, the title exaggerates the contrast between the implied and the obvious. The deceptive simplicity, like that evoked in the MacLeish poem plays on the aural-visual. The birds rest on a stand that weakly supports them with its devilish prongs, the weight of which is overbalanced on the right-hand side, a semblance of a stand precariously standing on another stand. As the only indication of perspective, this technical device suggests the metaphorical as something hiding beneath or beyond the flatness. The birds may at any moment plunge into or against this platform, which, if they turn round with the crank, rather than bobbing up and down, their fragile heads will be lopped off. Thus, the child's toy becomes a suggestion of technology gone awry, and on a deeper level, there is the threat of annhiliation—to the contraption or to the birds—the impending death and "nothing—nothing at all." The smudged canvas, the carelessness, may indicate a squeaky crank and the birds in response to this seem to have a panicky shrillness about their unsteady manner of perching. In his highly symbolic language, Klee gives all the necessary clues to indicate the impending noise as well as the impending silence of death. One of the birds seems to have a hook or arrow in its throat, and one is attempting to swallow an exclamation point—a subtle indication of a burst of sound. Stripped of their defenses in their simplistic presentation, they seem vulnerable to the threats. They stand in anticipation, poised, like MacLeish's audience, receiving the exclamation point and the pointing of the drum in their expectation of the end.

In both works, this language of expectation functions from a distant or initial impression as well as from a subsequent or closer examination. Though peculiar to each medium, this dual perception process evinces similarities in the translation from one to another. Likewise, the perception of the audience is manipulated by the artist who is aware of certain predictable aspects of the metaphorical and technical indications. In the artistic process as with language, there must be an active participation in the examination of the art work to dig below the obvious. In a verbal exchange, there are similar levels of interpretation available that lie below the outer, more literal, indications of the words.

In order to decipher the Klee painting as an art work the almost purely symbolic must interact with the simplistic. In the English language, the phrase "I do," may carry blatant implications that push the meaning into a ritualistic area that sets it apart from similar linguistic constructions. It becomes a sentence and acquires various levels of meaning much in the way an art work functions. Artistic appreciation is an adjunct of just this type of gestalt formation. It requires a willingness on the part of the observer to inquire beyond the easy symbol to reach the more technically governed system of concepts. In this process of appreciation, the observer retains the original immmpression, which is modified by closer, more sophisticated information. The memory aids the process, as further reflections on the art work may not necessarily occur in the actual presence of the work itself. The possible translations that make the work comprehensible, and that relate it to other artistic media, are a result of the integration of the various levels of perception.

In Béla Bartók's (1881-1945) *Allegro Barbaro* for piano, the technical procedure bears a similar distant-close contradiction as in the poem and the drawing. On first hearing, the listener is primarily aware of the barbaric disturbance of the banging chords, the loud dynamic level and the thickness or heaviness of the low register of the instrument. The opening chords establish a duple pattern that is then overlaid with a conflicting melodic pattern. The melody is characterized by three repeated notes that interrupt the meter established by the opening chords. (On a technical level these may be heard as a new metrical grouping against the duple meter, or the first note may be grouped with the duple as an anacrusis or upbeat. Bartók gives credence more to the first option by placing accents on all three notes, so that each time the melody enters, it sounds like a new beginning.)

The plainness of the melody, its reduction to simple elements, recalls the symbol birds in the Klee drawing. Where the birds have been reduced to a few gestures, the melody concentrates primarily on one note, moving away briefly, but always returning. The system of accents at first supports the bassline, then shifts to the melody, adding further complications to the interpretation—both on the part of the performer as well as the listener. The focal point, or primary element begging for audibility, appears to shift with the accentuation, both the natural accentuation implied by the rhythmic grouping as well as the imposed accentuation of the accent marks. After each segment

\

of the theme, the opening chords come back, at first retaining the duple grouping, then extending the phrase, so that it appears as if the lower chords actually govern the piece, while the melody vies for second place.

The repeated melody note, through its continual reassertion, gains in stature as the focal point. Since the bassline moves in contrary motion against the simplified movements of the melodic fragment, the result is a more stringent dissonance or disagreement whenever the primary melody note is left for another note. Harmonically, this is perceived as a higher dissonance level in an already dissonant context. Theoretically, the main dissonance consists of a major seventh and a tritone. (The tritone in the medieval period was known as *diabolus in musica*, an interval to be avoided because of its clashing sound. It was generally understood by performers that when this interval appeared, even hidden within the inner voices, that one of the singers would raise or lower one note of the interval to make it consonant.

Consonance and dissonance are determined by the space between two or more sounding notes. Certain intervals are more dissonant than others, depending on the syntactical relationship toward the tonic, the central harmonic place of rest in the piece. The tonic, like the poetic metaphor, exerts an underpinning of meaning during a musical work. Like the gestalt, it may remain in the periphery of the mind's ear as an outline governing movement toward and away from this point of resolution. Depending on the challenge exerted by other harmonic areas against this tonic area, its function may be made more or less obvious during the journey of the piece.

Part of the "barbaro" quality is hidden in the noise and fast tempo of the work, since the semantic disagreement of these intervals is momentary. The bassline, which normally makes the harmonic foundation evident, exhibits a conservative and traditional dominant-tonic movement, a syntactical indication that works somewhat like a transitive verb that must take its object. The melody becomes audible against this, at first only as a contradiction, then as the piece progresses, the theme is transposed or repeated on other pitches in the same corresponding arrangement, and the gravitational pull of the repeated note takes on new connotations. What results acoustically is that the dissonant notes in the treble begin to maintain their harmonic identity independently of the lower notes, and the resulting dissonance approximates a microtonal melody. Because of the upper overtones produced in the bassline, these upper melody notes conflict, producing notes that disagree with those produced by the bass. As the waves are out of phase with each other, the beats produced create notes of their own. These notes are not actually even available on the piano, as they would have to appear in the cracks between the keys. The phenomenon that, in the "Lux Aeterna" example, produces a shimmer of consonance (the upper sounding notes duplicating the nonsounding but physically ringing notes), in the Bartók produces a tinny, out-of-tune sound in the melody that resembles an authentic folk instrument.

Like the focal point in the picture, the melody pulls the attention back just as the eye is pulled back to the more striking aspect in the composition of the drawing. The musically implied double meaning is that between the non-traditional structure of the folklike melody and the traditional structure of the underlying harmony. The visually implied double meaning in the Klee is between the traditional representational system that carries its own set of expectations, versus the nonrepresentational dissonance that counters it and drives the metaphorical focal point into other interpretive areas (the smudges, the flatness, the single use of perspective).

Bartók, after intensive study of traditional composers and research into the radically different folk music of the Magyar people, was well aware of the implied characteristics of each. The "barbaro" quality is a result of this deliberate juxtaposition. In a temporal sense, the piece moves back and forth between these levels of dissonance, just as the melody and rhythm move in a simultaneous contradiction. The title, *Allegro Barbaro*, implies or suggests a sonata-allegro or first movement, a developmental formula in which two or more themes are presented, fragmented, and recombined according to rather prescribed harmonic requirements. Because Bartók adds a tempo indication (tempo giusto, which means a strict tempo), it is clear that the title does not merely mean an allegro speed.

The folklike melody is not used in a developmental manner but in an additive sense, where there is no actual second theme but a generic variant of the primary melody. The sectional repetition additively presents the melody and its offshoots in combinations with changes in accompaniment, register, harmony, and textural alterations that make it seem thinner or thicker. Whereas sonata-allegro offers a dramatic structure (it has been compared by some to the tension curve of Greek tragedy) that contains a magnetic harmonic scheme, the folk tradition offers only a principle of contrast to relieve the tedium that would result from merely repeating the melody. The gestalt of large and small areas, areas that recede and then come forward, opposes the sonata-allegro gestalt that is more all-encompassing and that maintains a more deterministic foundation.

The texture that has been elevated to the level of structure presents more evidence of the folk-melody's opposition to the traditional harmony in the lower parts. The loud, heavy chords, to offer contrast, move upward into the higher treble register where the strings are shorter and there are fewer audible overtones. As more separation is heard between the parts, they become more audible as two different or bitonal harmonic areas. After the closer harmonic guise of the new section, the repetitions of the original harmonization in the bass are reinterpreted also as a bitonal move, even though it does not lie in a territory quite as evident to the ear.

The opening chords, which represent the traditional aspect of the work, return throughout the work, as though they are interruptions of all the other harmonizations or approaches to the melody, as if to assure the listener of their tonal (focal point) stability. In this manner, the folk element governs the structure, melody, harmony, and rhythm, but it has to fight continually against the expectations of the competing traditional system. The opening chords form framing sections around the melody and its generic variants much like the "quite unexpectedly" recurs in the MacLeish poem. The semantic meaning therefore accumulates and metamorphoses, like layers of allegory. The frame of traditional syntax that links sections, yet sets them apart in clearly delineated subgroups, eats away at the implied opposition of the competing harmonic systems, and offers different interpretive possibilities in the overall gestalt of the work.

In the MacLeish poem, the governing dramatic element is highlighted by the contrast between the narrative forward-moving opening (traditional harmony also has functional forward-moving tendencies) and the suspended delaying action of the closing (non-Western or nontraditional harmony has a static nonfunctional quality). The couplet, in relation to the traditional rhyme scheme, has the same accumulative relationship—it is an interruption of the form, but the reader does not know this until after the last line. The trick has not been "given away" in advance.

MacLeish pits the structural possibilities of the Petrarchan and Shakespearean sonnet against each other much like Bartók uses the two musical approaches. The structural division of the poem follows the Italian form (Petrarchan) of octave and sestet, but the rhyme scheme (which sets off the couplet) follows the Shakespearean tradition. The psychology of the poem follows the Italian form: the octave states the situation and the sestet provides the solution. (There may be a direct comparison between octave/exposition and between sestet/resolution, but sometimes the sestet presents not so much a resolution of the exposition as an intensification or elaboration of it.) The sestet may also reinforce the situation by making an abstract reference to the first section, like a nonliteral recapitulation. MacLeish offers the psychological pattern of the Petrarchan bipartite division with the rhyme scheme of the Shakespearean form, but adds a little twist at the end regarding the dual resolution or intensification possibilities of the sestet.

The title foreshadows this twist as "The End of the World" indicates a time frame soon to be ending. The verb constructions in the first section ("was lighting" and "was engaged in biting") emphasize the temporal quality as if the event, the title, had already taken place, but at the same time they provide the narrative setting—the situation or problem. The notable absence of the verb in the second section signals both a temporal and structural reversal. If the Italian sonnet expectation is accepted, the second section may be interpreted as a complement to the first, as an answer to the problem posed in the first half. In retrospect, the ending line does not so much form a couplet with its preceding line as it forms a unit with the framing device of "Quite unexpectedly." The last line of the first section contains the only functional verb, its action encompassing the totality of the scene-setting verbs of the first section. The final line of the poem is separated in the same parenthetical way from the verb "blew off." The intervening section, by the close of the poem, may be clearly seen as a delaying device, so that what is read in a sequential manner as a couplet, is reinterpreted in retrospect as an answer or completion of the verb. In the Shakespearean tradition, the couplet traditionally forms a semantic relationship to the rest of the poem, summarizing or distilling or commenting on what has been presented before. The couplet in this case only summarizes in retrospect, so that its focal point function is that of an interruption, a puncture and subsequent deflation of expectation.

Wallace Steven's "Thirteen Ways of Looking at a Blackbird" presents a series of thirteen tableaulike sections, all of which mention the blackbird. Like enigma variations on a theme, the theme is not varied but alluded to, thus the process aspect of variation technique is nonexistent. Each tableau is like a translation of some exotic language, as if the act of poeticizing would contaminate the original meaning. The stilted, unadorned language resembles English versions of Oriental poetry, or English translations of Zen koans. The presentation is flat, static, the opening reference to the "twenty snowy mountains" offering a further allusion to Oriental art. In the poem, there is no movement but that of the blackbird, and the only sounds are the implied sounds that relate to the blackbird. From both distant and close perceptual stances the poem appears disjunct, purposely vague, a chain of fragile words barely held together by the presumed relationship of the title.

It would appear from the wealth of juxtapositions of the literal and figurative that the blackbird functions in the sense of an *Ur-motif* rather than a theme followed by variations. This motive forms a source that sets the background of the poem, the *Ursatz* or principle that recedes or comes forward in its successive stages. Some critics take this a step further and compare the poem to a cubist layering of perspectives so that each individual side is present to the eye at once. This view still retains an element of variation of the whole, rather than the subtle suggestive quality of a tiny detail, the blackbird, that takes on larger and larger dimensions in the mosaic. Although the tableaux follow one another sequentially in the poem, the temporal aspect is neutralized by the absence of connectives or parallel relationships between sections. The gestalt reveals a process in which the multiple views are like an act of memory. Each statement takes on new meaning in the changing context; each mention of the blackbird takes on new coloring, creating a shape that is not sequential but organic and all-encompassing. The effect is somewhat akin to that produced by a Jackson Pollock (1912-1956) painting in which the outward or initial appearance of the work is senseless and chaotic. The colors move in and out of the layers of paint in a physical sense, as warm colors move toward the eye and cool colors move away from the eye, and a patient study reveals an illusory persepective in the otherwise arbitrary lines and splashes. The colors themselves take on degrees of dominance against one another.

In the Stevens work, the impulsive throwing together is absent, but the arbitrariness seems at first to predominate. Patterns may be found but they do not seem to point to anything that affects the overall composition of the piece. Unlike the language of expectation set up by the MacLeish poem, the Stevens example is a negation of the process-oriented gestalt. Rather than a contrast between narrative and delaying techniques on a time-bound visual and temporal plane, the effect is that of a pull of the reflection and stasis against the fleeting, ephemeral quality of the now distinct, now vanishing images and suggestions.

In Edward Hopper's (1882-1967) painting *Early Sunday Morning*, there is a similar technical stasis. The barrenness of the street has been reduced to a deliberately bland, uneventful presentation. The light is the only theatrical suggestion, but this creates a metaphorical tension rather than a dramatic implication. There is no sense that anything is about to happen. There is no sense of the hidden, the enigmatic, as in the Klee work. There is merely existence. As in the Stevens poem, the blackbird is a fact of his own (Stevens' or the blackbird's) existence. The atmosphere of the poem and painting shares the quality of unreality that lies at the edges of the simplicity, the ordinariness.

In the Hopper painting, the outward guise of realism sets up a similar defense against the overpowering unreality. The slightly critical implication in the shabbiness of the street is absorbed into the play of shadows, verticals and horizontals of the street and building. The highly organized, carefully governed placement of objects that negate one another achieves a neutrality like the Stevens poem. The two works are groomed with care to give the impression of carelessness, randomness. The muted colors, the nonsignifying aspect of the empty street, the balance that appears accidental through the subtle touch of the slightly leaning barber pole, all offer an unprepossessing curtain to the wrenching associations, the melancholy, and in their technical control of the nonverbal, these elements cancel out the drama. The consciously objective stands between the personal and the audience like the flat language of the Stevens poem. There is a similar impression even of the nonpoeticizing. The picture is the thing itself, as the blackbird is the thing itself. The Oriental suggestiveness of the Stevens poem works like the light in the Hopper painting. Both add another dimension to the interpretive possibilities, but neither gets in the way of the seemingly factual presentation.

Unlike the Bartók piece, which works on a sophisticated intellectual system of tonalities and harmonic systems, the Samuel Barber (1910-　　) *Adagio for Strings* offers a counterpart to the Stevens and Hopper art works. The first hearing presents none of the aesthetic "inaudibility" problems that the Bartók does. It seems, like the Hopper, to be all there, evident, in plain sight—a realistic placing together of tones. The formal organization is based on a melodic line which extends and interweaves pulling the listener's attention effortlessly along. Each time the melody begins again, it does so against a different voice or line that forms a gentle pull, a melody that does not move but insists on its syntactical function. This steady voice persuades the melody to its cadence. The cadence, a hallmark of the classical style, is comparable to a rhetorical commonplace. It is there for signaling purposes and carries ordinary indications, a sort of glue to bind together the more imaginative aspects of the language.

The cadence, like expectations of the sonata-allegro format, marks off phrases into their symmetrical patterns. Barber takes this aural commonplace as a point of departure rather than a place of rest or coming together. The entire work at each moment is controlled by this ordinary functional move. The syntax of the dominant-tonic relationship discussed above works here in the gravitation of the second voice. The melody begins against a simple move in a lower voice to a note or chord that exerts this pull, producing a drone effect that is not consonant, but not unpleasantly dissonant. The interval employed is within the range of the tonality, and though it creates a disagreement between the drone voice and the upper moving part, the level of consonance is high. The result is a serene journey of the moving line that resembles the mental landscape of the Stevens poem and the emotional landscape of the Hopper painting.

The only event in the Barber piece is the climax of the work, brought about by the almost imperceptible thickening of moving parts and the gradual move into the upper register of the strings. The music grows toward this peak and is followed by an abrupt silence. Because of the gradual build, which has progressed uninterrupted from the beginning of the work, this length of time, the fullness of the strings, the busy motion of the increased movement of the parts, all contribute to the sudden emptiness of the silence. This silence seems, in contrast, louder than the preceding fortissimo sound. The moment, like the overall serenity of the work, has parallels in the technical devices of the Stevens and Hopper, with its simplicity and straightforwardness. Like the Klee, the simplicity hides the underlying profundity, and even like the MacLeish, the movement emphasizes the sudden cessation of motion.

This aspect of silence, however, points to a critical difference that sets the MacLeish, Klee, and Bartók works slightly apart from the Stevens, Hopper, and Barber works. In the second group of works and analyses, there is less reliance on a sequential process-oriented thinking and more use of intuitive structures. In this discussion, the detail has purposely been sacrificed in the second group for the larger element, to illustrate how these less verbal aspects determine the shape on a more conceptual level. For example, whereas the silence in the MacLeish poem is led in a dramatic sense, something implied then snatched away, it is a component of the Stevens in a nondramatic almost coloristic sense. The tone or mood of the Stevens has the quality of a motion picture still, a frozen segment of time, whereas the tone of the MacLeish has an encroaching intensity. The MacLeish moves, gains momentum, then stops right in the midst of its increasing momentum. The Stevens never moves, never alters its frozen sensation, and rather than coming to a stop, the end seems to be a continuation of the silence—having begun in silence, it merges with the silence and just as silently ends in the silence.

The silence in the Klee brims over with potentialities for interruption. The silence in the Hopper, like the Stevens, is a mere glimpse of the continuum, a moment, silent in its sameness. The Bartók is an active interruption of the silence, blundering in with its insinuating loudness, and each successive section further interrupts each new attempt at continuity. As the melodies vie for harmonic priority, the rhythms vie for phrase priority, thus bumping against one another on vertical and horizontal planes. The abrupt ending, having returned once more to the assertive opening chords, just as agressively pounds its last insult, without pedal—a marking specifically indicated—to exaggerate the sudden end. The final chord is preceded by the slightest pause, as if to frame the shock. Dramatic, like the Klee and MacLeish, the Bartók ends without warning.

The Barber, like the Hopper and Stevens, comes out of stillness making hardly a ripple of sound. The event, after the growth of moving parts, falls into the silence not as an interruption but as a completion, a full satisfying gasp before the final stillness, a reference to the opening. Though there are more possibilities for cross relationships with the Barber and both groups, there is a closer affinity with the Stevens and Hopper when viewed as a whole. The motion in the Barber is as though held back by the harmonic motion of the lower cadence-seeking voices. Each new journey of the moving voice has its cadential function implied by the second beat or pulse, and the underlying voice that determines this move toward completion gently asserts its harmonic place. The result is not dramatic but controlled, reined in, subdued. The space or gap, between the build and the ensuing soft return of the string voices, is not so much a result of the climax as it is a climax itself, an apotheosis of the nontemporal, of the silence.

Unlike the detailed technical analyses of the MacLeish, Klee, and Bartók examples, the latter analyses are more subjective. It is the subjective quality that separates art from other aspects of human endeavor. The intuitive has a more elusive nature, like the joke that sometimes produces convulsions of laughter and sometimes falls flat. Like a translation, there is a process of incorporating an intuitive yet technical procedure that, while working with both subjective and objective elements, does have definable, recognizable characteristics.

The process is similar to looking up the words of a sentence in a foreign language and finding multiple definitions available, realizing gradually that the choice of a certain word may carry connotations in several different areas.

The words interact with one another on numerous levels, while the person responsible for the translation, who has looked up each individual word, may have more information than he can necessarily convey in the translation. The humor of a joke may hinge on the tiniest detail that tips the understanding or expectation over into an area of surprise. The artistry may come from an awareness of this detail or the more subjective feel for the overall impact.

As someone in the first throes of learning a new language quickly notices, fluency is attained through a plateau effect, rather than through an orderly progression from vocabulary words acquired, to conjugations mastered, and idioms memorized. From the distance of newness, the details of grammar and vocabulary are merely a wash of sound or letters on a page. With the art work there is a similar elementary involvement that creates the initial aesthetic blur—only a line or two of the poem may attach itself to the memory, only the general shape of the painting, drawing, or sculpture, only a fragment of melody may remain—until the distance is overcome and, as with language, certain fundamental relationships are internalized.

The artist plays a conscious but nonverbal game with these levels of perception, creating impressions that deliberately contradict the first experience of the art work with further details on a more intimate perception level. What may seem intuitive or poetic to the lay audience, or to an artist whose familiarity lies in another medium, may be the result of this internalization of the language of artistic possibilities. As a child is taught the language of his parents, he learns not only the words and structures but also the cultural nonverbal attachments that exhibit influences.

Thus, to say that intuition is nonverbal does not necessarily place it in the realm of magical potions. Artistic intuition is like the body language that, although it defies categorization or definition in many areas, does exhibit recognizable patterns. It is on the intuitive level that the arts share common possibilities, where the tile of a head may convey more than the words themselves, and the underlying impact of a work of art may transcend the technique, the use of the medium, the "words" of the artistic process.

Like languages, artistic norms fluctuate from fashion to fashion and style to style. Contradictory approaches prosper alongside one another, each taking the dominant role at one time or another. Like grammatical forms that alter with usage, and like vocabularies that ameliorate over long periods of time, so do the arts modify the intrinsic creative process.

The extrinsic influences should be questioned carefully as the media barriers are crossed, in order to separate the cultural and historical influences that may color the interpretation of particular artistic languages. The awareness of these varying levels of perception may be shared by viewer, creator, and critic, as each has the capacity for the technical as well as the nontechnical. Like the sculptor who takes a chance and leans his piece just a bit more each time, until the clay gives way, or until the oven causes a crack such that nothing can repair or hide, so must the critic and the audience be willing to go as far to seek the limits of the artistic process. A closer examination of the fundamental elements, the foundations of the art impulse, reveals a "physiology of creativity" that approximates man's mental apparatus as it manifests itself in the creative act.

Diane Moody

APPROACHES TO EXPLICATING POETRY

Explicating poetry begins with a process of distinguishing the poem's factual and technical elements from the reader's emotional ones. Readers respond to poems in a variety of ways which may initially have little to do with the poetry itself but that result from the events in their own lives, their expectations of art, and their philosophical/theological/psychological complexion.

Every serious reader hopes to find poems that can blend with the elements of his or her personal background in such a way that for a moment or a lifetime his or her relationship to life and the cosmos becomes more meaningful. This is the ultimate goal of poetry, and when it happens—when meaning, rhythm, and sound fuse with the reader's emotions to create a unified experience—it can only be called the magic of poetry, for something has happened between reader and poet which is inexplicable in rational terms.

When a poem creates such an emotional response in a reader, then it is at least a partial success. To be considered excellent, however, a poem must also be able to pass a critical analysis to determine whether it is mechanically superior. Although twentieth century criticism has tended to judge poetic works solely on their individual content and has treated them as independent of historical influences, such a technique often makes a full explication difficult. The best modern readers realize that good poetry analysis observes all aspects of a poem: its technical success, its historical importance and intellectual force, and its effect on the reader's emotions.

Students of poetry will find it useful to begin an explication by analyzing the elements which poets have at their disposal as they create their art: dramatic situation, point of view, imagery, metaphor, symbol, meter, form, and allusion. The following outline will help guide the reader through the necessary steps to a detailed explication.

I. THE INITIAL READINGS
   A. Before reading the poem, the reader should:
      1. Notice its form and length.
      2. Consider the title, determining, if possible, whether it might function as an allusion, symbol, or poetic image.
      3. Notice the date of composition or publication, and identify the general era of the poet.
   B. The poem should be read intuitively and emotionally and be allowed to "happen" as much as possible.
   C. In order to establish the rhythmic flow, the poem should be reread. A note should be made as to where the irregular spots (if any) are located.

II. EXPLICATING THE POEM
II. A. *Dramatic situation*. Studying the poem line by line helps the reader to

discover the dramatic situation. All elements of the dramatic situation are interrelated and should be viewed as reflecting and affecting one another. The dramatic situation serves a particular function in the poem, adding realism, surrealism, or absurdity; drawing attention to certain parts of the poem; and changing to reinforce other aspects of the poem. All points should be considered. The following questions are particularly helpful to ask in determining dramatic situation:

1. What, if any, is the narrative action in the poem?
2. How many personae appear in the poem? What part do they take in the action?
3. What is the relationship between characters?
4. What is the setting (time and location) of the poem?

B. *Point of view.* An understanding of the poem's point of view is a major step toward comprehending the poet's intended meaning. The reader should ask:

1. Who is the speaker? Is he or she addressing someone else or the reader?
2. Is the narrator able to understand or see everything happening to him or her, or does the reader know things that the narrator does not?
3. Is the narrator reliable?
4. Do point of view and dramatic situation seem consistent? If not, the inconsistencies may provide clues to the poem's meaning.

C. *Images and metaphors.* Images and metaphors are often the most intricately crafted vehicles of the poem for relaying the poet's message. Realizing that the images and metaphors work in harmony with the dramatic situation and point of view will help the reader to see the poem as a whole, rather than as disassociated elements.

1. The reader should identify the concrete images (that is, those that are formed from objects that can be touched, smelled, seen, felt, or tasted). Is the image projected by the poet consistent with the physical object?
2. If the image is abstract, or so different from natural imagery that it cannot be associated with a real object, then what are the properties of the image?
3. To what extent is the reader asked to form his or her own images?
4. Is any image repeated in the poem? If so, how has it been changed? Is there a controlling image?
5. Are any images compared to each other? Do they reinforce one another?
6. Is there any difference between the way the reader perceives the image and the way the narrator sees it?
7. What seems to be the narrator's or persona's attitude toward the

image?

D. *Words.* Every substantial word in a poem may have more than one intended meaning, as used by the author. Because of this, the reader should look up many of these words in the dictionary and:

1. Note all definitions that have the slightest connection with the poem.
2. Note any changes in syntactical patterns in the poem.
3. In particular, note those words that could possibly function as symbols or allusions, and refer to any appropriate sources for further information.

E. *Meter, rhyme, structure, and tone.* In scanning the poem, all elements of prosody should be noted by the reader. These elements are often used by a poet to manipulate the reader's emotions, and therefore they should be examined closely to arrive at the poet's specific intention.

1. Does the basic meter follow a traditional pattern such as those found in nursery rhymes or folk songs?
2. Are there any variations in the base meter? Such changes or substitutions are important thematically and should be identified.
3. Are the rhyme schemes traditional or innovative, and what might their form mean to the poem?
4. What devices has the poet used to create sound patterns (such as assonance and alliteration)?
5. Is the stanza form a traditional or innovative one?
6. If the poem is composed of verse paragraphs rather than stanzas, how do they affect the progression of the poem?
7. After examining the above elements, is the resultant tone of the poem casual or formal, pleasant, harsh, emotional, authoritative?

F. *Historical context.* The reader should attempt to place the poem into historical context, checking on events at the time of composition. Archaic language, expressions, images, or symbols should also be looked up.

G. *Themes and motifs.* By seeing the poem as a composite of emotion, intellect, craftsmanship, and tradition, the reader should be able to determine the themes and motifs (smaller recurring ideas) presented in the work. He or she should ask the following questions to help pinpoint these main ideas:

1. Is the poet trying to advocate social, moral, or religious change?
2. Does the poet seem sure of his or her position?
3. Does the poem appeal primarily to the emotions, to the intellect, or to both?
4. Is the poem relying on any particular devices for effect (such as imagery, allusion, paradox, hyperbole, or irony)?

The following is an example of how these step-by-step procedures may be applied systematically to a difficult poem by Edwin Arlington Robinson. The reader should proceed carefully through the steps towards an explication, assimilating the information which is needed to synthesize a full experience of the poem.

"Luke Havergal"

Go to the western gate, Luke Havergal,
There where the vines cling crimson on the wall,
And in the twilight wait for what will come.
The leaves will whisper there of her, and some,4
Like flying words, will strike you as they fall;
But go, and if you listen, she will call.
Go to the western gate, Luke Havergal—
Luke Havergal.   8

No, there is not a dawn in eastern skies
To rift the fiery night that's in your eyes;
But there, where western glooms are gathering,
The dark will end the dark, if anything: 12
God slays Himself with every leaf that flies,
And hell is more than half of paradise.
No, there is not a dawn in eastern skies—
In eastern skies.   16

Out of a grave I come to tell you this,
Out of a grave I come to quench the kiss
That flames upon your forehead with a glow
That blinds you to the way that you must go. 20
Yes, there is yet one way to where she is,
Bitter, but one that faith may never miss.
Out of a grave I come to tell you this—
To tell you this.   24

There is the western gate, Luke Havergal,
There are the crimson leaves upon the wall.
Go, for the winds are tearing them away,—
Nor think to riddle the dead words they say, 28
Nor any more to feel them as they fall;
But go, and if you trust her she will call.
There is the western gate, Luke Havergal—
Luke Havergal.

1897
E. A. Robinson

STEP I-A: *Before reading*

1. "Luke Havergal" is a strophic poem composed of four equally lengthened stanzas. Each stanza is long enough to contain a narrative, and involved description or situation, or a problem and resolution.

2. The title raises several possibilities: Luke Havergal could be a specific

person; Luke Havergal could represent a type of person; the name might have symbolic or allusive qualities. Thus, "Luke" may refer to: Luke of the Bible; "Luke-warm": meaning indifferent or showing little or no zeal. "Havergal" could be a play on words. "Haver" is a Scotch and Northern English word meaning to talk foolishly. It is clear from the rhyme words that the "gal" of Havergal is pronounced as if it had two "l's," but it is spelled with one "l" for no apparent reason unless it is to play on the word "gal," meaning girl. Because it is pronounced "gall," meaning something bitter or severe, a sore or state of irritation, or an impudent self-assurance, this must also be considered as a possibility. Finally, the "haver" of "Havergal" might be a perversion of "have a."

3. Published in 1897, the poem probably does not contain archaic language unless it is deliberately used. The period of writing is known as the Victorian Age. Historical events which may have influenced the poem may be checked for later.

STEP I-B: *The poem should be read*

STEP I-C: *Rereading the poem*
The frequent use of internal caesuras in stanzas one and two contrast with the lack of caesuras in stanzas three and four. There are end-stopped lines and much repetition. The poem reads smoothly except for line twenty-eight and the feminine ending on lines eleven and twelve.

STEP II-A: *Dramatic situation*
In line one of "Luke Havergal" an unidentified speaker is addressing Luke. Because the speaker calls him by his full name there is a sense that the speaker has assumed a superior (or at least a formal) attitude toward Luke and that the talk which they are having is not a casual conversation.

In addition to knowing something about the relationship in line one, the reader is led to think, because of the words "go to the western gate," that the personae must be near some sort of enclosed house or city. Perhaps Luke and the speaker are at some "other" gate, since the western gate is specifically pointed out.

Line two suggests that the situation at the western gate is different from that elsewhere—there "vines cling crimson on the wall," hinting at some possibilities about the dramatic situation. (Because flowers and colors are always promising symbols, they must be carefully considered later.)

The vines in line two could provide valuable information about the dramatic situation, except that in line two the clues are ambiguous. Are the vines perennial? If so, their crimson color suggests that the season is late summer or autumn. Crimson might also be their natural color when in full bloom. Further, are they grape vines (grapes carry numerous connotations and symbolic values), and are the vines desirable? All of this in line two is ambiguous. The only certainty is that there is a wall—a barrier which closes something in and something out.

In line three, the speaker again commands Luke to go and wait. Since Luke is to wait in the twilight, it is probably now daylight. All Luke must do is be passive because whatever is to come will happen without any action on his part.

In line four, the speaker begins to tell Luke what will happen at the western gate, and the reader now knows that Luke is waiting for something with feminine characteristics, possibly a woman. This line also mentions that the vines have leaves, implying that crimson denotes their waning stage.

In line five, the speaker continues to describe what will happen at the western gate: the leaves will whisper about "her," and, as they fall, some of them will strike Luke "like flying words." The reader, however, must question whether Luke will actually be "struck" by the leaves, or whether the leaves are being personified or being used as an image or symbol. In line six, the speaker stops his prophecy and tells Luke to leave. If Luke listens, "she" will call, but if he does not, it is unclear what will happen. The reader might ask the questions, to whom is "she" calling, and from where?

In summarizing the dramatic situation in stanza one, one can say that the speaker is addressing Luke, but it is not yet possible to determine whether he or she is present or whether Luke is thinking to himself (interior monologue). The time is before twilight; the place is near a wall with a gate. Luke is directed to go to the gate and listen for a female voice to call.

From reading the first line in the second stanza, it is apparent that Luke has posed some kind of question, probably concerned with what will be found at the western gate. The answer given is clearly not a direct answer to whatever question was asked, especially as the directions "east" and "west" are probably symbolic. The reader can expect, however, that the silent persona's response will affect the poem's progress.

Stanza three discloses who the speaker is and what his relationship is to Luke. After the mysterious discourse in stanza two, Luke has probably asked "Who are you?" The equally mysterious reply in stanza three raises the issue of whether the voice speaking is a person or a spirit or whether it is Luke's imagination or conscience.

Because the voice says that it comes out of the grave, the reader cannot know who or what it is. It may be a person, a ghost, or only Luke's imagination or conscience. Obviously the answer will affect the dramatic situation.

In line eighteen the reader learns that the speaker is on a particular mission: "to quench the kiss," and the reader can assume that when the mission is complete he or she will return to the grave. This information is sudden and shocking, and because of this sharp jolt, the reader tends to believe the speaker and credit him or her with supernatural knowledge.

In stanza four it becomes apparent that Luke and the speaker have not been stationary during the course of the poem because the western gate is now visible; the speaker can see the leaves upon the wall (line twenty-six).

The wind is blowing (line twenty-seven), creating a sense of urgency, because if all the leaves are blown away they cannot whisper about "her." The speaker gives Luke final instructions and the poem ends with the speaker again pointing toward the place where Luke will find the female persona.

In summary, one can say that the dramatic situation establishes a set of mysterious circumstances which are not explained or resolved on the dramatic level. Luke has been told to go to the western gate by someone who identifies himself or herself as having come from the grave in order to quench Luke's desire, which seems to be connected with the estranged woman who is, perhaps, dead. The dramatic situation does not tell whether the commanding voice is an emissary from the woman, or from the devil, or is merely Luke's conscience; nor does it suggest that something evil will happen to Luke at the western gate, although other elements in the poem make the reader afraid for him.

The poet, then, is using the dramatic situation to draw the reader into questions which will be answered by other means; at this point, the poem is mysterious, obscure, ambiguous, and deliberately misleading.

STEP II-B: *Point of view*

There are a number of questions which immediately come to mind about the point of view. Is the speaker an evil seducer, or is he or she a friend telling Luke about death? Why is the poem told from his or her point of view?

From a generalized study, readers know that the first-person singular point of view takes the reader deep into the mind of the narrator in order to show what he or she knows or to show a personal reaction to an event.

In "Luke Havergal," the narrator gives the following details about himself and the situation: a sense of direction (lines one and nine); the general type and color of the vegetation, but not enough to make a detailed analysis of it (line two); a pantheistic view of nature (line four); a feeling of communication with the leaves and "her" (lines five and six); a philosophic view of the universe (stanza two); the power to "quench the kiss," a sense of mission, and a home—the grave (line eighteen); special vision (line twenty); a sense of destiny (lines twenty-one and twenty-two); and a sense of time and eternity (lines twenty-seven through twenty-nine).

Apparently, the narrator can speak with confidence about the western gate, and can look objectively at Luke to see the kiss upon his forehead. Such a vantage point suggests that the speaker might represent some aspect of death. He also knows the "one way to where she is," leaving it reasonable to infer that "she" is dead.

There is another possibility in regard to the role of the speaker. He might be part of Luke himself—the voice of his thoughts, of his unconscious mind— or of part of his past. This role might possibly be combined with that of some sort of Spirit of Death.

The poem, then, is an internal dialogue in which Luke is attempting to cope with "she," who is probably dead and who might well have been his lover, though neither is certain. He speaks to another persona, which is probably Luke's own spirit which has been deadened by the loss of his lover.

Once it is suggested that Luke is a man who is at the depth of despair, the dramatic situation becomes very important because of the possibility that Luke may be driving himself toward self-destruction.

The dramatic situation, therefore, may not be as it originally seemed; perhaps there is only one person, not two. Luke's psychological condition permits him to look at himself as another person, and this other self is pushing Luke toward the western gate, a place which the reader senses is evil.

If the voice is Luke's, then much of the mystery is clarified. Luke would have known what the western gate looked like, whereas a stranger would have needed supernatural powers to know it; furthermore, Luke had probably heard the leaves whispering before, and in his derangement he could believe that someone would call to him if he would only listen.

Establishing point of view has cleared up most of the inconsistencies in this poem's dramatic situation, but there is still confusion about the grave and the kiss. It is easy to make the grave symbolically consistent with point of view, but the reader should look for other possibilities before settling on this explanation.

In stanzas one and two there is no problem; the dramatic situation is simple and point of view can be reconciled since there is no evidence to prove that another person is present. If, however, the voice is that of Luke's other self, then why has it come from the grave, and where did the kiss come from? At this point, it is not possible to account for these inconsistencies, but by noting them now, the reader can be on the alert for the answers later. Quite possibly accounting for the inconsistencies will provide the key for the explication.

STEP II-C: *Images and Metaphors*

Finding images in poems is usually not a difficult task, although seeing their relation to the theme often is. "Luke Havergal" is imagistically difficult because the images are introduced, then reused as the theme develops.

In stanza one the reader is allowed to form his own image of the setting and mood at the western gate; most readers will probably imagine some sort of mysterious or supernatural situation which is related to death or the dead. The colors, the sound of the words, and the particular images (vines, wall, whispering leaves) establish the relationship between the living and the dead as the controlling image of the entire poem.

Within the controlling death-in-life image, the metaphors and conceits are more difficult to handle. Vines clinging crimson on the wall (line two) and waiting in the twilight for something to come (line three) are images requiring no particular treatment at this point, but in lines four and five the reader is forced to contend directly with whispering leaves which are like flying words, and there are several metaphorical possibilities for this image.

First, there is the common image of leaves rustling in a breeze, and in a mysterious or enchanted atmosphere it would be very easy to imagine that they are whispering. Such a whisper, however, would ordinarily require a moderate breeze, as a fierce wind would overpower the rustling sound of leaves; but there is more ambiguity in the image: "The leaves will whisper there for her, and some,/ Like flying words, will strike you as they fall";

Because of the syntactical ambiguity of "some,/ Like flying words, will strike," one cannot be sure how close or literal is the similarity or identity of "leaves" and "words." The reader cannot be completely sure whether it is leaves or words or both that will strike Luke, or whether the sight of falling leaves might be forcing him to recall words he has heard in the past. There is a distinct metaphoric connection between leaves and words, however, and these in some way strike Luke, perhaps suggesting that the words are those of an argument (an argument in the past between Luke and "her" before her death) or perhaps meant to suggest random words which somehow recall "her" but do not actually say anything specific.

In stanza two, the poet forces the reader to acknowledge the light and dark images, but they are as obscure as the falling leaves in stanza one. The dawn which the reader is asked to visualize (line nine) is clear, but it is immediately contrasted with "the fiery night that's in your eyes"; Luke's smoldering, almost diabolic eyes are imagistically opposed to the dawn.

Line eleven returns to the western gate, or at least to the "west," where twilight is falling. The "western glooms" become imagistic as the twilight falls and depicts Luke's despair. Twilight is not "falling," but dark is "gathering" around him, and glooms not only denotes darkness, but also connotes Luke's emotional state.

The paradox in line twelve, "The dark will end the dark," beckons the reader to explore it imagistically, but it is not easy to understand how darkness relieves darkness, unless one of the two "darknesses" is symbolic of death or of Luke's gloom. With this beckoning image, the poet has created emphasis on the line and teases with images which may really be symbols or paradoxes. The same thing is true for lines thirteen and fourteen, which tempt the reader to imagine how "God slays Himself" with leaves, and how "hell is more than half of paradise."

The beginning of stanza three does not demand an image so much as it serves to tell where the narrator comes from, and to present the narrator's method for quenching the kiss. Line nineteen however, presents an image which is as forceful as it is ambiguous. The kiss, which may be the kiss of the estranged woman, or "the kiss of death," or both, flames with a glow, which is also paradoxical. The paradox, however, forms an image which conveys the intensity of Luke's passion.

Stanza four returns to the imagery of stanza one, but now the whispering leaves take on a metaphorical extension. If the leaves are whispering words from the dead, and if the leaves are "her" words, then once the wind tears all the leaves away, there will no longer be any medium for communication between the living and the dead. This adds a sense of urgency for Luke to go to the western gate and do there what must be done.

In summary, the images in "Luke Havergal" do more than set the mood; they also serve an important thematic function because of their ambiguities and paradoxical qualities.

STEP II-D: *Words*

Because the poem is not too old, the reader will find that most of the words have not changed much. It is still important, however, for the reader to look up words as they may have several diverse meanings. Even more important to consider in individual words or phrases, however, is the possibility that they might be symbolic or allusive.

"Luke Havergal" is probably not as symbolic as it at first appears, although poems which use paradox and allusion are often very symbolic. Clearly the western gate is symbolic, but to what degree is questionable. No doubt it represents the last light in Luke's life, and once he passes beyond it he moves into another type of existence. The west and the twilight are points of embarkation; the sun is setting in the west, but even though the sun sets there will not be a dawn in the east to dispel Luke's dark gloom. Traditionally the dark, which is gathering in the west, is symbolic of death (the west is also traditionally associated with death), and only the dark will end Luke's gloom in life, if anything at all can do it.

There is one important allusion in the poem, which comes in stanza three; the kiss which the speaker is going to quench may be the "kiss of death," the force which can destroy Luke.

In both concept and language, stanza three is reminiscent of the dagger scene and killing of Duncan (Act II, Scene 1) in William Shakespeare's *Macbeth* (1606). Just before the murder, Macbeth has visions of the dagger:

> Art thou not, fatal vision, sensible
> To feeling as to sight? or art thou but
> A dagger of the mind, a false creation,
> Proceeding from the heat-oppressed brain?
> I see thee yet, in form as palpable
> As this which now I draw.
> Thou marshall'st me the way that I was going;

And a few lines later (Act II, Scene 2) Lady Macbeth says:

> That which hath made them drunk hath made me bold;
> What hath quench'd them hath given me fire.

The reversal in point of view in "Luke Havergal" gives the poem added depth, which is especially enhanced by the comparison with Macbeth. The line, "That blinds you to the way that you must go" is almost a word-for-word equivalent of "Thou marshall'st me the way that I was going," except that in "Luke Havergal" whoever is with Luke is talking, while Macbeth himself is talking to the dagger.

The result of the allusion is that it is almost possible to imagine that it is the dagger that is talking to Luke, and the whole story of Macbeth becomes relevant to the poem because the reader suspects that Luke's end will be similar to Macbeth's.

The words of Lady Macbeth strengthen the allusion's power and suggest a male-female relationship which is leading Luke to his death, especially since, in the resolution of *Macbeth*, Lady Macbeth goes crazy and whispers to the spirits.

If the reader accepts the allusion as a part of the poem, the imagery is enhanced by the vivid descriptions in *Macbeth*. Most critics and writers agree that if a careful reader finds something that fits consistently into a poem, then it is "there" for all readers who see the same thing, whether the poet consciously put it there or not. Robinson undoubtedly read and knew Shakespeare, but it does not matter whether he deliberately alluded to *Macbeth* if the reader can show that it is important to the poem.

There is a basic problem with allusion and symbol which every explicator must resolve for himself: Did the poet intend a symbol or an allusion to be taken in the way that a particular reader has interpreted it? The New Critics answered this question by coining the term "intentional fallacy," meaning that the poet's *intention* is ultimately unimportant when considering the finished poem. It is possible that stanza three was not intended to allude to *Macbeth* and it was simply by accident that Robinson used language similiar to Shakespeare's. Perhaps Robinson never read *Macbeth*, or perhaps he read it once and those lines remained in his subconscious. In either case, the reader must decide whether the allusion is important to the meaning of the poem.

STEP II-E: *Meter, Rhyme, Structure, and Tone*

Because "Luke Havergal" is a poem that depends so heavily upon all the elements of prosody, it should be scanned carefully. Here is an example of scansion using the second stanza of the poem:

No, there/ is not/ a dawn/ in eas/tern skies

To rift/ the fie/ry night/ that's in/ your eyes;
But there,/ where wes/tern glooms/ are gath/ering,
The dark/ will end/ the dark,/ if an/ything:
God slays/ Himself/ with eve/ry leaf/ that flies,
And hell/ is more/ than half/ of par/adise.
No, there/ is not/ a dawn/ in east/ern skies—
In eas/tern skies.

The basic meter of the poem is iambic pentameter, with frequent substitutions, but every line except the last in each stanza contains ten syllables.

The stanza form in "Luke Havergal," is very intricate and delicate. It is only because of the structure that the heavy *a* rhyme (aabbaaaa) does not become monotonous; yet it is because of the *a* rhyme that the structure works so well. The pattern for the first stanza works as follows:

Line	Rhyme	Function
1	a	Sets up ideas and images for the stanza.
2	a	Describes or complements line one.
3	b	Lines three-four-five constitute the central part of the mood and the fears. The return to the *a* rhyme unifies lines one-five.
4	b	
5	a	
6	a	Reflects on what has been said in one-five; it serves to make the reader stop, and it adds a mysterious suggestion.
7	a	Continues the deceleration and reflection.
8	a	The repetition and dimeter line stop the stanza completely, and the effect is to prepare for a shift in thought, just as Luke's mind jumps from thought to thought.

Stanza two works in a similar manner, except for lines thirteen and fourteen, which tie the stanza together as a couplet. Thus, thirteen and fourteen both unify and reflect, while fifteen and sixteen in the final couplet continue to reflect while slowing down.

Line	Rhyme	Function
9 & 10	a	Opening couplet.
11 & 12	b	Couplet in 11-12 contains the central idea and image.
13 & 14	a	Couplet in 13-14 reflects on that in 11-12, but the autonomy of this third couplet is especially strong. Whereas

in stanza one only line five reflects on the beginning of the stanza to create unity, this entire couplet is now strongly associated with the first, with the effect of nearly equating Luke with God.

15 & 16   a   Final couplet reflects on the first and completes the stanza.

Stanza three works in the same manner as stanza two, while stanza four follows the pattern of stanza one.

Each stanza is autonomous and does not need the others for continuation or progression in plot; each stanza appears to represent a different thought as Luke's mind jumps about.

The overall structure focuses on stanza three, which is crucial to the theme. Stanzas one and two clearly present the problem: Luke knows that if he goes he will find "her," and the worst that can happen is that the darkness will remain. With stanza three, however, there is a break in point of view as the narrator calls attention to himself.

With stanza four there is a return to the beginning, reinforced by the repetition of rhyme words; the difference between stanzas four and one is that the reader has felt the impact of stanza three; structurally, whatever resolution there is will evolve out of the third stanza, or because of it.

The stanza form of "Luke Havergal" achieves tremendous unity and emphasis; the central image or idea presented in the *b* lines is reinforced in the remainder of the stanza by a tight-knit rhyme structure. There are several types of rhymes being used in the poem, all of which follow the traditional functions of their type. Stanza one contains full masculine end rhyme, with a full masculine internal rhyme in line two (*There where*). Lines two and three contain alliteration (*c* in line two, *t* in line three) also binding the lines more tightly.

With "go" occurring near the end of stanza one and "No" appearing as the first word in stanza two, this rhyme becomes important in forming associations between lines. Lines nine, ten, fifteen, sixteen, and eighteen form full masculine end rhyme, with line fourteen "paradise" assonating with a full rhyme. Lines eleven and twelve are half falling rhymes; these lines also contain a full internal rhyme ("there," "where") and alliteration ("g" and "w" in line eleven). "Dark" in line twelve is an exact internal rhyme. The "l" and "s" in "slays" and "flies" (line fourteen) create an effect similar to assonance; there is also an "h" alliteration in line fifteen.

In stanza three, the plosive consonants "c" and "q" make an alliterative sound in line eighteen, binding "come" and "quench" together; there is also an "f" alliteration in line nineteen. All of the end rhymes are full masculine in stanza three except line twenty-one, which assonates. Stanza four contains full masculine end rhyme, with one internal rhyme ("they say") in line twenty-eight, one alliteration in line twenty-nine, and consonance ("will call") in line thirty.

In addition to its function in developing the stanza, rhyme in "Luke Havergal" has important influence on sound, and in associating particular words and lines.

In lines one and two of "Luke Havergal," there are a number of plosive consonants and long vowels, in addition to the internal rhyme and "c" alliteration. The cadence of these lines is slow, and they reverberate with "cling" and "crimson." The tone of these lines is haunting (which is consistent with the situation), and the rhythm and sound of the poem as a whole suggest an incantation; the speaker's voice is seductive and evil, which is important to the theme, because if Luke goes to the gate he may be persuaded to die, which is what the voice demands.

Through its seductive sound, the poem seems to be having the same effect on the reader that it does on Luke; that is, the reader feels, as Luke does, that there is an urgency in going to the gate before all the leaves are blown away, and that by hearing "her" call, his discomfort will be relieved. The reader, unable to see the evil forces at work in the last stanza, sympathizes with Luke, and thinks that the voice is benevolent.

Whereas sound can be heard and analyzed; tone is a composite of a number of things which the reader can feel only after coming to know the poem. The poet's attitude or tone may be noncommittal or it may be dogmatic (as in allegory); sometimes the tone will affect the theme, while at other times it comes as an aside to the theme.

Poems that attempt to initiate reform frequently have a more readily discernible tone than poems which make observations without judging too harshly, although this is not always true. "Luke Havergal" is, among other things, about how the presence of evil leads toward death, but the poet has not directly included his feelings about that theme. If there is an attitude, it is the poet's acceptance of the inevitability of death and the pain which accompanies it for the living.

Perhaps the poet is angry at how effectively death can seduce life; it is obvious that Robinson wants the poem to haunt and torment the reader, and in doing so make him conscious of the hold death has on humanity.

Luke must meet death part way; he must first go to the gate before he can hear the dead words, which makes him partly responsible for death's hold over him. The tone of "Luke Havergal" is haunting and provocative.

STEP II-F: *Historical Context*

Finished in December, 1895, "Luke Havergal" was in Robinson's estimation a symbolist poem. It is essential, then, that the explicator learn something about the symbolist movement. If his explication is not in accord with the philosophy of the period, the reader must account for the discrepancy.

In a study of other Robinson poems, there are themes parallel to that of "Luke Havergal." One, for example, is that of the alienated self. If Robinson believes in the alienated self, then it is possible that the voice speaking in "Luke Havergal" is Luke's own, but in an alienated state. This view may add credence to an argument that the speaker is Luke's past or subconscious, though it by no means proves it. Although parallelisms may be good support for the explication, the reader must be careful not to misconstrue them.

STEP II-G: *Themes and Motifs*, or correlating the parts

Once the poem has been placed in context, the prosodic devices analyzed, and the function of the poetical techniques understood, they should be correlated, and any discrepancies should be studied for possible errors in explication. By this time every line should be understood, so that stating what the poem is about is merely a matter of explaining the common points of all the area, supporting it with specific items from the poem, secondary sources, other poems, other critics, and history. The reader may use the specific questions given in the outline to help detail the major themes.

Walton Beacham

AN EXPLANATION OF POETICAL TERMS

Accented syllable. See *Stressed syllable.*

Accentual meter: One of four base meters used in English (accentual, accentual-syllabic, syllabic, and quantitative), accentual meter is the system in which the occurrence of a syllable marked by a *stress* determines the basic unit, regardless of the number of unstressed syllables. In other words, it is the stresses and not the unstresses that determine the metrical base. An example from modern poetry is "Blue Moles" by Sylvia Plath, the first line of which *scans*: "They're out of the dark's ragbag, these two." Because there are five stressed syllables in this accentually based poem, the reader can expect that many of the other lines will also contain five stresses per line. The most prominent use of accentual meter in English poetry is in *Old English versification*.

Accentual-Syllabic meter: By far the most common base meter for English poetry, accentual-syllabic measures the pattern of stressed syllables relative to the unstressed ones. In the first line of William Shakespeare's sonnet 130, "My mistress' eyes are nothing like the sun," we can see that a pattern of alternating unstressed with stressed syllables is evolving, although there is a *substitution* of an unstressed syllable for a stressed syllable at the word "like." In the accentual-syllabic system, stressed and unstressed syllables are grouped together into *feet*, of which there are six varieties.

Allegory: One of the "figures of speech," allegory represents an abstract idea in concrete imagery, almost always in the form of a humanized character. Gluttony, for example, might be allegorized by a character who eats all the time, while Christian love might be allegorized by a character who does charitable deeds. The traditional use for allegory is to make it possible for the poet to show how abstract ideas affect real people who are in contact with them, or how abstract emotions affect each other within a human being. Thus, a narrator might watch two opposite sides of his personality fight for dominance. One of the most popular poetic devices during the Middle Ages, allegory fell out of favor in more modern times, but was given new credibility when Sigmund Freud explained the mind allegorically as the "id," "ego," and "super-ego." Allegory works on two levels: the literal, in which the story is complete and sensible without further interpretation, and the allegorical, in which the poet endeavors to convey religious, moral, political, personal, or satiric principles by showing how concepts mold our view of life. An example of medieval allegory is *Roman de la Rose* (1360-1372, *Romance of the Rose*), and a modern example of allegory can be found in "The Idea of Order at Key West" by Wallace Stevens.

Alliteration: When consonant repetition is focused at the beginning of sylla-bles, the repetition is called alliteration, as in: "Large *m*annered *m*otions of his *m*ythy *m*ind." Alliteration is used when the poet wishes to focus on the details of a sequence of words, and to show meaning relationships between words within a line. Because a reader cannot easily skim over an alliterative line, it becomes more conspicuous and demands greater emphasis. *Old English versification* used alliteration extensively, and it is sometimes refered to as "alliterative versification." Alliteration is also a principal characteristic of vowel music, and is used in all poetry for its sound effect.

Allusion: When a reference is made to a historical or literary event whose story or outcome adds dimension to the poem, then poetical allusion occurs. "Fire and Ice" by Robert Frost alludes to the biblical account of the flood and the prophecy that the next destruction will come by fire, not water. Without recognizing the allusion and understanding the biblical reference to Noah and the surrounding associations of hate and desire, the reader cannot fully appreciate the poem. Some allusions are important for their *connota-tions*, or for the cumulative reaction that our culture has built around the event alluded to, as much as for the details of the event itself. For example, the biblical prophecy of another doomsday or day of judgment has hung over the Western world for so long that it has spawned several apocalyptic religious groups which anticipate world destruction, and Frost's "Fire and Ice" uses the weight of this fear as well as the story of the Flood itself. One of the most popular devices in modern poetry, allusion can be found everywhere, but two prime examples are "Leda and the Swan" by W. B. Yeats and *The Journey of the Magi* (1927) by T. S. Eliot.

Anacreontic verse: Using the *trochee* as the *base foot*, this four-line stanza adapted from the Greek poet Anacreon, has a falling rhythm which creates an aura of softness and musical lightness. Many songs are written in this form; in his *Songs of Innocence* (1789), William Blake uses trocaic quatrains to give lightness and innocence to situations which are often awesome and terrifying, thus creating *irony*.

Anacrusis: The opposite of *truncation*, anacrusis occurs when an extra unstressed syllable is added to the beginning or end of a *line*, as in the line: "their shoul/ders held/the sky/suspended." This line is described as iambic tetrameter with terminal anacrusis. Anacrusis is used to change a rising meter to falling, and vice versa, in order to change the reader's emotional response to the subject. Falling rhythms, particularly in rhymed poems, are frequently used for soft, soothing endings, while rising rhythms caused by terminal anacrusis are more disturbing, as in the line, "Down the/rivers/of the/windfall/light."

Anapest: One of six standard rhythmic units in English poetry, the anapestic foot associates two unstressed syllables with one stressed syllable, as in the line, "With the sĭft/ĕd, hărmón/ĭoŭs paŭse." The anapestic foot is one of the three most common in English poetry and is used to create a highly rhythmical, usually emotional, line.

Approximate rhyme: The two categories of approximate rhyme are assonance and half (slant) rhyme. Assonance occurs when words with identical vowel sounds but different consonants are associated. "Stars," "arms," and "park" all contain identical "a" (and "ar") sounds, but because the consonants are different, *full rhyme* cannot occur. Half or slant rhymes contain identical consonants but different vowels, as in "fall" and "well." "Table" and "Bauble" constitute half rhymes; "law," "cough" and "fawn" assonate. Generally speaking, approximate rhyme is not as satisfying as full rhyme and is sometimes frustrating for the reader because it approaches rhyme without achieving it. For the same reason, however, approximate rhyme is well-suited to poems in which despair or anxiety are important, as in many of the poems of Emily Dickinson and E. E. Cummings. While approximate rhymes are effective in poems connoting anxiety, they are not always used this way, and poets will frequently choose good approximate rhymes rather than use mediocre full rhymes.

Assonance. See *Approximate rhyme*.

Autonomy: When the end of a line signifies the end of a complete statement, the line is said to be "autonomous" even if there is no punctuation indicating *end-stop*. In the lines, "O sages standing in God's holy fire/ As in the gold mosaic of a wall," line 1 completes a statement which is complemented by line 2; so it is said to be autonomous even though there is no punctuation after "fire." If a line is not autonomous and carries over into the next line, *enjambment* has occurred. Autonomy and enjambment are two of the poet's most important tools for creating tension within the poem.

Ballad: The ballad stanza, a type of *quatrain*, may alternate its rhyme scheme as abab or abcb. If all four lines contain four feet each (*tetrameter*), the stanza is called a "long ballad"; if one or more of the lines contain only three feet (*trimeter*), it is called a "short ballad." Ballad stanzas, which are highly *mnemonic*, take their origin from verse adapted to singing. For this reason, the poetic ballad is well suited for presenting simple stories. Popular ballads are songs or verse which tell tales, usually impersonal, and they usually imply the wisdom of the folk. Supernatural events, courage, and love are frequent themes, but any experience which appeals to common people is acceptable material. By using the ballad form, the poet can establish expectations of simplicity and suspense; perhaps the most famous example for many readers is *The Rime of the Ancient Mariner* (1798), by Samuel Taylor Coleridge. The long ballad is also a popular stanza form for hymns, and because the ballad has been so closely associated with religious music, it carries with it the connotation of openness and sincerity. Some modern poets have created *irony* in their poetry by *counterpointing* traditional expectations of the hymn stanza with secular or antireligious subject matter.

Ballade: The French "Ballade," a popular and sophisticated form, is commonly (but not necessarily) composed of an eight-line stanza rhyming ababbcbc. Early ballades usually contained three stanzas and an *envoy*, but there was no consistent syllable count. Other common characteristics of the ballade are a refrain occurring at the end of each stanza and an envoy, usually addressed to a nobleman, priest, or the poet's patron. The refrain is likely to contain the recurring motifs of the poem, while the envoy climaxes or restates the theme. The widest use of the ballade came in France during the fourteenth and fifteenth centuries, and the form was perfected by its greatest practitioner, François Villon. In English the ballade was imitated by Geoffrey Chaucer and John Gower, and was revived in the nineteenth century by Austin Dobson and Algernon Charles Swinburne.

Base meter (or metrical base): Poems in English and in most European languages which are not *free verse* are written in one of four base meters (*accentual*, *accentual-syllabic*, *syllabic*, or *quantitative*), measured by the number, pattern, or duration of the syllables within a line or stanza. Accentual base meter counts the number of stressed syllables, as in Sylvia Plath's "Blue Moles"; accentual-syllabic base meter indicates the relationship of unstressed to stressed syllables, as in Shakespeare's sonnets; syllabic base meter counts the number of unstressed syllables, as in Dylan Thomas' "Fern Hill"; and quantitative base meter counts the amount of time it takes to read a line, as in Thomas Campion's "Rose-Cheeked Laura." Rhythm in verse occurs because of *meter*, and the use of meter depends upon the type of base into which it is placed. Readers should never underestimate the power of meter to influence and shape responses to a poem, and careful readers will want to *scan* the poem to see how it achieves its metrical effects.

Blank verse: Although many variations can occur in the *meter* of blank verse, its *base meter* is iambic pentameter. Blank verse lines are unrhymed, and are usually arranged in *stichic* form (that is, not in stanzas). Most of Shakespeare's plays are written in blank verse, but in poetry it is often used for subject matter that requires much narration or reflection. In both poetry and drama, blank verse elevates emotion and gives a dramatic sense of importance to almost every theme. In his comedies, Shakespeare knew well how to use the elevated diction possible through employment of blank verse to create absurd situations. Readers familiar with Shakespeare will almost automatically associate blank verse with him, and thus a kind of metrical *allusion* occurs. Although the base meter of blank verse is iambic pentameter, the form is very flexible, and *substitutions, enjambments, feminine endings,* and extra syllables can relax the rigidity of the base. In fact, the flexibility of blank verse gives the poet an opportunity to use a formal structure without seeming unnecessarily decorous, and many of the best lines in English are written in this form. Even with its great flexibility, however, blank verse is taxing because it demands grace and beauty without the benefit of rhyme, while requiring elevated emotion and profound observations about life. Because of Shakespeare's dominance of English literature, modern poets have been reluctant to risk using blank verse in its strict form; thus, they have taken great liberties, adding or subtracting feet or interspersing three-foot lines within the five-foot structure. Poets who take such liberties usually maintain the *iambic* base while varying the length of the line, and some critics have tagged these "*variable verse*" poems as "free verse." Clearly, this form is not "free" since it relies so heavily on a traditional form. T. S. Eliot's "Burnt Norton" is one example of a modern blank verse poem.

Bobs. See *Standard Habbie.*

Brace stanza: The brace stanza consists of four lines of *iambic* pentameter rhyming abba. The form is seldom used except in *Italian sonnets* because it has a tendency to cause the poem to build toward a climax very quickly, and unless some *resolution* is found after two or three stanzas, the reader becomes frustrated. For the poem which needs to move quickly to a resolution, however, the brace is ideal, although it is difficult to write. It is especially well-suited to sonnets which must establish a situation and quickly resolve it.

Cadence: The rhythmic speed or tempo with which a line is read is its cadence. All language has cadence, but when the cadence of words is forced into some pattern, it then becomes *meter*, thus distinguishing poetry from prose. *Prose poetry* may possess strong cadence, combined with poetic uses of imagery, symbolism, and other poetic devices, but it cannot become a poem without meter or the intentional absence of it.

Caesura: When the poet imposes a pause or break in the poem, whether or not he uses punctuation marks, a caesura has occurred. The comma, question mark, colon, and dash are the most common signals for pausing, and are properly termed "caesuras"; but pauses may also be achieved through syntax, *lines, meter, rhyme,* and the sound of words. The type of punctuation determines the length of the pause. Periods and question marks demand full stops;

colons take almost a full stop; semicolons take a long pause; commas a short pause. The end of a line usually demands some pause even if there is no punctuation. Caesuras are used to change the natural emphasis of the *line* in order to emphasize a portion of the poem or line which might not otherwise be noticed. Caesuras can also be used very effectively and subtly to alter the reader's natural breathing cycles in order to build tension in the poem. The most obvious use of caesura, however, (See *Dieresis*, *Split foot*, *Enjambment*) is simply to clarify syntax.

Catalexis. See *Truncation*.

Cinquain: Any five-line stanza, including the *mad-song* and the *limerick*, is a cinquain. Cinquains are most often composed of a *ballad* stanza with an extra line added to the middle, as in Coleridge's *The Rime of the Ancient Mariner*.

Conceit: One of several types of *metaphor*, the conceit is used for comparisons which are highly intellectualized. Simple metaphors compare objects whose common properties are clear. When Shakespeare says, "My mistress' eyes are nothing like the sun," the reader can understand that eyes and the sun are comparable: they both radiate, they have similiar shapes, they are bright and warm, they are the means by which we can see. When Eliot, however, says that winding streets are like a tedious argument of insidious intent, there is no clear connection between the two, and so the reader must apply abstract logic and fill in the missing links between the *tenor* and the *vehicle* of this conceit. The conceit serves both as a focusing and a shocking device, forcing the reader to impose his own logic on the poem. Often, as in the poetry of John Donne, the missing links of the conceit contain the hidden meaning of the poem.

Connotation: Words convey meaning in three ways: through their sound (apply the sound of "cat" and "dog" to the characteristics of the animals), through their formal, *denotative* definitions, and through their use in context. When a word takes on an additional meaning other than its denotative one, it achieves connotation, and much of the communication that writers achieve, especially in poetry, is the result of the implied use of language. The word "mercenary," for example, simply means a soldier who is paid to fight in an army not of his own region, but connotatively a mercenary is an unprincipled scoundrel who kills for money and pleasure, not for honor and patriotism. Thus, in A. E. Housman's poem, "Epitaph on an Army of Mercenaries," the reader brings negative associations to the subject matter by virtue of con- notation alone, without ever having read the poem. Connotation is one of the most important devices for achieving *irony*, and many a reader has been fooled into believing the poem has one meaning because he has missed the connotations which reverse the poem's apparent theme. (See the author entry about Robert Frost for examples of how connotation reverses meaning.)

Consonance: When the final consonants of stressed syllables agree, but the preceding vowels are different, consonance occurs. "Chair star" is an example of consonance, since both words end with "r" preceded by different vowels. Terminal consonance creates half or slant rhyme (see *Approximate rhyme*). Consonance differs from *alliteration* in that the final consonants are repeated rather than the initial consonants. In the twentieth century, when *full rhyme* seems inappropriately traditional, consonance has become one of the principal rhyming devices, and is used to achieve formality without seeming stilted or old-fashioned.

Consonants: Consonants are among the most important sound-producing devices in poetry, and there are five basic effects which certain consonants will produce: resonance, harshness, plosiveness, exhaustiveness, and liquidity. Resonance, exhaustiveness, and liquidity will tend to give the words—and consequently the whole line if several of these consonants are used—a soft-sound effect, while plosiveness and harshness tend to create tension. Resonance is the property of long duration produced by nasals, such as "n," "m," "ng," and voiced fricating consonants, such as "z," "zh," "v," and the voiced "th" as in "them." Compare, for example, the amount of time it takes to pronounce "man" and "cat." Resonanting words tend to ring throughout the line, and they can be used to establish either harmony or cacophony. Exhaustiveness is created by the voiceless fricating consonants and consonant combinations, such as "h," "f," and the voiceless "th," "s," "sh." If enough exhaustive consonants are grouped together, the reader must pause to catch his breath, which circumstance may in turn be used by the poet to establish the narrator's attitude or the theme of the poem. In the line, "These sudden ends of time must give us pause," the preponderence of exhaustive consonants, combined with the resonating "n" and "m" consonants in "sudden," "ends," and "time," and the plosive consonants in "time," "must," and "pause," force us to stop breathing and consider the physical nature of the end of time. Liquidity results from using the liquids and semivowels "l," "r," "w," and "y,' as in the word "silken." When liquid consonants hover between syllables, as in "solemn," they seem especially flowing. When resonant, exhaustive, and liquid words are forced together, they give the line a soft, sensuous quality, as in the line, "The summer palaces on slopes, the terraces." Plosiveness occurs when certain consonants create a stoppage of breath before releasing it, especially "b," "p," "t," "d," "g," "k," "ch," and "j." They are particularly noticeable in terminal positions, as in "top," "putt," or "tag." Plosives tend to make a word hard and restrained, causing the line to reverberate with bitterness, as in the lines: "Six hands at an open door dicing for pieces of silver,/ and feet kicking the empty wine-skins." Poets frequently use consonant groupings to create special effects, and when this occurs, it is important for the reader to determine what phonic emotion the poem is creating.

Controlling image/controlling metaphor: Just as a poem may include as structural devices form, theme, action, or dramatic situation, it may also use imagery for structure. When an image runs throughout a poem, giving unity to lesser images or ideas, it is called a "controlling image." Usually, the poet establishes a single idea, such as the spinning wheel in Edward Taylor's "Huswifery," then expands and complicates many aspects of weaving until the reader begins to see life as a tapestry. Poets use a controlling image or metaphor when they want to develop a single idea, usually didactic, or to illustrate the intrinsic and complex connection between various facets of life. While only a few poets have been able to sustain successfully complex controlling metaphors, much inspirational poetry has used the device, such as Joyce Kilmer's "Trees." Robert Frost's poem "The Silken Tent" is one of the finest examples of a controlling image and *extended metaphor*.

Counterpointing: When a shift occurs within a line, or from one line to the next, causing the meter to change from rising to falling, or vice versa, it is called "counterpointing." This unexpected reversal of rhythm can create complex effects, marking unanticipated movement, discovery, change, or new direction. Whatever it suggests, it is almost always accompanied by the release of some emotion. Generally, because of the prevalence of the iamb in English, the characteristic reversal is achieved by a trochaic *substitution*, particularly in the first *foot*, but any type of counterpointing will have a similar effect. Almost all accomplished poets use counterpointing, but E. E. Cummings offers clear examples of its best use, as in: "my father moved through dooms of love/ . . . singing each morning out of each night."

Couplet: Any two succeeding lines which rhyme form a couplet, but because the couplet has been used in so many different ways, and because of its long tradition in English poetry, various names and functions have been given to types of couplets. One of the most common is the decasyllabic (ten-syllable) couplet, used by Robert Browning in "My Last Duchess:" "That's my last Duchess painted on the wall,/ Looking as if she were alive. I call." When there is an *end-stop* on the second line of a couplet, it is said to be "closed"; an *enjambed* couplet is open, as in the example from "My Last Duchess." An end-stopped decasyllabic couplet is called a "heroic couplet," because the form has often been used to sing the praise of heroes. The heroic couplet was the form most used by the neoclassical poets of the eighteenth century, and lends itself to the pithy, aphoristic, ordered statement so prized by that century. It also lends itself to monotony if not varied masterfully, and some of the greatest poets have proved their metrical skills by making the heroic couplet brilliantly fresh. Because it is so stately and sometimes pompous, the heroic couplet invites satire, and many poems have been written in "mock heroic verse," such as Alexander Pope's *The Rape of the Lock* (1712). Another commonly used couplet is the octasyllabic (eight-syllable) couplet, formed from two lines of iambic tetrameter, as in "L'Allegro" by John Milton: "Come, and trip as we go/ On the light fantastic toe." First used for serious poetry, the light, sing-song tone of the octasyllabic couplet also invited satire, and in the seventeenth century Samuel Butler wrote one of the most famous of all satires, *Hudibras* (1663, 1664, 1678) in this couplet, giving it the name by which it is known today, "Hudibrastic verse." The *feminine* and *multiple* rhymes, combined with ludicrous rhyme words, have established a tradition which makes it nearly impossible for poets since Butler to use the form seriously, a curse which the writer of birthday-card verse have not quite understood. Because the rhymes immediately follow each other in couplets, the juxtaposition of closely associated lines sets up an opportunity for witty antithesis or observation; the poet can make a statement and then, with identical form, make a comment on it. For example, Pope says: "Laugh where we must, be candid where we can," and then makes an observation as to what we must do: "But vindicate the ways of God to man." When a couplet is used to break another rhyme scheme, it generally produces a summing-up effect, and has an air of profundity. Shakespeare found this characteristic particularly useful when he needed to give his newly invented *Shakespearean sonnet* a final note of authority and purpose. Modern poets who have used internal couplets brilliantly are Frost and Eliot, while Yeats adopted stanza forms which ended in couplets, such as *ottava rima*.

Curtal sonnet: Although a number of variations have been made on the English and Italian sonnet forms, none has distinguished itself enough to become standard except the Miltonic and the Spenserian (see *Sonnet* for a full discussion). Gerard Manley Hopkins, however, developed a new form which rejects the English and Italian influence. It is called a "curtal" (curtailed) sonnet and consists of a six-line "octave" rhyming abcabc, and a four and a half line "sestet" rhyming dbcdc. Hopkins wrote only two sonnets of this sort, both in *sprung rhythm*, and there have been no successful attempts to imitate this form.

Dactyl: The dactyl, formed of a stress followed by two unstressed syllables ($\prime$$\smile$$\smile$), is fairly common in isolated words, but when this pattern is included in a line of poetry, it tends to break down and rearrange itself into components of other types of feet. Isolated, the word "méan-ĭng-lĕss" is a dactyl, but in the line, "Políte/meaning/léss words" the last syllable becomes attached to the stressed "words" and creates a *split foot*, forming a *trochee* and an *iamb*. Nevertheless, a few dactylic poems do exist, as in "Aftĕr thĕ/pángs ŏf ă/ despĕrăte/lóvĕr."

Denotation: The explicit, formal definition of a word, exclusive of its implications and emotional associations (see *Connotation*), is its denotation or denotative meaning. In Kenneth Rexroth's lines, "We lie here in the bee filled, ruinous/ Orchard of a decayed New England farm" ("When We with Sappho"), the denotative meaning of the word "ruinous" is: "in a state of collapse, neglect, or decay." The *connotations* of the word "ruinous," however, are rich with romantic emotional associations. By association with the word "ruins" in particular, the "ruinous" orchard suggests the transience of all human things—one of the themes of Rexroth's poem.

Depressed foot: Occasionally, two syllables occur in a pattern in such a way as to be taken as one syllable without actually being an *elision*, thus creating a depressed foot. In the line: "Tŏ eăch/thĕ boúl/dĕrs (thăt hăve)/fállĕn/tŏ each" the *base meter* consists of five iambic feet, but in the third foot there is an extra syllable which disrupts the meter but does not break it, so that "that have" functions as the second half of the iambic foot. Clearly there are three syllables in the foot, but the linguistic quality of "that have" allows it to be depressed into the iambic base so that the regular meter can be maintained. The effect of a depressed foot is to change the balance of the line, and it serves as an effective means by which the meter can be interrupted without being broken.

Diction: John Dryden defined diction concisely as the poet's "choice of words." In Dryden's time, and for most of the history of English verse, the diction of poetry was elevated, sharply distinct from everyday speech. The diction of twentieth century poetry, however, ranges from the banal and the conversational to the highly formal, from obscenity and slang to technical vocabulary, sometimes in the same poem. The diction of a poem often reveals its persona's values and attitudes. In Philip Larkin's "Church Going," for example, the narrator enters a church "which has fallen out of use" and observes "some brass and stuff up at the holy end." It is clear from the narrator's diction that he is not a regular churchgoer and that he feels both uncomfortable and a bit contemptuous as he stands behind the lectern, "perusing a few large scale hectoring verses."

Dieresis: *Caesuras* which come after the foot (see *Split foot* for a discussion of caesuras which break feet), called "dieresis" (although the technical name is seldom used), can be used to create long pauses in the *line*, and they are often used to prepare the line for *enjambment*. Any caesura creates a pause, but dieresis tends to create a longer pause because it gives the foot more unity, especially when it comes after a syllable of long *duration*. The effect of dieresis is to slow the line and to emphasis a particular foot.

Dramatic dialogue: When two or more personae speak to each other in a poem or a play, they engage in dramatic dialogue. Unlike *dramatic monologue*, both characters speak, and in the best dramatic dialogues, their conversation leads step by step to a final resolution in which both characters and the reader come to the same realization at the same time. The focus is on both personae, who learn from each other and reveal their emotions and insights in the process. In most *lyric poetry* the narrative persona is alone with his thoughts, struggling to deal with life as an isolated being, whereas in *narrative poetry* the narrator measures life against someone else. Dramatic dialogue and monologue are devices which allow characters in poetry and drama to reveal their inner feelings which would seem ridiculous if verbalized without the presence of an onstage listener.

Dramatic monologue: In dramatic monologue, the narrator addresses a silent persona who never speaks but whose presence greatly influences what the narrator tells the reader. The principal reason for writing in dramatic monologue is to control the speech of the major persona by the implied reaction of the silent one. The effect of dramatic monologue is one of continuing change and often surprise. In "My Last Duchess," for example, the Duke believes that he is in control of the situation when in fact he has revealed to the emissary terrible insights about the way he treated his former Duchess. The emissary, who is the silent persona, has asked questions which the Duke has answered, and in doing so he has given away secrets. The reader is just as surprised and horrified as the emissary at this revelation of the Duke's character. Dramatic monologue is like hearing one side of a telephone conversation, in which the reader learns a great deal about both participants. Dramatic monologue is especially useful for revealing characters slowly and involving the reader almost as another silent participant. Most dramatic monologues are working for *irony* to create *theme*.

Dramatic situation: Closely linked with *point of view*, dramatic situation is the setting in which the poem occurs, and it is one of the most important devices for establishing the poem's tension and theme. Who are the personae of the poem? Where are they? What does it (and they) look like? Why are they there? When does it take place? Once these questions are answered, the dramatic situation can be reduced to a prose statement. For "Stopping by Woods on a Snowy Evening" by Robert Frost, the statement might be: "A man in a carriage drawn by a horse has stopped by woods to watch the snow fall. There is no one around, and there is no farmhouse between the woods and the lake. The owner of the woods is not present to witness the narrator stopping here. The only noises are the sound of the horse shaking his harness bells and the wind blowing easily. The narrator seems to be talking to someone who is not in the poem." This statement of the dramatic situation raises as many questions as it answers: Where has the narrator come from, and where is he going? Why did he stop? What time of day is it? Why is he in a horse-drawn carriage? Why does he think he knows whose woods these are? These implied questions about the dramatic situation, when answered, will lead to a fuller understanding of the theme. Not all poems have a dramatic situation, and in some poems the action will shift from the immediate setting. The dramatic setting of *The Rime of the Ancient Mariner* is before a church where three wedding guests who are about to enter the festivities have been stopped by an old man who holds them with his eye. Most of the poem, however, takes place on board ship, so that the dramatic situation shifts, and each time it does the careful reader must establish the relationship between the narrator and his setting.

Duration: The measure of *quantitative meter* is the duration or length of the syllables. Duration can alter the tone and the *relative stress* of a line and influence meaning as much as the *foot* can. Long durational stresses slow the meter and make the stressed syllables less prominent, as in the word "cól/umn," a two-syllable word with the natural stress falling strongly on the first syllable. The two resonating *consonants*, "m" and "n," however, create such a long duration that the second syllable takes almost as much stress as the first.

Elegy: The elegy and pastoral elegy are distinguishable by their subject matter, not their form. The elegy is usually a long, rhymed, *strophic* poem whose subject is meditation upon death or a lamentable theme, while the pastoral elegy uses the natural setting of a pastoral scene to sing of death or love. Within the pastoral setting the simplicity of the characters and the scene lend a peaceful air despite the grief which the narrator feels. Although elegies and *odes* were better suited for other poetic ages, modern poets use the elegy for putting complex feelings into a simple setting so that they can be examined closely or placed in a complicated modern setting, such as a great city, in order to create *irony* or compare the past with the present. *For the Union Dead* (1964) by Robert Lowell is one example of a modern elegy.

Elision: The two types of elision are synaeresis and syncope; they occur when a poet who is attempting to maintain a regular *base meter* joins two vowels into a single vowel, or omits a vowel altogether. In the line "Of man's first disobedience, and the fruit" the "ie" in "disobedience" is pronounced as a "y" ("ye") so that the word reads dis/o/bed/yence, thereby making a five-syllable word into a four-syllable word. This process of forming one vowel out of two is synaeresis. When a vowel is dropped altogether, rather than combining two into one, it is called "syncope," as when "natural" becomes "nat'ral" and "hastening" becomes "hast'ning." Elisions indicate that the poet is especially sensitive to his base meter, and that any variations in it are deliberate and important. In these lines by Alexander Pope, "True ease in writing comes from art, not chance/ As those move easiest who have learned to dance./ 'Tis not enough no harshness gives offense,/ The sound must seem an echo of the sense," the poet adds a syllable to the ten-syllable base meter of line 2 and makes frequent *substitutions*, giving the sensation of dancing through his meter gracefully in order to reinforce the meaning of lines 3 and 4. Pope deliberately does not elide "easiest" while he does elide "It is" into "'Tis," so that when we compare the beauty of line 2 with the starkness of line 3, we realize what Pope thinks about the widely held eighteenth century idea that the best poetry conforms to a rigid ten-syllable line. Much less frequent uses of elision are to change the sound of a word, or to spell words as they are pronounced, or to indicate dialect.

Emphasis: Through a number of techniques, such as *caesura*, the *line*, *relative stress*, *counterpointing*, and *substitution*, poets are able to alter the usual emphasis or meaning of words. Whenever the *metrical contract* is intentionally broken through one of these techniques, certain words or the entire line will be highlighted or emphasized for the purpose of calling attention to the most important parts of the poem. Whenever the poet creates emphasis, he is signaling to the reader that the most important keys to the theme lie there.

End-stop: When a punctuated pause occurs at the end of a line, the line is said to be "end-stopped." The function of end-stops is to show the relationship between lines, and to create *emphasis* on particular words or on a particular line. In the lines "The water, like a witch's oils,/ Burnt green, and blue, and white." the long *duration* of the *consonants* in "oils," combined with the end-stop, cause the reader to ponder over the word and to consider the mystifying effect of "witch's oils." End-stop in rhymed poems creates much more emphasis on the rhyme words, which already carry a great deal of emphasis by virtue of their rhymes. Unless the rhymes are especially important and deserve attention, or are used so skillfully as to give pleasure, end-stops should not be used. With *enjambment*, the opposite of end-stopping, and internal caesuras, the poet can reduce the attention which rhymes demand. This method is very effective when the poet wants to maintain the associative power of rhymes without calling attention to them.

Enjambment: When a line is not *end-stopped*, so that it carries over to the following line, the line is said to be "enjambed," as in: "Avenge, O Lord, thy slaughtered saints, whose bones/ Lie scattered on the Alpine mountains cold." Enjambment is used to change the natural emphasis of the *line*, to strengthen or weaken the effect of *rhyme*, or to alter *meter*. In the lines of the example, Milton has managed to place emphasis on all three sections of the first line by combining internal *caesuras* with enjambment. The effect is that the lines become deliberate, and the horror of the massacre is reinforced by the enjambed phrase: "whose bones Lie scattered." In the twentieth century, caesura has been especially important in allowing the poet to create a conversational tone which breaks down the formality of poetry while, at the same time, maintaining the advantages of rhyme and the line.

Envoy: Generally, an envoy is any short poem or stanza addressed to the reader as a beginning or end to a longer work. Specifically, the envoy is the final stanza of a sestina or a *ballade* in which all of the rhyme words are repeated or echoed.

Extended metaphor (see *Controlling image/controlling metaphor*): When *metaphors* are added to one another so that they run in a series, they are collectively called an "extended metaphor." Frost's poem "The Silken Tent" is one extended metaphor which compares the "she" of the poem to the freedom and bondage of a silken tent.

Eye rhyme: Words which appear to be identical because of their spelling, but which sound different, are known as "eye rhymes." "Bough, enough, cough" are examples. Because of changes in pronunciation, many traditional poems appear to use eye rhymes but do not. For example, "wind" (meaning moving air) once rhymed with "bind" and "find." Eye rhymes which are intentional and do not result from a change in pronunciation, are often used to create discomfort or a disconcerting effect. "Ballet" and "pallet" are examples.

Falling rhyme: Rhymes in which the correspondence of sound comes only in the final unstressed syllable which is preceded by another unstressed syllable (see *Masculine* and *Feminine rhyme*) are known as "falling rhymes." Eliot rhymes "mĕ-tíc-ŭ-loŭs" with "rĭ-díc-ŭ-loŭs" and creates a falling rhyme. (See *Rhyme* for a discussion of the uses of various types of rhyme.)

Falling rhythm: A line in which feet move from a stressed to unstressed syllables (*trochaic* or *dactyllic*) is said to "fall," as in this line from "The Naming of Parts": "Glĭstĕns/líke cór/ăl ĭn/áll ŏf thĕ/néighbŏrĭng/gárdĕns." Because English and other Germanic-based languages naturally rise, imposing a falling rhythm on a rising *base meter* creates *counterpointing* and is important for establishing *emphasis* and the *tone* of the poem. Lines ending with an unstressed syllable are known as "feminine endings," the effect of which is to create a soft, soothing feeling.

Feminine ending. See *Falling rhythm*.

Feminine rhyme: Feminine rhyme occurs when the final accented syllable is followed by a single unaccented syllable. The accented syllables rhyme, while the unaccented syllables are phonetically identical, as with "flick-er/snick-er" and "fin-gers/ma-lin-gers." Feminine rhymes are often used for lightness in tone and delicacy in movement; while *masculine rhyme* is forceful and sure, feminine rhymes seem soft. The softness may or may not indicate a lack of assurance, but it does indicate a lack of brusqueness and brutality. In "The Love Song of J. Alfred Prufrock," Eliot uses many feminine rhymes and *feminine endings* to reinforce Prufrock's indecisiveness.

Figure poetry: Also called "pattern poetry" and "Carmen figuratum," figure poetry attempts to represent visually the subject of the poem. Thus, George Herbert's "Easter Wings" is shaped like birds' wings, and John Hollander's "For a Thirtieth Birthday, with a bottle of Burgundy" is constructed in the shape of a wine bottle. Although figure poetry offers pleasure through the cleverness of its shape, the poet sacrifices the advantages of the *line*; consequently, there are few successful figure poems. In spite of the failure of the true figure poem, however, poets have used the visual appearance of the type on the page very dramatically, and in the twentieth century typography has been used as an integral part of many successful poems. E. E. Cummings is the most famous practitioner of effective typography, amounting to a variation on figure poetry.

First person: This *point of view* has been particularly useful in short, lyrical poems which tend to be highly subjective, taking the reader to the depths of the narrator's thoughts. Normally, though not necessarily signaling the use of the first person through the pronoun "I," first-person poems allow the reader direct access to the narrator's thoughts, or they provide a character who can convey a personal reaction to an event. When a poem is written in the first person, the poet wants the reader either to identify with the narrator or to understand an event through the narrator's reaction to it. First-person poems often strive to make the narrator the central point of the poem so that the reader's reaction is determined as he identifies with the narrator. The meaning of the poem may lie in the difference between the narrator's and the reader's thoughts, emotions, and reactions to the situation. When the narrator is speaking only to the reader or musing to himself, he is engaged in interior monologue, thus revealing his own thoughts.

Foot/Feet: The natural speech pattern in English and other Germanic-based languages is to group syllables together in family units. In English, the most common of these rhythmic units is composed of one unstressed syllable attached to one stressed syllable (an *iamb*). When these family groups are forced into a line of poetry, they are called "feet" in the *accentual-syllabic* metrical system. In the line "My mis/tress' eyes/ are noth/ing like/ the sun" there are four iambic feet (˘ ´) and one pyrrhic (˘ ˘) foot, but in the line "There where/ the vines/ cling crim/son on/ the wall" there are three *substitutions* for the iamb, in the first, third, and fourth feet. The six basic feet in English poetry are the iamb (˘ ´), trochee (´ ˘), anapest (˘ ˘ ´), dactyl (´ ˘ ˘), spondee (´ ´), and pyrrhus (˘ ˘). Recognizing the *base meter* of the poem (that is, which type of foot dominates the line) and noticing when the poet has intentionally altered the base for effect, will help explain where the *emphasis*, and thus the meaning, of the poem lies. (See *Base meter, Substitution, Split feet, Relative stress, Scansion*.)

Form: The form of a poem is determined by its arrangement of lines on the page, its base meter, its rhyme scheme, and occasionally its subject matter. Poems which are arranged into *stanzas* are called "strophic," and because the strophic tradition is so old (see the chart on page 3571 for a list of the traditional stanzas) a large number of commonly used stanzas have evolved very particular uses and characteristics. Poems which run from beginning to end without a break are called "*stichic*," and they, too, possess certain characteristics and uses. The form of *pattern poetry* is determined by its visual appearance rather than by lines and stanzas, while the definition of "*free verse*" is that it has no form at all. Some poem types, such as the sestina, *sonnet*, and *ode*, are written in particular forms, and frequently are restricted to particular subject matter, but because form greatly influences the reader's emotional response, poets carefully select and manipulate the form of all poems. (See *Nonce forms*.)

Found poetry: Found poetry such as David Antin's "Code of Flag Behavior," is created from language which is "found" in print in nonliterary settings—on menus, tombstones, fire extinguishers, even on shampoo bottles. Any language which is already constructed, but especially language which appears on artifacts that characterize society, such as cereal boxes, provides the material from which the found poem is created. The rules for writing a found poem vary, but generally the found language is used intact or altered only slightly. Words may be eliminated from the instructions on a fire extinguisher, but none may be added. The typography may be rearranged, so that a pizza menu might appear in the form of a pizza plate or a wedge, but whatever else the poet does with the found language, he may not alter the language itself—only rearrange it to make it serve some purpose other than its original utilitarian one. Found poetry almost always depends on *irony*, pointing out the differences between the way society uses that particular language and the way more sensitive people apprehend it.

Free verse: A poem which does not conform to any traditional convention, such as meter, rhyme, or form, and which does not establish any pattern within itself, is said to be a "free verse" poem. There is, however, great dispute over whether free verse exists. Eliot said that by definition poetry must establish some kind of pattern, and Frost said that free verse was like playing tennis without a net: you still have to hit the ball as though the net were there if the game is to make any sense at all. It is clear, however, that modern poets have attempted to break down the formal structures of poetry to present serious subjects in ordinary language. Free verse depends more on cadence than on meter; there is rhythm in free verse, but it does not follow the strict rules of meter. Street verse and *variable verse* might be thought of as "free verse," although the closest example to free verse is *prose poetry*.

Greek feet: In Greek literature, in which the poetical *foot* originates, there are a number of other types of feet in addition to those common in English poetry. When those Greek feet are forced into a two-syllable base meter in English, they tend to divide into major English feet, and it is doubtful whether Greek feet exist in English poetry. For example, the Greek antipast (˘ ´ ´ ˘) might divide into an *iamb* (˘ ˘) and a *trochee* (´ ˘). The Greek amphibrach, however, has some claim to consideration as a pattern in English, as in Robert Browning's "How They Brought the Good News from Aix to Ghent." The amphibrach (˘ ´ ˘) is a unit tight enough to be used for *substitution*, as with the word "rŏ-mán-tĭc."

Haiku: Haiku is a Japanese form which appeared in the sixteenth century and is still practiced in Japan. A haiku consists of three lines of five, seven, and five syllables each; in Japanese there are other conventions regarding content which are not observed in Western haiku. The traditional haiku took virtually all of its *images* from nature, using the natural world as a *metaphor* for the spiritual. Because it depends on the strength of its imagery, on implication rather than statement, and because its syllabic form lends itself to *free verse* in translation, the haiku appealed to early twentieth century poets such as Ezra Pound. Pound and the Imagists, particularly Amy Lowell, helped to popularize the form in England and America, but the influence of haiku on early modern poetry was international and enormous and cannot be attributed to any one group or movement.

Half rhyme. See *Approximate rhyme*.

Hemistich. See *Old English versification.*

Heroic couplet. See *Couplet.*

Hudibrastic couplet. See *Couplet.*

Hymn stanza. See *Ballad.*

Hyperbole: When the poet deliberately overstates in order to heighten the reader's awareness, he is using hyperbole. As with *irony*, hyperbole works because the reader can perceive the difference between the importance of the dramatic situation and the manner in which it is described. In Alfred, Lord Tennyson's "The Eagle" we come to understand the narrator's awe for the eagle because of the hyperbole describing the azure world which the eagle occupies. Hyperbole usually causes the reader to identify with the narrator, and it is almost always the narrator as a person rather than other elements of theme which hyperbole explores.

Iamb: The basic *foot* of English speech, the iamb associates one unstressed syllable with one stressed (˘ ´). The line: "Šo long/as men/can breathe/or eyes/can see," is composed of five iambs. In the line "Ă cold/coming/we had/ of it" a *trochaic* foot has been *substituted* for the expected iamb in the second foot, thus emphasizing that this is a "coming" rather than a "going," a crucial distinction in Eliot's poem *The Journey of the Magi.*

Identical rhyme: Identical rhyme occurs when the entire final stressed syllables contain exactly the same sounds, such as "break/brake," or "bear" (noun), "bear" (verb), "bare" (adjective), "bare" (verb). Usually, identical rhyme is used to indicate weariness, defeat, or dullness, for which purpose it can be very effective; but identical rhyme can also create problems with *punning*. In Geoffrey Chaucer's time identical rhyme was used somewhat indiscriminately for a variety of purposes, but by the time of the Renaissance, poets had learned that it was most successful when used sparingly.

Imagery: Imagery is traditionally defined as the verbal simulation of sensory perception. Like so many critical terms, "imagery" betrays a visual bias: it suggests that a poetic image is necessarily visual, a picture in words. In fact, however, imagery calls on all of the five senses, although the visual is predominant in many poets. In its simplest form, an image re-creates a physical sensation in a clear, literal manner, as in Robert Lowell's lines, "A sweetish smell of shavings, wax and oil/ blows through the redone bedroom newly aged" ("Marriage"). Imagery becomes more complex when the poet employs *metaphor* and other figures of speech to re-create experience, as in Seamus

Heaney's lines, "Right along the lough shore/ A smoke of flies/ Drifts thick in the sunset" ("At Ardboe Point"), substituting a fresh metaphor ("A smoke of flies") for a dead one (a cloud of flies) to help the reader visualize the scene more clearly in his mind's eye. Such imagery is usually called "figurative imagery," as opposed to the "literal imagery" of the lines from Lowell quoted above. Heaney's "smoke of flies," although a figurative image, re-creates a physical perception which the reader can easily share. Much figurative imagery, however, especially in modern poetry, is not intended to evoke a particular sight, sound, or some other physical sensation. Tomas Tranströmer's lines, "Friends! You drank some darkness/ and became visible" ("Elegy"), do not evoke a physical perception. Instead, the poet uses physical images for their *symbolic* associations. "Darkness" suggests the depths of life—not the mere surface of things. The act of drinking is voluntary; to drink darkness is to deliberately experience life more fully—in mystery, in suffering, in all its complexity. Paradoxically, it is by "drinking *darkness*" (instead of light) that the poet's friends become visible. To become visible is to become real; one becomes real (that is, fully human) by drinking some darkness.

In Memoriam stanza: Closely related to the lamentation or seriousness of the *heroic* quatrain is the "In Memoriam" stanza, which consists of four tetrameter lines rhyming abba. The rhyme scheme creates much of the effect of the stanza: the "a" rhymes grip the internal *couplet*, giving the stanza a feeling of restraint or introversion, making In Memoriam (which takes its name from the title of a poem by Tennyson) well-suited to introspective or meditative subjects. Because of the couplet arrangement and the shortness of the lines, the third line of the stanza demands great *emphasis*, giving the poet a natural area of focus.

Initial rhyme. See *Rhyme*.

Intentional fallacy: The intentional fallacy is the process of applying the author's intentions to the work of art. Sometimes authors say what they think their poem means; at other times readers speculate about why the author included certain elements of the poem. A number of modern literary critics, representing various critical schools or factions, have held that a poem should be judged only by its intrinsic qualities, not by what the author hoped it would achieve. According to these critics, when a poet finishes his work, it no longer belongs to him, and whatever he says about it is no more (or less) reliable than what any other informed reader might say.

Interior monologue. See *First person*.

Internal rhyme. See *Rhyme*.

Irony: Irony is among the three or four most important concepts in modern literary criticism. Although the term orginated in classical Greece and has been in the vocabulary of criticism since that time, only in the nineteenth and twentieth centuries has it assumed such central importance. The term "irony" is used by critics in many different contexts with an extraordinary range of meanings, eluding precise definition. In its narrowest sense, irony is a figure of speech in which the speaker's real meaning is different from (and often exactly opposite to) his apparent meaning. In Andrew Marvell's lines, "The Grave's a fine and private place,/ But none I think do there embrace" ("To His Coy Mistress"), the speaker's literal meaning—in praise of the grave— is quite different from his real meaning. This kind of irony, the easiest to define, is often called "verbal irony." Another kind of irony is found in narrative and dramatic poetry. In the *Iliad* (c. 800 B.C.), for example, the reader is made privy to the counsels of the gods, which greatly affect the course of action in the epic, while the human characters are kept in ignorance. This discrepancy between the knowledge of the reader (or spectator) and that of the characer (or characters) is called "dramatic irony." Beyond these narrow, well-defined varieties of irony there are many wider applications. The contrast between the achievements of the past and the squalor of the present which informs T. S. Eliot's *The Waste Land* (1922), Ezra Pound's *Cantos* (1925-1972), and the late poems of William Butler Yeats, is a form of irony, as is the contrast between ideal visions of human life and its harsh realities. In this sense, irony is pervasive in modern literature.

Light rhyme: Words in which final stressed vowels and all succeeding consonants are identical, but in which stressed syllables do not correspond, constitute "light rhymes." Light rhyme is comparable to full rhyme except that the rhyming syllables are not primary stresses, as in "pant/ignorant" and "sing/beckoning," where in one word the rhymed syllable is stressed while in the other word it is unstressed.

Limerick: The limerick is a comic five-line poem rhyming aabba in which the third and fourth lines are shorter (usually five syllables each) than the first, second, and last lines, which are usually eight syllables each. The limerick's *anapestic* base makes the verse sound silly; modern limericks are almost invariably associated with bizarre indecency, or with ethnic or anticlerical jokes. (See *Mad-song*.)

Line: A line has been defined as a poetical unit characterized by the presence of *meter*, and lines are categorized according to the number of *feet* they contain. A pentameter line, for example, contains five feet. This definition does not apply to a great deal of modern poetry, however, which is written in *free verse*. Ultimately, then, a line must be defined as a typographical unit which performs various functions in different kinds of poetry. A single line has no real poetical function by itself, and must be placed in context before it can be properly considered. As an autonomous unit, the line normally places more *emphasis* at its begining and end than in the middle. Because of this natural emphasis, the poet has an important regularity at his disposal, and he can play the natural emphasis of the line against the subject of his poem and the tools of meter in order to change the focus. *Caesuras, enjambment, rhyme,* and *substitution* are the poet's principal tools for altering the emphasis a line places on its subject. In Milton's line, "Avenge, O Lord, they slaughtered saints, whose bones," the use of caesuras and enjambment has increased the emphasis on the middle of the line.

Lyric poetry: The two ancient roots of poetry are the narrative and lyric traditions. Narrative poetry, such as the *Iliad*, relates long stories, often historical, which preserve information, characters, and values of a culture. Lyric poetry developed when music was accompanied by words, and although the "lyrics" were later separated from the music, the characteristics of lyric poetry have been shaped by the constraints of music. Lyric poems are short, more adaptable to metrical variation, and usually personal compared with the cultural functions of narrative poetry. While narrative poetry preserves traditions, lyric poetry sings of the self; it explores deeply personal feelings about life. During various periods of literature, lyric poetry has fallen in and out of favor, enjoying great popularity during the Renaissance and practically none during the eighteenth century. All poetry, and perhaps all literature, falls within the spectrum whose poles are narrative and lyric, and the characteristics of an age can, in part, be measured by its attitude toward these two traditions.

Mad-song: The mad-song—verse uttered by the presumably insane—usually expresses a happy, harmless, inventive sort of insanity. The rhyme scheme is of the mad-song abccb, and the unrhymed first line helps to set a tone of oddity and unpredictability, since it controverts the expectation that there will be a rhyme for it. The standard mad-song is patterned this way: lines 1, 2, and 5 are iambic trimeter; lines 3 and 4 are iambic dimeter. The shortness of the lines also helps to suggest benign madness, since 'simple' people are associated with uncomplicated sentence patterns. Frequently, lines 2 and 5 will have *feminine rhyme* and any of the lines may contain *anapestic substitutions*. The mad-song was particularly popular during the Renaissance and was used by Elizabethan playwrights for comic relief.

Masculine rhyme: Masculine rhyme occurs when the correspondence of rhyme occurs in the stressed syllables. "Men/then" constitute masculine rhyme, but so do "af-ter-noons/spoons." Masculine rhyme is generally more forceful than *feminine* and *multiple* rhyme, and while it has a variety of uses, it generally gives authority and assurance to the line, especially when the final syllables are of short duration. Because readers expect rhymes to be masculine, as they expect the *meter* to be *iambic*, whenever there is a deviation from masculine rhyme, it causes greater emphasis.

Metaphor: Metaphor, like *irony*, is one of a handful of key concepts in modern literary criticism. Like irony, the term "metaphor" is used by critics in such a wide variety of contexts that any precise, all-encompassing definition is impossible. In its narrowest sense, metaphor is a figure of speech in which two strikingly different things are identified with each other, as in T. S. Eliot's lines, "The whole earth is our hospital/ Endowed by the ruined millionaire" ("East Coker," from *Four Quartets*, 1943). How is the earth like a hospital—especially a hospital endowed by "the ruined millionaire"? This metaphor is part of an *extended metaphor* in which Eliot is describing the human condition from a Christian point of view. All human beings are sick with sin, and to save them Christ had to take the burden of that sin on Himself and die. Thus Eliot says that "we" are cared for by "the wounded surgeon" and "the dying nurse," who constantly reminds her patients "that, to be restored, our sickness must grow worse"—that is, all men must die before they can be raised to eternal life. "The ruined millionaire" (not *a* ruined millionaire) is God the Father, whose "absolute paternal care" for mankind extended to the sacrifice of His own Son. In Eliot's metaphor, the "tenor" (the subject of the metaphor) is the whole earth and the "vehicle" (the *image* by which the subject is presented) is the hospital. In D. H. Lawrence's lines, "Reach me a gentian, give me a torch/ let me guide myslef with the blue, forked torch of this flower" ("Bavarian Gentians"), the tenor is the gentian and the vehicle is the torch. This relatively restricted and well-defined meaning of metaphor as a figure of speech by no means covers the usage of the word in modern criticism. Some critics argue that metaphorical perception underlies *all* figures of speech. Others dispute the distinction between literal and metaphhorical description, saying that language is essentially metaphorical. Still others assert that every use of language can be plotted between two poles, two radically opposed linguistic tendencies: the metaphoric and the metonymic (see *metonymy*). The term "metaphor" is widely used to identify analogies of all kinds in literature, painting, film—even in music—so that one reads, for example, that Dublin in James Joyce's *Ulysses* (1922) is a metaphor for the city as it has developed in Western civilization.

Meter: Meter is the pattern of language when it is forced into a *line* of poetry. All language has rhythm, but when that rhythm is organized and regulated in the line so as to affect the meaning and emotional response to the words, then the rhythm has been refined into meter. Because the lines of most poems maintain a similiar meter throughout, poems are said to have a *base meter* and to establish a *metrical contract* with the reader. The meter is determined by the number of syllables in a line and by the relationship between them. Much of the message of a poem is conveyed through its meter, and poets have learned through centuries of use which meters and *forms* can be used to arouse particular emotions in their readers. Meter usually works subconsciously on readers, but it is often manipulated quite deliberately by the poet, and until the reader can analyze how the meter operates, he cannot fully appreciate the poet's craft.

Metonymy: When an object which is closely related to an idea comes to stand for the idea itself, such as saying "the crown" to mean the king, it is called "metonymy." When a part of the object stands for the entire object, such as using "heart" to mean the man, it is called "synecdoche." Synecdoche is normally but not necessarily used as a metaphor, as in "He has a heart of gold,"—meaning that he is kind and generous, qualities which are treasured as gold is treasured. Metonymy and synecdoche are used in poetry to emphasize a particular part of the whole or one particular aspect of it. For example, in the lines "Six hands at an open door dicing for pieces of silver,/ And feet kicking the empty wine-skins." the poet wishes to call attention to the part of the body performing the action. The soldiers who are part of the Crucifixion are depicted by their hands and feet because they are men who do not use their hearts and brains.

Metrical contract: Once the poet has established the *base meter* of his poem, readers may expect that the base meter will be maintained unless there is a specific reason to alter it. In agreeing not to alter the meter without reason, the poet forms a "metrical contract" with the reader which, when understood by both parties, becomes an important means for creating *emphasis*: whenever the poet breaks the metrical contract, the reader can assume that there is an important reason for it.

Miltonic sonnet: The Miltonic sonnet is a variation of the *Petrarchan* sonnet. It maintains the same structure and rhyme scheme, and differs only in its frequent use of enjambment, especially at the end of the octave, and in its positioning of the turn. (See *Sonnet*.) By not clearly defining where the turn will come, the Miltonic sonnet attempts to overcome the reader's expectation of an automatic shift in tone after the octave. The result is to help create a more natural *resolution* while working within the highly structured form of the Petrarchan sonnet, giving the poem more of an emotional rather than a structural unity. There are, of course, many advantages to having a defined position for the turn, but the less formal line created by enjambment, combined with the undefined turn (which can come anywhere between the ninth and eleventh lines), give the Miltonic sonnet some flexibility to create an emotional surprise.

Mnemonic verse: Poetry in which rhythmic patterns aid memorization but do not effect meaning is called "mnemonic verse." "Thirty days hath September/ April, June, and November" is an example of using rhyme and meter to help memorize information. In his important study of oral poetry, Albert Lord postulates that bards were able to remember long poems because of stock phrases, these and other mnemonic devices allowing the singer of tales to insert local lore and update information as cultural and historical changes occurred.

Mock-heroic. See *Couplet.*

Multiple rhyme. See *Rhyme.*

Nonce forms: Whenever a poet uses one of the standard *forms* he is doing so for one of three reasons: (1) the characteristics of the form fit his material and approach to the poem; (2) the associations which accompany the form will enhance the poem; or (3) the associations give him a standard form which he can deviate to achieve emphasis. Although many poems are written in a standard form, many others are not; yet they achieve unity even though the form may never have been used before, or may never have been used so successfully that it has acquired associations. Such improvised poetic forms are called "nonce" forms.

Occasional verse: Broadly defined, occasional verse includes any poem written for a specific occasion, such as a wedding, a birthday, a death, or a public event. Edmund Spenser's *Epithalamion* (1595), which was written for his marriage, and John Milton's "Lycidas," which commemorated the death of his schoolmate Edward King, are examples of occasional verse, as are W. H. Auden's "September 1, 1939" and Frank O'Hara's "The Day Lady Died." The term "occasional verse" is also used in a narrower and often deprecatory sense to refer to poems written on order, so to speak, such as the royal birthday poems which the *poet laureate* was once obliged to write.

Ode: The ode is a *lyric* poem which treats a unified subject with elevated emotion, usually ending with a satisfactory *resolution*. There is no set *form* for the ode, but it must be long enough to build intense emotional response. Often the ode will address itself to some omnipotent source, and will take on a spiritual hue. When explicating an ode, readers should look for the relationship between the narrator and some transcendental power to which the narrator must submit in order to find contentment despite his failure.

Modern poets have used the ode to treat subjects which are not religious in the theological sense but which have become innate beliefs of society. When modern poets use the ode, they usually maintain the elevated emotion and high seriousness of purpose but use these ode characteristics as a foil for ironic situations which depict deficiencies in society. Allen Tate's "Ode to the Confederate Dead" is one example of a modern ode.

Old English versification: The most extensive use of *accentual meter* came in Old English poetry (before A.D. 1100), in which the *line* rather than the *stanza* served as the basic verse unit, since no end rhyme was used. The Old English line was composed of four stressed syllables with a varying number of unstressed syllables; the line was normally divided into two parts (each half line is called a "hemistich"), separated by a *caesura*, with two of the four stressed syllables falling on each side of the line. The hemistichs are bound by *alliteration*, with the *stressed* syllables falling on the alliterated syllables. The two stresses in the first hemistich often alliterate with each other, and at least one must alliterate with the first stressed syllable in the second hemistich. In Old English the alliteration may not be continued to the fourth stressed syllable, although in Middle English it frequently does. In Middle English alliterative verse the rules were loosened, but the following line from *The Vision of William, Concerning Piers the Plowman* (c. 1395) is similiar to the Old English line form. "In a summer season when soft was the sun." Both the number of stresses per line and the position in which they fall are important. The unstressed syllables, however, are not used for measuring the line. After the Norman conquest (A.D. 1066), during the period between 1100 to 1300, poets began counting the number of syllables per line, as is done in French *syllabic verse*, and by the time Chaucer wrote *The Canterbury Tales* (1387-1400), poetry had begun to settle into a four-stress line with eight or nine syllables, or a five-stress line with ten or eleven syllables. The extensive use of poetry which counted both accents and syllables was to follow soon, beginning the *accentual-syllabic* system of meter. Use of the four-stress line continued, however, especially in popular verse and nursery rhymes, although the rules for alliteration were loosened or dropped, as in: "This is the cock that crowed in the morn/ That waked the priest all shaven and shorn."

Ottava Rima: Ottava rima is an eight-line *stanza* of *iambic* pentameter, rhyming abababcc. Probably the most famous English poem written in ottava rima is Lord Byron's *Don Juan* (1819-1824), and because the poem was so successful as a hilarious spoof, the form has come to be associated with delightful hijinks. The stanza is very well suited to episode with commentary; the six lines of interlocking rhyme are adequate to build a situation at which the closing couplet can poke ridicule. The first six lines in ottava rima seem to inflate and swell, so that when they are followed by a couplet they tend to burst into *mock-heroic* (see *Couplet*). While ottava rima has found its renown in the delightfully facetious *Don Juan*, the stanza has also been used brilliantly for just the opposite effect: seriousness and meditation. The stanza is long enough for detailed meditation as well as narration, and the couplet can be used for observation and profundity. Especially in the hands of Yeats, ottava rima became lyrical, intense, and meditative, as in the poems "Among School Children" and "Sailing to Byzantium."

Oxymoron: Closely related to paradox, an oxymoron occurs when two paradoxical words are placed in juxtaposition, such as "wise fool" or "devilish angel." An oxymoron is neither as profound nor as important as paradox, and it is not used so much for calling attention to a new level of truth as it is to call attention to the line which contains it.

Poet Laureate: The poet laureate is the official poet of England, appointed for life by the English sovereign and expected to compose poems for various public occasions. The first *officially* appointed poet laureate was John Dryden, although precedence is often granted to Ben Jonson, who served as the laureate in effect and was so recognized by his peers. In the eighteenth century, the laureateship was granted to a succession of mediocrities, but since the appointment of William Wordsword in 1843, the office has generally been regarded as a substantial honor. Since the term of Robert Southey (1813-1843) there have been few formal expectations of the poet laureate, but the current laureate, John Betjeman, has been unusually active in his official capacity, writing a great many poems which commemorate events of state or celebrate the royal family.

Poetical intrusion: Occasionally a voice other than the narrator's will intrude on the poem in order to correct or clarify what the narrator is telling the reader. Particularly popular among eighteenth century novelists, poetical intrusion was used to remind readers that the story being told was only art, no matter how true to life it might seem. In poetry, intrusion breaks the intimacy which has been formed between the narrator and reader; it is used to discredit the narrator or to change the *tone* of the poem. The presence of poetical intrusion often suggests that the poem is developing *irony*.

Poetical voice: Sometimes the speaker in a *first-person* poem seems so far removed from the poem that it is difficult for the reader to identify him as a person, or as being distinct from the poet himself, resulting in a poetical rather than a personal voice. When the poet wants to convey as little emotion as possible—when the absence of emotion is more forceful than portraying it—then poetical voice is a suitable *point of view*.

Point of view: Point of view may be simply defined as the eyes through which we see the *dramatic situation*, and consists only of those elements which can be determined through the narrator's senses. Point of view can be thought of as a special motion-picture camera which can see, hear, touch, taste, and smell, but which cannot think. Whatever the camera photographs is the dramatic situation; whenever it moves from one place to another, the point of view has changed. What the narrator thinks about the dramatic situation is his interpretation of it, and that is called "point of interpretation." The differences between the point of view, the narrator's point of interpretation, and the reader's point of interpretation will often reveal the meaning of the poem (see *Irony*). In general English usage, "point of view" means "one's opinion," but in poetry it is restricted to the camera-eye. How the narrator interprets what he sees is crucial to the reader's understanding of his character and situation in the poem. As in fiction, poems may be told from first, second, or third person point of view, singular or plural, limited or omniscient. Limited point of view means that the narrator can see only what the poet wants him to see, while omniscient means that the narrator can know everything, including the thoughts and motives of others.

Polysyllables: Words adopted into English from the Romance languages tend to be multisyllabic, fluid, and soft; while words adopted from German are often monosyllabic or disyllabic, relying more often on plosive or harsh *consonants*. Thus, many poems endeavoring to be conventionally sensuous might use polysyllabic rather than monosyllabic words. Polysyllabic words generally have the same effect on a line as the soft consonants, and poets like to use polysyllabic words because they give variety to prevent an overabundance of soft consonants. Poems which use a number of polysyllabic words will usually be trying to create smooth or pleasing sounds rather than abrupt or cacophonous ones, although the poet may use the pleasant sound for *irony*. Forced into an *iambic base meter*, polysyllabic words are usually split, and unless the poet is careful, the *split foot* might counteract the softness of the word. The following line contains three polysyllabic words: "Monuments of unaging intellect." When forced into the pentameter base meter of "Sailing to Byzantium," the polysyllables tend to regroup themselves into disyllables: "Monu/ ments of/ unag/ing in/tellect." Polysyllabic words are frequently used to create vowel music.

Prose poem: Prose poems range in length from a few lines to three or four pages; most prose poems occupy a page or less. When the term is applied to much longer works it becomes meaningless. The distinguishing feature of the prose poem is its typography: it appears on the page like prose, with no line breaks. There are no formal characteristics by which a prose poem can be distinguished from a piece of prose. Many prose poems, such as those by

Arthur Rimbaud, employ rhythmic repetition and other poetic devices not normally found in prose, but many others, such as those of the Polish poet Zbigniew Herbert, use such devices sparingly if at all. Prose poems constitute a distinct genre of poetry within which there is enormous variety, from the cubism of Pierre Reverdy to the realistic sketches of Aleksandr Solzhenitsyn, which are rather like miniature stories.

Pun: A pun occurs when words which have similar pronunciations have entirely different meanings. Thus, by use of a pun the speaker establishes a connection between two meanings or contexts that the reader would not ordinarily make. The result may be a surprise recognition of an unusual or striking connection, or, more often, a humorously accidental connection. During certain literary periods, the pun was admired and widely used for serious as well as for comic purposes, as it is throughout Shakespeare's sonnets. An example of a pun is: "They went and told the sexton and the sexton tolled the bell."

Pyrrhus: When two unstressed syllables comprise a foot, it is called a "pyrrhus," as in the line "Appear/and dis/appear/in the/blue depth/of the sky," where foot four is a pyrrhus. Because the syllables are unstressed, pyrrhic substitutions are used more for meter than for meaning, or to call attention to other more important feet.

Quantitative meter: Quantitative meter is measured by the duration of pronunciation; in other words, syllables of the same quantitative length take the same amount of time to pronounce. While there have been a few attempts in English to imitate classical quantitative verse, notably in the poetry of Thomas Campion, English does not adapt satisfactorily to the system. Quantity is very important, however, in explaining why certain syllables demand more *emphasis* and create the *tone* of the poem (see *Consonants*). The effect of long durational stresses on a line is to slow the meter and make the stressed syllables less prominent, giving the line a more somber and less emotional character.

Quatrain: Any four-line stanza is a quatrain; aside from the *couplet*, it is the most common stanza type. The quatrain's popularity among both sophisticated and unsophisticated readers suggests that there is something inherently pleasing about the form: something even in the arrangement of four lines to a stanza that makes people think of poetry. For many readers, poetry and quatrains are almost synonymous. Balance and antithesis, contrast and comparison not possible in other stanza types are indigenous to the quatrain. With quatrains more than with other stanza types, it is possible to develop a poem linearly, as with ballads, where one action leads to the next. Most quatrains are rhymed, adding even greater unity and balance to the form; the rhyme scheme determines where the *emphasis* lies and what subjects are best suited to the particular type of quatrain.

Regular meter: A *line* of poetry which contains only the same type of *foot* is said to be "regular." Only the dullest of poems maintains a regular meter throughout; skillful poets create interest and *emphasis* through *substitution*.

Relative stress: When more emphasis is placed on one syllable in a pattern than on another, that syllable is said to be "stressed." Once the dominant stress in the line has been determined, every other syllable can be assigned a stress factor relative to the dominant syllable. The stress factor is created by several aspects of prosody: the position of the syllable in the *line*, the position of the syllable in its word, the surrounding syllables, the type of vowels and consonants which constitute the syllable, and the syllable's relation to the *foot*, *base meter*, and *caesura*. Since every syllable will have a different stress factor, there could be as many values as there are syllables, although most prosodists *scan* poems using primary, secondary, and unstressed notations. In the line "I am there like the dead, or the beast" the anapestic base meter will not permit "I" to take a full stress, but it is a more forceful syllable than the unstressed ones, so it is assigned a secondary stress. Relative to "dead" and "beast," it takes less pressure; relative to the articles in the line, it takes much more.

Resolution: Generally, a resolution is any natural conclusion to a poem, especially in a short *lyric* poem which establishes some sort of dilemma or conflict which the narrator must solve. Specifically, the resolution is the octave stanza of a Petrarchan *sonnet* or the couplet of a Shakespearean sonnet where the first part of the poem presents a situation which must find balance in the resolution.

Rhyme: Rhyme is the correspondence of sound between syllables within a line or between lines whose proximity to each other allows rhymed sounds to be sustained. The function of rhyme depends in part upon its type, which is classified according to: (1) the sound relationship between rhyming words, (2) the position of the rhyming words within the line, and (3) the number and position of the syllables within the rhyming words. Rhyme classified by sound includes: (a) full rhyme, which is defined as two or more words which have the same vowel sound, followed by the same consonants in their last stressed syllables, and in which all succeeding syllables are phonetically identical. "Hat/cat" are full rhymes, as are "laughter/after"; and (b) *approximate rhyme*, whose categories are *assonance, slant, alliterative, light, eye,* and *identical*. Rhyme classified by its position in the line includes end, internal, and initial rhyme. End rhyme occurs when the last words of two lines rhyme, whether the rhymes are full or approximate. The most important effect of end rhyme is to bind or associate lines. By *end-stopping* rhymed lines, the poet can generate even greater emphasis and binding power. Internal rhyme occurs when two words within the same line or within various lines recall the same sound, as in "Wet, below the snow line, smelling of vegetation" where "below" and "snow" rhyme. The effect of internal rhyme is to give unity to the line. When used in conjunction with end rhyme, it creates very tight lines; when used in the absence of end rhyme, it subtly knits portions of lines together. Internal rhyme can also be used effectively to give the line a more musical or rhythmic quality than it might otherwise have. Initial rhyme occurs when the first syllables of two or more lines rhyme, and although it is rarely used for entire poems, it creates the same binding effect as end rhyme. Rhymes classified by the number and position of syllables include: *masculine*, *feminine*, and multiple rhymes. Multiple rhymes occur when more than the last two syllables rhyme, as in "me/tic/u/lous" and "ri/dic/u/lous." Multiple rhymes can be used only sparingly for poems of a serious nature because they tend to produce a comic effect, but when used appropriately they can reinforce pathos or defeat.

Rhyme scheme: Poems which establish a pattern of rhyme have a "rhyme scheme," designated by lowercase letters; the rhyme scheme of *ottava rima*, for example, is abababcc. To a large extent, the focus and most appropriate subject matter for a stanza is determined by its rhyme scheme. Traditional stanza forms (see the table of forms on page 3571) are categorized by their rhyme scheme and *base meter*.

Rime couée: Also called "tail rhyme," rime couée is a six-line stanza rhyming aabccb where the "a" and "c" lines are tetrameter and the "b" lines trimeter. The form is made highly flexible by adding as many "a" and "c" lines as desired while maintaining the "b" lines, as in Tennyson's "The Lady of Shalott." Because the "b" lines are a foot shorter, and because they break the established rhyme, they call attention to themselves and are frequently used for a punch-line effect, as in Thomas Gray's "On the Death of a Favorite Cat, Drowned in a Tub of Goldfishes," where the tail rhymes create a devastatingly comic effect. In serious poems, such as Tennyson's "The Charge of the Light Brigade," the "b" lines—particularly the final "b" line—are used to evoke an emotional response or profound comment to the material which has been presented in the stanza.

Rime royal: The only standard seven-line stanza in English prosody is rime royal, composed of iambic pentameter lines rhyming ababbccc. Shakespeare's *The Rape of Lucrece* (1594) is written in this form. The only variation permitted is to make the last line hexameter. Rime royal is capable of great unity because of the central couplet (lines 4-5) and because the stanza seems to be composed of two fused *quatrains* (abab and bbcc) which are bound together by the fourth line; that is, the fourth and fifth "b" lines seem to belong to both halves of the stanza, acting as a transition between the parts. Because the final couplet is not anticipated by the preceding rhyme, it can act as an element of surprise or passion, making the form ideally suited to romance. Indeed, rime royal flourished during the period from 1375 to 1600 and is closely associated with the imaginative world of romance and with the narration of high and noble matters.

Rondeau: One of three standard French forms assimilated by English prosody, the rondeau generally contains thirteen lines divided into three groups. A common stanzaic grouping rhymes aabba, aabR, aabbaR where the "a" and "b" lines are tetrameter while the R (refrain) lines are dimeter. The rondel, a second French form, contains fourteen lines of trimeter with alternating rhyme: abababa bababab, and is divided into two stanzas. Lines 1 and 2 are repeated exactly as lines 6 and 7, and 13 and 14. The rondeau and rondel forms are always light and playful.

Rondel. See *Rondeau*.

Rubaiyat stanza: Rubaiyat stanzas contain four lines of iambic pentameter rhyming aaba. In Edward Fitzgerald's rendering of the *Rubáiyát of Omar Khayyám* (1859), from which the stanza takes its name, the fourth line is generally used to make some profound, and often cynical, comment on life and death. For the purpose of profundity the Rubaiyat stanza works well because it returns to the original rhyme after the stanza has built to crescendo in the third line. When the fourth line returns to the original rhyme, it seems to be reflecting on the situation which was presented in the first three lines. Because the Rubaiyat stanza is so rigidly associated with one particular poem whose theme is commonly taken to be "eat, drink, and be merry," and because the last line in the stanza purports to be profound, the Rubaiyat stanza is seldom used successfully except as satire or for comic effect. Robert Frost modifies the Rubaiyat stanza in poems such as "Stopping by Woods on a Snowy Evening" to create a wry, ironic tone.

Sapphic stanza: The English Sapphic stanza resulted from an attempt to reproduce in English the stanza form of the Greek poet Sappho. The original stanza was *quantitative*, making translation into English verse difficult. Sapphic stanzas contain three eleven-syllable lines and a fourth five-syllable line.

Scansion: Scanning is the process of assigning *relative stresses* and meter to a line of poetry, usually for the purpose of determining where variations, and thus emphasis, in the *base meter* occur. Scansion can help explain how a poem generates tension and offer clues as to the key words. E. E. Cummings' "singing each morning out of each night" could be scanned in two ways: (1) singing/each morn/ing out/of each night or (2) sing/ing each/morning/out of/ each night. Scansion will not only affect the way the line is read aloud, but will also influence the meaning of the line.

Secondary stress. See *Relative stress*.

Seguidilla: Like the Japanese *haiku*, the Spanish seguidilla is a mood or imagistic poem whose success hinges on the reader's emotional recognition or spiritual insight. Although there is no agreement as to what form the English seguidilla should take, most of the successful ones are either four or seven lines with an alternating *rhyme scheme*: ababcbc. Lines 1, 3, and 6 are trimeter; lines 2, 4, 5, and 7 dimeter.

Shakesperean sonnet. See *Sonnet*.

Simile: Loosely defined, a simile is a type of metaphor which signals a comparison by the use of the words "like" or "as." Shakespeare's line, "My mistress' eyes are nothing like the sun" establishes a comparison between the woman's eyes and the sun, and is a simile.

Slant rhyme. See *Approximate rhyme*.

Sonnet: The most important and widely used of traditional poem types, the sonnet is almost always composed of fourteen lines of iambic pentameter with some form of alternating rhyme, and a turning point which divides the poem into two parts. Because of its length, the sonnet is able to present a problem and then reflect upon it, while being short enough to maintain an elevated state of emotion throughout. Divided into two distinct parts, the situation and the resolution, the sonnet's most important feature is its balance, reflecting the Renaissance world which engendered the form. The original sonnet form, known as the "Petrarchan" (adopted from the poetry of Petrarch) or "Italian" sonnet, presented a problem or situation in the first eight lines, then resolved it in the last six. The "octave" is composed of two *quatrains* (abbaabba), the second of which complicates the first and gradually defines and heightens the problem. The "sestet" then proceeds to diminish the problem slowly until by the end of the poem a satisfying resolution is achieved. Because of the similar lengths of the octave and sestet, the problem and resolution seem proportionate, resulting in a logical and satisfying ending.

During the fifteenth century, the Italian sonnet became an integral part of the courtship ritual, and most sonnets during that time consisted of a young man's description of his perfect lover. The young man usually compared his intended to some beautiful and miraculous part of nature, this comparison becoming known as the "Petrarchan conceit." Because so many unpoetic young men had generated a nation full of bad sonnets by the end of the century, the form became an object of ridicule, and the English sonnet developed as a reaction against all the bad verse being turned out in the Italian tradition. When Shakespeare wrote "My mistress' eyes are nothing like the sun," he was deliberately negating the Petrarchan conceit, rejoicing in the fact that his loved one was so much more interesting and unpredictable than nature. Shakespeare also altered the sonnet's formal balance. Instead of an octave, the Shakespearean sonnet has three quatrains of alternating rhyme, and is resolved in a final couplet. This imbalance, giving so much more space to the problem than to the resolution, places great strain on the couplet to be witty or profound. Both the Petrarchan and Shakespearean sonnets tend to reflect rhetorical logic on an almost legalistic level, and part of the wit of the Shakespearean couplet is to alter the logical basis of the argument presented in the first part. During the sixteenth century, long stories were told in sonnet form, one sonnet after the next, to produce "sonnet sequences," and during the Romantic period William Wordsworth and Percy Bysshe Shelley created long poems using the sonnet as the basic stanza. Sonnets have been produced in every period since the Renaissance, although the constrictions of the form have made it less popular during modern times. Variations on the sonnet are the *Miltonic* and the *Spenserian*. Although most sonnets contain fourteen lines, some (the *curtal sonnet*) contain as few as ten, or as many as seventeen. The principal characteristic of the sonnet is balance, signaled by a turn which comes between the problem and the resolution.

Spenserian sonnet: A variation on the Shakespearean sonnet, the Spenserian attempts to interlock the quatrains through internal couplets, rhyming abab bcbc cdcd   ee. The result is a very tightly bound exposition of the problem which demands an equally tight, definitive couplet. Because of the demands made by the rhyme scheme of the quatrains and the profound response of the couplet, there are few successful Spenserian sonnets.

Split foot: A split foot occurs when the natural division of a word is altered as a result of being forced into a metrical base. For example, the words "point/ĕd," "lád/dĕr," and "stick/ĭng" have a natural falling rhythm, but in the line "My long/twó-point/ĕd lád/dĕr's stick/ĭng through/ă tree" the syllables are rearranged so as to turn the falling rhythm into a rising meter. The result of splitting feet is to create an uncertainty and delicate imbalance in the line.

Spondee: When two relatively stressed syllables occur together in a foot they are called a "spondee" or "spondaic foot," as in the line "Appear/and dis/appear/in the/blue depth/of the sky."

Sprung rhythm: If *accentual* poetry is taken to its extreme, one can never predict the patterns of succeeding stresses: it is only possible to predict a prescribed number of stresses per line. This extreme of unpredictability characterizes sprung rhythm, first described near the end of the nineteenth century by Gerard Manley Hopkins. In sprung rhythm "any two stresses may either follow one another running, or be divided by one, two, or three slack syllables." The tendency in sprung rhythm is to group stresses, as in: "sheer plod makes plough down sillion/ Shine." This grouping of stresses tend to make the reader spring from one stress to the next because there are few slack stresses to give pause or relief. Groups of stresses occurring in a line create tension, and Hopkins often used sprung rhythm to describe tenseness or excitement. Hopkins' "The Windhover" is an excellent example of sprung rhythm.

Standard habbie: A variation of *rime couée*, the standard habbie rhymes aaabab, where the "a" lines are iambic tetrameter and the "b" lines are dimeter. The flourish of tetrameter rhymes often creates a ridiculous effect, but the great master of this form, Robert Burns, was able to use it to portray everything from open freshness to impudent irony. His freshness is evident in "To a Mountain Daisy, on Turning One Down with a Plow in April, 1786"; his irony is apparent in "To a Mouse on Seeing One on a Lady's Bonnet at Church." The "b" lines are called "bobs" or "tails" and are most often used for a comic effect.

Stanza: When rhymed lines are meant to be taken as a unit, and the unit recurs throughout the poem, that unit is called a "stanza." Poems divided into fairly regular and patterned stanzas are called "strophic"; poems which appear as a single unit, whether rhymed or unrhymed, or which have no predictable stanzas, are called "stichic." Both strophic and stichic units represent a logical division within the poem, and the difference between them lies in the formality and strength of the interwoven unit. Short stanzas are generally most appropriate for concentrated ideas or moments of emotion, or for narration when the action is steadily progressing. Short stanzas also give the impression of organized thought or emotion expressed in long strophic or stichic divisions. Poems composed of longer stanzas (six or more lines per stanza) tend to complete a thought or action within the unit and then complicate the situation with the following stanza, while shorter stanzas tend to build from or reflect off one another in order to complete the thought. Because strophic verse allows pauses at regular and predictable intervals, the climactic effect is usually at the end of the stanza, whereas with stichic divisions the poet can build the material to a climax at any point or points he likes. The length of the lines and the *rhyme scheme* of traditional stanza forms greatly affect the emotions which the poet can convey, so that certain forms have come to be associated with certain types of subject matter.

Stave of six: Rhyming ababcc, the stave of six is the most common six-line stanza; its final couplet produces a summing-up effect, but its brevity pushes the reader onward to the next stanza. Wordsworth's "I Wandered Lonely as a Cloud" is one of many famous poems written with the stave of six.

Stichic verse. See *Stanza*.

Stress. See *Relative stress*.

Strophic verse. See *Stanza*.

Substitution: Substitution, one of the most common and effective methods by which the poet can emphasize a foot, occurs when one type of foot is replaced with another within a *base meter*. For example, in the line "Thy life/a long/ dead calm/of fixed/repose," a spondaic foot (ˊ ˊ) has been substituted for an iambic foot. Any foot may be substituted for another foot, but before substitution is possible, the reader's expectations must have been established by a base meter so that a change in those expectations will have an effect. In the following line, for example: "one hand/did nothing on/the vest" there are three different types of feet, and were the poet depending on substitution for effect, he could not get it, because no base meter has been established. There are three basic types of substitution: (1) substitution of stressed syllables for expected unstressed syllables, (2) substitution of unexpected unstressed syllables, and (3) substitution for the purpose of temporarily reversing rhythm (*counterpointing*). The substitution of unexpected stressed syllables can create a sense of strength, heaviness, or weariness, and to slow down the line (see *Sprung rhythm*). In the lines: "When A/jax strives/some rock's/vast weight/ to throw,// The line/to la/bors, and/the words/move slow"; the spondaic substitution in foot four of line 1 helps to slow the line and make the reader feel the difficulty of labor, while the spondees in line 2 illustrate how lines can be made to move slowly. When unexpected unstressed syllables are substituted, the line almost always takes on lightness and quick movement. Substitution which causes an unexpected reversal of rhythm can create complex effects, marking unanticipated movement, discovery, change, new force, or new direction of power. Whatever it suggests, it is almost always accompanied by the release of some emotion.

Syllabic binder: When assonance occurs in consecutive syllables, as between "*green*" and "*freedom*" in "The green freedom of a cockatoo," the syllables are bound together in a way that gives greater emphasis to the unit than does *alliteration* or *consonance*; this link is called a "syllabic binder" (See *Approximate rhyme*.)

Syllabic meter: The system of meter which measures only the number of syllables per line, without regard to stressed and unstressed syllables, is called "syllabic meter." In English and other Germanic-based languages, the *base meter* usually measures the relationship of stressed to unstressed syllables (see *Relative stress*), but in Latinate languages (and some Oriental languages) only the number of syllables per line establishes the metrical base. In some English poems, however, such as Dylan Thomas' "Fern Hill," the *accentual-syllabic* pattern is so irregular that the metrical effects can be explained only by syllabic meter.

Symbol: Loosely defined, a symbol is any sign which two people agree stands for something, as with mathematical notation. Unlike mathematical symbols, poetic symbols cannot be rigidly defined; a poetic symbol typically evokes a cluster of meanings rather than a single specifiable meaning. For example, the rose, which suggests fragile beauty, gentleness, softness, and sweet aroma, has come to symbolize love, eternal beauty, or virginity. Because symbols are established by consensus and are valid only when many readers understand them, most symbols have evolved through many years of use in which their properties have been slowly established. As the ideas of Christ became associated with the Crucifixion, the cross became the symbol for those ideas, standing for resurrection and the salvation of man. Symbols have also evolved from natural *imagery*, such as the tide, which symbolizes, among other things, time and eternity. Symbols which have grown out of common religious, folk, or cultural tradition, such as the cross, or out of some common understanding among men, such as the tide, or which have been used frequently enough so that every informed reader will recognize them, such as the Statue of Liberty, are usually referred to as "traditional symbols." If a poet includes a cross in his poem, for example, he must assume that it will bring to mind the passion and beauty of Christian suffering and forbearance. Whatever else the poet does with the cross, he must first deal with the traditional associations. Traditional symbols are ideal for poems whose subject matter is myth. The poet can introduce the symbol which represents the myth, a favorite technique for *allegory*. Although traditional symbols have been used effectively in great poetry, they are not as forceful today as they were in the hands of Dante Shakespeare, Milton, and many others principally because they have been used so often and so well that to use them again turns them into platitudes rather than meaningful concepts. Most poetry depending entirely on traditional symbols has not survived, and traditional symbols rarely exist in serious modern poetry except when they are being used for satire or to evoke a mythology. Because traditional symbols are not particularly useful to modern poets, writers have turned to personal symbols which offer greater flexibility and contact with the reader. Whereas readers automatically ascribe symbolic qualities to traditional symbols, personal symbols can be created only in the context of the poem or the poet's *oeuvre* and only when they are reinforced throughout. It is only through constant reinforcement that swans in Yeats's poetry finally mean as much to the reader as they do to the narrator. The following lines from James Dickey's poem "In the Mountain Tent" illustrate how an image is converted into a traditional symbol, only to become a highly personal symbol: "I am hearing the shape of the rain/ Take the shape of the tent and believe it." The *dramatic situation* is that the narrator is in a tent in the mountains listening to the rain as it runs down the canvas top and sides. The taut canvas allows the narrator to hear every trickle of water, and because the rain follows the curves of the tent, the water takes the same shape. When the narrator and reader begin to see the tent as made of water, the canvas overhead seems to disappear so that the narrator is enclosed in water, not fabric. Because the image in the context of the poem makes the reader feel enclosed, almost submerged, he may extend the image to that of submersion in water. So far, this water tent is only an image, but if the reader attaches submersion to baptismal ritual, the rain then becomes symbolic of baptism and all of its religious connotations. At this point, the symbol of the rain is a traditional one, with all its attached history and theology. The narrator of the poem, however, is not as interested in John the Baptist as he is in the power of self-redemption, so the poem's *theme* becomes how men redeem themselves through a release of their spirits from a bodily form. Having created a traditional symbol in the first two lines, the poet illustrates how man must break tradition in order to redeem himself, and thus the symbol of the water tent takes on an entirely different set of personal symbolic properties.

Synaeresis. See *Elision.*

Syncope. See *Elision.*

Synecdoche. See *Metonymy.*

Tails or Tail rhymes or Bobs. See *Rime couée* and *Standard habbie.*

Tenor. See *Metaphor.*

Terza rima: Terza rima is a three-line stanza in which the middle line of one stanza rhymes with the first line of the following stanza, and whose rhyme scheme is aba bcb cdc. . . . Since the rhyme scheme of one stanza can be completed only by adding the next stanza, terza rima tends to propel itself forward, and as a result of this strong forward motion it is well-suited to long narration, maintaining a feeling of unity even though the poem is composed of short *strophic* stanzas. The final stanza of a poem in terza rima is usually a *couplet* or *quatrain* completing the rhyme anticipated in the last tercet. Thus, the final couplet gives a note of authority. The most famous of all poems written in terza rima is Dante's *La Divina Commedia* (c. 1320, *The Divine Comedy*).

Theme: Loosely defined as what a poem means, "theme" more specifically refers to recurring elements, and the term is sometimes used interchangeably with "motif." A motif is any recurring pattern of images, symbols, ideas, or language and is usually restricted to the internal workings of the poem. Thus, one might say that there is an animal motif in Yeats's poem "Sailing to Byzantium." Theme, however, is usually more general and philosophical; so that the theme of "Sailing to Byzantium" might be interpreted as the failure of man's attempt to isolate himself within the world of art.

Third person: When the narrator has not been part of the event or affected it, and if he is not probing his own relationship to it but is only describing what happened and has not allowed intrusion of the word "I," then he is using third-person narration. There are three principal reasons why a poet uses the third person, either limited or omniscient (see *Point of view*): (1) to establish a distance between the reader and the subject; (2) to give credibility to a large expanse of narration which would be impossible for one person to experience; and (3) to allow the poem to include a number of characters who can comment on one another as well as be commented on by the participating narrator. Although the third-person narrator does not feel directly affected by the poem's events, as does the *poetical voice* narrator, his response to the events can be crucial for explicating the poem. The poet will sometimes use the narrator's response to an event in the poem to call attention to it, and the narrator's attitude will help to determine what the reader is supposed to think. In W. H. Auden's poem, "Musée Des Beaux Arts," for example, the narrator looks at a painting and points out the ironies of history through it, but the real interest of the poem lies in the *tone* with which he relays seemingly impersonal material. His tone contributes more to the *theme* and the reader's emotional response than does the irony.

Tone: Strictly defined, tone is the author's attitude toward his subject, his persona, himself, his audience, or his society. It is the expression or the reflection of attitude, and if the ultimate aim of art is to control emotions and attitudes, then tone is one of the most important elements of poetry. Tone in poetry is created in two ways: through the meaning of words, either *denotatively* or *connotatively*, and through the sound of language (principally, *Rhyme*, *Consonants*, and *Diction*). Adjectives such as "satirical," "compassionate," "empathetic," "ironical," "condescending," and "sarcastic" are used to describe tone, which is one of the most difficult and subjective poetic elements to define. Tone and *theme* are often linked and must be explicated simultaneously.

Transitional poetry: When poets radically change styles, themes, or philosophy, they are considered to have made a "transition." Usually the transition is a result of a changing world when the values and uses of poetry are a reflection of new attitudes, such as during the 1890's when poetry was emerging from Victorian to modern.

Triplets: Triplets are three lines of any length which rhyme aaa. In English poetry triplets are difficult to sustain because they usually result in a comic effect. In serious poems, triplets are rare, although they have been used in an attempt to suggest musical tempo. Triplets, however, have been used successfully for satire or for parts in *verse plays* when a comic character speaks. Used sparingly, triplets have also been successfully interspersed in long poems as a means to affect *tone*.

Tristichs: Tristichs are three unrhymed lines which form a *stanza*. Except as an occasional breaker in *stichic* poems, tristichs are seldom used.

Trochee: One of the most common feet in English poetry, the trochee associates one stressed syllable with one unstressed syllable (′ ˇ), as in the line: "Doŭble/doŭble, tói and/troŭble." Trochaic lines are frequently *substituted* in an iambic *base meter* in order to create counterpointing. Four-line stanzas whose base meter is trochaic are called "*Anacreonic*."

Truncation: Truncation occurs when the last, unstressed syllable of a falling line is omitted, as in the line: "Týgeř,/týgeř/búrniňg/bright," where the "ly" has been dropped from "bright." Often in rhymed poems in falling meters the rhyme will demand truncation so that there will be no preponderance of feminine or multiple rhymes (see *Rhyme*) which would lighten an otherwise serious poem.

Variable verse: If a poem establishes some sort of expectation of *meter*, and if the meter affects the meaning or *tone*, then it is more useful to think of the verse-form as "variable" rather than "*free*." Although the line-length and metrical base of Eliot's poem *The Journey of the Magi* vary considerably from line to line, both *syllabic* and *accentual-syllabic* meters help explain *emphasis*;

thus the poem is not free verse in any sense except in its irregularity. The advantage of variable verse is that it can be regulated according to the shifting demands of ideas and images. *Polysyllabic* words can be used without concern as to how they fit into meter, and variable verse offers the opportunity for sudden variations—an effect which traditional verse achieves through *substitution*. Anticipated by the Romantic poets in England and by Walt Whitman in America, variable verse is the most widely used metrical system for modern poetry.

Vehicle. See *Metaphor.*

Venus and Adonis stanza: When a foot is added to each line of the *stave of six*, making all the lines pentameter (and recalling the *heroic quatrain*), the stanza is called "Venus and Adonis," named for Shakespeare's poem of that title. The stanza works something like the last six lines of the Shakespearean sonnet, in which the couplet is used to make a profound observation on the previous *quatrains*. The four-line quatrain, however, does not provide enough space to build a situation which can sustain a conclusion, so that the couplet is normally used as an extension of the quatrain rather than a reflection on it (see *Sonnet* and *Ottava rima*).

Verse: Verse is a generic term for poetry, as in *The Oxford Book of English Verse* (1939). Verse also refers in a narrower sense to poetry that is humorous or merely superficial, as in "greeting-card verse." Finally, English critics sometimes use "verse" to mean "*stanza*," or, more often, to mean "*line.*"

Verse drama: Drama which is written in poetic rather than ordinary language, and which is characterized and delivered by the *line*, is called "verse drama." Before the twentieth century, much if not most drama was composed in verse, and for many centuries, when poetry and drama were used for ritual, plays almost always contained a great amount of poetry. Verse drama flourished during the eighteenth century when the *couplet* became a standard literary form.

Verse paragraphs: The divisions which are created within a stichic poem (see *Stanza*) by logic or syntax, rather than form, are called "verse paragraphs." They are important for determining the movement of a poem and the logical association between ideas.

Villanelle: The villanelle, like the rondeau and the rondel, is a French verse form assimilated by English prosody. It is usually composed of nineteen lines divided into five tercets and a quatrain, rhyming aba, bba, aba, aba, abaa. The third line is repeated in the ninth and fifteenth lines. Dylan Thomas'

"Do Not Go Gentle into That Good Night" is a modern English example of a successful villanelle.

Walton Beacham

INDEX FOR STANZA POEMS

No. of lines in stanza	Rhyme scheme	No. of feet in line	Type of stanza
varying	any or none	any	stichic
equal from stanza to stanza	any or none	any	strophic
	aa	any	couplet
2	aa	5	heroic couplet
	aa	4, varied	Hudibrastic verse
	aaa	any	triplet
	none	any	tristichs
3	aba	any	tercet
	aba bcb	any	terza rima
	none	syllables line 1 = 5 line 2 = 7 line 3 = 5	haiku
	any	any	quatrain
	abab or abcb	4 ll. 1,3 3 ll. 2,4	ballad
	abab or abcb	4	long ballad
	abcb	3 ll. 1,2,4 4 line 3	short ballad
	abab	5	heroic quatrain
4	abba	4	in memoriam
	abba	5	brace
	aaba	4	Rubaiyat
	none	any	unrhymed quatrains
	abab or aabb	trochaic tetrameter	trochaic quatrain
	varies	syllables ll. 1,2,3 = 11 line 4 = 5	Sapphic stanza

No. of lines in stanza	Rhyme scheme	No. of feet in line	Type of stanza
4 to 7	ababcbc or variations	3 ll. 1,3,6 2 ll. 2,4,5,7	seguidilla
5	abccb or variations	3 ll. 1,2,5 2 ll. 3,4	mad-song
	aabba or variations	anapestic	limerick
	any	any	cinquain
6	ababcc	4	stave of six
	ababcc	5	Venus and Adonis
	aabccb or variations	4 ll. 1,2,4,5 3 ll. 3,6	rime couée
	aaabab	3 ll. 1,2,3,5 2 ll. 4,6	standard habbie
7	ababbcc	5	rime royal
8	abababcc	5	ottava rima
9	ababbcbcc	5 6 (last l.)	Spenserian
10	abcabc dbcd	sprung rhythm	curtal sonnet
13	aabba aabR aabbaR	4 ll. a,b 2 ll. R	rondeau
14	abababa- bababab	3	rondel
	any	any	sonnet
	abbaabba- cdecde or variations	5	Petrarchan sonnet
	ababcdcdefef gg	5	Shakesperian sonnet

No. of lines in stanza	Rhyme scheme	No. of feet in line	Type of stanza
14	same as Petrarchan	5	Miltonic sonnet
	ababbcbc-cdcd ee	5	Spenserian sonnet
19	aba aba bba aba aba abaa	5 or variations	villanelle
39	repetitions: abcdef faebdc cfdabe ecbfad deacfb bdfeca eca	5 or variations	sestina

Walton Beacham

CRITICAL SURVEY
OF
POETRY

INDEX

I

II

birletta, 465.
Birney, Earle, 174-180; "David," 176-177; "For George Lamming," 179-180; "Trial of a City," 178.
"Birthday, A" (Creeley), 682-683.
"Birthplace Revisited" (Corso), 576-577.
Bishop, Elizabeth, 181-190; "Anaphora," 187; "The Burglar of Babylon," 187-188; "Crusoe in England," 189; "Faustina," 187; "Filling Station," 189; "The Fish," 183; "Four Poems," 189; "From the Country to the City," 188; "The Gentleman of Shalott," 185; "The Imaginary Iceberg," 184, 188; "In the Village," 181; "In the Waiting Room," 188; "Large Bad Picture," 186; "Love Lies Sleeping," 185; "The Man-Moth," 184; "Manuelzinho," 189; "The Map," 188; "The Monument," 186-187; "Over 2000 Illustrations and a Complete Concordance," 185-186; "Paris, 7 a.m.," 184; "Poem," 186; *Questions of Travel*, 187; "The Riverman," 186; "Sandpiper," 182-183; "Seascape," 184; "Sleeping Standing Up," 185; "12 O'Clock News," 188; "Wading at Wellfleet," 188; "The Weed," 184.
"Bishop Blougram's Apology" (Browning, R.), 341.
"Bishop Orders His Tomb at St. Praxed's Church, The" (Browning, R.), 339-341.
"Black Art, The" (Sexton), 2524.
Black Arts Movement, 3398.
Black Christ, The (Cullen), 697-698.
"Black Cross Farm" (Howells), 1426.
"Black Jackets" (Gunn), 1173.
"Black Poet, White Critic" (Randall, D.), 2316, 2317.
Black Pride (Madhubuti), 1892-1893.
Black Rock, The (Fletcher, J. G.), 1028.
"Black Sketches" (Madhubuti), 1894-1895.
Blackberries (Allingham), 45.
Blackburn, Paul, 191-202; *Against the Silences*, 199-200; "Clickety-Clack,"

199; "December Journal: 1968," 201; "The Hour," 195; "How to Get Through Reality," 196; "How to Get Up Off It," 198; "Light," 195-196; "Lines, Trees, and Words," 197; "Mestrović and the Trees," 196; "The Mint Quality," 200; "Monday, Monday," 200; "The Net of Moon," 198; "The Once-Over," 199; "A Permanence," 195; "The Purse Seine," 198; *The Reardon Poems*, 200-201; "Ritual I," 196-197; "Ritual IV," 197; "The Sea and the Shadow," 198; "So Deep We Never Got," 200.
"Blackrunners/blackmen or run into blackness" (Madhubuti), 1895.
"Black-Smith, The" (D'Urfey), 912.
"Blackstone Rangers, The" (Brooks, G.), 315-317.
Blackwood, Caroline, 1797, 1798, 1799.
Blake, William, 203-219, 3335, 3342, 3429, 3428; *America*, 213-214; *The Book of Ahania*, 216; *The Book of Los*, 215; *The Book of Thel*, 209; *Europe*, 214-215; *The [First] Book of Urizen*, 215; *The Four Zoas*, 217; *The French Revolution*, 213; "The Garden of Love," 3428; "Infant Sorrow," 3439-3440; *Jerusalem*, 218-219; "The Lamb," 209, 210; *The Marriage of Heaven and Hell*, 211-213; *Milton: A Poem*, 217-218; "The Sick Rose," 3416-3417, 3419, 3420-3423, 3424, 3425, 3427-3428; *The Song of Los*, 215-216; *Songs of Experience*, 207, 208-209; *Songs of Innocence*, 207, 208-209; "The Tiger," 209-211; *Visions of the Daughters of Albion*, 216-217.
blank verse, 350, 3046-3047, **3533-3534**.
"Blasphemies" (MacNeice), 1869.
"Blessed Damozel, The" (Rossetti, D. G.), 2427-2428.
"Blessed Is the Man" (Moore), 2047.
"Blessing, A" (Wright, J.), 3168.
"Blessing, The" (Kizer), 1620-1621.
"Blight, A" (Newman), 2104.
Blind Harry; *The Wallace*, 3278.

brace stanza, **3534**, 3571.
"Bracelet, The" (Stanley), 2728.
Bradstreet, Anne, 163, **257-264**, 1375, 3371, 3384; "As weary pilgrim, now at rest," 261; "Contemplations," 261-262; "The Flesh and the Spirit," 260-261; "In Honour of Du Bartas," 259-260; "In memory of my dear grand-child Elizabeth Bradstreet," 262-263; "To the memory of my dear and ever honoured Father Thomas Dudley," 260, 261.
"Brahma" (Emerson), 957-958.
Branches of Adam (Fletcher, J. G.), 1027-1028.
Brathwaite, Edward Kamau, 265-273; "Alpha," 272; *The Arrivants*, 268-271; "Caliban," 266; "The Cracked Mother," 270; "Islands," 271; *Mother Poem*, 272-273; "Nametracks," 272-273; "New World A-Comin," 271; *Rights of Passage*, 268; "Shepherd," 270-271.
Bravery of Earth, A (Eberhart), 928.
"Break, The" (Sexton), 2525.
Breakers and Granite (Fletcher, J. G.), 1027.
"Breasts" (Simic), 2592.
Brébeuf and His Brethren (Pratt), 2284-2285.
"Breefe balet touching the traytorous takynge of Scarborow Castell, A" (Heywood, J.), 1335-1336.
Breton, Nicholas, 274-282; *The Arbor of Amorous Devices*, 279; *Breton's Bowre of Delights*, 278; *The Countess of Pembroke's Passion*, 280; *Hate of Treason*, 282; *Honour of Valour*, 282; *I Would and Would Not*, 281; *Longing of a Blessed Heart*, 281; *Pasquil's Foole's Cappe*, 281; *Pasquil's Madcappe, Thrown at the Corruption of These Times*, 281; *Pasquil's Mistresse*, 281-282; *Passionate Shepheard*, 279; "Phillida and Coridon," 278-279; *The Phoenix Nest*, 278; *Pilgrimage to Paradise*, 279-280; *The Ravisht Soule, and the Blessed Weeper*, 280-281; *A Solemne Passion of the Soule's Love*, 280; *Soule's Immortal Crowne*, 282; "A

Sweet Lullabie," 279.
Breton's Bowre of Delights (Breton, N.), 278.
"Bridal Photo, 1906" (Ciardi), 503.
"Bride's Prelude, The" (Rossetti, D. G.), 2428-2429.
Bride's Tragedy, The (Beddoes), 111.
Bridge, The (Crane, H.), 651-652, 3365-3366, 3391.
"Bridge of Sighs, The" (Hood), 1388-1389.
Bridges, Robert, **283-291**; *The Growth of Love*, 287; "London Snow," 285-286; "Low Barometer," 286-287; *Milton's Prosody*, 289-290; "On a Dead Child," 286; *The Testament of Beauty*, 288-289.
"Briefcase History" (Middleton, C.), 1990.
Briggflatts (Bunting), 367, 371.
"Bright Field, The" (Walcott), 3006.
"Bristowe Tragedie: Or, The Deth of Syr Charles Bawdin" (Chatterton), 471.
Britannia's Pastorals (Browne), 320.
"Broken Connections" (Oates), 2119.
"Broken Dark, The" (Hayden), 1248-1249.
"Broken Ground, The" (Berry), 150.
Broken Ground, The (Berry) 149-150.
Brontë, Emily, **292-300**; "Aye, There It Is! It Wakes To-night," 298-299; "No Coward Soul Is Mine," 298; "Oh Thy Bright Eyes Must Answer Now," 297-298; "The Philosopher," 297; "The Prisoner," 299; "Remembrance," 296-297.
Brooke, C. F. Tucker, 1903.
Brooke, Fulke Greville, First Lord. *See* **Greville, Fulke**.
Brooke, Rupert, **301-308**; "The Dead" (I), 306; "The Dead" (II), 306; "The Old Vicarage, Grantchester," 304-305; "Peace," 306; "Safety," 306; "The Soldier," 306.
Brooks, Cleanth; *The Well Wrought Urn*, 3433-3434, 3435-3436.
Brooks, Gwendolyn, **309-317**; "The Blackstone Rangers," 315-317; *In the Mecca*, 3393; "Mentors," 3397; "The Mother," 313-314; "Sermon on

"Faithless Sally Brown" (Hood), 1385-1386.
"Fall of a City" (Spender), 2698.
Fall of America, The (Ginsberg), 1093-1094.
Fall of Hyperion, The (Keats), 1550-1551.
"Falling" (Dickey, J.), 789-799.
falling rhyme, **3543**.
falling rhythm, **3543-3544**.
Falls of Princes (Lydgate), 1805, 1810-1811.
"Falstaff's Lament over Prince Hal Become Henry V" (Melville), 1950.
Familiar Epistle to the Author of the Heroic Epistle to Sir William Chambers, A (Sheridan), 2566.
"Familiar Epistles to a Friend" (Byrom), 396.
familiar letter, 833.
fancy, 2851-2852.
Fanshawe, Sir Richard, 995-1003; *The Faithful Shepherd*, 1000-1002; *The Lusiads*, 1002-1003; "An Ode upon Occasion of His Majesty's Proclamation in the Year 1630," 998; "Presented to His Highness," 999; "The Rose," 999-1000; "The Royalist," 999; "The Saint's Encouragement," 998-999.
"Far East" (Snyder), 2673.
"Far Rockaway" (Schwartz), 2490.
"Far West, The" (Snyder), 2672.
Farewell and Return, The (Crabbe), 646.
"Farewell to Tobacco, A" (Lamb), 1636.
"Farewell Without a Guitar, A" (Stevens), 2750-2751.
"Farmer's Daughter, The" (D'Urfey), 913.
Farming (Berry), 152-153.
Fatal Interview (Millay), 2001.
Fate of the Jury, The (Masters), 1933.
Fates of the Apostles, The (Cynewulf), 715-717.
Father Hubburd's Tale (Middleton, T.), 1995-1996.
"Faustina" (Bishop), 187.
"Fears in Solitude" (Coleridge, S. T.), 541.

"Feast of Stephen, The" (Hecht), 1282.
"February 1st, 1842" (Coleridge, H.), 529-530.
"Felix Randal" (Hopkins), 1401.
"Female, Extinct" (Beer), 121-122.
feminine ending. *See* falling rhythm.
feminine rhyme, **3544**.
Ferlinghetti, Lawrence, 1004-1010, 3381; "Dog," 1008-1009; "Underwear," 1007.
"Festival, The" (Duncan), 901.
"Fictive Wish, The" (Everson), 989.
"Fido: An Epistle to Fidelia" (Browne), 321.
Field Work (Heaney), 1265, 1267,1272-1273.
"Fifty Males Sitting Together" (Bly), 227.
Fig for Momus, A (Lodge), 1733.
"Fig Tree" (Merwin), 1982-1983.
Fighting Terms (Gunn), 1169, 1170.
figure poetry, **3544**.
Figures for an Apocalypse (Merton), 1975.
Figures of the Human (Ignatow), 1473-1474.
"Figures of Thought" (Nemerov), 2089.
Figures of Transition (Hicks), 3410.
"Filling Station" (Bishop), 189.
"Fin du Globe" (MacBeth), 1832.
Finding Them Lost and Other Poems (Moss), 2066.
Findings (Berry), 151-152.
"Fire and Ice" (Frost), 1048.
"Firebombing, The" (Dickey, J.), 798.
Fireside Poets, 1745, 1747-1748.
"First Anniversary" (Donne), 3492.
[First] Book of Urizen, The (Blake), 215.
"First Confession" (Kennedy), 1571.
"First Death" (Justice), 1533-1544.
First Fowre Bookes of the Civile Warres, The (Daniel), 723, 729, 3295.
"First of April" (Warton), 3038.
first person, **3544**.
"First Sight" (Larkin), 3455.
First Will and Testament (Patchen), 2181.

XLII

INDEX

"Rest" (Newman), 2104.
Restoration, 2399.
Restoration period, 3315-3317.
Restoration poet, 126-127.
"Return, The" (Berry), 151.
"Return of Aphrodite, The" (Sarton), 2461.
"Return of the Goddess" (Graves), 1132.
"Return to Hinton" (Tomlinson), 2909.
Returning to Earth (Harrison), 1233-1234.
reversed consonance, 2980.
"Revolution in the Revolution in the Revolution" (Snyder), 2674.
Rexroth, Kenneth, **2348-2355**; *The Collected Longer Poems*, 2352; *The Collected Shorter Poems*, 2351; *The Dragon and the Unicorn*, 2353; *The Heart's Garden, The Garden's Heart*, 2353; *The Homestead Called Damascus*, 2352-2353; "A Letter to William Carlos Williams," 2352; *The Phoenix and the Tortoise*, 2353; *A Prolegomenon to a Theodicy*, 2353; "Thou Shalt Not Kill," 2352; "When We with Sappho," 2351; "Yin and Yang," 2351.
Reznikoff, Charles, **2356-2362**; *Holocaust*, 2361-2362; *Jews in Babylonia*, 2361; *Testimony*, 2361-2362.
"R. F. at Bread Loaf His Hand Against a Tree" (Swenson), 2798.
"Rhodora, The" (Emerson), 959.
"Rhotruda" (Tuckerman), 2939.
Rhyme, **3558-3559**.
"Rhyme" (Bogan), 235.
Rhyme scheme, **3559**.
Rhymes of a Red Cross Man (Service), 2514.
Rich, Adrienne, **2363-2371**; "Diving into the Wreck," 2368-2369; "The Images," 2371; "Snapshots of a Daughter-in-Law," 2366-2368; *Twenty-One Love Poems*, 2369.
"Richard Hunt's 'Arachne'" (Hayden), 1251.
"Rick of Green Wood, The" (Dorn), 841-842.

"Ridotto of Bath, The" (Sheridan), 2566.
Riede, David G., 2813.
Riffaterre, Michael, 3450-3451.
Right Madness on Skye, The (Hugo, R.), 1452-1453.
Riley, James Whitcomb, **2372-2383**; *The Flying Islands of the Night*, 2372; "Knee-Deep in June," 2379; "Leonainie," 2375; "Little Orphant Annie," 2381; "Nothin' to Say," 2379; "The Old Man and Jim," 2379-2380; "The Old Swimmin'-Hole," 2381-2382; "The Raggedy Man," 2380-2381; "When the Frost Is on the Punkin," 2378-2379.
rime couée, **3559**, 3572.
"Rime of the Ancient Mariner, The" (Coleridge, S. T.), 536-539.
rime royal, **3559-3560**, 3572.
Ring and the Book, The (Browning, R.), 344-346.
"Ringing the Bells" (Sexton), 2521.
"Rite, The" (Randall, D.), 2316-2317.
"Rites of Passage" (Gunn), 1176.
Rites of Passage (Brathwaite), 268.
"Ritual IV" (Blackburn), 197.
"Ritual I" (Blackburn), 196-197.
Riven Doggeries (Tate, J.), 2839-2840.
"River, The" (Patmore), 2189.
"Riverman, The" (Bishop), 186.
"Roan Stallion" (Jeffers), 1492.
Robinson, Edwin Arlington, **2384-2394**, 3388; "Eros Turannos," 2389-2391; "The House on the Hill," 2388-2389; "How Annandale Went Out," 2391, 2392-2393; *Lancelot*, 2393; "Luke Havergal," 3518-3529; *Untriangulated Stars*, 2384-2385; "The Whip," 2391-2392.
Rochester, John Wilmot, Earl of, **2395-2404**; Epistolary Essay from M. G. to O. B. upon their Mutual Poems," 2403-2404; "Fair Chloris in a pigsty lay," 2400; "A Ramble in St. James's Park," 2400-2401; "A Satire Against Mankind," 2402-2403; "A Song: My dear Mistress has a heart," 2399-2400; "Timon," 2401-2402.
"Rocks, The" (Creeley), 682.

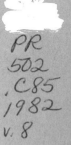